Brauner / Hamblock / Heinrich / Popp / Schwindt / Spörl

IT´S ALL PART OF THE JOB - Lehrbuch

W0400379

IT´S ALL PART OF THE JOB

Englisch
für die Polizei

von
Norbert Brauner
Dr. Dieter Hamblock
Friedrich Schwindt
unter Mitarbeit von
Eva Heinrich
Michael Popp
Udo Harry Spörl

VERLAG DEUTSCHE POLIZEILITERATUR GMBH
Buchvertrieb

Bibliografische Information der Deutschen Nationalbibliothek

Die Deutsche Nationalbibliothek verzeichnet diese Publikation in der Deutschen Nationalbibliografie; detaillierte bibliografische Daten sind im Internet über http.//dnb.d-nb.de abrufbar.

10. Auflage 2011
© VERLAG DEUTSCHE POLIZEILITERATUR GMBH Buchvertrieb; Hilden/Rhld., 2011
Alle Rechte vorbehalten
Satz: VDP GMBH Buchvertrieb, Hilden
Druck und Bindung: Griebsch & Rochol Druck, Hamm
Printed in Germany
ISBN: 978-3-8011-0659-1

Vorwort

Das Lehrbuch IT'S ALL PART OF THE JOB – Englisch für die Polizei – ist sowohl für den berufsbezogenen Englischunterricht an den verschiedenen Ausbildungsstätten der Polizei in der Bundesrepublik Deutschland und im deutschsprachigen Ausland als auch für das Selbststudium konzipiert.

Ziel des Lehrbuches ist es, Polizeibeamtinnen und Polizeibeamten die für viele berufliche Situationen notwendige sprachlich-kommunikative Kompetenz in der englischen Sprache zu vermitteln.

IT'S ALL PART OF THE JOB setzt allgemeinsprachliche Kenntnisse voraus, die in etwa denen entsprechen, die in ca. sechs Jahren Unterricht erworben wurden. Daher wurde im Vokabelverzeichnis auf die Kennzeichnung der Aussprache (Lautschrift), auf die Angabe der Wortarten und größtenteils auf den Grundwortschatz und Wörter, die in beiden Sprachen identisch sind, verzichtet. Das Vokabelverzeichnis ist für das ganze Buch alphabetisch geordnet, wobei angeführt wird, wann ein Wort zum ersten Mal vorkommt.

Was die Aussprache anbetrifft, wird auf allgemeinsprachliche Wörterbücher hingewiesen, da Fachwörterbücher normalerweise keine Aussprachehinweise enthalten; dies gilt auch für das unter dem gleichen Titel IT'S ALL PART OF THE JOB erschienene polizeifachliche Wörterbuch.

Aufgrund der langjährigen Unterrichtserfahrung der Verfasser in polizeilichen Bildungseinrichtungen wurden in jede Unit eine kurze Grammatikübersicht und Übungen aufgenommen.

IT'S ALL PART OF THE JOB ist ein Lehrbuch für die Praxis. Deshalb haben die Verfasser in fast allen Units eine oder mehrere in Gesprächsform gehaltene Situation(en) angeführt, die der praktischen Polizeiarbeit entlehnt sind. Diese handlungsorientierte didaktische Konzeption ließ es auch sinnvoll erscheinen, jedes Gespräch sofort in der englischen Sprache beginnen zu lassen und die englische Sprache auch dann zu benutzen, wenn sich, wie z.B. in 3.9, nur Deutsche unterhalten.

Die in IT'S ALL PART OF THE JOB genannten Personen sind fiktiv, auch wenn sich die dargestellten Sachverhalte genauso oder so ähnlich ereignet haben. Bei namentlich gekennzeichneten Beiträgen ist dies natürlich nicht der Fall.

Aufgrund des föderalen Aufbaus der Bundesrepublik Deutschland und der Tatsache, dass die Polizei Ländersache ist, sind die Anforderungen an die Vorkenntnisse der Polizeianwärter(innen) und die Dauer und der Umfang des Englischunterrichts während der Ausbildung in den einzelnen Bundesländern sehr unterschiedlich. Daraus ergibt sich, dass in der zur Verfügung stehenden Unterrichtszeit nicht die gesamte Stofffülle von IT'S ALL PART OF THE JOB behandelt werden kann. Für die Unterrichtenden bietet sich nun die Möglichkeit an, eine entsprechende Auswahl zu treffen, die sich nach der Zahl der Unterrichtsstunden, nach pädagogischem Ermessen und nach Kenntnisstand und Lernfortschritt der Studierenden richtet.

Die Autoren wünschen beim Lernen viel Spaß und Erfolg!

Danksagung

Herausgeber und Verfasser möchten an dieser Stelle all denen danken, die mit Anregungen, Informationen, Kommentaren, Quellenmaterial und auf andere Weise zum Entstehen dieser 9. Auflage von IT'S ALL PART OF THE JOB beigetragen haben.

An erster Stelle sind hier natürlich die Ehepartner(innen) der Autoren zu nennen, ohne deren Verständnis und Wohlwollen die zeitraubende Erstellung dieses Buches wohl kaum möglich gewesen wäre.

Unser besonderer Dank gilt:

Albrecht, Jimmy, pensionierter Deputy Inspector des NYPD, ist seit über einem Jahr Leiter der Kriminalabteilung von EuLex im Kosovo, USA

Beck, Anna, Politesse, Eichstätt

Becki, Steffen, POK, Wasserschutzpolizei Rheinland-Pfalz, Station Ludwigshafen/Rhein

Bennet, Charles, Police Chief (ret.), Lynchburg, Virginia, USA

Bilgeri, Dieter, PHK, PP Rheinpfalz, VD Rheinpfalz, PASt Ruchheim

Brady, Nicola, Sergeant, Dublin, Irland

Brauner, Gisela, Diplom-Übersetzerin, Wittlich

Brauner, Dr. Thomas, Diplom-Physiker, Berlin

BMW AG, München

Casselman, William L., Patrolman, Director Public Safety, Senior Investigator, Moose Pass, Alaska, USA

Clemenz, Helmut, PK, PP Rheinpfalz, VD Rheinpfalz, Schifferstadt

Club Mobil, München

Connor, Steve, New Scotland Yard, Präsident IPA Britische Sektion, London, England

Crockard, Stephen, Vizepräsident IPA Britische Sektion, Belfast, Nordirland, International Assistant Secretary General

Damaske, Peter, POK, Polizeistation Vitte, Insel Hiddensee

Danik, Jeffrey A., S. A., FBI, West Palm Beach, Florida, USA

Delong, Mike, Deputy Sheriff, Palm Beach Gardens, Florida, USA

Dräger Safety AG & Co KgaA, Lübeck

Feller, Stefan, LKD, Police Commissioner, Leiter der EU-Polizeimission in Bosnien und Hercegovina

Frauenkron, Peter, KHK, PP Köln

Fresemann, Dieter, EPHK a. D., Generalsekretär IPA Deutsche Sektion a. D., Präsident des Deutschen Polizeimuseums in Salzkotten, Goslar

Fromm, Wolfgang, Polizeipräsident, PP Rheinpfalz, Ludwigshafen/Rhein

Geib, Rüdiger, Gemeindeverwaltung Mutterstadt/Pfalz

Geiling, Erik, EKHK, PP Duisburg

Gowitzke, Werner, Europol, Den Haag, Niederlande

Grebe, Thomas, KHK, PP Duisburg

Greschek, Hans, EKHK, PP Rheinpfalz, Kriminalinspektion Neustadt/Weinstraße

Hadeler, Uwe, PHK, Landesamt für Zentrale Polizeiliche Dienste (LZPD) NRW, National Football Information Point, Neuss

Hamblock, Barbara, Diplom-Betriebswirtin, BA, Witten

Hamblock, Heather, MA, Witten

Harms, Anne-Claudia, KHK'in, BKA, Berlin

Helbing, Stefan, KHK, Innenministerium NRW, Düsseldorf

Henk, Horst, PHK, Polizeistation Vitte, Insel Hiddensee

Hitz, Uwe, EPHK, PP Bochum

Humphries, Gavin, PC, Cleveland, England

Hynes, Jerry, (ret), United States Capitol Police, Washington D.C., USA

Jähne, Mathias, PHK, PP Rheinpfalz, PD Ludwigshafen/Rhein, PI Schifferstadt

James, Dr. Earl, †, J.D., Ph.D., First Lieutenant, Michigan State Police, Lansing, Michigan, USA

Jarkiewicz, Martin, PHK, PP Rheinpfalz, VD Rheinpfalz, Schifferstadt

Jones Beti, †, Police Inspector a. D., Ruthin, North Wales

Karbstein, Albert, POK, PP Rheinpfalz, VD Rheinpfalz, PASt Ruchheim
Keeling, Simon, New Scotland Yard, IPA Britische Sektion, London, England
Klein, Volker, KHK, PP Rheinpfalz, PD Ludwigshafen, PI Frankenthal
Klös, Jürgen, Internationaler Präsident IPA a. D., Berlin
Konze, André, POR, Landesamt für Aus- und Fortbildung und Personalangelegenheiten der Polizei NRW
Kral-Özdemir, Mine, KK'in, PP Bochum
Kreutz, Karlheinz, PHK, PP Rheinpfalz, VD Rheinpfalz, Schifferstadt
Kulow, Günter, EKHK, PP Duisburg, Leiter KK 33
Langangke, Arno, POR, DPKO United Nations, New York, USA
Lauerbach, Dieter, PHK, PP Rheinpfalz, Stabsbereich 13, Verkehrspuppenbühne, Ludwigshafen/Rhein
Litges, Tom, PHK, Landesamt für Ausbildung, Fortbildung und Polizeiangelegenheiten der Polizei NRW, Brühl, z.Zt. Afghanistan
Maurer, Ralf, KHK, PP Wuppertal
Mayer, Karl, Chefinspektor, BMI, Wien, Österreich
Meißner, Wolfgang, EPHK, PP Rheinpfalz, VD Rheinpfalz, Leiter PASt Ruchheim
Mergl, Kay, PHK, Wasserschutzpolizei Rheinland-Pfalz, Station Ludwigshafen/Rhein
Mokros, Reinhard, Vizepräsident FHöV NRW, Gelsenkirchen
Mönninghoff, Martin, PD, Deutsche Hochschule der Polizei, Münster - Hiltrup
Müller, Bernd, POK, PP Rheinpfalz, VD Rheinpfalz, PASt Ruchheim
Munsteiner, Klaus, PHK, Bundespolizeidirektion, Koblenz, bpold.presse@polizei.bund.de
Narindal, Jean Philipp, Aigle, Schweiz
Nieder, Klaus, Direktor IPA Bildungszentrum Schloss Gimborn
Nöllenburg, Martin, EKHK, PP Duisburg, Leiter KK 44
Peter, Jo, PHK, Polizeipräsidium Essen
Pommer, Alois, Oberst, Landeskriminalamt Wien, Österreich, z.Zt. Frontex, Warschau, Polen
Reichel, Harald, EPHK, PP Rheinpfalz, Abteilung Polizeieinsatz, Ludwigshafen/Rhein
Ritter, Dr. Markus, PD, Kaiserslautern, z.Zt. Afghanistan
Sawatzki, Horst, PHK, PP Rheinpfalz, Abteilung Polizeieinsatz, Diensthundestaffel, Edenkoben
Schäfer, Hans-Willi, EKHK, PP Bochum, Direktion Kriminalität
Schayen, Karl Heinz, KD a. D., Kleve
Schleyer, Daniel, Deputy Scheriff, Brawley, California, USA
Schmittat, Peter, EPHK, Polizei beim Deutschen Bundestag, Berlin
Schmitz, Heinz, Kaufmann, Wittlich
Scholz, Bernd, KOR, Landesamt für Ausbildung, Fortbildung und Personalangelegenheiten der Polizei NRW, Selm
Schulte-Schrepping, Michael, PHK a. D., z.Zt. Criminal Justice & Police Law Expert EUPOL COPPS Ramallah, Palästinensische Autoritätsgebiete
Schumacher, Olaf, Königswinter
Schwarz, Wolfgang, KHK, PP Rheinpfalz, KI Neustadt/Weinstraße
Shaw, Bernie, Wellingborough, England
Spanheimer, Horst, Polizei Bayern, München
Spörl, Frederik, PK, PP Rheinpfalz, PD Ludwigshafen/Rhein, PI Schifferstadt
Steele, Steve, Major (ret), Tulsa Police Department, Tulsa, Oklahoma, USA
Stoller, Jürgen, PK, PP Rheinpfalz, VD Rheinpfalz, Schifferstadt
Thiel, Wolfgang, EKHK, Hilden
Tiemann, Horst, LPD a. D., Präsident IPA Deutsche Sektion a. D., Selm
Tschentscher, Dr. Frank, Diplom-Biologe, LKA NRW, Düsseldorf
Vigneault, Daniel, C/E, Team's Chief, Sûreté du Québec, Bezirk Charlevoix, La Malbaie, Canada
Vilímovský, Jaromír, Polizeioberkommissar, Kriminalpolizei Olomouc, Tschechische Republik
Vowe, Peter, LKD a. D., Görsroth
VW Kuhlo, Wittlich
Witte, Karla, LAFP NRW, z.Zt.Training Officer, UNLB, Brindisi, Italien

7 Traffic enforcement/control

8 Traffic control and on-the-spot fine

9 Traffic checks and fixed-penalty notices

13 Theft of and from vehicles

14 Shoplifters, pickpockets, thieves, description of persons

15 Robbery, mugging

16 Burglary

17 Punch-ups, riots, hooliganism, criminal damage to property

22 Organized crime and terrorism

23 Weapons

24 Murder, manslaughter

Development of the Police in Germany

This unit deals with

- the origin and meaning of the word "police"
- tasks of the police
- the history of the police in Germany and
- the gender and the plural of nouns.

1.1 Police on TV

Some TV programmes

a) "Behind Bars", "CSI Miami", "Spartan", "Police, Camera, Action", "Judge Judy", "America's Most Wanted", "Cars, Cops and Bailiffs", "Honour Kills", "The Bill", "Columbo", "Video Justice", "Road Wars", "Diagnosis Murder", "The Jury"

b) "The Simpsons", "Who Wants to Be a Millionaire?", "Friends", "News, Weather", "The Daily Politics", "Master Chef", "Deal or No Deal", "Darts Extra", "Shark Mountain", "Travel Shop", "Star Trek", "Impossible Bridges", "The Chaplin Revue"

1. Questions

1. What is the difference between the programmes in group a and group b?
2. Do you know any of these programmes?
3. How many hours a week do you watch TV?
4. At what time do you/your parents/your friends usually switch on the TV?
5. What sort of programmes do you like?
   (films, documentaries, serials, sports, quiz shows, comedy programmes, detective stories/series, music programmes, chat shows, cartoons, others …)

2. Complete the following sentences

1. My favourite channel is ....
2. Life without TV ....
3. I would never ever watch ....
4. People who take part in chat shows are ....
5. My favourite commercial is ....
6. The police on TV are ....
7. A detective in the media spends his time ....

3. Compare your answers with those of your neighbour, then tell the group what you have in common / where you have different opinions

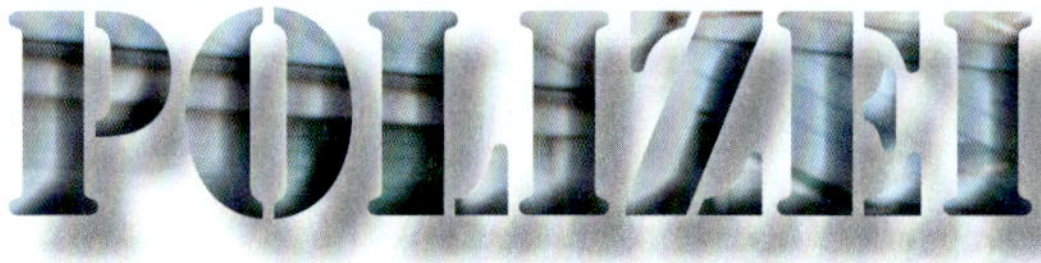

1.2 The word "Police"

The word "police", which exists in different forms in many languages ("Politie", "Polis", "Polizia", "Policja"), is derived from the Greek "Polis" = town. In the city states of ancient Greece, "Politeia" signified municipal order and administration generally.

Later the city states developed into territorial states, but the meaning of "Politeia", which the Romans called "Politia", and which was called "Polizey" in the Middle Ages, did not change; the word meant "state, government, politics, administration, order, monitoring of morality".

Later the word was used less widely, and since the beginning of the 19th century the word "Polizei" has gradually acquired its present meaning (the police are responsible for public safety), but terms like "baupolizeiliche Vorschriften" (= building regulations) still reflect its former, much more comprehensive meaning.

Find at least ten nouns from the police/judicial language which can also be used as verbs. Example: work – to work

1.3 Tasks of the police in the Federal Republic of Germany

The chief task of the police is to stave off any danger to "public security", which means protecting the public against dangers to life and limb as well as property. For this reason, the German penal code comprises a great number of penal provisions to cover all spheres of life.

Broadly, policing can be divided into prevention of danger, crime control and road traffic safety. Checking drunk driving at night serves to detect cases of crime (crime control/prosecution) on the one hand and to increase road traffic safety through the deterrent effect of such checks on the other. The same goes for speed checks.

Nocturnal patrols by plain-clothes officers likewise pursue several goals. Such patrols are intended to catch burglars in the act and to prevent further misdeeds.

Since policing is the responsibility of the German "laender" (states), police officers are, as a matter of principle, only allowed to operate within their respective states. There are exceptions based on agreements between the federal government and state governments, e.g. for riot police operations, certain cases of investigative work and essential emergency measures. In addition, there are exceptions in border areas, based on interstate agreements.

1. Which answer is correct?

"If the chief task of the police is to stave off any danger to public security", this means that

a) the police are responsible that the citizens can feel safe.
b) the police protect the citizens against foreign armies.
c) the police must be present whenever a dangerous situation could occur.

"The German penal code comprises a great number of penal provisions" means

a) there are not enough possibilities to punish an offender.
b) there are many ways to punish an offender.
c) there are ways to punish offenders but they are not severe enough.

"The same goes for speed checks" means

a) the same police officers go to the checkpoints.
b) speed checks also increase traffic safety and deter drivers from speeding.
c) speed checks have no effect on speeding.

"Nocturnal patrols by plain-clothes officers" means that

a) uniformed police officers patrol at night.
b) the police officers concerned do not wear uniform and work the early morning shift.
c) the police officers concerned do not wear uniform and patrol the streets at night.

2. What does the text say about

a) checking drunk drivers?
b) nocturnal patrols?
c) the consequences of the German federal system on policing?

1.4 A typical task for the police?

Mrs Alexandra Berger from Malchin drove to a local supermarket to do her weekend shopping. Her three-year-old daughter was in the child's seat behind her. In the parking area of the supermarket she got out of the car, but left the car key in the ignition lock. She closed the door, and went to get a shopping trolley. When she came back to the car about 20 seconds later, she could not open the rear door, because young Susie had pressed the door button, and Mrs Berger was locked out. A police car was soon on the scene, and one of the officers drove Mrs Berger back home to retrieve her spare keys while the other one stayed with the girl, playing peek-a-boo with her. And what happened? When mother arrived, little Susie was fast asleep!

1. Questions on the text

1. Where is Malchin?
2. Did Mrs Berger act negligently? Give reasons for your answer.
3. Is this a typical task for the police? Give reasons for your answer.

2. Text production

Here are some headlines from German newspapers:

What might have happened? Choose one of the headlines above, decide what happened, explain what it says in English and write a short report

1.5 History of the police in Germany

Until the end of the Weimar Republic, policing was a matter for the individual German states. From 1933 to 1945 it was centralized by the totalitarian state.

After the end of World War II, the Allies continued the Weimar Republic tradition by establishing new state police services. At first, police officers operated in plain clothes under military police supervision, later in army uniforms which had been dyed blue. They were initially armed with just a wooden baton.

In the four occupation zones, the police developed in different ways because each occupying power wanted to copy its own system. Thus the Gendarmerie in Rhineland-Palatinate was organized on the French model, whereas the police in the British zone was modelled on the British police.

Bavarian police officer (beginning of 20th century)

The Allies also separated policing powers from those of public administration by e.g. transferring the fire brigade, the residents' registration offices and passport offices as well as other public order functions to the local governments. The police were, therefore, left with the task of maintaining security. This separation principally applies in all federal states, although there are minor differences.

The standby police services were also based on the idea of the police being a matter for the individual states. There were also federal police services: the Federal Criminal Police Office, whose main task in the beginning was to collect and collate crime-related data, the Federal Border Guard and as special police services, the "Hausinspektion beim Deutschen Bundestag" (today: Police of the German Bundestag), the "Bahnpolizei" (transport police) and the Postal Inspection Service of the German Postal Services.

After the terrorist attack on Israeli sportsmen and women in the Munich Olympic village in 1972, the federal special intervention group GSG 9 (Grenzschutzgruppe 9) and the state special intervention groups in the individual states were set up.

After 1972, police organization in the federal states was largely standardized, while local government police forces and the Gendarmerie were abolished. Moreover, from 1976, standardized beige-green uniforms were introduced throughout the Federal Republic, with the respective coats of arms of the states being the only apparent difference. Since 2007, some federal states have again introduced blue uniforms for reasons of European standardization.

Over to you. Find out more about the history of the police in

1. your home town
2. your federal state
3. the old Federal Republic of Germany
4. the former German Democratic Republic
5. other countries.

1.6 The lost child

Characters: PK'in Tina Hagers (TH), KOK Carl Hausmann (CH), Hong Kong Detective Meng Tam (MT), girl Ju-Ching Tam (JU)

Police officers are expected to act sensitively and professionally, especially when they have to deal with children. The following scene gives a first impression.

During a visit to Hong Kong, Carl Hausmann's passport was stolen. Detective Meng Tam had to deal with the case. A close friendship developed from this. At the moment, Meng Tam and his wife Lan and their two children are staying with the Hausmanns.

The Hausmanns live in a detached house in a quiet residential area. Close to their house is a playground which is frequented by their children Lea, 6, and Dominique, 8, without either of their parents being present. Today eight-year-old Liang and five-year-old Ju-Ching are with them. Lea and Dominique are riding their bicycles, Liang is skateboarding, and Ju-Ching is pushing a bobby car using her short legs. After a while Ju-Ching rolls from the playground onto the pavement and rolls away. She sometimes turns right or left into a side street, and a short time later she doesn't know where she is.

The other children haven't noticed that she has disappeared. Some residents become aware of her loud crying. As the child does not answer their questions and continues to cry loudly, they call the police. A short time later a patrol car arrives. PK'in Tina Hagers addresses the girl and manages to win her confidence, and as a result of skilled questioning the parents are found and are on their way to the police station.

TH: Well, little lady. You see, everything will be fine soon. Your mummy and your daddy and aunt Hausmann will be here soon to pick you up.

JU: Are you a real police officer?

TH: Yes, I'm a real police officer.

JU: Do you also have a pistol?

TH: Every police officer has a pistol.

JU: Why?

TH: You know, Yu-Ching, sometimes there are very bad people. I have the pistol to protect myself.

JU: Do you also know how to box and do jui-jitsu?

TH: Of course. Once I accidentally hit my boyfriend, so he got a black eye. That was funny.

JU: Is your boyfriend a police officer as well?

TH: Yes, he's a good police officer. His name is Frederik. Many call him Freddy.

JU: Is Freddy here, too?

TH: No, he works at another police station.

JU: Where's mummy?

TH: She'll be here soon, she's on her way.

Tina Hagers takes Ju-Ching in her arms.

JU: Are these your police clothes?

TH: Yes, that's my shirt, and these are my trousers. And over there's my cap.

JU: Can I put it on?

TH: Of course. Put it on, but it's a bit too big for you.

JU: What have you got on your belt?

TH: These are all things which I need. A torch, gloves, handcuffs for very bad people, and some other things. Here's a ballpoint pen for you.

JU: Thank you. Have you also got a prison here?

TH: We put very bad persons into the basement. We've got a few rooms there.

JU: Do you catch many burglars?

TH: Of course.

JU: And you lock them in the basement?

TH: Exactly.

JU: Tell me, how many police cars have you got?

TH: We've got five.

JU: And you're allowed to drive all of them?

TH: Yes, I'm allowed to drive all of them. But the other officers drive them as well. Everyone gets his turn.

JU: In Hong Kong the lights are red and blue. The same here?

TH: No. We've got only blue flashing lights.

JU: Is this your room?

TH: When I'm at work, I sit here. But when I'm off, somebody else sits here.

JU: Do you have to work at night, too?

TH: Yes, because the bad guys do bad things during the night. And we want to catch them.

JU: Yes, that's right – and lock them up in the basement. Can I have a look there?

TH: No, we want to be here when your mum comes. She'll be here in a minute. Here, can you draw me a police officer or a police car? Would you like to do that?

JU: Fine. I'll do that.

Some minutes later the station sergeant knocks at the doorframe. Ju-Ching's parents have come. Ju-Ching runs to meet them immediately. Lan Tam starts crying and holds her daughter very firmly.

JU: Mummy, why are you crying? Look, this is my friend Tina.

Her husband addresses Tina Hagers.

MT: We're greatly indebted to you. We cannot make up for what you've done for Ju-Ching. I know we have taken too much of your time already.

CH: Would you like to come to our house while our Chinese friends are still here?

TH: Thanks a lot for the invitation. I'll certainly accept it.

MT: I'd like to tell you that I'm a police officer as well. I'm a CID officer in Hong Kong. Therefore it's rather embarrassing for me that this has happened. But my wife and I, and also the Hausmanns, never thought that something like this could happen in a small residential area. Their children often play in front of the house or on the playground. Nothing like this has ever happened before. But you certainly know better as this is your area. I think we've all learned something today.

TH: OK, let's not talk about it any more here and now. We'll do that when I come to see you. But you, as a colleague, are invited to look at our police station. I'll be glad to show you around. Please call me so that we can arrange a date. Here's my card.

JU: Daddy, see, Tina is a nice friend. Here, Tina, I've drawn you and your police car. The picture is for you.

Creative writing

1. Write a dialogue between Tina Hagers and Mrs Lan Tam on the occasion of their meeting a week later.
2. How might the story have continued?

1.7 Word comb

Complete the word comb using the clues below

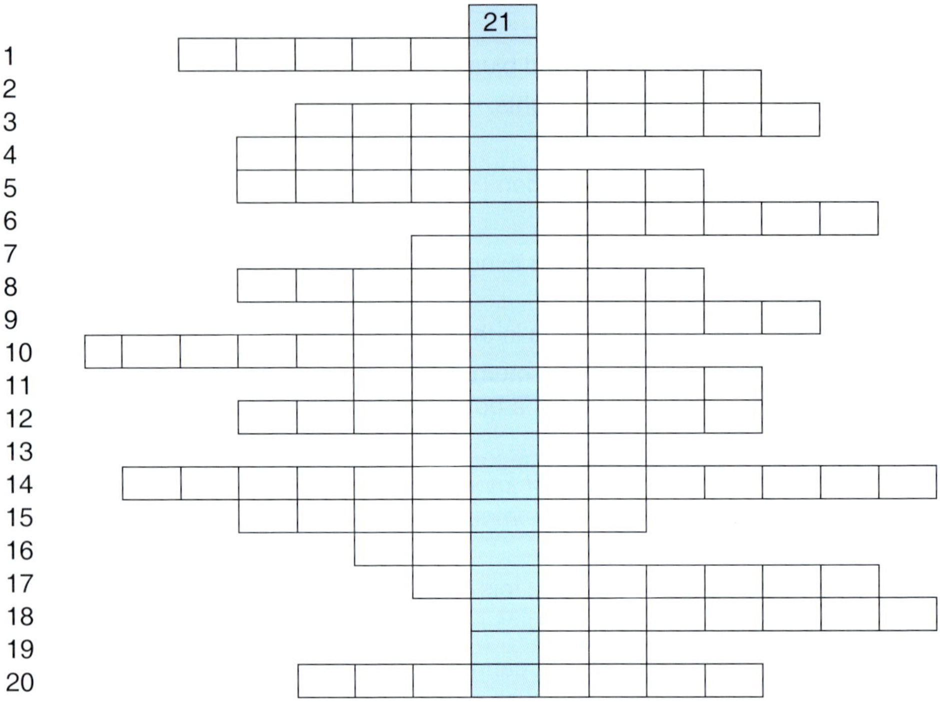

1. you wear them on your hands
2. British word for flashlight
3. to go away suddenly
4. the stick policemen carry
5. a person who lives in an area
6. a person who enters a house illegally
7. to change the colour of your hair
8. a document of identification
9. something that is owned by someone, e.g. land
10. a policeman who works with dogs
11. trained, clever
12. the police use these two very special metal rings and a chain
13. you wear it around your waist
14. a department that controls everything and does a lot of paperwork
15. to keep someone safe
16. a group of people in a trial who decide whether a person is guilty or not guilty
17. one or more reasons why the police believe that something is true or not true
18. to get bigger
19. you wear it on your head
20. the part of your house that is often underground
21. after training, most police officers spend some time in this service

1.8 Gender of nouns

Grundregel

Männliche Personen = *he;* weibliche Personen = *she;* Tiere, Sachen etc. = *it*

The police constable *arrested the thief.*	***He*** *arrested the thief.*
Mrs Steele *is a police lieutenant.*	***She*** *is a police lieutenant.*
The nearest police station *is round the corner.*	***It*** *is round the corner.*

Besonderheiten

Tiere sind im allgemeinen sächlich

The elephant *in the zoo has died.* ***It*** *has died.*

Haustiere werden meist als „Familienmitglieder“ angesehen und sind daher männlich oder weiblich; dies gilt natürlich auch für Polizeihunde

PC Janet Morris, a dog handler, has a new ***dog****.* ***He*** *is a German shepherd.*

Ländernamen sind oft weiblich

Britain *used to be known for* ***her*** *shipbuilding industry.*

Kraftfahrzeuge, Schiffe, Flugzeuge usw. sind oft weiblich

At the petrol station you "fill ***her*** *up" when you want the tank of your* ***car*** *filled up completely.*

Besondere Wörter, Endungen oder Zusätze für das Geschlecht

uncle – aunt, waiter – waitress, lady teacher, woman police constable (WPC).

1.9 Plural of nouns

Grundregel

Anhängen von -s

*One truncheon – five truncheon****s***

Besonderheiten (Eselsbrücke FOXY)

F – Substantive auf -f und -fe bilden den Plural häufig mit *-ves*
*calf – cal****ves****, thief – thie****ves****, knife – kni****ves****; aber: roof – roof****s****, chief – chief****s****.*
O – Substantive auf -o bilden den Plural häufig mit *-es*
*potato – potato****es****, tomato – tomato****es****; aber: photo – photo****s****, radio – radio****s***
X – Substantive auf -s, -x, -ch usw. (Zischlaute) hängen *-es* an
*boss – boss****es****, box – box****es****, match – match****es****, bush – bush****es***
Y – Substantive auf -y nach Konsonant bilden den Plural auf *-ies*
*family – famil****ies****, lady – lad****ies***

Unregelmäßige Pluralformen

foot – ***feet****, man –* ***men****, woman –* ***women****, child –* ***children****, mouse –* ***mice****.*

1.10 Fill-in exercise

Fill in the feminine or plural form

A Chicago detective

John Darms is a detective with the Chicago Police. He has a son and three ...., two brothers and three ...., an uncle and an .... and five nephews and .... He started his professional career more than 20 years ago and since then, serving under half a dozen different (chief) ...., has not only arrested many (thief) .... and burglars, but also a number of murderers and even one .... You cannot imagine how many men and .... are involved in crime. For example, there was the case when two (German) .... broke into an apartment and killed a young (widower) ...., who worked as a (waiter) .... They stabbed her with two carving (knife) ...., but did not harm the two (baby) .... who were sleeping in their cots and did not wake up despite their mother's loud (cry) .... The two killers, one male and one ...., in fact they were husband and ...., fled from the scene of the crime on foot, climbing over a number of (roof) .... and dashing through various rows of (bush) .... They were arrested in the house of a friend, an (actor) ...., who informed the police because she noticed two blood-stained (scarf) .... around the woman's (calf) .... She had injured herself while committing the crime, so the authorities had enough evidence. The two are now serving their sentences at the Illinois State Penitentiary.

1.11 Useful phrases

Übersetzen Sie

1. Das Wort Polizei kommt aus der griechischen Sprache.

   ....

2. Es bedeutete ganz allgemein städtische Ordnung und Verwaltung.

   ....

3. Erst im 19. Jahrhundert erhielt es seine heutige Bedeutung.

   ....

4. Die Aufgabe der Polizei ist es, Gefahren abzuwehren, der Kriminalität vorzubeugen und für Verkehrssicherheit zu sorgen.

   ....

   ....

5. In Deutschland ist die polizeiliche Tätigkeit Angelegenheit der einzelnen Länder.

   ....

6. Die Bereitschaftspolizeien wurden nach dem 2. Weltkrieg aufgestellt.

....

7. Spezialeinsatzkommandos wurden erst nach dem Münchner Terroranschlag von 1972 aufgestellt.

....

8. Es wird erwartet, dass Polizeibeamte in jeder Situation sensibel und professionell handeln.

....

9. Dies ist besonders wichtig, wenn sie mit Kindern oder Opfern umgehen müssen.

....

10. Seit 2007 werden blaue Uniformen eingeführt.

....

11. Teile der Ausrüstung eines Polizeibeamten sind unter anderem: Handschuhe, Taschenlampe, Handschellen, Waffe und Schlagstock.

....

....

1.12 Key words and phrases

administration – baton – burglar – CID officer – constable – crime control – deterrent – dog handler – evidence – Federal/State Criminal Police Office – guilty – handcuffs – judge – life and limb – plain-clothes officer – policing – property – public safety/security – riot police – scene of the crime – special intervention group – standby police service – thief – truncheon

Unit 2 Police organization in Germany

This unit deals with

- the structure of the police in Germany
- police organization in Bavaria and North Rhine-Westphalia
- the federal police services in Germany
- other governmental and private police and security services and
- the English genitive.

2.1 Sixteen state and three federal police services

The Federal Republic of Germany consists of 16 federal states or "laender". Each state or "land" has its own police service. Future police officers are, therefore, recruited and trained at state level. The duties and powers of the state police services are defined by the respective state legislation, which is, however, largely identical throughout the Federal Republic. Someone who is not involved with the police would not notice any difference. In addition, there are three federal police services: the Federal Police, the Federal Criminal Police Office, and the Police of the German Bundestag.

True or not true?

1. Each German federal state has its own police service.
2. Police officers in Germany are recruited and trained in the same way.
3. In some German states a police officer has more power than in others.
4. The federal police services have greater powers than the state police services.

Fill in the right number on the map

1 = Baden-Wuerttemberg
2 = Bavaria
3 = Berlin
4 = Brandenburg
5 = Bremen
6 = Hamburg
7 = Hesse
8 = Lower Saxony
9 = Mecklenburg-Western Pomerania
10 = North Rhine-Westphalia
11 = Rhineland-Palatinate
12 = Saarland
13 = Saxony
14 = Saxony Anhalt
15 = Schleswig-Holstein
16 = Thuringia

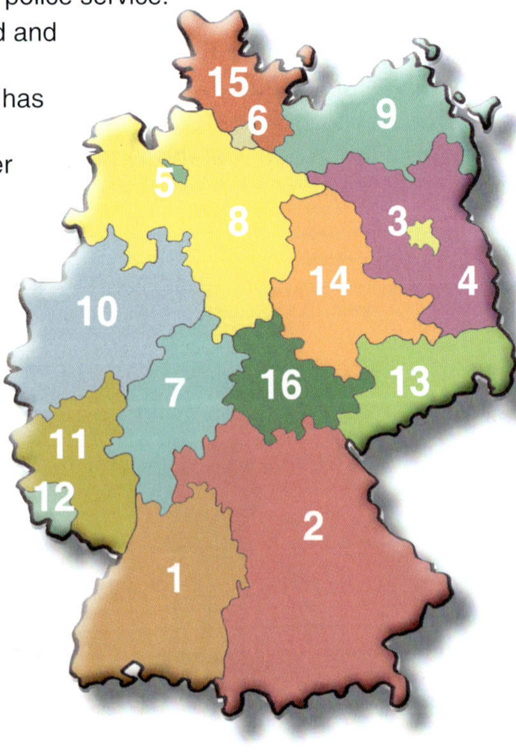

2.2 Different branches of the state police services

There is no such thing as "the police". The word "police" usually suggests uniformed police officers. When the "police" are called, it is the uniformed police who start dealing with the matter in question. They are responsible for all traffic-related matters (prevention, monitoring, recording accidents). Officers in uniform also act as investigators and collect and secure evidence. In some federal states, the uniformed police also deal with medium-level and petty crime. The riot police offers one of several possibilities for officers to specialize within the police service. The respective officers are specially equipped for large-scale crowd management like sports events or major demonstrations, or they support their colleagues at local police stations.

In case of criminal offences, the CID (Criminal Investigation Department) are called. In TV films, these officers solve even the most sophisticated crime within 90 minutes. CID officers wear plain clothes. This division has specialists in the most diverse fields.

The river police are in charge of safety and security on navigable rivers, canals, lakes and in ports.

2.3 Police organization in Bavaria

In the past Bavaria had a four-tier police structure, with the Bavarian Department of the Interior being the first tier. The second tier consisted of seven regional police presidencies, the third of 35 police directorates and the fourth of several hundred police inspectorates.

In the course of a major reform, from 2007 to 2009 the police presidencies and the police directorates were merged, so a three-tier system was established with the Department of the Interior, ten new police presidencies and the existing police inspectorates. The new presidencies are:

Munich for the state capital Munich
Nuremberg for Central Frankonia
Würzburg for Lower Frankonia
Bayreuth for Upper Frankonia
Regensburg for Upper Palatinate
Straubing for Lower Bavaria
Rosenheim for Upper Bavaria South
Ingolstadt for Upper Bavaria North
Augsburg for Swabia North
Kempten for Swabia South/West.

The new presidencies are the control centres for their areas, where all emergency calls are received and all operations are directed from; but the operations are carried out by the local police inspectorates. Thus the local inspectorates have more time and possibilities for immediate action.

2.4 Police organization in North Rhine-Westphalia

North Rhine-Westphalia's reorganization of the police in 1994, which was aimed at integrating all police functions under the heading of "danger prevention/law enforcement", did not totally meet expectations. Therefore the state government developed a product-oriented directorate model which concentrates on the main duties of crime control, danger prevention and operations, traffic matters and central tasks. Within this framework, the local police authorities are allowed ample scope so that local traditions can be maintained. At present, North Rhine-Westphalia has eight different directorate models.

2.5 Where would you go to?

Match the questions and answers

a)	Where would John Davies go to if his car was broken into?	1	complaints management
b)	Where would Sheila Crowe go to if she witnessed a burglary?	2	special traffic
c)	Where would Gemma Adams go to if she found a broken refrigerator and a lot of cans of old motor oil in a car park?	3	KK 16 Trickdelikte
d)	Where would the demonstrators go to if they wanted to complain about an officer's actions?	4	public relations department
e)	Where would Woman Police Constable (WPC) Yvonne Sharman go to if she did not get promoted because of her sex?	5	traffic supervision group
f)	Where would an American tourist go to if he lost 500 euros in a shell game?	6	theft
g)	Where would the kindergarten teacher go to if she found a bag with syringes and sachets of white powder?	7	identification service
h)	Where would the manageress of a crane company go to if she had to transport a very large crane from A to B?	8	traffic commissariat
i)	Where would an old-age pensioner go to if he thought some girls were working as prostitutes in the next-door flat?	9	environmental crime
j)	Where would a witness go to if he had to identify a suspected criminal?	10	vice
k)	Where would a motorcyclist go to if he got a speeding ticket and thought that the radar set did not work properly?	11	drug squad
l)	Where would a motorist go to if he suspected that someone intentionally crashed into his car?	12	burglary crime squad
m)	Where would a group of students go to if they wanted information about the police for a school project?	13	equal opportunities

2.6 Uniforms

In the past, the state police services in Germany had many different uniforms. A standard uniform was only introduced in 1976; police officers were issued with green tunics and beige trousers. In 1990, after reunification, the police in the five new eastern states of Germany adopted this standard uniform as well.

German police officers wear a patch on the top left sleeve displaying the respective state's coat of arms. The same applies to the emblem on the cap star. There are also slight differences with regard to rank insignia.

Since 2006 several German state police services have decided to change the design and the colour of uniforms again. The new uniforms will be more practical for street and office duty, and the colour is blue, following the example of most European police services.

2.7 The Federal Police

The former Federal Border Guard (Bundesgrenzschutz BGS) was a product of the Cold War. It was established in 1951, at a time when the Federal Republic of Germany did not yet have armed forces; its purpose was to counter potential acts of aggression from the Communist East below the threshold of a military conflict. Therefore the Federal Border Guard was equipped with military weaponry and trained in a military style. They had military ranks and their own rank insignia. When, in 1956, the Bundeswehr was established, nearly half of the BGS personnel chose to join the Bundeswehr. In the course of time the tasks for the remaining members of the BGS changed. Their first great test was the great flood in Hamburg in 1962, when 4,000 members were deployed.

After the terrorist attack on the Israeli team during the Olympic Games in Munich in 1972, the GSG 9 – as the first SWAT-like unit – was established, which five years later freed 86 hostages from a Lufthansa airliner at Mogadishu Airport in Somalia. In 1976 training was adapted to the training of police forces in the federal states. The BGS also decided to join the nationwide rank system with civilian ranks and rank patches. However, the new nationwide rank insignia were not adopted before 1990, and only then did the BGS switch to the standard police uniform. On 1st October 1987, the first women joined the BGS. After reunification in 1990, border patrols and checks of persons at the inner-German border were no longer necessary; also about 7,000 members of the Border Patrols of the former German Democratic Republic were integrated. In 1992, the BGS took over the duties of the transport police, and about 3,000 railway police officers were also integrated. On 1st July 2005 the name was changed to Federal Police.

2.8 The Federal Criminal Police Office

The Federal Criminal Police Office (Bundeskriminalamt BKA) was founded in Hamburg in 1951. It evolved from the "Criminal Police Office for the British (occupation) Zone". Later Wiesbaden was chosen as location for the new headquarters.

The main task at that time was to serve as the central agency for police communication and information between the federal states as well as for international co-operation.

The Federal Criminal Police Office has grown with its tasks. During the seventies, information technology, material evidence and computerization were its main challenges. During the seventies and eighties, the terrorism threat of the Red Army Faction kept the Federal Criminal Police Office busy, and during the nineties it played a leading role in developing the new state criminal offices in the five new laender after German reunification and in dealing with crimes committed by members of the GDR government and its agencies. Nowadays the threat of international Islamic terrorism poses the greatest challenge.

The Federal Criminal Police Office is prepared to cope with growing tasks. In 2004, a "Joint Counter-Terrorism Centre" was introduced. A new "International Coordination" division was developed in 2007 to coordinate the work of BKA liaison officers throughout the world, to support EU twinning activities and to streamline all international BKA activities.

From humble beginnings, the Federal Criminal Police Office has become an efficient agency with more than 5,500 employees, with specialists in many different fields. Its headquarters are in Wiesbaden, with branch offices in Berlin and Meckenheim near Bonn.

2.9 The Police of the German Bundestag

With about 135 officers, who are supported by 25 officers of the Federal Police, the Police of the German Bundestag in Berlin is Germany's smallest police service. They are responsible for security and order on all premises of the German Federal Parliament, and also other premises that are only used temporarily, for example, during international conferences. They are answerable to the President of the German Bundestag.

Find out about other countries

2.10 A state visit

Part 1

Briefing between unit commander Peter Reiser (PR) of a close protection unit of the Bundestag Police and Commander Jack Hurst (JH) on the occasion of a state visit to the Bundestag.

PR: Hello, my name is Peter Reiser. I'm the police officer in charge at the Bundestag. I'm glad you've contacted me in good time, so that we can discuss the details of your president's visit.

JH: Pleased to meet you. My name is Jack Hurst. I'm in charge of the close protection unit for the president. Please tell me about your programme for the visit. The best thing would be to walk around all the places in question.

PR: It's always easier if you know the local conditions. Even so, I have to draw your attention to some special aspects. Under the constitution of the Federal Republic, the Bundestag Police are the only police service authorized to act within the entire parliamentary precinct. No other security organization or agency is allowed to act here, which means that we're in charge of close protection within these premises.

JH: I'm afraid that's not good enough. Like that, I can't fulfil my protection duties.

PR: I suppose there are similar rules in your country. I can't imagine that German bodyguards would provide protection in your parliament.

JH: Of course not, so how are we to solve the problem?

PR: I suggest that, as unit commander, you stay with your president. Mind you, I cannot allow any of your team to carry a firearm. You'll have to leave them in your vehicle or deposit them in the safe provided for this purpose. Close protection will be provided by the Bundestag police.

JH: OK, but I've got to be right next to the president at all times.

PR: I'll introduce you to my team so the officers will be able to identify you, and nobody will obstruct you. After that, we'll walk the whole length of the way envisaged by the programme for the visit. And there is one more detail: you'll have to leave the conference room with us after we've escorted the representatives of the press outside.

JH: I'm with you as far as the assignment is concerned. Thanks for all the information.

Part 2

Close protection in Germany

Every German (1) .... is entitled to close protection, depending on the assessment of danger. Broadly speaking, state politicians are (2) .... by state police officers and federal politicians by federal police officers. However, there are certain (3) .... As a rule, the Chancellor insists on being protected by officers from his/her (4) .... state, as was/is the case with Helmut Schmidt, Gerhard Schröder, Dr. Helmut Kohl or Dr. Angela Merkel. The number of officers (5) .... for this purpose depends on the danger level; protection can amount to permanent (24/7) protection of the politician concerned, (6) .... family members and other people living within his/her household.

The tasks of protection can also be divided, e.g. protection of (7) .... by members of the local police and close protection by the Federal Police.

Danger assessment also covers residential buildings and security (8) .... like stronger doors and windows as well as plate-glass panes.

Complete the above text with words from this list

1.	VIP	politician	statesman
2.	protected	secured	safe
3.	rules	exceptions	irregularities
4.	home	individual	private
5.	sent	deployed	engaged
6.	near	narrow	close
7.	premises	landscape	zone
8.	means	works	measures

2.11 Voluntary police services

In Germany, there are voluntary police services in Baden-Württemberg, Hesse, Brandenburg, Saxony and Bavaria. Voluntary policing is restricted to a few hours per week or month, and is – as a matter of principle – strictly voluntary. The tasks and powers of these voluntary services vary from state to state. Their members are chiefly deployed to support uniformed police officers at station level, to protect premises and during major events.

2.12 Public order police services

While the police are responsible for staving off public danger and maintaining law and order, the public order authorities are in charge of staving off civil dangers and maintaining public order. This division is chiefly due to the fact that many fields of responsibility were transferred from the police to other authorities after World War II. However, this principle is handled in different ways in Germany's federal states. It is only in North Rhine-Westphalia that the two authorities have different powers. Depending on the federal state concerned, the public order authorities are responsible for the law of registration, aliens law, the fields of law relating to trade, building, water, infectious diseases, animal diseases and dead bodies, as well as the law relating to food, waste, soil protection and emissions. The interface between the police and other public authorities in their everyday work lies in their respective powers of investigation, prosecution and punishment of public order offences, e.g. with regard to stationary traffic.

After the public authorities had, for a long time, depended on official assistance by the police, there is now a nationwide tendency to carry out such tasks as a local authority police force with their own uniformed and partly even armed personnel, with the uniforms and service vehicles resembling their police equivalents to such an extent that, for instance in Hesse, one has to have a close look to see which is which. It is in the spirit of the philosophy of community policing that joint patrols are more and more frequently being carried out in order to ensure that the citizens' problems are also registered immediately by the authority in charge.

2.13 Services with policing functions

In Germany, other authorities with policing functions are:

the **Border Customs Service**, which is authorized – within the customs surveillance zone (within 30 km of the federal border) – to check vehicles and persons even after they have passed the border and – if there are reasonable grounds for suspicion – to search vehicles and demand evidence of the origin of goods carried,

the **Customs Investigation Service**, which investigates and institutes proceedings in cases of criminal and other offences concerning customs and tax matters, the **Tax Investigation Service**, which combats tax evasion, tax crimes and tax offences,

the **Joint Drugs Investigation Groups**, in which police and customs authorities act jointly against the smuggling of drugs from abroad,

the **Joint Financial Investigation Groups** of the state criminal police offices, federal police and state tax authorities, whose remit it is to investigate money-laundering offences,

the **Military Police** – the members of which are soldiers who serve in a police capacity in the military sector. Their work impacts on the civil sphere, for instance in connection with manoeuvres and major events.

2.14 Private security services

In law, private security services are traders. Their employees are required to prove that they are reliable and also to furnish evidence of knowledge in certain fields in accordance with established trading standards. They are specialists in a variety of tasks and fill a gap between governmental responsibilities and the protection of private rights. The main legal basis of their work is the law of proprietorship. It is on this basis that e.g. employees of a plant's protective service are empowered to deny unauthorized persons access to a company's premises. The interface between private security services and the police are semi-public spheres, e.g. in trams and stations, where private security services and the police often cooperate in security partnerships. While the Hamburg police academy traditionally trains junior commissioned police officers, it has, since October 2007, also been offering "security management" courses for the middle management of private security services.

As a matter of principle, private security services are unarmed. There are exceptions, e.g. when valuables are transported or when private individuals are to be protected.

2.15 The control room

The control room is a security area with sophisticated equipment which only authorized persons are allowed to enter. It is the centre of any police station, and all police activity is controlled from here.

In a modern control room there are many monitors, keyboards, telephones, microphones and many white and coloured flashing buttons. They are all integrated into a radio and control desk.

The officers who work here must have the necessary knowledge of the equipment and the ways police respond to an incident, they must know their area, must be articulate – and always fully concentrate. They must react, in a professional manner, to every 110 call, to every silent bank alarm, to every other call and request they receive.

The officer is the coordinator and contact for his colleagues on the beat, during operations, and also inside the building. He/she opens doors, security airlock systems, and the gates for police vehicles which leave or enter the station, monitors the CCTV cameras which protect the premises, and is the telephone operator. Phones are ringing, radio calls are being sent and received; everything seems to be very hectic.

The interior of a control room is more or less the same everywhere, and an insider immediately knows what to do. The control desk is in the centre of the room.

The desk is secured by a bullet-proof glass pane and a pass-through hatch, usually a deep drawer. Talking is done by means of an intercom. A magnetic board serves to pass on pieces of information, to show the number of officers present, the names of officers present and absent, the number of patrol cars and their radio call signs. In motorway police stations, there is a large map of the operational area and the roadworks sections.

Office furniture contains the necessary documents and also reference books. One cupboard contains hand-held radios, photo and video equipment, cases with equipment to secure traces, cases with forms and other equipment used at the scene of an incident, breathalyzer equipment, glow sticks to direct traffic and other things for everyday routine operations. There are also compartments for the documents and keys of the patrol cars.

There is also a weapons locker, either in the control room or in an adjoining room. Here, additional weapons and ammunition are stored, but also handcuffs and shackles for arrested persons.

Everywhere electronic data processing prevails, everything is done electronically and digitally.

But nothing would work without the officers who work here. It's human beings who control everything.

2.16 A shift at a police station

Characters: shift leader = SL, control desk = CD, patrol 1 = P1, patrol 2 = P2, patrol 3 = P3, plain-clothes patrol = PCP, officers at the station, processing of cases = OSPC, custody service = CS, recording charges = RC, additional shift service = ASS

Morning shift

06.00	SL	taking over from shift leader of night shift, checking that all the equipment is there, checking the number of officers present, taking over and checking detained persons, making entries in the logbook, report number of officers to acting police chief
06.00	CS	checking on detained persons, at least every half-hour, by officers at the station, until the detained persons are released
06.10	P1	beginning of patrol
06.25	P1	executing a warrant
06.45	P1	recording an accident (accident with injured persons)
07.15	P1	recording an accident (damage-only accident)
07.20	RC	recording a charge at the station (property damage)
07.35	P1	investigation in a case of theft, the charge has already been recorded
08.00	P1	investigation in a hit-and-run case, the charge has already been recorded
08:00	P2	beginning of patrol
08.00	ASS	beginning of traffic checks (alternately stationary and mobile checks), briefing
08:25	P1+P2	response to bank alarm
08:25	ASS	bank alarm, dispatching unmarked car with two plain-clothes officers
08:30	RC	recording a charge at the station (bicycle theft)
09:00	P1+P2	false bank alarm
09:00	SL	informing chief
09:10	P1+ASS	return to station, end of patrol
09.15	P3	beginning of patrol
09:25	P3	traffic enforcement (especially use of mobile phones and seatbelt offences)
09:30	ASS	departure to first checkpoint
09:35	P2	recording an accident (accident with injured persons)
09:50	ASS	checkpoint installed and in operation
10:00	RC	recording a charge at the station (bodily harm)
10:10	P2	investigations in hospital after recording of accident
10:15	SL	briefing with chief, community beat officer and juvenile crime department (police checks at points where offenders meet to plan offences, reports about suspicious persons and vehicles)
10:30	P3	recording a charge at a filling station (filling station fraud)
11:00	P2	end of patrol
11:20	RC	recording a charge at the station (hit-and-run accident)
11:25	P3	fire at a flat
11:25	P2	responding to fire at flat (backup by P3)
11:25	ASS	stopping checkpoint duty, block street and control traffic at site of fire
12:00	P2+P3	fire at flat extinguished, end of patrol
12:00	SL	passing on responsibility to shift leader of following shift

Continue the day. Write down what might happen in the late and night shifts

2.17 Whose responsibility is it?

Until 1975, the country police wore green uniforms and the city police wore blue uniforms in Bavaria. In 1959, the following case happened in a county town:

The dead body of a male was found in a ditch. Later it became known that the man had been walking and had suddenly died as a result of a heart attack. One half of the dead body was on the territory of the county town, the other half on country territory. Who was, therefore, in charge of the investigation? Well, in this case, the decision was soon taken. A high-ranking police officer of the country police passed the scene by chance and said to his lower-ranking city police colleagues: "That's your case, because the head is on your territory."

2.18 Genitive

's-Genitiv	
Bildung	
's im Singular	*Peter's book*
' im Plural auf -s	*the five constables' uniforms*
's bei unregelmäßigem Plural	*the policemen's truncheons*
' oder *'s* bei Eigennamen auf -s	*James' tunic* oder *James's tunic*
Anwendung	
bei Personen und Personengruppen	*the neighbour's garden, the police chief's house, the special unit's office*
bei Staaten, Städten und Tieren	*England's industry, New York's police, the dog's tail, New York City's police department*
häufig bei Zeit- und Ortsangaben	*today's newspaper, Scotland's new parliament, this week's wanted persons list*
house, shop, store usw. entfallen meist	at *my brother's (house); to the baker's (shop)*
of-Genitiv	
Bildung	
	the end of the war; the door(s) of the house(s)
Anwendung	
bei Sachen	*the lock of the door*
in Objektfällen	*the assassination of the president*
nach Zahlwörtern und Mengenangaben	*five of the suspects, a pound of heroin*
nach bestimmten Substantiven	*the City of London, the Isle of Man, the rank of PC*

2.19 Fill-in exercise

Fill in the correct form of the genitive

John and Sally are spending an evening out: John has taken (car – his father) .... but hasn't bothered to close the (garage – door) .... First they go to (pub – Jim) .... where John buys a (coke – bottle) .... and a (wine – glass) .... for Sally. A few minutes later (friends – Sally) ....

Tina and Joan come in with their boyfriends. As John and Sally haven't met the two (girls – boyfriends) .... before, they are quite surprised to learn that (boyfriend – Tina) .... Charles is a police constable and that (boyfriend – Joan) .... Warren also works in the (crime prevention – field) ....; he is a store detective. And (father – Charles) .... is a detective with the local CID. They have (a couple – drinks – rounds) .... and enjoy themselves very much. However, John only drinks coke as tonight it's his turn to drive back home. And when driving the car into the garage, he makes an unpleasant discovery: both his and (bike – his father) .... have gone. "That's your fault," says Sally, "because you couldn't be bothered to close the (garage – door)."

2.20 Useful phrases

Erklären Sie einem ausländischen Kollegen, dass

1. – es in Deutschland 16 Länder- und 3 Bundespolizeien gibt.

   ....

2. – man, grob gesprochen, zwischen Bereitschaftspolizei, uniformierter Polizei, Kriminalpolizei und Wasserschutzpolizei unterscheidet.

   ....

   ....

3. – fast überall die grünen Uniformen durch blaue ersetzt werden/wurden.

   ....

4. – die Bundespolizei unter anderem für die Sicherheit auf Flughäfen und Bahnanlagen zuständig ist.

   ....

   ....

5. – das Bundeskriminalamt unter anderem für die Zusammenarbeit mit dem Ausland und die Terrorismusbekämpfung zuständig ist.

   ....

   ....

6. – es in einigen Bundesländern freiwillige Polizeidienste gibt.

   ....

7. – in Deutschland der ruhende Verkehr von den Ortspolizeibehörden überwacht wird.

   ....

8. – die Wache das Herzstück einer Polizeiinspektion ist.

   ....

2.21 Key words and phrases

CID – close protection – control (room) – customs service – federal police (service) – liaison officer – public order police service – rank insignia – shift – state police service – SWAT team – uniformed police officer – warrant

Unit 3

Police training and ranks in Germany

This unit deals with

- some positive and negative aspects of being a police officer
- applications for a position in the police
- the subjects taught at a police academy
- police ranks and
- all the verb forms.

3.1 Two true stories?

Story 1

At an international meeting at the IPA information centre at Gimborn all the participants from a dozen European countries were asked to tell the other participants why they had become police officers. A lady from Sweden told the others: "When I graduated from high school, I wanted to become a nurse or a supermarket manager or a police officer. I got three favourable replies on the same day. So I took three new envelopes, put the letters inside, and after having shuffled them around I opened one envelope with my eyes closed. That's how I became a police officer."

Apparently it was the right choice, because she now holds a leading position in the police service of her country.

Story 2

A personnel officer interviews three candidates who have applied for the position of detective. To test their skills in recognizing a suspect, he shows the first candidate a picture of a man for five seconds and then hides it. "How would you recognize that man?" The first candidate answers, "That's easy, he's only got one eye." The personnel officer says: "That's because the picture shows his profile."

He then flashes the picture for five seconds at the second candidate, who says, "That man's easy to catch because he only has one ear." The officer responds angrily, "What's the matter with you two? Of course only one eye and one ear are showing because it's a picture of his profile. Is that the best answer you can come up with?"

He then shows the picture to the third candidate, saying, "This is your suspect. How would you recognize him?" He quickly adds, "Think hard before giving me a stupid answer." The candidate looks at the picture intensely for a moment and says, "Hmmm ..... the suspect wears contact lenses."

The personnel officer is surprised and speechless because he really doesn't know himself whether the suspect wears contacts or not. He leaves the room and goes to his office, checks the suspect's file on his computer, and comes back with a big smile.

"Wow! I can't believe it ..... it's true. Good work. How did you know?"

"Easy," says the candidate, "he can't wear regular glasses because he has only one eye and one ear."

1. Have a look at the headline again. Are these stories true? What do you think?

2. Explain in your own words

a) international meeting
b) manager
c) envelope
d) choice
e) detective
f) suspect
g) profile
h) contact lenses

3. Find synonyms

a) reply
b) apparently
c) recognize
d) skill
e) flash

4. Say it in a different way, avoiding the words in bold type

a) ... with my **eyes closed** ...
b) ... she **holds a leading position** ...
c) ... the officer **responds angrily** ...
d) ... the best answer you **can come up with** ...
e) ... **think hard before giving** me **a stupid answer** ...
f) ... she is **surprised and speechless** ...
g) ... he **checks** the suspect's **file** on his computer ...

5. Find three jokes about the police on the internet and tell them to your colleagues

3.2 Police officer – a good job?

Why I joined the police

Make a list of the advantages and disadvantages of being a police officer. Afterwards discuss the pros and cons and write an essay

The following words and phrases will help you:

administration – bad reputation in certain neighbourhoods – CASTOR – chances of promotion – crime scene officer – danger – deal with people in extreme situations – decent salary later – decision-making – demonstrations – dog handler section – enforce the law – good pay during training period – help other people – help to prevent crime and accidents – income of one's own from the very beginning – interesting job – leadership – learning on the job – lifelong learning – lifetime employment – mounted police – no military or alternative service – overtime – responsibility – secure pension – shift work very strenuous – social life difficult due to shift work – specialists – standby duty – technician – uniform – various career paths

3.3 Police training in Bavaria

Bavaria has a three-tier police career system: candidates are trained for the intermediate, higher intermediate and senior services. In some other federal states there is no intermediate service, training is for the higher intermediate and senior services only.

Every applicant for the police must meet the following conditions:

- he/she must be of German nationality, although exceptions are possible
- he/she must be at least 165 cm tall
- he/she must be between 17 and 24, although there are exceptions with regard to the maximum age, for example for ex-soldiers of the Bundeswehr who have served for a limited number of years
- he/she must be medically fit
- he/she must not be overindebted and must also have an unblemished reputation
- he/she must have passed the entrance examination.

The educational requirements for training for the intermediate service are:

- secondary school certificate and qualified vocational training or
- General Certificate of Secondary Education (GCSE) or
- vocational baccalaureat diploma or
- A levels.

The educational requirements for the higher intermediate service are:

- vocational baccalaureat diploma or
- A levels.

Training for the intermediate service

Training for the intermediate service lasts 29 months and is divided into 5 modules.

In the first module of six months, the trainees receive theoretical and practical tuition in 18 different subjects, they learn how to read and interpret law texts. They also learn how to use their service weapon, and great emphasis is placed on physical fitness. And they do a one-week practical training course at a police station.

In the second module (6 months), the emphasis is on police casework in cross-departmental lessons with a high degree of practical exercise. The thematic areas concerned are: "service operations", "traffic", "patrols" and "combating crime". Students do practical exercises in police intervention as well as PC skills, and there is an achievement test. Students are required to pass the class B driving test by the end of this module.

In the third module (6 months), students take simple police measures, e.g. issuing penalty tickets or questioning witnesses. They also take part in real police actions, albeit under supervision. They do a four-week practical training course at a police station.

In the fourth module (6 months), they do a twelve-week practical training course at a police station, during which period they are deployed, together with a patrol partner, for all assignments that might develop. They do a road safety training course with blue lights and siren, they are tested with respect to safely handling firearms, and they acquire techniques that allow them to cope with stress.

In the fifth and last module (5 months), students practise difficult police situations, e.g. arresting a fugitive suspect or criminal or securing evidence at the crime scene. In addition, there is an intensive week of English and very demanding subjects like dealing with mentally ill people or informing relatives of a death.

The training course ends with a final examination consisting of four written papers, a practical examination and an oral examination in English.

The thematic areas above are divided into law (general police law, criminal law, traffic law, special security law, civil service law), police practice (criminalistics, case handling, information technology, weapons training and marksmanship, deployment in groups, driving training), personal development (professional ethics, political education and current events, communication and conflict resolution, deployment-related self-defence and measures for one's own security, sports, English) and police conduct in deployment situations (comprehensive training from emergency call to the end of a case file).

After passing the employment examination, each trainee is appointed police constable.

Training for the higher intermediate service

This training course lasts three years and takes place at the University of Applied Sciences: Public Administration and Administration of Justice in Bavaria at the Fürstenfeldbruck and Sulzbach-Rosenberg locations.

The first year consists of basic practical course 1 (6 months) and basic practical course 2 (6 months).

Basic practical course 1 chiefly covers a course of law, plus a four-week internship (vocational part) at a police station and a two-week internship at a CID inspectorate.

Basic practical course 2, which takes place at a riot squad department, covers a basic course in police service theory and closed-formation operations. In addition, there are courses in weapons handling and marksmanship, driver training and sports.

The second year consists of a basic course (6 months) at the university of applied sciences and the main internship (6 months).

The basic course chiefly covers legal matters.

In the main internship, students are taught managerial skills as well as case handling at the higher intermediate service level, with ten weeks being devoted to deployment tactics training with the riot squad and ten weeks to tasks of a shift at a police station plus eight weeks devoted to the tasks of a shift leader at a police station.

The third year of the course is divided into main course 1 and main course 2 of six months each. The subjects are: laws on using administrative force, state and constitutional law, criminal law and law of public order offences, civil law, traffic law, general administrative law, public service law, procedural law, budget law, criminalistics, criminology, operations management, traffic management, tactical behaviour, police management, sociology, psychology, communication and conflict resolution, professional ethics, police information and communication systems.

The course ends with an employment examination, which consists of a written and an oral part. Having graduated, the students concerned obtain the degree of "Diplom-Verwaltungswirt(in) (FH)" and are appointed police inspectors.

It is interesting to note that approximately 75 % of all applicants for the intermediate service have A levels or the vocational baccalaureat diploma and could, therefore, be instantly recruited for training for the higher intermediate service. Apparently, the shorter training period and, as a result, the possibility of earning a living (as well as earning more money) at an earlier stage are a great incentive especially since, after a while, also members of the intermediate service are admitted to the basic course at the university of applied sciences, where they constitute the great majority. Admission to the university of applied sciences is granted the earlier, the better the results of the training course and the continuous assessment are. Many chief superintendents' careers in Bavaria began this way.

Training for the senior service

Training for the senior police service takes place at the German Police University, formerly "Polizeiführungsakademie", at Hiltrup, a borough of Münster.

Higher intermediate service officers from all German state and federal police services can be enrolled by their respective ministries of the interior, if they meet the requirements set by their state or organization, and the requirements of the university.

The studies at the German Police University take two years, and when graduating, the officers receive a master's degree in "Public Administration – Police Management."

The first year of studies, which is run by the federation and the federal states, is divided into ten modules; the students become acquainted with different public safety organizations and get to know their role and setup.

The second year is undertaken at the German Police University; it consists of nine modules.

Students have to study the following subjects: police operations, leadership, business administration, organizational management, human resources management, psychology, crime, criminology, law and traffic in order to be prepared for their future role.

As this role is mainly a managerial role, the main skills and capabilities to be acquired are

- commanding regional police districts and major police units
- running police operations at command and control centres
- being responsible for managerial functions in central and high-level agencies of either the federation or a federal state
- being involved in providing police training and development.

One particular benefit of the German Police University is the fact that students from all German police services study together and thus share common ideas and experience differences in local laws, customs and traditions. Policing problems are more or less the same all over Germany and in the democratic states all over the world, but there are different ways to tackle these problems. Therefore, students also become acquainted with policing philosophies in other countries.

German Police University at Hiltrup

3.4 Subjects at a police academy

Find the pairs

1	Ausländerrecht	a	aliens law
2	Beamtenrecht	b	business administration
3	Betriebswirtschaftslehre	c	civil law
4	Eingriffsrecht	d	civil service law
5	Einsatzlehre	e	criminal law
6	Einsatztraining	f	criminalistics
7	Erste Hilfe	g	criminology
8	Fremdsprachen	h	first aid
9	Führungslehre/Management	i	foreign languages
10	Informations- und Kommunika-tionstechnik	j	information and communication technology
11	Kriminalistik	k	law of assembly
12	Kriminologie	l	operational theory
13	Öffentliches Dienstrecht	m	operational training
14	Polizeirecht	n	physical education (PE)
15	Psychologie	o	police law
16	Selbstverteidigung und Eingriffstechniken	p	police management (theory)
17	Soziologie	q	police powers
18	Sport	r	policing in formations
19	Staats- und Verfassungsrecht	s	psychology
20	Strafrecht	t	public and constitutional law
21	Verbandstraining	u	public service law
22	Verkehrsrecht	v	self-defence and restraint techniques
23	Versammlungsrecht	w	sociology
24	Waffenkunde	x	traffic law
25	Zivilrecht	y	weapons handling

1. **Do you think that all these subjects are necessary? Which of them are the most important? Give reasons.**
2. **Should other subjects be taught?**
3. **Which of the above is your favourite subject?**
4. **Which of the above are you not so keen on?**

3.5 Foreign languages

Migration within Europe, and especially within the European Union, is something which influences our everyday lives in many fields, and the .... are no exception. Every police officer should be able to communicate in at .... one other language. Here is an .... :

Since the expansion of the European Union in 2004 many people from .... European countries have come to work and live in the United Kingdom (and also Ireland), especially from Poland as there are no immigration restrictions within the EU. However, their knowledge of the English language is very .... When such a person, for example, dials 999 to report a severe road traffic accident and is put through to the police service, he or she cannot talk to the control room officer directly but has to wait until an interpreter becomes ...., and thus vital time might be lost. So an English police service is now advertising for Polish-speaking operators. And, by the way, in some areas in England information panels in Polish have been put up in danger spots in order to .... accidents caused by Polish drivers.

1. Fill in the gaps. Choose from the following words:

available	eastern	example	good
last	least	limited	police
prevent	ready	roads	southern

2. Do you think that it is really necessary to hire operators who can answer calls in another language?

3. Even if you have a phrasebook and can ask questions in another language, will you be able to understand the answers?

3.6 Police ranks in Germany

In most federal states and also in the Federal Police Service the career structure consists of three tiers. However, some federal states have so-called two-tier structures, i.e. there is no longer the intermediate service, but only the higher intermediate service and the senior (command) service.

Mittlerer Dienst (intermediate service)

Polizeimeisteranwärter
Polizei-/Kriminalmeister
Polizei-/Kriminalobermeister
Polizei-/Kriminalhauptmeister

Gehobener Dienst (higher intermediate service)

Polizeikommissarsanwärter
Polizei-/Kriminalkommissar
Polizei-/Kriminaloberkommissar
Polizei-/Kriminalhauptkommissar
Erster Polizei-/Kriminalhauptkommissar

Höherer Dienst (senior service or senior command service)

Polizeiratsanwärter (nur für Seiteneinsteiger)
Polizei-/Kriminalrat
Polizei-/Kriminaloberrat
Polizei-/Kriminaldirektor
Leitender Polizei-/Kriminaldirektor
Direktor des Landeskriminalamtes und evtl. anderer Landesoberbehörden
Inspekteur der Polizei

The designations of rank are – in the end – untranslatable, since there are significant differences all over the world with regard to size, structure, tasks, etc. Thus, in Great Britain, the lowest rank is that of constable, which would correspond to "Polizeimeister" in federal states with a three-tier career structure or "Polizeikommissar" in federal states with a two-tier career structure.

3.7 A policeman's career

Leitender Polizeidirektor Herbert Adler is going to retire. You have been asked to compose a speech for the occasion in English, as there will be guests from England at the farewell party. The following details will help you:

1955 born on ..... at .....
family background – parents – brothers and sisters – relatives
1971 high school – intermediate level
1972 joining the police – training with standby police in .....
1975 Polizeihauptwachtmeister – standby squad in .....
1977 police station in ..... – patrol duty
1982 promotion to Polizeihauptmeister
1983 police station in ..... – patrol duty – supervisor
1985 promotion to Polizeikommissar after successful qualification – police headquarters in ..... – administrative work
1992 command course at Deutsche Hochschule der Polizei (German Police University) in Hiltrup
1993 promotion to Polizeirat – commander of standby squad
1996 promotion to Polizeioberrat and transfer as chief of staff in the county of ....
1999 promotion to Polizeidirektor – chief of police in the county of .....
2005 head of traffic section in the ministry of the interior
2008 promotion to Leitender Polizeidirektor and transfer as chief of police in .....

- hobbies: martial arts, shooting, cycling, cooking
- travelling: Canada, Alaska, down under
- always nice and friendly, helpful, reliable
- family, wife, children, one son also police officer
- police union, IPA
- member of local council in .....

Discuss your career etc. with that of a foreign colleague from your twin town in another country

Pair work

20 years from now, what would your CV be like? Write a list with the details of your own – possible – career. Then work with your partner. Student A tells student B about his/her career, student B asks for as many details as necessary to get a good picture of his/her partner, then they take turns.

3.8 Application for a Europol position

Write an application for Europol describing your professional career. An application form might look like this:

Application form

Name			
First name(s), surname(s)			
Date of birth			
Nationality			
Civil status			
Education (1) – institution – date(s) – degree/diploma Institution			
Education (2) – institution – date(s) – degree/diploma Institution			
Education (3) – institution – date(s) – degree/diploma Institution			
Language skills 1 = fluent 5 = basic	spoken	written	passive
German			
English			
French			
Spanish			
Other			
Membership in professional bodies			
Other skills			
Current position			
Years with the agency			
Key qualifications			
Relevant experience in non-EU member states (1) – country, date, brief description of project			
Relevant experience in non-EU member states (2) – country, date, brief description of project			
Professional experience (outside the police) (1) – company/agency – location – date – position – description			
Professional experience (outside the police) (2) – company/agency – location – date – position – description			
Publications			
Other			

3.9 Maximilian Arnolds wants to become a police officer

Maximilian Arnolds (MA) has just started in the 13th form of his school in Ratingen. He knows that, next year, 1,100 young men and women are to be recruited by the North Rhine-Westphalian police. His school has offered its prospective A level candidates to take a test which is supposed to provide information about interests, abilities and qualifications for certain professions. M.A.'s test revealed that he is well qualified for a career with the police.

Thereupon the school's careers master arranges for an interview with Kriminaldirektor Rainer Stumpf (RS), head of Mettmann CID, about police training and career prospects.

Part 1

RS: Hello Max, come in. Your teacher has informed me about your visit. So you would like to become a police officer?

MA: Yes, I'm thinking about it. I did the school's aptitude test, which showed that I was qualified for a career with the police. I don't know anything about police training and career prospects.

RS: Career prospects are quite good in the service. Police officers have a secure and interesting job, and there are good chances of promotion.

MA: I'd like to join the CID, but I don't know much about the things I have to do as a police officer.

RS: Being a police officer chiefly means working round the clock. Working shifts can be disagreeable and some operations can be a real strain, but it's the best job in the world if you want to help people and prevent crime and accidents. It can also be quite dangerous. On the other hand, you can specialize in so many fields, so we're talking about a variety of "professions" within the police profession.

MA: What sort of position could I achieve then?

RS: The basis is the uniformed radio patrol, which deals with emergencies. Our colleagues in uniform are always the first to arrive on the scene if there is a road traffic accident, if there is a fire in a house, if there is a case of shoplifting or if someone has locked himself out. Our colleagues analyze the situation, cordon off the scene, secure evidence, or render assistance. They decide whether to handle the case themselves or what specialists to call.

MA: What specialists are there?

RS: We have many specialists. The riot police are specialized in dealing with demonstrations and major events with many members of the public. The traffic commissariats are specialists in clearing hit-and-run traffic accidents. The homicide squad solves cases of murder, the helicopter squad helps clear up environmental offences and many other crimes, photographers secure traces, chemists and physicists, who are not police officers in most cases, evaluate evidence and prepare expert opinions, the river police are in charge of inland waterways – well, we have so many specialists –, and you can decide at a later stage whether you want to join the special intervention group or mobile intervention group, or to be employed as a dog handler. As you can see, our profession really offers a great many possibilities.

MA: Sounds very interesting and it might be a good job for me.

Part 2

RS: Perhaps I'd better explain how to apply. The easiest method is to apply online on your PC. I'll show you on my computer. We'll go for the home office website, and then the police website and then click "application", where you will find all the necessary information.

MA: What requirements do I have to meet?

RS: First of all, A levels, because the North Rhine-Westphalia police only recruit for the higher intermediate service. Now for the requirements. For a start you must be a German citizen or citizen of a EU member state and, of course, you must not have a criminal record.

MA: So, other aliens are not accepted?

RS: Well, they are, but there are special regulations, which I can explain at a later stage. In this case, you must have A levels or the certificate of maturity for universities of applied sciences, which you've got anyway.

MA: What other requirements must be met?

RS: Have you got the German sports badge? That would be another requirement, and of course the lifeguard badge and driving licence class B, but the latter can still be taken during the first year of your studies. Moreover, you must be able to type on a PC with at least 80 characters per minute.

MA: That's asking for quite a few things, but so far I'm all right.

RS: Then there is a medical, which tests whether you are suitable from a medical point of view, and a test to evaluate your analytical memory and your analytical and logical ability to think.

MA: And then?

RS: Well, then we can start. You'll be recruited and seconded for a course of studies at the university of applied sciences for public administration. Two sites, i.e. Duisburg and Cologne, are quite close to where you live.

MA: What's the course of studies like? Is it hard?

RS: Studying means constant and consistent learning, else you'll fail. At least, that's my experience as chairman of a board of examiners.

MA: Will I have to live in barracks while studying?

RS: No, we don't do that any more. Like other students, you'll have to travel to your university of applied science for public administration, or perhaps move if it's too far from home. The course is for three years and you'll graduate as a bachelor. The course itself is divided into theoretical and practical parts. The practical parts take place at the state office for vocational and advanced training and human resources of the police at Bork and Brühl. In addition, there'll be practical training periods at operational police authorities where theory can be applied in practice and where the students get first experience in real-life police work.

MA: And where will I be deployed after the examination?

RS: That depends on where there is a need. Basically, you can be deployed throughout North Rhine-Westphalia, although, if possible, you would be deployed near your home town.

You'll first have to work shifts at a police station. After a year, you're likely to be seconded to a riot squad for three years. Later you might be in a position to specialize in your favourite field.

MA: We haven't talked about earnings and promotion prospects. My mother thinks that a police officer cannot afford to feed a family.

RS: In the private sector, people often earn more, but here you have a crisis-proof job. That's something to bear in mind and consider. In North Rhine-Westphalia, we've abolished the intermediate service and raised standards. Police officers are paid like any other member of the higher intermediate service in public administration. A Polizeihauptkommissar's salary allows you a decent standard of living, and if you make use of your opportunities, you can be promoted to Erster Polizeihauptkommissar or even get into the senior service. Like everything else, all this depends very much on your own efforts.

MA: That was very interesting. I've made up my mind and would like to apply.

RS: In that case, we'll carry on on the home office website and complete your electronic application.

1. Talk about the entrance requirements in your federal state and in other countries

2. How and why did you join the police?

3.10 Verb forms – active/passive

Present tense – Präsens – Gegenwart

	alle Verben	un-regelmäßig	to have	to be	Verlaufsform	Passiv
I	work	go	have	am	am working	am beaten
he*, she*, it*	works	goes	has	is	is working	is beaten
we, you, they**	work	go	have	are	are working	are beaten

Besonderheiten beim Anhängen von -s – z.B. he finishes;

* oder Hauptwort Einzahl; ** oder Hauptwort Mehrzahl

Past tense – Imperfekt – Vergangenheit

I				was	was working	was beaten
he, she, it	worked	went*	had	was	was working	was beaten
we, you, they				were	were working	were beaten

* = 2. Form

Present perfect – Perfekt – Vollendete Gegenwart

I	have worked	have gone*	have had	have been	have been working	have been beaten
he, she, it	has worked	has gone*	has had	has been	has been working	has been beaten
we, you, they	have worked	have gone*	have had	have been	have been working	have been beaten

* = 3. Form

Past perfect – Plusquamperfekt – Vollendete Vergangenheit

I, he, she, it, we, you, they	had worked	had gone*	had had	had been	had been working	had been beaten

* = 3. Form

Future I – Futur I – Zukunft

I, he, she, it, we, you, they	will work	will go	will have	will be	will be working	will be beaten

Conditional I – Konditional I – Möglichkeitsform

I, he, she, it, we, you, they	would work	would go	would have	would be	would be working	would be beaten

Future II – Futur II – Vollendete Zukunft

I, he, she, it, we, you, they	will have worked	will have gone	will have had	will have been	will have been working	will have been beaten

Conditional II – Konditional II – Vollendete Möglichkeitsform

I, he, she, it, we, you, they	would have worked	would have gone	would have had	would have been	would have been working	would have been beaten

3.11 Facing a "tense" problem

Determine the tense forms in red bold face and translate the sentences into German

1. I **would like** to apply for a traineeship with the police.

   ....

2. I **have** always **been interested** in sports and dealing with people.

   ....

3. An unsuccessful applicant said: "I'**ve** always **wanted** to help to prevent crime and accidents and enforce the law."

   ....

4. My mother being Polish, I **was brought up** bilingually in English and Polish.

   ....

5. At my school, Gaelic **is offered** as the first foreign language, so I **am** quite fluent in this language.

   ....

6. After we **had moved** to Killester, I **joined** the local rugby club.

   ....

7. I **would have liked** to become a professional player, but I **did** not **make** it.

   ....

8. I **was told** about police training while I **was staying** with a superintendent's family.

   ....

9. Even if I **do** not **get** into the senior command service, I **will be able** to earn a decent living.

   ....

10. Sometimes shift work **causes** problems, as it **can** also **affect** your social life.

    ....

11. But by the end of my traineeship, I **will have got** used to irregular working hours.

    ....

12. If I **pass** all the tests, I **will be invited** for an interview and a medical check-up.

    ....

3.12 Using the passive

Police constable Dram is sipping his usual dram of whisky after his late shift and tells his wife about the day.

"Today we stopped a Mr Merry from Beer in Devon in the pedestrian precinct. We asked him to show us his papers. As he seemed to be drunk, we breathalyzed him and then asked him to get out of his car. Then we left his car where it was and escorted him on foot to the police station. There we called a doctor who took a blood sample. Finally we put him in our detention cell to sober up."

Two days later Mr Merry tells his wife: "The day before yesterday I was stopped ....."

Continue the story, using the passive voice

3.13 Useful phrases

Bei einem internationalen Treffen von Polizeibeamten erklären Sie den ausländischen Teilnehmern:

1. Ich wollte schon immer Polizeibeamter werden.

   ....

2. Ich machte die Ausbildung bei der Bereitschaftspolizei in Göppingen.

   ....

3. Die Ausbildung dauerte zweieinhalb Jahre.

   ....

4. Meine Lieblingsfächer waren Polizeirecht, Selbstverteidigung und Eingriffstechniken.

   ....

5. Die Ausbildung war nicht nur theoretisch, sondern beinhaltete auch zwei Praktika.

   ....

6. Anschließend wurde ich nach Stuttgart versetzt und war dort im Streifendienst eingesetzt.

   ....

7. Nachdem ich die Ausbildung zum Hundeführer abgeschlossen hatte, arbeitete ich bei der Hundestaffel.

   ....

8. Ich habe mich für das SEK beworben und habe nächste Woche ein Vorstellungsgespräch.

   ....

9. Ich halte den Polizeiberuf für sicher, weil man eine Einstellung auf Lebenszeit erhält, aber man muss sich immer auf neue und manchmal gefährliche Situationen einstellen.

   ....

   ....

10. Die Schichtarbeit ist zwar anstrengend, hat aber den Vorteil, dass man während der Woche freie Tage hat.

    ....

3.14 Key words and phrases

deploy – enforce the law – hit-and-run accident – internship – promotion – secure evidence – university of applied sciences for public administration – and all the subjects mentioned in 3.3 and 3.4

Unit 4 Road traffic

This unit deals with

- roads and motorways
- the highway codes in different countries
- traffic signs in different countries and
- questions and negations in English.

4.1 Types of roads

A road is a wide carriageway leading from one place to another, especially one which vehicles can use; a street is a public road in a village, town or city, typically with pavements and houses and buildings on one or both sides. Most countries in the world have a classification system which distinguishes, in various stages, between national motorways, highways and local country roads.

Germany	United Kingdom	United States
(Bundes)Autobahn – A 1	motorway – M 25	freeway, interstate, turnpike, expressway – I 20
Bundesstraße – B 2	A road – A 68	U.S. road – U.S. 1
Landesstraße – L 34	B road – B 632	state road – Texas 12
Kreisstraße – K 26	C road – C 37	county road – Klamath 17
Gemeindestraße – G 23	D road – D 38	farm road, country road

Find out about other countries

4.2 Road vocabulary

1. Find out the meanings of the following words (use your dictionary or the internet), and explain them in English

acceleration lane
carriageway
cone
crossroads
curve
deceleration lane
drive(way)
emergency telephone
fast lane
footpath

bend
central reservation
contraflow (system)
crosswalk
cyclepath
diversion
dual carriageway
entrance
flyover
grade crossing

bypass
centre lane (*US* center lane)
crash barrier
cul-de-sac
dead-end street
divided highway
emergency lane
exit
footbridge
guard rail

hard shoulder	highway	hump(back) bridge
intersection	junction	lane
main road/street	major road/street	median
middle lane	mobile roadworks	one-way street
outside lane	overpass	path
pavement	pedestrian crossing	pelican crossing
railroad crossing	railway level crossing (controlled or open)	
ramp	rest area	road shoulder
rotary	roundabout	rumble strips
service area / services	side road/street	sidewalk
sleeping policeman	slip road	slow lane
soft shoulder	spaghetti junction	subway
thoroughfare	through road	toll bridge/toll road
traffic circle	trunk road	underpass
works entrance	works exit	zebra crossing

2. Find the right word

a road passing around a town	
one of the two halves of a very fast and wide road, e.g. of a motorway	
two roads meet here	
it is often built along the edge of a road/the two sides of a large road are often separated by it	
a (narrow) route from one place to another, often for special road users like cyclists, pedestrians etc.	
people, cars and trains can cross a river on a	
an important road that connects cities or towns	

3. Find the American term

bend	
central reservation	
roundabout	
level crossing	
cul-de-sac	
pavement	
pedestrian crossing	
slip road	
crossroads	
flyover	

4.3 The highway code

The highway code lays down the rules which apply to all road users, whether pedestrians, cyclists, drivers, motor cyclists, horse riders or the persons in charge of a horse-drawn vehicle. Many of the rules in the highway code are legal requirements. Disobeying the rules means committing an offence which will be punished appropriately, with fines, penalty points, disqualification from driving for a certain period, and even prison.

4.4 Traffic signs

Road traffic signs regulate, warn and guide traffic. International signs with symbols have been developed to avoid misunderstanding because of language difficulties. However, they are not used everywhere. For example, in the USA there are many signs with a text, and you can't understand them if you don't speak the language.

In Germany, there are three categories of signs:

- warning signs: these signs warn of (possible) dangers, for example slippery road or steep hill downwards
- signs giving orders (white road markings on the road surface belong to this category): these signs either give orders what to do, or they are prohibitive and tell you what you must not do
- information signs: these signs give information to facilitate traffic.

In addition, there are additional panels which give more details about an individual sign.

In Great Britain, the Highway Code speaks of

- signs giving orders (signs with red circles are mostly prohibitive)
- warning signs (mostly triangular)
- direction signs (mostly rectangular)
- information signs (all rectangular)
- roadworks signs.

Draw the following signs

roundabout – riding of pedal cycles prohibited – steep hill downwards – give way to oncoming vehicles – give way – road narrows on both sides – no vehicles except bicycles being pushed – turn right ahead

4.5 Renting a car

John Williams (JW), an American tourist, enters a rent-a-car office in Nuremberg; he plans to drive around southern Germany for a fortnight. He asks the employee of the rental agency, Roland Ries (RR), about differences between the German and American road regulations.

JW: Are there any important rules about driving here in Germany which I have to pay special attention to?

RR: Not really. But we do have far more traffic signs than you do, but they are all self-explanatory. Maybe there's one exception, the "yield" sign. That's a white triangle with red rims, and the point of the triangle is at the bottom. When you approach an intersection or junction and you see this sign, it means that you must yield to traffic on the other road, but you needn't stop if there's no traffic on the other road.

JW: Well, that's a new one for me. We don't have such a sign in Texas.

RR: In Germany, priority is normally indicated by signs. The diamond-shaped yellow square informs you that you are on a major road, and all traffic coming from the left or right has to yield. If there are no signs at all, we have the "priority from the right" rule, which means that you have to yield to any vehicle coming from the right, even cyclists. And it doesn't matter how wide both roads are.

JW: Well, I'll have to concentrate on that. We usually have four-corner stops, at least in residential areas.

RR: The idea is to make drivers slow down in such areas with the "priority from the right" rule; drivers have to slow down at every intersection and watch for traffic coming from the right.

JW: What about speed? Is it really true that you don't have speed limits on your freeways?

RR: First of all, the national speed limit is 100 kph on any road outside built-up areas, if not otherwise posted. Within built-up areas it is 50 kph, and the yellow sign with the place name tells you that you are not allowed to drive faster than 50 kph. You're right, we don't have a speed limit on our autobahns; however, on many sections there are maximum speed signs for various reasons. And very often traffic is so heavy that you can't drive real fast.

JW: I'm looking forward to driving faster than at home.

RR: Be careful. The car you've just rented has a maximum speed of about 170 kph, which is about 100 mph. Travelling at about 120 to 130 kph is what most motorists in Germany do. However, the number of drivers who are slower is on the increase, they want to save gas with the price of gas being so high.
And a very important point: a basic rule in Germany is "drive on the right and pass on the left". This also applies to the freeways. Even on six- or eight-lane highways you're not allowed to pass on the right.

JW: Well, that's different from the States. Our basic rule is "Keep your lane", and any driver who wants to change lanes must make sure he can do so safely. Passing on the right is quite normal.

RR: One more detail. In your country turning right at a red traffic light is allowed if there isn't the sign "No turn on red". In Germany this is generally not allowed, except for those intersections where beside the red light you see a green arrow. Before 1990 the green arrow existed only in the former GDR, but now we have it all over Germany.

Compare traffic signs in Germany and the USA. Use the internet

4.6 Word order, questions, negation

Die normale Wortstellung im Aussagesatz ist

(Zeitangabe) –	Subjekt –	Verb –	Objekt –	(Ortsangabe) –	(Zeitangabe)
(Every day)	*PC Miller*	*drives*	*his patrol car*	*(along the M 25)*	*(at 8 a.m.).*

Fragebildung mit 'to do'

Entscheidungsfragen (= Fragen, die mit „ja" oder „nein" beantwortet werden) und Fragen mit Fragewörtern werden immer durch ein Hilfsverb eingeleitet. Ist keines vorhanden, wird mit to do umschrieben. Dadurch wird mit dem Vollverb die Wortstellung Subjekt – Verb – Objekt (SVO) eingehalten.

Can you afford a Rolls-Royce?

Does she like Chinese food?

When is he leaving?

How did you find the defect?

Ist das Fragewort Subjekt/Teil des Subjekts des Fragesatzes, wird nicht mit to do umschrieben, weil die Wortstellung Subjekt – Verb – Objekt eingehalten wird.

Who speaks Hungarian?

Which of you works night shifts this week?

Verneinung mit 'to do'

Enthält der verneinte Satz kein Hilfsverb, wird mit *do/does/did not* verneint.

Police officers do not like paperwork.

The air ambulance did not land because of the fog.

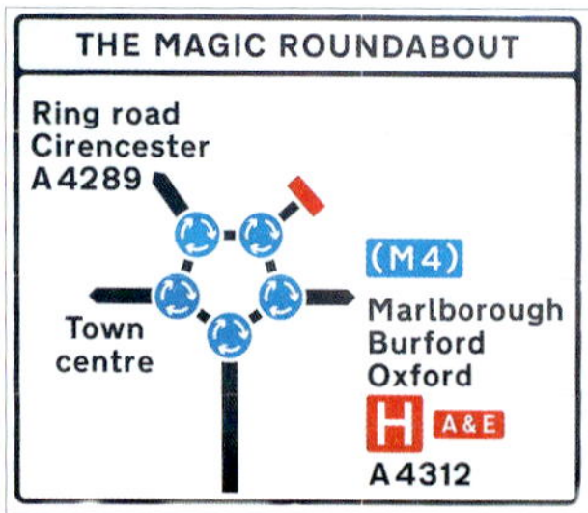

Confusing, isn´t it?

What language is this?

Self-explanatory

Which way?

4.7 Exercises

1. Write the sentences in the correct order

1. armed – with guns – are – most British police officers – not

....

2. truncheons – carry – they – always – but – CS spray – only sometimes

....

3. their unarmed colleagues – armed specialist officers – at any time – may support

....

4. handle – they (British Telecom) – a year – in the UK – over 6 million emergency calls (999)

....

5. began to pay – the City of London – in 1663 – watchmen

....

6. Sir Robert Peel – his force – in 1829 – established – of 3,000 bobbies

....

7. no women – were – until 1914 – in the police service

....

8. the work of men – the first female volunteers – took on – during World War I

....

9. police officers – until 1908 – worked – seven days a week

....

10. in a special blue bag – were allowed to – they – bring – their food and drink – at that time

....

2. Write the sentences in the correct order

History of British traffic signs

1. at its crossroads – in 1648 – each community – signposts – had to place

....

2. became – these guides – after the General Turnpike Act of 1773 – more common

....

3. riding bicycles – in the 19th century – more and more popular – on public roads – became

4. steep hills – were – for early cyclists – and sharp bends – extremely dangerous

5. therefore – signs showing skull and crossbones – at the most dangerous places – were erected

6. had installed – by the end of the 19th century – about 4,000 warning signs – local authorities

7. their effectiveness – began – they – because of this over-use – to lose – eventually

8. warning and prohibitive signs – after the Motor Car Act 1903 – at crossroads – were placed

9. A and B – in 1921 – the roads – all over the country – and given a number – were classified

10. warning signs – and double bends – were introduced – at the same time – level crossings – for schools

3. Form long sentences as in the example below

Halloween – pirate costume – find – motel

On a cold morning after Halloween a fair-haired seven-year-old wearing a torn pirate costume was found murdered near a shabby motel.

1. two students – launch – attack – school – pepper spray – resistance
2. driver – too fast – accident – tree – ditch – passenger – injured
3. teacher – police college – questions – not answer – because

4.8 Useful phrases

Erklären Sie einem britischen Kollegen, dass

1. in Deutschland die öffentlichen Straßen in Autobahnen, Bundes-, Landes-, Kreis- und Gemeindestraßen eingeteilt sind.

   ....

2. eine Autobahn aus zwei durch einen Mittelstreifen getrennten Fahrbahnen besteht und jede Fahrbahn zwei oder drei, manchmal auch mehr Fahrstreifen hat.

   ....

3. in Baustellenbereichen auf Autobahnen die Fahrstreifen oft schmaler/schmäler als normal sind.

   ....

4. die Zahl der Kreisverkehre in Deutschland immer mehr zunimmt.

   ....

5. die Vorschriften der Straßenverkehrsordnung für alle Verkehrsteilnehmer gelten.

   ....

6. Verstöße gegen die Straßenverkehrsordnung mit einem Bußgeld und eventuellen Fahrverbot geahndet werden können.

   ....

7. man bei den Verkehrszeichen zwischen Warnzeichen, Vorschriftzeichen und Informationszeichen unterscheidet.

   ....

8. viele Leute behaupten, dass es in Deutschland viel zu viele Verkehrszeichen gibt.

   ....

9. das Stoppschild das einzige achteckige Verkehrszeichen ist.

   ....

10. in Deutschland Markierungen auf der Straße genauso beachtet werden müssen wie Verkehrszeichen.

   ....

4.9 Key words and phrases

air ambulance – carriageway – crash barrier – crossroads – disqualification – dual carriageway – emergency telephone – hard shoulder – highway – highway code – junction – lane – motorway – pavement – pedestrian crossing – penalty point – roundabout – slip road – and all the traffic signs

Unit 5

Waiting and Parking

This unit deals with

- the difference between waiting and parking
- no-parking
- the parking system in a small town
- parking tickets and being towed off and
- the concord between noun and verb.

5.1 Definitions

In Germany, "waiting" (Halten) is defined as stopping the vehicle for a short time. If the driver stops for more than three minutes, or if he/she leaves the vehicle, this would be defined as "parking" (Parken).

5.2 No waiting or parking

Drivers of motor vehicles cannot stop or park where they want. In Germany, waiting and parking are generally prohibited, to name just a few examples,

- on motorways
- outside built-up areas, if there is a white line at the side of the road
- on cyclepaths and pavements
- on the carriageway if the vehicles are left two abreast
- on or near road junctions
- on or near pedestrian crossings
- on or near level crossings
- on or near tramlines or railway tracks
- on bus lanes and at bus stops
- in tunnels
- in places where visibility is obstructed, e.g. on or before bends or hill crests
- in front of driveways.

And, of course, where there are the corresponding signs.

Nearly all parking offences are committed knowingly while others are committed as a result of negligence, lack of attention, or because drivers are under pressure. Drivers should be familiar with the highway code and also be able to obey the many prohibition signs which are clearly visible. Drivers are often prepared to accept a warning fine. However, when they are confronted with a traffic warden, or if their vehicle has been towed off, drivers often engage in discussions, bargaining, intimidation and insults or even attempts of bribery. As a rule, drivers tend to make objections and rarely accept that they were wrong. Many react in an irritated and/or aggressive manner, if and when they find a parking ticket behind their wiper(s) or if they are reminded of their offence by the administrative authority in charge at a later date. It is up to them to terminate proceedings instantly by paying the warning fine; otherwise the fixed-penalty office will take action.

1. **Find out about all the rules concerning waiting and parking in Germany**
2. **Compare with other countries**
3. **In some countries, single or double yellow or red lines on the edge of the carriageway indicate that you are not allowed to wait or park there. Should such lines be introduced in Germany as well?**
4. **Explain the following words**

negligence: ....
familiar: ....
traffic warden: ....
bribe: ....
objection: ....

5.3 Stationary traffic

As a matter of principle, staving off dangers is a matter for the federal states within the Federal Republic. The authorities concerned are the police as well as public order and administrative authorities. Since the 1960s the federal states have made a distinction between staving off danger by the police on the one hand and public order authorities on the other. In some federal states the police have since then no longer primarily been concerned with preventing breaches of public order. Examples of public order offences are parking in a no-parking area, speeding and other offences against the highway code, offences against local ordinances which do not constitute offences against public security.

In Germany's federal states the public order authorities are organized, trained and equipped in different ways. In Frankfurt, for example, the members of the public order authority (traffic wardens/auxiliary police) wear uniforms which differ from those of the police merely having different coats of arms on their sleeves as well as different cap stars. Moreover, they are armed. In Frankfurt they also prosecute public order offences committed in non-stationary traffic.

In some federal states there are combined patrols consisting of a police officer and a public order official. In keeping with the idea of a citizen-oriented police force, all relevant problems of citizens are thus to be channelled to the proper authorities.

No-parking signs

5.4 Parking in Eichstätt

The town of Eichstätt in Bavaria has about 14,000 inhabitants. It is situated in the Altmühl valley, and many tourists visit the town during the summer months, many of them cyclists who ride on the famous "Altmühltal Cycling Route" and spend a night at Eichstätt. The town, which is also a bishop's see, has many attractive baroque buildings, gardens and parks. It has a Catholic university, the only one in Germany, and it is also the home town of the second Bavarian standby division.

Like in many towns, Eichstätt does not have enough parking space. Without strict surveillance and the corresponding tickets and fines, the parking situation in the town would be an unmitigable disaster. Therefore the town employed a traffic warden already 20 years ago.

Eichstätt engaged Mrs Anna Beck, a trained office clerk, and this was a wise decision. First, for three months, she accompanied her colleagues of the uniformed police division, learning a lot about their daily tasks. Then she had to take a course in law in a nearby city. Her colleagues from the Eichstätt police inspectorate, where she also has her office, now have a a helpful fellow officer who is specialized in stationary traffic. But paperwork is only a small part of her job. "I mostly have to deal with people who have a complaint to make." Most of her work is in the streets.

She can't complain about lack of work. Eichstätt has about 1,200 parking spaces in the centre or rather close to it, only some of which are free; in addition, there are 70 spaces for motorhomes and 200 for residents only. Mrs Beck is responsible for all these spaces, except those in multi-storey car parks or underground garages. The parking areas outside the town centre often have empty spaces, whereas, especially near the university, there are not enough spaces, and cars are often parked illegally.

In addition, motorists often park their cars in places which are reserved for taxis, buses, doctors or in fire lanes. For her it does not matter if a car is parked in a no-parking area, if the parking time is exceeded or if a car is parked in a fire lane: she will always put a parking ticket behind the windscreen wipers.

Her job also includes vehicle checks. She checks whether the TÜV and AU decals are still valid and also if the tyres have enough tread. If necessary, she will issue a vehicle defect form.

In her long career Mrs Beck has experienced many different situations with other people. Occasionally situations (about one in ten) became critical when the driver of the car challenged her while she was issuing the parking ticket. Many won't accept the ticket, and it isn't rare that she is sworn at or even insulted. However, she has learnt to deal with such sitations and usually stays quite calm.

Sometimes people come into her office because they believe that the ticket was wrongly issued. "Women are generally less aggressive than men. I've never had a really aggressive or nasty confrontation with a woman."

Mostly her encounters with other people are friendly, sometimes even funny. "Some months ago, a driver shouted at me when he noticed me: What a pity, I've just paid the parking fee, so for once you can't give me a ticket."

Many lonely people like to talk to her, they tell her about their private lives and the latest news; for them the traffic warden is a welcome partner.

And she clearly remembers an English driver, who asked her for help as he couldn't find his car any more. It took the two of them quite some time until they found the vehicle. "Once more I was confirmed in my opinion that proficiency in English is so important nowadays – and not only in my job as a traffic warden."

Find the words in the text whose explanation is given below

1. area governed by a bishop or archbishop: ....
2. sum of money to be paid as a penalty for a petty offence: ....
3. event causing great and often sudden damage or suffering: ....
4. not moving: ....
5. statement expressing dissatisfaction about something: ....
6. competence in doing something, especially a foreign language: ....
7. speak or treat someone rudely and with disrespect: ....
8. thick moulded part of a tyre that grips the road: ....
9. high-level educational institution in which students study for degrees: ....
10. given or available without charge: ....

5.5 A parking ticket

A car with British licence plates is parked in front of a butcher's shop in Bremen, partly on the pavement, so that it is an obstacle for pedestrians. Traffic warden Melanie Becker (MB) has noticed it, and after about fifteen minutes she decides to write a warning ticket. As she does so, the driver of the car, Welsh tourist Buddug Prydderch (BD) from Llanfairfechan approaches her vehicle.

BD: What are you doing to my windscreen wipers?

MB: My name is Becker. I've just written a ticket because you've parked your car on the pavement.

BD: But I was only in the butcher's shop for two minutes.

MB: That's not possible. I've seen your car parked here for at least fifteen minutes.

BD: Fifteen minutes? Never! I only went in to buy some sausages and some cooked meat to take back home. There were only three people in front of me when I entered the shop.

MB: Your car has been parked here for at least fifteen minutes. It was 10.45 when I first spotted it, and now it's 11 o'clock. Your car is obstructing pedestrians. While some people may be able to squeeze through between the car and the shop, what about prams or wheelchairs, or an elderly lady with her rollator?

BD: Well, there's plenty of room on the carriageway.

MB: Are you telling me that small children and handicapped people should be exposed to the traffic in this busy street?

BD: Why not? The traffic doesn't look so bad, does it?

MB: There's always a lot of traffic here, and you've been obstructing pedestrians. Parking on the pavement causing an obstruction to pedestrians carries an on-the-spot fine of 20 euros.

BD: Hm, I suppose there's nothing I can do about it. Here's your 20 euros.

MB: And here's your receipt.

BD: That's what happens if you buy German sausages on Friday 13th.

5.6 Towing off an illegally parked vehicle

The "stolen" car

Brynmor Rhys (BR) and his wife Gwen (GR) from Cardiff call at a Berlin police station because they believe their car has been stolen. The officer in charge is Siegfried Mawritzki (SM).

SM: Good afternoon, what can I do for you?

GR: Our car has been stolen! With all our belongings! We've only had it for a few months!

BR: ... and in broad daylight, too!

SM: Now calm down, tell me where you left it.

BR: We left it in Unter den Linden, close to the Brandenburg Gate, about two hours ago.

GR: And there were no double yellow lines.

SM: As far as I know, it's a no-parking area. I am pretty sure you must have overlooked the no-parking signs.

BR: So what's happened to our car then? Do you mean to say it's been towed away?

SM: I can find out in a minute. What make of car was it and what was the licence plate number?

BR: A blue Vauxhall Insignia. The licence plate number is CF59XYZ.

SM: Just a minute, I'll phone to find out whether it's been towed off....... . Yes, it has. It's in the car pound in Berlin Mitte, Rheinpfalzallee 83.

GR: Oh dear, that'll cost quite a bit, won't it?

SM: It'll be about 150 euros all told. I can't give you an exact figure because illegal parking and towing are not a matter for the police, but for the local authority. You'll have to go to the car pound to retrieve your car there after paying them the exact amount. This amount consists of the fine for illegal parking, towing costs and administrative costs.

BR: How do we get to the car pound?

SM: There's an underground station nearby.

BR: Oh well, it's one of those things!

GR: I told you we couldn't park in that place, didn't I? You're always doing things like that!

5.7 Role play

Simulate various situations of illegal parking. Take the role of the offender, his wife, the traffic warden, the driver of the tow truck, the police officer, the official at the car pound

Think of a situation when

- a parking offence is committed knowingly
- a parking offence is committed through negligence
- a prohibition sign is not clearly visible
- a tourist is bargaining with a policeman
- a driver is intimidating a traffic warden
- a driver is insulting a policewoman
- a driver is trying to bribe a traffic warden
- a biker is making objections
- a driver wants to prevent the departure of the tow truck with his vehicle
- a driver talks to the official at the car pound
- a driver and his wife argue because their vehicle has been towed to the car pound.

5.8 Noun and verb – concord

Grundregel

Das Verb richtet sich nach dem Substantiv

The car is new. – The cars are new.

Besonderheiten

Bei Sammelbegriffen steht das Verb normalerweise im Plural

Cattle, people, police, clergy
– The police are coming.

Auch bei Substantiven ohne Pluralform steht das Verb in der Regel im Plural, es sei denn, es handelt sich um ein Einzelexemplar

Sheep, deer, hair
– Five deer are crossing the street.
– The detective found two black hairs on the dead body.

Bei Substantiven, die eine Gruppe von Personen bezeichnen, wie
family, team, party, majority, crew usw.

steht das Verb im Singular, wenn die Gruppe als Einheit betrachtet wird
– The family is an institution.

steht das Verb im Plural, wenn an jedes einzelne Mitglied gedacht wird
– The family have left the house.

Bei einer Reihe von Begriffen steht das Substantiv im Plural, das Verb zumeist im Singular *barracks, works, headquarters*
– The police headquarters is round the corner.

5.9 Fill-in exercise

1. The Jacobs family (travel) .... to Italy every year.
2. The Ford works (be) .... at Cologne.
3. People often (not, know) .... the law.
4. Watch out! Cattle (cross) .... the road.
5. The wanted woman has black hair which (be) .... dyed pink.
6. The motorway crew (be used) .... to severe accidents like this.
7. Our team (win) .... the first prize every year since 1995.
8. The two black hairs on the body of the dead woman (be)......................... almost certainly from the murderer.
9. The Munich police headquarters (be) .... in Ettstraße.
10. The majority of the CID officers (not, like) .... the new pay system.

5.10 Useful phrases

1. Sagen Sie dem Fahrer, dass er hier nicht parken darf, weil er die Fußgänger behindert.

   ....

2. Weisen Sie ihn darauf hin, dass auf dem Bürgersteig wegen des parkenden Fahrzeuges nicht genügend Platz für Kinderwagen und Rollstuhlfahrer ist.

   ....

   ....

3. Erklären Sie ihm, dass er nicht unmittelbar vor dem Zebrastreifen parken darf, weil er dadurch sowohl Autofahrern als auch Fußgängern die Sicht versperrt.

   ....

   ....

4. Teilen Sie ihm mit, dass hier in der Hauptverkehrszeit Haltverbot besteht.

   ....

5. Erklären Sie ihm, dass er grundsätzlich nicht an Stellen parken darf, wo er andere Verkehrsteilnehmer gefährdet oder behindert.

   ....

   ....

6. Erklären Sie ihm, dass sein Fahrzeug abgeschleppt wurde, weil es auf den Straßenbahnschienen stand.

....

7. Sagen Sie ihm, dass 300 m weiter ein großes Parkhaus steht.

....

8. Empfehlen Sie ihm, das Auto hier zu parken und öffentliche Verkehrsmittel zu benutzen.

....

9. Erklären Sie, dass er sein abgeschlepptes Fahrzeug auf dem Stellplatz abholen kann.

....

10. Machen Sie darauf aufmerksam, dass das Parken in einer Tiefgarage bei weitem nicht so teuer ist wie das Abschleppen.

....

....

11. Sagen Sie dem Fahrer, dass er zuerst am Parkscheinautomaten ein Ticket ziehen muss.

....

12. Erklären Sie, dass neben und hinter dem Fahrzeug eines Behinderten ein größerer Abstand zu halten ist, und dass nur bei bestimmten Fahrzeugen das Halten in der zweiten Reihe erlaubt ist.

....

....

5.11 Key words and phrases

administrative costs – car pound – hill crest – insult – licence plate number – multi-storey car park – local ordinance – no-parking area – no-parking sign – obstruct pedestrians – parking ticket – stationary traffic – tow away – towing costs – traffic warden – two abreast

Unit 6

Asking the way

This unit deals with

- finding your way
- places on and along the road
- giving directions and
- the present and past tenses.

6.1 Who tampered with the signpost?

More than 30 years ago my wife and I were on holiday in Ireland. We had flown to Dublin, where we picked up our rental car and started touring the country. We enjoyed the beautiful and sometimes spectacular countryside, had a look at many of the historic sites and spent nice evenings in small country pubs over two or three pints of stout. The weather was typically Irish: beautiful sunshine was followed by heavy rain, stormy winds drove thick clouds across the sky and whipped the sea against the shores, fog and even brief spells of snow made driving difficult at times. Spring was in the air, the daffodils were in full bloom, and so were the rhododendrons in the south-west of the country.

There was not much traffic in those days, and when we were on small country roads, we were often quite alone. We had found accommodation in Killarney and were touring the surrounding mountain areas. The road was getting narrower and narrower, there were fewer and fewer isolated farms, only the number of sheep on both sides of the road increased. We were in a valley with mountains to the right and left, and also in front of us. More and more we had the impression that we were reaching a dead end, but the signpost – it was an old one, consisting of a pole and two hands pointing in different directions – at the last crossroads had clearly told us to go in that direction, and so we were confident that we were on the right road. We were sure that we would soon be back on the main road again, there would be some hidden hairpin bends, and we would be out of that valley.

But we were too optimistic. Suddenly the road just ceased to exist. There was a fence with hundreds of sheep behind it, not a building, not a human being was to be seen. Our only choice was to go back. Turning on the narrow road with deep ditches on either side was impossible, so we had to back the car for about 500 metres. When we finally found a space where we could turn around, a French car came along the road. The French tourists had also followed the signpost and arrived at the same dead end as we had. When we had a closer look at the signpost a few minutes later, we all agreed that we had taken the right direction. Somebody must have turned it in such a way that motorists were sent in the wrong direction.

When we told our story to some regulars in the pub in the evening, they just laughed: "Don't you know that we Irish don't like the English too much? Most of the tourists over here are from England, and what's wrong with sending them in the wrong direction once in a while?"

Questions

1. How had the couple travelled to Ireland, and how were they travelling in Ireland?
2. What do you think of the Irish weather?
3. What kind of road were the couple travelling on?
4. Why did they have to go back?
5. Why had they gone in the wrong direction?
6. What would you have done in that situation?
7. Would you have followed the instructions of a modern navigation system instead? Why? Why not?
8. Why had somebody turned the signpost?
9. Do you have any idea why the Irish "don't like the English too much"?

6.2 Finding your way – no problem with a modern satnav system

Due to sophisticated navigation systems getting lost in strange towns and cities or trying to find the right way to a particular destination is no longer a problem.

The GPS global positioning system is a satellite-based navigation system which was developed by the Defense Department of the United States and which has continually been modernized since 1995, when it came into full operation. More than 30 satellites in orbit transmit signals to GPS receivers. A GPS receiver in a car can thus not only determine the exact location of the car, but also its speed and its direction. The European Union, together with some other nations, is to have its own "Galileo" satellite navigation system by 2011.

GPS receivers for cars, either built-in or mobile, have extensive software showing maps with roads and streets etc. on a small display, and a voice tells the driver which way to go and where to turn left or right. Thus the driver can easily find his/her destination and can just concentrate on driving. Specially equipped satellite navigation receivers, hidden somewhere in a vehicle, can also help prevent vehicle theft as the location of a stolen vehicle can easily be determined.

However, by just selecting options for the route such as "shortest", "fastest" and "make maximum use of motorways" in random combinations, the advice given by your satnav can sometimes be misleading. You could end up on a single-track country lane with grass down the middle, or end up in an impassable ford or do 150 km on motorways instead of the usual 50 km on ordinary roads. So even if your car is equipped with a navigation system, do not throw away your road atlas and maps! They might come in handy when checking out where this modern device has taken you.

Navigation systems are becoming more and more sophisticated almost daily. For example, the route and directions are shown semi-transparently on the windscreen rather than on a small display. Future systems will no longer show a map, but real live views of the road; a camera in the car will photograph what is happening in front of the car, and in darkness infra-red sensors will do so. The pictures are transmitted to the navigation system, which compares the data of the position of the car and its software, and is thus able to project the necessary information onto the windscreen.

Many systems also inform the driver about famous sights or hotels, restaurants, fuel stations, shops and businesses along his/her route, or inform the driver when he/she is speeding or turning into a road with a speed limit. And, of course, these systems will show and inform drivers about traffic jams and will provide information on how to avoid them.

Don't forget: the driver – rather than the satnav – is responsible for his car. He/she must still obey the traffic rules, and it is his/her fault if he causes an accident because his/her satnav gave misleading information or he/she was distracted by looking at the display.

Questions

1. What are the advantages and disadvantages of a navigation system?
2. Have you ever used it and what is your experience?
3. How could the police make use of a GPS system?
4. "I'm completely lost" – Tell a story!
5. A Ukrainian driver, who was transporting a load of paper to Ireland, followed the directions of his satnav and got stuck in a small village in England; his articulated lorry had to be towed away by a tow truck. He could not understand the warning on a sign which had been put up to warn truck drivers that many navigation systems were wrong with regard to this village.
   a) Will the driver get a fine?
   b) Who will pay for the tow truck?
   c) What will the driver tell his company in the Ukraine and the recipients of the paper in Ireland?
   d) Could the driver or his company sue the manufacturers of the navigation system?
6. Will we get "driverless" cars in the future?

6.3 Landmarks to help you find your way

Following directions is a lot easier if you know what to look out for along the way. Write the words in the table below and add other landmarks that come to your mind

bridge	bus station	bus stop
canal	castle	chemist's
church	cinema	city hall
convention centre	department store	drugstore
exhibition centre	factory	farm
fast-food restaurant	forest	fountain
gas station	gym(nasium)	high-rise building
hill	hospital	hotel
kiosk	kindergarten	lake
lighthouse	marketplace	multi-storey car park
museum	office block	opera house
palace	park	petrol station
pharmacy	post office	pub
public toilets	railway station	restaurant
river	school	shopping centre
skyscraper	stadium	supermarket
telephone box	tower	town hall
train station	tramlines	zoo

Fill in the table

public buildings	shops	sights	work	leisure	other

6.4 Explaining the route

Part 1

After a severe road traffic accident, an English couple, Mr and Mrs Winterbottom from Manchester, are being treated in Wittlich hospital. Their son John Winterbottom (JW) and his wife Lesley (LW) are coming by car to see them. They have just left the motorway at Wittlich-West when they notice a speed check. They stop and ask police officers Theo Boerner(TB) and Roland Caspari (RC) how to get to Wittlich hospital.

Due to a computer virus, the sentences have been mixed up. Put them in the right order

JW: Good evening, officer, could you please tell us how we can get to the hospital here in Wittlich?

JW: O.K., third exit at the first roundabout and second exit at the second roundabout.

JW: We also call it a hole-in-the-wall machine.

LW: Well, you certainly have a lot of roundabouts!

LW: Oh, is there an ATM on our route? We only have English pounds on us.

LW: An ATM, an automated teller machine, a cash machine – you know.

LW: Thank you very much. Good-bye.

TB: Well, that's quite easy. Follow this road until you get to the second roundabout. That's a double roundabout. Take the third exit of the first and the second exit of the second roundabout.

TB: Yes. Then you are in a street leading to the town centre. Drive straight on, pass the pelican crossing at the elementary school, and you get to another roundabout.

TB: Take the first exit at that roundabout and drive up the hill. The hospital is on the left just outside the town.

RC: Yes, we have, madam. They've become very popular in recent years.

RC: What exactly are you looking for? I didn't get that.

RC: Ah, I see. Yes, on the street into the town there's the branch of a bank on the left. There is a zebra crossing in front of it.

Part 2

Due to an accident on the L 113 the road is blocked; police officers are securing the scene and directing traffic.

Driver: What's wrong, officer?

Police officer: Sorry, sir, you cannot drive through here, the road is blocked because of an accident. Please turn round, go back to the next roundabout. Enter the roundabout, take the third exit and then drive straight on for about 1.5 kms. Turn left after the traffic lights and follow the road, it will take you to the L 113.

1. **Describe the route from the police training centre to your home town**

2. **Take the map of a big city. Describe the way from police headquarters to the town hall/hospital/vocational school/train station/waste water treatment plant/motorway**

6.5 Exercises – Vocabulary

Part 1

Which word is correct?

1. The police station is **next/nearby/near** the local court.
2. What is the building we have just passed, **next to/close to/through** the town gate?
3. Drive **over/round/at** the corner and make a right turn.
4. Every morning, they share a ride to town, as they work in **adjacent/near/opposite** buildings.
5. I live **into/in/at** Main Street, just **opposite/into/nearest** the post office.
6. Drive **at/over/onto** the roundabout and then take the first exit.
7. Turn right **into/round/along** the main street.
8. You can't see the station, walk **at/past/across** the big building, then you'll see it on your right.
9. Excuse me, is there a travel agency **close/near/nearby**?
10. You can get maps **by/into/at** the tourist information centre.
11. The police station is **at/within/on** easy reach, just walk a little **on/farther/further**.
12. A police officer often walks **along/over/through** the streets when he is **at/in/on** the beat.

Part 2

Explain the words by giving a short definition

1. A crossroads is ....
2. A crosswalk is ....
3. A level crossing is ....
4. A pavement is ....
5. An underpass is ....
6. A hairpin bend is ....
7. A stadium is a place where ....
8. A lighthouse is ....
9. A gas station is ....
10. A hotel is ....

Part 3

Which word does not exist? Cross out the incorrect word

1. ice-cream parlour – pizza parlour – hair parlour – massage parlour
2. federal authority – prosecuting authority – average authority – administrative authority
3. newsagent – flower agent – travel agent – FBI agent – estate agent
4. pelican crossing – zebra crossing – duck crossing – elephant crossing – level crossing
5. fixed-penalty office – beggar's office – front office – head office – post office

6.6 Use of the tenses 1

Present Tense – Präsens/Gegenwart

Eigenschaften – Dinge, die immer so sind

This road leads to Bautzen.

Handlungen, die (mehr oder weniger) regelmäßig vor sich gehen, Fahrplansituationen

The chief constable's sons go to public school.

The train departs at 5.50 a.m. Officer Sharp's night shift starts at 9.00 p.m.

Handlungsketten = mehrere Handlungen, die nacheinander ablaufen (typisch für Witze)

The driver of an Irish car, who is lost in a German city, spots a traffic warden, drives up to her, asks her for directions how to get to the City hotel, gets the information, thanks her and drives on....

Handlungen, die nur einen kurzen Augenblick andauern

The car keys fall to the ground. The traffic lights change from green to amber and red.

Beckham passes the ball to Rooney who scores his second goal.

Verben des Glaubens, Denkens, Fühlens, Hoffens, der sinnlichen Wahrnehmung etc. sowie die Verben, die auf Grund ihrer Bedeutung nicht in der Verlaufsform stehen können

I hope he will tell the truth.

This minivan belongs to Mr Jones.

Present Continuous – Verlaufsform Präsens

Handlungen, die gerade im Augenblick vor sich gehen (verlaufen)

She is talking to the traffic warden.

They are discussing the best way to get to the museum.

Geplante Handlungen in der nahen Zukunft

Police constables Miller and Thompson are going on a refresher course next week.

Past Tense – Imperfekt/Vergangenheit

Abgeschlossene Handlungen, insbesondere mit entsprechender Zeitangabe

Yesterday the crew of patrol car "Emil 36" guided the Ukrainian lorry driver to his destination.

Past Continuous – Verlaufsform Imperfekt

Mehrere Handlungen verliefen gleichzeitig

While father and mother were discussing which route to take, the children were playing Nintendo in the back of the car.

Eine Handlung war im Gange (Hintergrundhandlung), eine weitere trat neu ein

Mr Jones was studying the map when his five-year-old son suddenly burst into tears.

6.7 Fill-in exercise

Part 1

Simple present or present continuous? Fill in the right verb

1. At the beginning of your career as a police officer you usually .... shift work.
2. As a police officer you .... drivers, you ....to help people in need but you .... not .... their cars.
3. You often .... reports at the local police station, but now you .... an English exercise.
4. A foot patrol officer regularly .... the beat; this policeman over there .... to people.
5. After an accident the policeman .... witnesses; look, there he .... a young lady.
6. This CID officer .... in his car waiting for the supect. The criminal police often .... suspicious people.
7. I think this is a plain-clothes officer who .... that group of young people.
8. The stand-by squad .... very irregular working hours. I think PC Lang .... this weekend.
9. Inspector Kurz is on the phone. He .... a colleague. They .... on a murder case.
10. I'm sorry, you can't speak to superintendent Schlau now. She .... an interview to the press.

Part 2

Simple past or past continuous?

1. Yesterday we (drive) .... down the road, when we (be called) .... to the scene of an accident.
2. As the car (travel) .... at very high speed, the driver (lose) .... control and (crash) .... into a lorry.
3. When we (arrive) ...., one passenger (stand) .... in the middle of the road, and the other (lie) .... in the ditch.
4. Normal traffic (cannot pass) .... the scene of the accident, so one of us (secure) .... it while the other (direct) .... the traffic.

Part 3

Fill in the correct tense

1. These days many drivers (use) .... modern satnav systems.
2. The number of cars stolen from the commuter car park behind the central station last year (show) .... an increase.
3. Police (know) .... what's going on in this part of the town.
4. Many teenagers (listen) .... to their favourite rock band when the roof of the concert hall (collapse) .... all of a sudden.
5. When we (arrive)...................., the two drivers (stand) .... in the middle of the road.
6. At present five junctions (be converted) .... into roundabouts.
7. We (conduct) .... a traffic check tonight and tomorrow night.
8. During last night's traffic check the uniformed officers (check) .... the drivers' papers while CID officers (search) .... them and their cars for drugs, when a minivan (crash) .... into one of the vehicles.
9. Right now the Wismar police (investigate) .... a double murder.

6.8 Asking questions

Form the adequate questions to the answers given

question	answer
1.	I live in Rastatt.
2.	I leave home very early, at about 6.30 a.m.
3.	Breakfast? I never have breakfast!
4.	Yes, I share a ride with a colleague, that way we can cut costs.
5.	Yes, I'm married and have two children.
6.	Yes, she works part-time.
7.	At the moment I'm not working as a policeman, I'm studying here.
8.	I have a small flat in Villingen – not far from here.

6.9 Useful phrases

Übersetzen Sie

1. Fragen Sie den Fahrer/die Fahrerin, ob Sie behilflich sein können.

2. Erkundigen Sie sich beim Fahrer nach seinem genauen Ziel.

3. Fragen Sie den Fahrer, ob er einen Stadtplan/eine Straßenkarte mit sich führt.

4. Fragen Sie ihn, ob er das Umleitungsschild an der letzten Kreuzung nicht gesehen hat.

5. Sagen Sie ihm, dass er zunächst geradeaus fahren und an der fünften Ampel links abbiegen muss.

6. Teilen Sie ihm mit, dass er zuerst durch die Unterführung fahren und dann die Brücke überqueren muss.

7. Sagen Sie ihm, dass die Abzweigung nach Querfurt nicht sehr weit ist.

8. Empfehlen Sie ihm, das Auto im Parkhaus abzustellen und den Rest des Weges zu Fuß zu gehen oder die Straßenbahn/den Bus/ein Taxi zu nehmen, weil es in der Innenstadt kaum Parkmöglichkeiten gibt.

9. Erklären Sie ihm, dass er sich in einer Einbahnstraße befindet und nicht wenden darf.

10. Bestätigen Sie dem Fahrer, dass er auf der richtigen Straße ist und die Autobahnauffahrt nach etwa einem Kilometer erreicht, wenn er den blauen Autobahnsymbolen folgt.

11. Reagieren Sie in angemessener Form auf den Dank des Fahrers/der Fahrerin.

6.10 Key words and phrases

amber – asking the way – destination – ditch – double roundabout – hairpin bend – satellite navigation system (satnav) – signpost – tamper with – and all the words from 6. 3

Traffic enforcement/control

This unit deals with

- traffic checks
- all types of road vehicles
- licence plates
- vehicle lights
- tyres
- keepers of motor vehicles
- cautions
- issuing of a vehicle defect form and
- present perfect, past perfect and future.

7.1 Traffic checks

In Germany, there are about 50 million registered motor vehicles. So it is not astonishing that many drivers do not obey all the traffic rules. Therefore the police are authorized to conduct traffic checks at any place and at any time. In the course of such a check the police check the driver's fitness (e.g. whether or not he/she is fit to drive), his/her documents (ID document, driving licence, vehicle registration certificate), compliance with traffic rules (e.g. whether driver and passengers are wearing seatbelts), certain details of the vehicle (e.g. tyres and lights), or, in the case of trucks and buses, they check driving times and rest periods.

Sometimes it is necessary to arrange for a blood sample to be taken or to secure or confiscate the driving licence.

Traffic checks are conducted either on the spot, i.e. the police set up a checkpoint, or they are mobile, i.e. a patrol car moves around in a certain area for random checks. Speed checks, either on the spot or mobile, are a special form of traffic check.

Sometimes uniformed police support CID officers, customs officers or other specialists in conducting special checks which are aimed at combating, for example, trafficking in human beings or the smuggling of drugs, cigarettes or money.

Questions

1. What are the principal aims of traffic checks?
2. What about other countries? Compare
3. Why are diesel-engined vehicles sometimes checked by customs officers?
4. What´s wrong with the photo on the right?

7.2 Checking documents

a) Driving licence

In Germany, the driver of any motor vehicle is required to carry his/her driving licence while driving and, on demand, to hand it over to a police officer. Failure to do so can result in a warning fine of ten euros or a producer being issued.

Since 1st January 1999, there have been the following main categories of driving licence in the European Union; they have replaced the former German categories 1 to 5.

category A – motorcycles
categories B and S – cars
category C – trucks
category D – buses and coaches
categories T and L – agricultural vehicles, tractors etc.

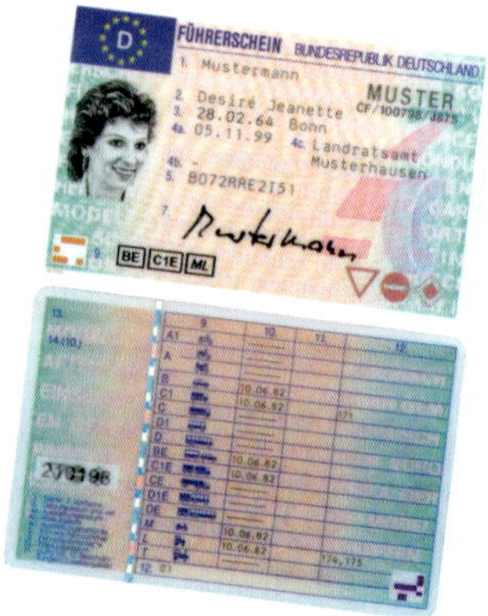

b) Identification document

During a traffic check, the driver's identity is established, normally by inspecting his national ID card or passport. The driving licence or any other document with a photograph may be accepted instead.

c) Other documents

First of all, the vehicle registration certificate for the vehicle and – perhaps – trailer will be checked. The police are also authorized to check the green insurance card, and, in the case of trucks, loading and transport documents, exemption permits, special safety documents when hazardous goods are being carried and insurance papers.

Offences may result in a warning fine of ten euros or in a charge being made out. A producer may also be issued.

7.3 Checking vehicles

Although motor vehicles and trailers are regularly inspected by the approved technical services (TÜV, DEKRA and others in Germany, MoT-approved garages and vehicle testing stations in Great Britain), their condition may be impaired through wear and tear, damage, rust etc. If, in the course of a roadside check, a small defect is detected, a vehicle defect form will be issued. If a severe defect is detected, the vehicle may be put out of operation. In case the load is not or not properly secured, the driver will have to secure it properly, and in case of overloading the vehicle will have to be (partially) unloaded.

7.4 Types of road vehicles

Find out the meanings (use your dictionary). Which terms are British and which are American English? Explain them

Example: An ambulance is a vehicle specially equipped for taking sick or injured people to hospital, especially in emergencies.

ambulance	articulated lorry/truck	auto(mobile)
bicycle	bike	buggy
bus	camper	car
caravan	chopper	classic car
coach	compact car	convertible
delivery van	drawbar combination	estate car
fastback	Hackney carriage	hardtop
hatchback	horse-drawn carriage	liftback
limo(usine)	lorry	minibus
minicar	minivan	moped
motor caravan	motor scooter	motorcycle
motorhome	passenger car	pickup
platform truck	quad	saloon
scooter	sedan	semitrailer
sidecar	sports car	sports utility vehicle (SUV)
station wagon	streetcar	stretch limo
tanker	three-wheeler	tractor (unit)
trailer	trailer truck	tram
transporter	tricycle	trike
truck	truck and trailer	van
vintage car		

Do you know other vehicles which are not in the list?

What sort of vehicle is it?

1. A large car, especially one driven by a chauffeur who is separated by the passenger(s) by a partition. In the USA it is also a car carrying people to and from an airport.
2. A vehicle composed of two wheels held in a frame one behind the other, propelled by pedals and steered with a handlebar attached to the front wheel.
3. A large heavy vehicle for transporting goods.
4. A vehicle equipped for living in, towed by a car, chiefly used for holiday and leisure time.
5. A wheeled container pulled by another vehicle.
6. A car produced between 1917 and 1930.
7. A car with a folding or detachable roof.
8. A trailer having wheels at the back but supported at the front by a towing vehicle.

9. A low-built and powerful car preferred by people who like driving fast.
10. A passenger road vehicle running on rails laid in a public road, powered by electricity conveyed by overhead cables.

1 ……………………… 2 …………………………….. 3 ………………………..

4 …………………….. 5 ……………………………... 6 ………………………..

7 …………………….. 8 ……………………………... 9 ………………………..

10 ……………………

7.5 Licence plates

Part 1

The vehicle licence plates are fixed at the front and at the back of a vehicle, except with motorcycles where they are at the back only. Such a licence plate comprises a series of letters and figures, and each state has its own system. In the EU member states, the nationality sign, together with the European coat of arms, is integrated into the licence plate. And, depending on each state, registration, test and insurance decals may be added.

List the names of the countries bordering on Germany together with their capitals as well as the corresponding nouns and adjectives

Example: DK Denmark Copenhagen Dane Danish

Complete the list for the following countries

AL, AND, BG, BIH, BY, E, EST, FIN, FL, GB, GE, GR, H, HR, I, IRL, KZ, LT, LV, MA, MD, N, P, RO, RSM, RUS, S, SK, SLO, SRB, TR, UA, UZ, V

Part 2

British vehicle number plates

Since January 1st, 1904, British motor vehicles have had to carry number plates, which consisted of a combination of numbers and letters, with the exception of the official car(s) of the reigning monarch.

Until 1963, they consisted of a combination of up to three letters and four numbers, which could be either way round, i.e. letters or numbers first. The only common feature was that the numbers were grouped together and the letters were grouped together. From 1st January 1963, the year of registration was identified by a suffix letter at the end of the registration, so a vehicle registered on that date would have been suffixed by the letter A. On 1st January of the following year the suffix letter was B and so on. The suffix letter F was used from January to July 1967, and from August 1st 1967 the next suffix letter was used. The letters I, O, Q, U and Z were not used as suffix letters, I and Z being reserved for Ireland. The suffix letters of the alphabet were exhausted on 31st July 1983.

As from 1st August 1983, the year of registration was identified by a prefix letter at the start of the registration number, again starting with the letter A and working through the alphabet, changing on 1st August of each year. Beginning in March 1999, the prefix letter was changed every six months on 1st March and 1st September. The last prefix Y was issued on 1st March and used until 31st August 2001.

The present system was introduced on 1st September 2001. A British vehicle number plate now consists of seven characters, a two-letter area code, a two-digit age identifier and a three-letter sequence. The first letter is the "local memory tag", showing the region: A for East Anglia, B for Birmingham, C for Wales (Cymru), D for Deeside, E for Essex, F for Forest and Fens, G for Garden of England (Kent), H for Hants and Dorset, K for Luton and Northampton, L for London, M for Manchester, N for Newcastle and North, O for Oxford, P for Preston and Pennines, Q for vehicles of unidentifiable age, R for Reading, S for Scotland, V for Vale of Severn, W for West country, and Y for Yorkshire. The letter T was not allocated to any region, but has been used in Scotland since 2007. The second letter (= local identifier) shows the local registration office. In the case of East Anglia, the letters A to N refer to the Peterborough registration office, the letters O to U refer to Norwich, and the letters V to Y refer to Ipswich. Northern Ireland has its own system.

The two letters are followed by the two-digit age identifier, which changes on March 1st and September 1st. It consists either of the year itself, for example 07 for March to August 2007, or it has 50 added, being 57, for September 2007 to February 2008. So, in 2024, it will be 24 for March to August, and 74 (24 + 50) for September to February.

The following three letters distinguish the cars with the same four character-area. Some combinations of letters are not issued as they might appear offensive; that is the reason why some Scottish cars do not have S but T as their memory tag.

British number plates now have black characters on white background in front, and black characters on yellow background at the rear.

As a rule, vehicle keepers obtain their registration number from the Driver and Vehicle Licensing Agency (DVLA), Swansea. On request, and at considerable extra cost, the DVLA will issue what is known as a "personalized" or "cherished" or "individual" registration number. Normally a vehicle will retain its licence plate when it is sold. However, owners may also keep their number, especially a personalized one, if they wish to transfer it to another vehicle. They may even sell it to anyone who is interested in it. In fact, there is a buoyant market in vehicle registration numbers. For example, in 2007, a company advertised DUI 96 for £ 999, and IT1 for £ 275 000; M1 was auctioned for £ 330,000.

Questions

1. What do British licence plates look like?
2. Can you imagine situations in which the British system could be helpful for the police?
3. Why are certain letters not used as suffixes or prefixes?
4. What are other systems like? Germany, France, Czech Republic, Switzerland .....?
5. Why might the following personalized numbers be attractive? B16 MUM; C14 CAT; M1 NUT; 666 BMW; H1 TEC; T33 BOY; 4 YOU; B8 FLY; LOV 3R.

7.6 Where the hell is Diplomat?

Our family lived in the USA for four years when my husband worked as the German Police Liaison Officer in Washington, D.C. During the long summer school breaks we used to travel around the country by car. On one of these trips we reached the mighty Mississippi just south of St. Louis. To experience the vastness of this river, we decided not to use a bridge for crossing but a ferry.

In the middle of nowhere we found a small craft that took people and vehicles across. It took quite some time to cross the river, and I noticed that one of the ferry personnel, a huge African American who looked as if just stepped out of the Tom Sawyer story, kept looking at our license plate. As we had diplomatic status, our car was not registered in the state of Maryland where we actually lived but with the State Department. The license plate looked like any ordinary license plate: only instead of mentioning the state of origin it simply said "Diplomat". Shortly before we reached the river bank on the other side, he braced up and finally asked the question that had been on his mind for the last ten minutes. He seemed confused about the number of states that constitute the USA and just wanted to know: "Where the hell is Diplomat?"

Questions

1. Who wrote this text?
2. What does D.C. stand for?
3. When did the couple travel around the country?
4. Why did the couple cross the river on a ferry boat?
5. Who was Tom Sawyer?

Translate the names of the following places and find out in which state of the USA they are situated. Find out more about these places

1. Truth or Consequences; 2. Broken Arrow; 3. Hungry Horse; 4. Branding Iron; 5. Frostproof; 6. King of Prussia; 7. Hot Coffee; 8. Goodnight; 9. Mexican Hat; 10. Burnt Ranch

7.7 Vehicle lights

In the course of a traffic check the vehicle lights are usually checked, too. If only a bulb has gone, a vehicle defect form will normally be issued. If the whole lighting system does not work, the driver might not be allowed to proceed, especially in darkness, fog, rain or snowfall.

Find out the meanings (use your dictionary). Which terms are British and which are American English?

additional headlights	back lights
backup lights	brake lights
bright lights (brights)	dimmed/dipped beam
dimmed/dipped lights	emergency warning lights
fog lights (front or rear)	front lights
full/high/main beam	hazard warning flashers/lights
headlights	high-intensity fog light(s)
(turn) indicators	licence plate / number plate light
parking lights	rear lights
reflectors	reversing lights
side lights	signals
stop lights	tail lights

7.8 Tyres

Fill in the following words

The roadworthiness of a (chlveie) .... largely depends on the (etsta) .... of its tyres. A loose top layer or cuts in the sidewall can be lethal for car (seagpsresn) .... and other (rtifafc) .... participants. In Germany, the minimum depth of tyre treads is 1.6 mm. There are summer tyres, winter tyres, and (tlaewelahr) .... tyres. Tyres used in winter must be (utbslaie) .... for wintry road conditions. Any serious (admeag) .... to even one tyre can lead to the (rdirve) .... no longer being (dlalowe) .... to proceed.

7.9 Identifying the keeper of a vehicle

The keeper (or registered owner) is a natural person or a distinct legal entity in whose name the vehicle is registered with the road traffic authority. The owner's personal data or the relevant data of the distinct legal entity are entered on the vehicle registration certificate. The keeper need not be the owner or the driver. The relevant data of all German vehicles are registered with the Federal Motor Transport Authority in Flensburg and can be retrieved by the police at any time. It is, therefore, possible to rapidly establish in the course of a check whether driver and registered owner are identical or whether the data provided by the driver are correct.

7.10 Routine traffic check

PHM Johannes Obstlander (JO) is going back to his station in Langenargen on Lake Constance. In Lindauer Straße, a driver is obstructing traffic as he continually slows down and accelerates again. When this car stops, he switches on the blue light, gets out of the patrol car and walks to the side window of the other vehicle, which has stopped. The driver is Eric Schaffer (ES) from the Midwest of the USA, who is visiting relatives.

JO: Good morning. I don't like the way you're driving. You're obstructing others and might cause an accident.

ES: Good morning. I'm sorry, but I can explain. I'm looking for my wife.

JO: Ah. The lost wife can get a husband very excited. I understand that. But one thing after the other. Could I have your driver's license and vehicle registration certificate?

ES: I'm American, of German origin, and we are visiting relatives here. Here you are, my American driver's license, and here the registration certificate of the rental car. I dropped my wife off in the city centre, close to the castle, and went to buy a souvenir. Now I'm driving around looking for her as she didn't show up at the meeting place we had arranged. And because I'm watching out for her, I'm probably a bit too slow. Sorry about that.

JO: It might be better to park the car and look for your wife on foot. The town center and the lake promenade aren't far from here, perhaps she's in the harbor area. There's also our police station. Are you satisfied with your rental car?

ES: Oh yes. It runs smoothly, and the service is very good.

JO: Let me have a look at the tires.

JO checks if the tires are damaged and if they have enough tread. He also checks the registration, AU and HU decals and walks around the car. Now he is in front of the car.

JO: Please get into the car and switch on the lights. Parking lights ..... dipped beam ..... full beam .... all right. Now turn signals left .... and right .....ok. And now the hazard warning flashers....all right.

He walks to the back of the car.

JO: Please step on the brake ......turn signal left ..... and right ......, and the rear fog light. All the lights are ok. Thank you. Now, in Germany you must have a warning triangle and a first-aid kit in the car at all times.

ES: Yes, I know. When I took over the car, they told me and also showed me where they are. Here, in the trunk, on the right.

JO: Everything is all right with the car. But what about your wife? I suggest that you park your car here and come with me to the harbor. Maybe we can spot your wife on the way. And with a patrol car I can drive slow and stop any time. You only have to tell me what your wife looks like.

When they arrive at the police station, a woman is waiting there.

ES: There she is, Catherine! Man, you must be a clairvoyant. Thank you very much. But one more thing: Can you please tell me where I parked my rental car?

7.11 Caution

If the driver of a vehicle admits that he or she has acted in breach of the relevant rules and regulations, and if it is a case of a minor public order offence, the officer in charge may exercise his discretion by just issuing an oral caution. This means that the driver concerned is cautioned with regard to the traffic offence committed without a warning fine being imposed.

7.12 Vehicle defect (rectification) form

If, in the course of a traffic check, a defect is detected, e.g. a defective rear light, the driver will be handed a postcard-size vehicle defect form identifying the defect and stipulating the date by which the latter is to be rectified. As soon as the defect has been rectified, this will, for instance, be confirmed by taking the vehicle to a police station, whereupon the card is to be returned to the issuing authority. If the defect has not been rectified or if the deadline has been exceeded, the road traffic authority concerned will take the appropriate steps.

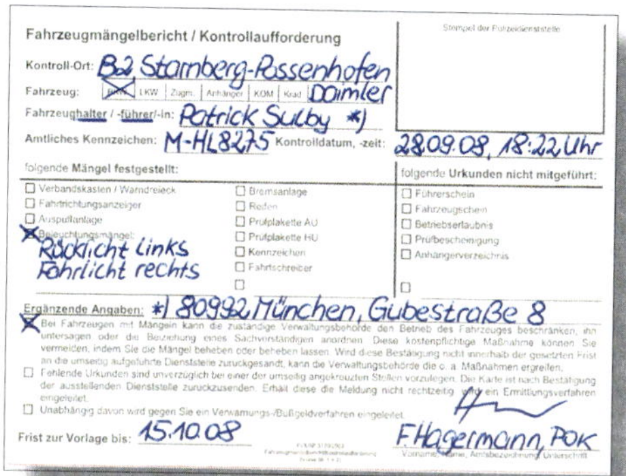

Fahrzeugmängelbericht / Kontrollaufforderung

Stempel der Polizeidienststelle

Kontroll-Ort: B2 Starnberg-Possenhofen

Fahrzeug: ☒ PKW ☐ LKW ☐ Zugm. ☐ Anhänger ☐ KOM ☐ Krad Daimler

Fahrzeughalter / -führer/-in: Patrick Sulby *)

Amtliches Kennzeichen: M-HL8275 Kontrolldatum, -zeit: 28.09.08, 18:22 Uhr

folgende Mängel festgestellt:

- ☐ Verbandskasten / Warndreieck
- ☐ Fahrtrichtungsanzeiger
- ☐ Auspuffanlage
- ☒ Beleuchtungsmängel: Rücklicht links, Fahrlicht rechts
- ☐ Bremsanlage
- ☐ Reifen
- ☐ Prüfplakette AU
- ☐ Prüfplakette HU
- ☐ Kennzeichen
- ☐ Fahrtschreiber
- ☐

folgende Urkunden nicht mitgeführt:

- ☐ Führerschein
- ☐ Fahrzeugschein
- ☐ Betriebserlaubnis
- ☐ Prüfbescheinigung
- ☐ Anhängerverzeichnis
- ☐

Ergänzende Angaben: *) 80992 München, Gubestraße 8

☒ Bei Fahrzeugen mit Mängeln kann die zuständige Verwaltungsbehörde den Betrieb des Fahrzeuges beschränken, ihn untersagen oder die Beziehung eines Sachverständigen anordnen. Diese kostenpflichtige Maßnahme können Sie vermeiden, indem Sie die Mängel beheben oder beheben lassen. Wird diese Bestätigung nicht innerhalb der gesetzten Frist an die umseitig aufgeführte Dienststelle zurückgesandt, kann die Verwaltungsbehörde die o. a. Maßnahmen ergreifen.

☐ Fehlende Urkunden sind unverzüglich bei einer der umseitig angekreuzten Stellen vorzulegen. Die Karte ist nach Bestätigung der ausstellenden Dienststelle zurückzusenden. Erhält diese die Meldung nicht rechtzeitig, wird ein Ermittlungsverfahren eingeleitet.

☐ Unabhängig davon wird gegen Sie ein Verwarnungs-/Bußgeldverfahren eingeleitet.

Frist zur Vorlage bis: 15.10.08

F. Hagermann, POK

Vorname, Name, Amtsbezeichnung, Unterschrift

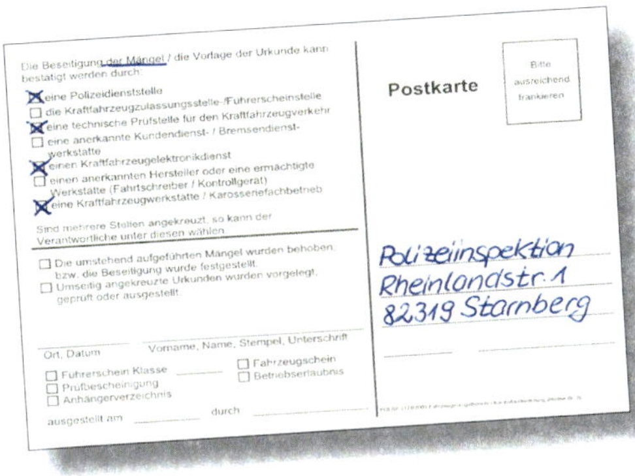

Die Beseitigung der Mängel / die Vorlage der Urkunde kann bestätigt werden durch:

- ☒ eine Polizeidienststelle
- ☐ die Kraftfahrzeugzulassungsstelle-/Führerscheinstelle
- ☒ eine technische Prüfstelle für den Kraftfahrzeugverkehr
- ☐ eine anerkannte Kundendienst- / Bremsendienst-werkstätte
- ☒ einen Kraftfahrzeugelektronikdienst
- ☐ einen anerkannten Hersteller oder eine ermächtigte Werkstätte (Fahrtschreiber / Kontrollgerät)
- ☒ eine Kraftfahrzeugwerkstätte / Karosseriefachbetrieb

Sind mehrere Stellen angekreuzt, so kann der Verantwortliche unter diesen wählen.

☐ Die umstehend aufgeführten Mängel wurden behoben bzw. die Beseitigung wurde festgestellt.

☐ Umseitig angekreuzte Urkunden wurden vorgelegt, geprüft oder ausgestellt.

Ort, Datum | Vorname, Name, Stempel, Unterschrift

☐ Führerschein Klasse ____ ☐ Fahrzeugschein ☐ Betriebserlaubnis ☐ Prüfbescheinigung ☐ Anhängerverzeichnis

ausgestellt am ____ durch ____

Postkarte

Bitte ausreichend frankieren

Polizeiinspektion
Rheinlandstr. 1
82319 Starnberg

7.13 Issuing a vehicle defect form

Patrick Sulby (PS) is from Port Erin on the Isle of Man. As a distributor/dealer for British sports cars, he lives in Munich. On a drive to Lake Starnberg, he realizes ground fog is spreading, so he switches on the dimmed lights of his classic car, a 1969 Ascot fawn-coloured Daimler 250 V8 (136 bhp, RHD, fluted radiator grille, Borg-Warner automatic, hemispheric Weslake combustion chamber, walnut dashboard, Conolly leather seats). He is overtaken and waved into a lay-by by a police motorcyclist. POK Freddie Hagermann (FH) parks his motorcycle and walks to the driver's side.

FH: Good afternoon, sir. My name is Hagermann of the Starnberg police. Traffic check. Please let me have your driving licence and the vehicle registration certificate.

PS: Good afternoon. Here you are. I'm from the Isle of Man, but I've been living in Munich for a long time.

FH checks the data listed on the driving licence and compares the photo with the driver. The Daimler has only recently been licensed.

FH: According to the vehicle registration certificate, the RBJ Royal British Jaguar firm of Munich is the registered owner. Is it a company car?

PS: Yes, it is. I'm the Jaguar area representative for Bavaria. Here's my calling card.

FH: Hm. Even with such an old car, which, by the way, is a beauty and I wish it was mine, everything should be in perfect working order. But the left-hand rear light is not on. As I was overtaking you, I also saw that only the right-hand headlamp parking light was on. Please alight so that we can both have a look at it, but leave the lights on, please.

They walk around the vehicle. Patrick Sulby taps the plastic cover of the rear light, but it won't come on. The same applies to the headlights.

PS: It can't be true! Two bulbs being gonners at the same time! Is that possible? I'll just check the fuses.

FH: Mr Sulby, we're close to the water here and dampness tends to impair cables and clip-on connections. A delicate thing like a bulb is soon gone, too. You're quite right to check the fuses to make sure, but there's nothing else you and I can do just yet.

PS: Am I still allowed to drive to my firm? I'll have the car checked at once in our garage.

FH: Of course you can, but you'll have to have the defect seen to. The vehicle lights must be in perfect working order. You might have heard the phrase: "See and be seen!" That's got something to do with road safety for you and for others, too.

PS: Yes, I'm aware of that.

FH: May I also remind you that law requires drivers to walk round their vehicle to check whether everything is in working order before they set off.

PS: But who does all that?

FH: You're right there. There aren't many people who do that. But that doesn't matter right now. You're here now with defective lights. Let's assume that the bulbs only went while you were driving, in which case you're not to blame. How could you have noticed? I'll make out a vehicle defect form. Just bear with me for a moment.

FH now enters some data of the driving licence and vehicle registration certificate on the vehicle defect form, adds some notes, ticks off a few items and signs the card. He detaches the card from his pad of vehicle defect forms and then stands next to Mr Sulby.

FH: Here you are. Just have a look. This is a vehicle defect form which doesn't cost you anything apart from the stamp for sending it back to my police station. Here, top left, I entered the name of the place where your car was checked. We're on federal road No 2 between Starnberg and Possenhofen. Below you can see a tick for your passenger car, and – next to it – the make of your vehicle, i.e. Daimler. One line below, I entered your name and the address of your firm, followed by the licence plate number, date and time of check. Here, in this part, let's say in the middle of the form, various frequently occurring defects are listed. I ticked "lighting defects", specifying the defects concerned as well as the respective lighting fixtures. Bottom left, I entered a date as deadline for re-submission of the card to me. A week should be enough time.

PS: All right, but how do I obtain confirmation that the defects have been rectified?

FH: Just look at the reverse of the card. You'll find several options ticked by me: a police station, MoT testing station, garage or an auto-electrician.

PS: As I said, our firm has its own garage, but will you believe me if our garage superintendent has signed the form?

FH: I'm sure your firm is a respectable enterprise, but you can also have your car inspected by any Munich police station. Here you are. This is where you've got to affix a stamp. That's our address: Polizeiinspektion Starnberg, Rheinlandstraße 1, 82319 Starnberg. Send the card back to me within a week, so I can strike you off our list. If there are any delays, just give me a ring to tell me, because if the card does not arrive at our police station, I'll have to forward the copy to the vehicle registration office in Munich. And you'll have to pay if we have to issue another demand. OK? Any questions? Bye then, and have a nice trip.

PS: Thanks. Bye.

Which answer is correct? Tick the box

1. The colour of Patrick Sulby's vehicle is a kind of

   - ☐ green
   - ☐ blue
   - ☐ beige
   - ☐ black

2. bhp stands for

   - ☐ British horse power
   - ☐ brake horse power
   - ☐ broad high pressure (tyres)
   - ☐ bifocal high-intensity point (lights)

3. Patrick Sulby is stopped because

   - ☐ he has been weaving in and out of slow-moving traffic
   - ☐ his lights were not on in foggy conditions
   - ☐ his steering wheel is on the wrong side
   - ☐ his lights are defective

4. The defect concerned is due to

   - ☐ missing bulbs
   - ☐ dampness and faulty clip-on connections
   - ☐ blown fuses
   - ☐ defective bulbs

5. The officer tells Mr Sulby that

   - ☐ the fine can be paid by cheque
   - ☐ it is OK for his garage to rectify the defect
   - ☐ his old Daimler must be inspected by the German equivalent of the MoT
   - ☐ the Starnberg division of the Munich police specialize in vehicle defects.

7.14 Role play

Simulate a traffic check in English with your colleagues. Use your private cars and follow the correct procedure. Issue the vehicle defect form used in your federal state. Record everything on video to see whether the check was conducted in accordance with the rules

7.15 Use of the tenses 2

Present Perfect – Perfekt/Vollendete Gegenwart

Handlungen, die in der Vergangenheit begonnen haben und noch andauern; besonders in Sätzen mit *for* und *since* wird dabei vorzugsweise die Verlaufsform verwendet

PC Plod has been waiting for his promotion since 2008.

They have been married for 15 years now.

Abgeschlossene Handlungen, deren Wirkung in die Gegenwart reicht

Inspector Williams has been promoted. She is now head of section.

I've been to Italy, that's why I know a few things about this country.

Handlungen, die sich kurz vor der Gegenwart ereignet haben

He has just arrived.

Past Perfect – Plusquamperfekt/Vollendete Vergangenheit

Handlungen, die vor einer anderen Handlung in der Vergangenheit bereits vorbei sind und damit in Verbindung stehen

When the CID officers arrived at the scene, the burglars had already left.

Future – Futur/Zukunft

Für zukünftige Handlungen gibt es mehrere Formen

going to + Infinitiv wird überwiegend in der Umgangssprache verwendet, besonders bei Absichten, Plänen und erwarteten Ereignissen

What are you going to do about the missing child?

It's going to rain.

will + Infinitiv wird vornehmlich in der Schriftsprache, in der Kurzform *'ll* auch in der Umgangssprache bei erwarteten Vorgängen verwendet

Tomorrow will be fine, with occasional showers.

Die Verlaufsform Präsens wird für geplante Handlungen in der nahen Zukunft verwendet

I'm attending a refresher course next week.

Das einfache Präsens wird für verbindliche Handlungen der Zukunft verwendet, insbesondere bei Fahrplänen

Our plane lands at Detroit at 7.20 a.m. next Wednesday.

The Spanish King visits Berlin tomorrow.

will be + -ing-Form wird vornehmlich für zukünftige Handlungen verwendet, die als selbstverständlich angesehen werden

I'll be seeing you then.

7.16 Exercises

1. Fill in the correct tense. Use the following verbs

arrive, be (2x), be fined, buy, deal, meet, read, want, work, write

1. He lost his butterfly knife shortly after he .... it from a fence, who was known to the police.
2. I (never) .... such rubbish in all my life.
3. I'm afraid he .... for exceeding the speed limit.
4. How many times (you) .... on night shift next month?
5. He .... as a clerk at the local magistrates' court for 20 years.
6. The drunk drifter in the detention cell .... fast asleep for three hours now.
7. When (you) .... with this matter? Tomorrow?
8. He .... to visit Bristol since you .... to him last May.
9. Let's have a break. The pizzas (just) ....
10. I'm sure we .... again.

2. The following answers were given by applicants for the police service during their interviews with the examiners' board. Form the questions

1. No, I haven't got my class B driving licence yet, but right now I'm having driving lessons, and the test is scheduled for May 15.
2. No, I haven't applied in another force, this is my first application.
3. Yes, I've been to France, Spain and Portugal.
4. I've been living in this town since 2006.
5. No, I've never committed an act of vandalism.
6. I've been studying English for ten years now.
7. I've known PC James Walker since 2005, when he moved into the next-door house.
8. Since I graduated from school, I've been helping my parents, who run a pub.
9. No, I've never been sent off the pitch with a red card when playing soccer.
10. Yes, I've already inquired about the many possibilities of a police officer's career.

7.17 Useful phrases

1. Begrüßen Sie den Fahrer/die Fahrerin, stellen Sie sich vor und sagen Sie ihm/ihr, warum Sie ihn/sie angehalten haben.

   ....

2. Bitten Sie den Fahrer, den Motor abzustellen und das Radio auszuschalten.

   ....

3. Teilen Sie dem Fahrer mit, dass die Polizei bei Verkehrskontrollen die Papiere, Beleuchtung und Bereifung sowie die Fahrtüchtigkeit des Fahrers überprüft.

   ....

   ....

4. Bitten Sie den Fahrer, Ihnen die Papiere auszuhändigen (Führerschein usw.).

   ....

5. Teilen Sie dem Fahrer mit, dass Sie ihn angehalten haben, weil das linke Rücklicht und das linke Abblendlicht nicht funktionieren.

   ....

6. Bitten Sie den Fahrer, die Beleuchtung einzuschalten (Standlicht, Abblendlicht, Fernlicht, Blinker rechts und links, Warnblinkanlage, Bremsleuchte, Nebelschlussleuchte).

   ....

   ....

7. Verweisen Sie den Fahrer an die nächstgelegene Werkstatt und empfehlen Sie, die Schäden so schnell wie möglich beheben zu lassen.

   ....

8. Teilen Sie dem Fahrer mit, dass alle Reifen nur noch sehr wenig Profil haben.

   ....

9. Erklären Sie das Prinzip des Mängelberichts / der Kontrollaufforderung.

   ....

10. Geben Sie dem Fahrer die Dokumente zurück und wünschen Sie ihm eine gute Fahrt.

   ....

7.18 Key words and phrases

caution – exemption permit – green insurance card – hazardous goods – keeper – mobile traffic check – on-the-spot traffic check – producer – registered owner – traffic enforcement – traffic offence – tyre tread – vehicle defect (rectification) form – vehicle registration certificate – and all the words from 7. 4 and 7. 7

Traffic control and on-the-spot fine

Unit 8

This unit deals with

- personal data
- some minor traffic offences
- warnings and on-the-spot warning fines and
- the comparison of adjectives.

8.1 Personal data

When dealing with members of the public, police officers have very often to write down the personal data of a person; and it doesn't matter if this person wants to make a complaint or whether he/she is a witness, a suspect or an arrested criminal.

According to German law, every person **must** give the following personal data:

- family name
- first name(s)
- date of birth (DOB)
- place of birth
- residential address
- occupation/profession.

The following data **may** be supplied on a voluntary basis:

- family status
- brothers and sisters
- children
- parents/legal guardian(s)
- honorary functions/posts
- income
- previous conviction(s)/criminal record.

Form the questions to match the answers given here

question	answer
1.	My family name is McDonald.
2.	My first names are Stephen John.
3.	I was born on 13th December 1986.
4.	I was born in Stranraer, Scotland.
5.	I live in 43 Parkstone Road, Hastings, Sussex, TN34 2AT, England.
6.	I'm a carpenter. I have my own workshop.
7.	Yes, I am. My wife's name is Jennifer. No, I'm not, I'm single. I'm a widower. I'm divorced.
8.	I've got an elder brother and two younger sisters.
9.	Yes, I've got a girl, aged 14, and a son, aged 12.
10.	My parents are Richard and Janet McDonald, they live in 3456 Mazama Drive, Klamath Falls, Oregon 97603, USA.
11.	No, I don't. I have a big garden, and taking care of it takes all my spare time.
12.	About € 50,000 a year.
13.	No, I don't. I always obey the law.

8.2 Warning and on-the-spot warning fine

In Germany police officers have powers, in case of minor offences, to caution the offender with an on-the-spot fine of 5 to 35 euros. The offences and fines are listed in a catalogue. The warning fine serves to persuade the offender not to commit this offence again without giving the impression that he is "punished". Most cautions are issued in road traffic. Sensible drivers see the error of their ways and pay the fine on the spot. Then the matter is settled. If a driver accepts the fine but has no or not enough cash on him, he will get a transfer form from the fixed-penalty authority. If he refuses to pay, he will make a statement to the police on the spot and will later receive a fixed-penalty notice from the fixed-penalty office. Offenders from abroad have to pay on the spot. If necessary, police officers escort them to an ATM. If the foreigner refuses to pay, police will demand bail from him immediately and start fixed-penalty proceedings.

8.3 In front of a school

Taxi driver Geoffrey Barney (GB) from Leicester is on a cure at Bad Sulza in Thuringia. For two days now he has been watching, from his hotel window, the scene in front of the school on the other side of the street when school starts in the morning. Community officer POK Hans Mansel (HM) is standing beside the zebra crossing at the school. He is talking to children, teachers and parents, and also watches the motorists. Across the road there are big banners with the slogans "Watch out for school children" and "School term has started". Geoffrey Barney knows the situation from his home town and wants to have a closer look. He walks down into the street. POK Mansel is just pointing out to school beginners that they have to use the pedestrian crossing. Mr Barney addresses him.

Part 1

GB: Good morning. I'm from Leicester in England. I've been driving a taxi there for 30 years, and I know about the situation in front of a school. May I ask a question?

HM: Good morning. Yes, of course. What I'm doing here is what we call "A safe way to school".

GB: And you watch the pupils?

HM: I make sure that the children use the pedestrian crossing and don't run across the street at other places or run across the street from between parked cars. The children should have learnt, from an early age, from their parents and also in kindergarten to use the zebra crossing. But sometimes they forget because they want to get quickly across the street for some reason. Then they just start running. This week I'm trying to show the children what to do and what they must not do. An accident with a child is a dreadful thing to happen.

GB: Yes, I can imagine. Then there would be lots of arguments how this could possibly have happened. But aren't the children often accompanied by a parent, or grandmother or grandfather, or aunt or uncle?

HM: At the beginning of a school year, the children are often accompanied by grown-ups, who show them where the way to school is dangerous, and they practise with them how to cross the street. In front of the school here I'm the nice bobby whom they tell proudly what they have already learnt. There, look! The little girl has held out her arm to show that she wants to use the zebra crossing. Her mother is standing behind her, watching her. The approaching car now stops.

GB: Yes, that's right. And there aren't any problems?

HM: Yes, there are. It doesn't always work smoothly, and I have to have a close look. But often it's the grown-ups who don't obey the traffic rules and set a bad example. Then I have to be very strict with the drivers; mostly it's the mothers who bring the children to school and pick them up again.

GB: Today's road traffic is really dangerous. Often it is too dangerous for children and elderly people. Children should learn from their parents what to do in such situations and what to avoid.

HM: You're right there. But excuse me for a moment. There comes a lady. She isn't wearing her seatbelt.

Geoffrey Barney now watches the scene with great interest. POK Mansel walks to the car, which has stopped. A child with a school satchel is about to get out on the left side.

HM: Stop. Stop, young man. You've to get out on the other side of the car, and you don't run across the street. First you walk the short distance on the pavement to the zebra crossing. After that you can get to the other side of the street together with the other children.

He addresses the woman:

Good morning. It would have been your job, as the mother of this boy, to teach him how to cross the street. As a driver you have to be very careful. I've just told this gentleman from England that another driver can easily overlook a small child. There is no need for that to happen. Please help us. It's also your child that might be involved. May I have your driving licence, please?

POK Mansel inspects the driving licence. The driver is Sandra Karbach (SK).

Part 2

HM: Mrs Karbach, why aren't you buckled up?

SK: Oh! I usually buckle up. But I've only driven a short distance, from home to the school here.

HM: Mrs Karbach, you certainly know what might happen if you don't wear your seatbelt. Without the seatbelt you might suffer severe injuries even at a low speed.

SK: Yes, I understand. I'm sorry.

HM: Mrs Karbach, do you agree to a warning fine of € 30?

SK: Is that really necessary? Can't you just waive it? Or can you make it less expensive?

HM: What are you trying to do? Do you want to haggle with me about your traffic infraction? The amount of € 30 is set by law.

SK: You asked me if I did agree to the fine. So I don't have to accept it, do I?

HM: Mrs Karbach, I'll explain as briefly as possible. You can accept it if you admit that you acted wrongly. Then you can pay directly to me, and the matter is settled. If you don't agree, the fixed-penalty office will start proceedings against you. You can then hire a lawyer. And you'll have to pay administrative fees. Mrs Karbach, think about it. Well, it has happened, and if you get excited about it, then perhaps you might remember it at a later date, and you'll always buckle up. So what are you going to do?

SK: I'll pay.

Shortly afterwards POK Mansel talks to Mr Barney again.

GB: Very interesting. I didn't understand everything, but I noticed that the lady wanted to argue with you. But in the end she paid. It was nice talking to you and watching you doing your job.

HM: My pleasure. Here's my card.

GB: Many thanks. Good-bye.

HM: Maybe we'll meet again tomorrow morning. I'll be here again. All the best.

1. Who, apart from the police, can help schoolchildren cross the street in Germany?

2. Find out about other countries

3. True or not true?

	true	not true
1. Geoffrey Barney drove a taxi 30 years ago.		
2. POK Mansel wants the children to use the pedestrian crossing.		
3. POK Mansel thinks that the grown-ups set a good example.		
4. The little boy got out of the door behind the driver.		
5. Mrs Karbach tries to talk POK Mansel out of fining her.		
6. It is more expensive if you pay on the spot.		

4. Find the synonyms in the text for:

1. to start talking to someone ....
2. students ....
3. terrible ....
4. plenty of ....
5. adults ....
6. police officer ....
7. senior citizens ....
8. school bag ....
9. to fasten the seatbelt ....
10. shortly ....

5. Explain the meaning of the following phrases

1. an approaching car: ....
2. something works smoothly: ....
3. can't you just waive it?: ....
4. you can hire a lawyer: ....

8.4 Adjectives: comparison

Steigerung mit *-er* und *-est*

Einsilbige Adjektive werden mit *-er* und *-est* gesteigert

Positiv *tall* Komparativ *taller* Superlativ *tallest*

Zweisilbige Adjektive werden normalerweise ebenfalls mit *-er* und *-est* gesteigert, soweit sie auf *-er, -le, -y, -some* und *-ow* enden oder auf der zweiten Silbe betont sind

clever – cleverer – cleverest *simple – simpler – simplest*
ugly – uglier – ugliest *narrow – narrower – narrowest*
severe – severer – severest *handsome – handsomer – handsomest*

Stummes -e am Wortende entfällt *simple – simpler – simplest*

Verdoppelung nach einfachem, kurzem und betontem Vokal *hot – hotter – hottest*

Nach einem Konsonanten wird -y zu -i: *easy – easier – easiest*

Steigerung mit *more* und *most*

Zweisilbige Adjektive mit Betonung auf der ersten Silbe sowie alle drei- und mehrsilbigen Adjektive werden mit *more* und *most* gesteigert

modern – more modern – most modern
difficult – more difficult – most difficult

Unregelmäßige Steigerung

good – better – best; bad/ill – worse – worst; many/much – more – most; little – less – least; far – farther/further – farthest/furthest; near – nearer – nearest/next; old – older/elder – oldest/eldest

Vergleich

Vergleich gleichwertiger Dinge *as ... as; not as ... as; not so ... as*
as safe as houses, not as/so bright as his sister

Vergleich unterschiedlicher Dinge *Komparativ + than*
better than, more beautiful than

Merke

the sooner the better = *je ... desto ...*
faster and faster = *immer schneller*

8.5 Fill-in exercise

Part 1

Fill in the correct forms

1. I haven't the (remote) .... idea why I'm being stopped.
2. What's the (near) .... way to the police station? – Take the (near) .... street on the right and then keep straight on.
3. She's lost all the money she had in her bag, and the (bad) .... thing is that it wasn't even hers.
4. Finding a parking space in our city is getting (difficult) .... these days.
5. Illegal parking can be (dear/expensive) .... than you think.
6. Working night shifts is (hard) .... than most people think.
7. A police officer's work can be (strenuous) .... than that of a lorry driver.
8. The speeding ticket cost him (little) .... than he had expected.
9. For (far) .... information contact the local authority.
10. The new patrol car is not as (comfortable) ....as the previous model.

Part 2

Fill in the correct forms. Choose from the following adjectives

bad (2x) – beautiful (2x) – clever – environmentally friendly – experienced – fast (2x) – large – loud – noisy – sharp – tall

1. PC Langley is the............................. officer at our police station, he must be nearly two metres.
2. WPC Soames is ...., but her daughter is even ....
3. The criminal thought that he was .... than the detective.
4. The New York City Police Department is one of the .... in the world.
5. The weather is getting .... and ....
6. The .... you drive, the .... the noise of the engine will be.
7. The murder case was solved by the .... detectives.
8. A bicycle is not as............................. as a motorcycle and ....
9. Bends can be .... than they appear.
10. Emergency vehicles are allowed to drive .... than the speed limit allows.

8.6 Useful phrases

Fragen Sie einen Mann/eine Frau nach

1. Vor- und Familiennamen, Geburtsdatum und Geburtsort

   ....

2. Wohnanschrift und Beruf

   ....

3. Familienstand, Geschwistern und Kindern

   ....

4. seinem/ihrem Einkommen, eventuellen Vorstrafen.

   ....

5. Belehren Sie ihn/sie darüber, dass nach deutschem Recht er/sie die ersten zwei Fragen beantworten muss, die restlichen aber nicht zu beantworten braucht.

   ....

   ....

6. Erklären Sie ihm/ihr, dass in Deutschland die Polizei bei geringfügigen Verkehrsverstößen eine Verwarnung mit Verwarnungsgeld bis zu € 35 aussprechen kann.

   ....

   ....

7. Weisen Sie Schulkinder darauf hin, dass sie immer den Zebrastreifen benutzen sollen.

   ....

8. Erklären Sie einem Elternpaar, dass sie beim Überqueren der Fahrbahn immer Vorbild für ihre Kinder sein sollten.

   ....

   ....

9. Fragen Sie eine Autofahrerin, warum sie nicht angeschnallt ist.

   ....

10. Erklären einem Fahrer, dass die Angelegenheit erledigt ist, wenn er das Verwarnungsgeld bezahlt hat.

    ....

11. Erklären Sie ihm auch, dass ein Bußgeldverfahren gegen ihn eingeleitet wird, wenn er nicht bezahlt.

    ....

12. Sagen Sie ihm auch, dass er jederzeit einen Anwalt hinzuziehen kann.

    ....

8.7 Key words and phrases

bail – buckle up – community beat officer – criminal record – fixed-penalty authority/office – on-the-spot fine – personal data – previous conviction – proceedings – suspect – wear the seatbelt – warning fine – witness – zebra crossing

Traffic checks and fixed-penalty notices

Unit 9

This unit deals with

- minor traffic offences and fixed-penalty notices
- the penalty points system
- speeding and speed checks
- using a mobile phone behind the wheel
- checking lorries
- bail and
- the adverb.

9.1 Two stories

Part 1 – A story from the United States

Sitting on the side of the highway waiting to catch speeding drivers, a police officer sees a car chugging along at 22 mph. He thinks: "This driver is just as dangerous as a speeder!" So he turns on his lights and pulls the driver over.

Approaching the car, he notices that there are five old ladies in the car, two in the front, and three in the back – wide-eyed and white as ghosts. The driver, obviously confused, says to him, "Officer, I don't understand why you've pulled me over, I was doing the maximum speed – exactly. What's the problem?"

"Madam," the officer replies, "You weren't speeding, but you should know that driving much more slowly than the speed limit can also be a danger to other drivers."

"Slower than the speed limit? No, sir, I was doing the speed limit exactly ... twenty-two miles per hour!", the old woman says proudly.

The police officer, trying to contain a chuckle, explains to her that "22" is the road number, not the speed limit.

A bit embarrassed, the woman grins and thanks the officer for pointing out her error.

"But before I let you go, Madam, I have to ask ... Is everyone in this car okay? Your companions seem awfully shaken, and they haven't said a single word the whole time," the officer asks.

"Oh, they'll be all right in a minute, officer. You see, we've just got off road 119."

1. **What do you think of this story?**
2. **If you had been the police officer, how would you have reacted?**
3. **What do you think of elderly drivers? Should there be an age limit for drivers?**

Part 2 – A story from Great Britain

In Cornwall, a female Jaguar driver was stopped because she had been driving at 90 mph – the speed limit being 70 mph. When asked by the police why she had been doing as much as 90 mph – almost a ton (100 mph) – she pointed to one of the dials on the dashboard and insisted that she had only been doing 40.

Which dial was she referring to?

9.2 Speeding

Exceeding the speed limit or failure to adapt one's speed to the situation are the main reasons for road traffic accidents. In 2006, more than 8.4 million traffic offenders were registered with the Central Register of Traffic Offenders at Flensburg, that's about 15 % of the more than 55 million vehicle keepers in the Federal Republic. Nearly 60 % of these registrations, which comprise fixed-penalty notices and court penalties, were made because drivers had exceeded the speed limit or they had been driving at excessive speed.

A driver exceeds the speed limit if he drives faster than the national speed limit allows, in other words: if he drives faster than 100 kph outside or faster than 50 kph inside built-up areas or if he drives faster than the maximum speed posted, for example, if he drives faster than the posted maximum speed of 80 kph in a roadworks area on the motorway.

A driver fails to adapt his speed to the situation if road and weather conditions, traffic density and visibility only allow a lower speed than is permitted. Doing 50 kph on the motorway in dense fog may be too fast. Apart from that, the driver has to adjust his speed to his abilities and also to the vehicle and its load.

9.3 Speeding fines and penalties in Germany

speed exceeding	outside built-up areas			within built-up areas		
	fine	penalty points	disqualification	fine	penalty points	disqualification
up to 10 kph	€ 10	–	–	€ 15	–	–
11-15 kph	€ 20	–	–	€ 25	–	–
16-20 kph	€ 30	–	–	€ 35	–	–
21-25 kph	€ 70	1	–	€ 80	1	–
26-30 kph	€ 80	3	–	€ 100	3	–
31-40 kph	€ 120	3	–	€ 160	3	1 month
41-50 kph	€ 160	3	1 month	€ 200	4	1 month
51-60 kph	€ 240	4	1 month	€ 280	4	2 months
61-70 kph	€ 440	4	2 months	€ 480	4	3 months
more than 70 kph	€ 600	4	3 months	€ 680	4	3 months

These fines and penalties apply to passenger cars and motorcycles. Other tables and fines apply to cars with trailers, vehicles of more than 3.5 tonnes and vehicles carrying hazardous cargo.

Foreigners travelling in Germany have to pay double the amount in cases of fixed-penalty fines, and, if bail is to be furnished, administrative costs have to be paid in addition. The police are only allowed to retain up to € 1,000, and the administrative costs are € 20 with lower fines, and 5 % of the total sum with higher fines.

9.4 The penalty points system in Germany

In this text there are seven mistakes re word order; find them

The Central Register of Traffic Offenders

The Federal Motor Transport Authority at Flensburg keeps the so-called Central Register of Traffic Offenders. There the penalty points, which get motorists because of offences against the code highway and/or the road licensing regulations, are registered nationwide. For offences minor, up to four penalty points will be registered, for serious traffic offences five to seven points.

If a person has reached 18 points, he/she will be disqualified.

Penalty points will be deleted after a time certain; the time is two years for minor offences and five or ten years for serious offences.

As the Central Register of Traffic Offenders is intended have to a preventive effect, a motorist who has reached eight to thirteen points will get a warning letter, and also will be informed that he/she can have up to four points deleted, once within a period of five years, if he/she attends a refresher course.

If 14 to 17 points have been registered, the motorist must attend such a course; if he/she has done so within the five previous years, he/she will be recommended to seek counselling from a psychologist traffic.

9.5 Speeding in the United States

Part 1

The number of German tourists to the United States is constantly increasing. Many rent a car or motorhome to see the country. The rules for driving are pretty similar to those in Germany, and if you drive carefully and use your common sense, you won't get into trouble despite the fact that each of the 50 states has its own highway code.

There is one field, however, where American police officers are not very tolerant: if you exceed the speed limit. Everywhere signs show you the maximum speed allowed, which usually varies between 55 and 75 mph on the freeways. In built-up areas the speed limit may be as low as 25 mph, and in school zones it is often even lower. And the speed limits are strictly enforced, even in desert areas where settlements may be a hundred miles apart.

Practically every police patrol car has a radar or laser set, and the troopers frequently make use of it. When the cruiser is stationary, the speed of cars passing in both directions can be recorded, and when it is moving, not only the speed of the car in front can be clocked but also that of an oncoming car.

Whenever a trooper detects a speeder, he follows the car and turns on his red and blue lights and, if necessary, also sounds his siren as a signal for the driver to pull over. In some areas, the red and blue lights are not on the roof of the car but either integrated into the outside mirrors or installed inside the car, so a driver won't notice that he is being followed by a police vehicle as long as the lights aren't switched on.

The driver should stop the car on the road shoulder and remain seated in his car, his hands on the wheel. After the police officer has informed his dispatcher about stopping a vehicle and given him the license plate number of the car, he walks to the window on the driver's side and talks to him. The driver should never reach down or to the side to get his driver's license or other papers before the officer talks to him as the latter might think he is reaching for a gun or other weapon. And the driver should not get out of his car. In either case he might be confronted by a police officer who has drawn his gun and levelled it at him.

1. **What do you think of the American way of dealing with speeders?**
2. **Have you ever been to the US and been stopped for speeding or other traffic offence?**
3. **Do you think that every German police patrol car should have a built-in radar set?**

Part 2

This text was translated by a computer into German

Der Anzahl deutsche Touristen zu den Vereinigten Staaten vermehren ständig. Viele mieten ein Auto oder motorhome und Reise durch das Land. Die Regeln für Treiben sind ziemlich ähnlich die in Deutschland, und, wenn Sie treiben vorsichtig und mit gemeinsamem Sinn, Sie in Schwierigkeit trotz der Tatsache nicht erhalten werden, die jedes von den 50 Staaten seinen eigenen Landstraße Code hat. Es gibt ein Feld aber wo Amerikaner Polizeioffizier nicht sehr tolerant sind: wenn Sie die Geschwindigkeit Grenze überschreiten. Überall zeigen Schilder Ihnen die maximale erlaubte Geschwindigkeit, die auf den Autobahnen gewöhnlich zwischen 55 und 75 mph ändert. In aufgebauten Gebieten kann die Geschwindigkeit Grenze so niedrig wie 25 mph, und in der Schule Zonen sein, die es oft sogar unter ist. Und die Geschwindigkeit Grenzen werden streng, sogar in Wüste Gebieten wo Siedlungen eine hundert Meilen abgesondert durchgesetzt können sein. Praktisch hat jedes Polizeipatrouille Auto ein Radar oder Laser Satz, und die Kavalleristen machen oft Gebrauch davon. Wenn der Kreuzer feststehend ist, kann die Geschwindigkeit der Autos, die an in beiden Richtungen vorbeigehen, aufgezeichnet werden, und, wenn es bewegt, kann nicht nur die Geschwindigkeit des Autos in Front sondern auch dass von einem entgegenkommenden Auto abgestoppt werden. Wenn ein Kavallerist einen speeder entdeckt, folgt er dem Auto und schaltet seine roten und blauen Lichter ein und, wenn auch notwendig, ertönt auch das verursachte als ein Signal für den Fahrer, über zu ziehen. In einigen Gebieten, sind die roten und blauen Lichter nicht auf dem Dach des Autos aber entweder eingegliedert in den Außenseite Spiegel oder installiert innerhalb des Autos, deshalb wird ein Fahrer, dass er von einem Polizeifahrzeug so lang wie die Lichter gefolgt wird, nicht auf nicht bemerken werden geschaltet. Der Fahrer soll das Auto auf der Straße Schulter aufhalten und soll gesetzt im Auto, seiner auf dem Rad bleiben reicht. Nachdem der Polizeioffizier seinen dispatcher um den Halt und gegeben ihn die Erlaubnis Plattenanzahl das Auto informiert hat, er zum Fenster auf dem läuft. Die Seite von Fahrer und alle notwendige Reden macht. Der Fahrer soll hinunter oder zur Seite nie erreichen, die Erlaubnis oder andere Papiere seines Fahrers zu erhalten, bevor der Offizier mit ihm spricht, als er denken dürfte, dass er für ein Gewehr oder andere Waffe erreicht. Und der Fahrer soll von seinem Auto nicht aussteigen. In jedem Fall dürfte er durch einen Polizeioffizier konfrontiert worden, der hat gezeichnet sein Gewehr und es an ihn nivelliert hat.

1. **What do you think of this translation?**
2. **Why are machine translations fraught with problems?**
3. **Translate the English text correctly**
4. **Find out the various meanings of the following words**

built-up area, clock, code – highway code, cruiser, dispatcher, draw, drive, field, gun, increase, low – low speed, might, officer, pass, pull over, radar set – laser set, rule, school zone, sense – common sense, settlement, shoulder, sound, speed limit – maximum speed, stationary, stop, switch on, travel, trooper, wheel

9.6 Speed cameras – moneymakers?

Police claim that speed cameras, either stationary or temporary, are only installed at accident black spots. Anti-speed camera campaigners, however, say that these cameras do little to help make roads safer, that they are nothing but "cash cows" and are only set up to make money. And at least in some cases this seems to be true. Here are two examples.

Over a period of ten weeks the "Mobil" club in Munich recorded the locations of all temporary speed cameras that motorists were informed about by the four Munich radio stations. The result: only one out of ten of these speed cameras was set up in streets which are among the most accident-prone in Munich. If accident prevention had been the main reason for setting up these cameras, they would have had to be set up in the "dangerous" streets. Extra money for the city of Munich?

Another example: On a motorway in England a temporary speed camera was put up to protect workers building a crawler lane as narrow lanes and heavy traffic posed a risk to them. Within eight weeks more than 30,000 motorists were caught exceeding the

40 mph limit, one of them a deputy chief constable. About 90 % of them had to pay a fine of £ 60 and got three penalty points, the other 10 % were so fast that they had to appear in court. It is estimated that the cameras netted more than £ 1.5 million for the state coffers. Of course, nobody wants to see road workers killed or injured, but why are the cameras also operational when there are no workers on the motorway, for example on Sundays?

1. **What do the authorities do with the money they get from traffic fines?**

2. **Have you ever had to pay a traffic fine for speeding?**

3. **Should speed cameras at construction sites be switched off when there is no work in progress?**

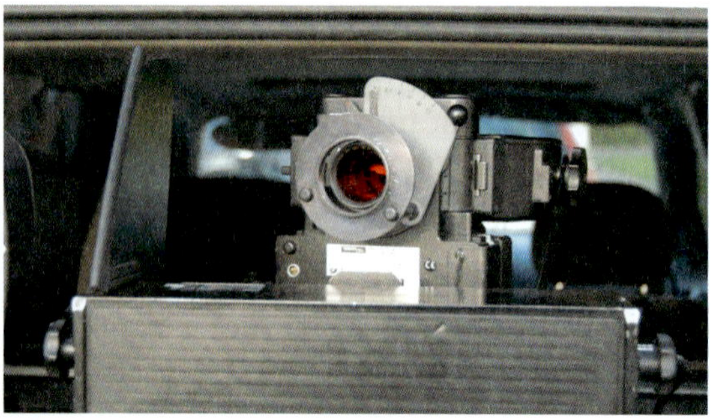

9.7 Caught speeding in Germany

Peter Hynes (PH) and his wife Mary (MH) from Nottingham are on holiday in Germany. They spent a night at Eisenach, another night at Weimar, and are now on the A 4 to Berlin. At the Hermsdorfer Kreuz junction they have to do a right turn of 270 degrees to get onto the A 9 to Berlin. On the slip road which takes them from the A 4 to the A 9 there is a speed limit of 60 kph. As many motorists have exceeded the speed limit there, and many accidents have happened there, some of them rather spectacular, especially those where lorries overturned and spilled their loads all over the carriageway, police often position a radar car there. After a few miles on the A 9, the Hyneses are overtaken by a police car and signalled to stop at Osterfeld rest area. Officers Franz Ebert (FE) and Günther Lachowsky (GL) approach their car. Mrs Hynes, who is behind the wheel, winds down the window.

FE: Good afternoon. Would you please turn off the engine?

MH: Okay. Why are we being stopped? Is anything wrong?

FE: Well, yes. You were much too fast on the slip road at Hermsdorfer Kreuz junction. There is a speed limit of 60 kph. Didn't you see the signs?

MH: Oh, yes, of course. They say not to drive faster than 60, and I was only doing about 50. So how can I have been too fast? That's impossible!

FE: Our radar car there recorded a speed of exactly 80 kph, and that's 20 kph above the speed limit of 60 kph.

MH: But my speedometer showed 50.

FE: That may be right. But the signs mean 60 kph and not 60 mph. When you were doing 50 mph according to your speedometer, which shows miles, you were doing exactly the 80 kph we recorded. In other words, you were 20 kph or 13 mph too fast. By way of tolerance we have to deduct 5 %, 4 kph, so you were 16 kph or 10 miles too fast.

MH: Gosh! You're right. I'll never get used to the metric system. What are you going to do now? Will you put me in the stocks or in a dungeon as they did in former times?

FE: Oh no, we have become much more civilized. You'll have to pay a fine, an on-the-spot fine because this slip road is an accident black spot. You can't imagine how many bad accidents we've had here, including overturned lorries carrying dangerous loads. Just last week we had to block the road here for five hours when a lorry from Spain overturned and about 20 tonnes of olive oil were spilled onto the carriageway. So we have to enforce the speed limit very strictly on this stretch of motorway. Could I please have your driving licence, vehicle registration certificate and passport?

MH: Here are the papers.

FE: Your papers are okay, Mrs Hynes. In Germany minor traffic offences like exceeding the speed limit by up to 20 kph outside built-up areas can be settled with an on-the-spot fine. In your case, this will be € 30. By the way, if you had been a little bit faster, this offence could not have been dealt with by an on-the-spot fine, we would have been obliged to bring a charge against you and you would have got a fixed-penalty notice.

An on-the-spot fine can only be imposed if you agree. If you don't, I'll have to bring a charge against you.

MH: All right, here are the € 30.

FE: Thank you. And here's your receipt.

PH: Why must coppers be the same all over the world?

1. **What must you do if the Hyneses don't agree to paying the fine but tell you they will wait for the fixed-penalty ticket?**

2. **What must you do if the Hyneses pay neither the warning fine nor the bail?**

3. **What must you do if the Hyneses are willing to pay, but don't have any euros on them?**

9.8 Using a mobile phone behind the wheel

Part 1

It is a proven fact that drivers using a mobile phone without a hands-free system while driving are a great danger to traffic safety. To prevent this, police often check on such drivers. A well-known form of such checks is an on-the-spot check.

Police officers spot drivers using their mobile phone, stop them, explain their offence to them and get their statement for the fixed-penalty proceedings. Such an offence entails a fixed penalty of € 40, and a penalty point will be entered into the Central Register of Traffic Offenders.

On busy federal road number 4 at Nordhausen in Thuringia two officers are waiting on the embankment behind a bend and inform, by radio, their colleagues who have set up a checkpoint a short distance further down the road. The two officers have a clear view of vehicles and their drivers, so they can easily spot drivers using their mobile phones. Such drivers can easily be identified, for example they are holding their mobile phone to their ear, they type in keys, they gesticulate, or they drive erratically.

The officer who receives the information by radio is the "stopper". He will stop the vehicle and direct it to the checkpoint where another officer will conduct the check.

Such a radio message might be like: "Black VW Passat, number plate LU-CC 123, driver is holding his mobile to his left ear".

The officer who does the check will get this information from the stopper. He will write down the exact time and then confront the driver with his offence. More than 90 % of the drivers stopped readily admit their offence.

Using a mobile phone while driving can be the cause of serious, sometimes even fatal, road traffic accidents as can be seen from the following example from England:

18-year-old Stephanie Shaddock, driving on the A 34 Newbury bypass dual carriageway in southern England, crashed into the back of the car in front of her, killing the driver instantly. Miss Shaddock, despite the fact that it was dark and raining, had texted her boyfriend while driving, and had not seen the car in front of her. She claimed she had not used her mobile phone at the time, but investigations revealed that she had used it several times immediately before the accident. She had passed her driving test only 8 weeks before.

In 2007, new rules came into force in the United Kingdom, forbidding making or receiving calls on the mobile phone behind the wheel. The offence is called "not being in proper control of one's vehicle". The rules also include eating behind the wheel. A driver caught eating a sandwich had his licence endorsed with three points and was fined £60.

1. **What do you think of the use of mobile phones while driving?**
2. **What about using it during stop-and-go on the motorway to inform family or friends that you will arrive late?**
3. **What about using a hands-free system?**
4. **If eating behind the wheel is an offence in Britain, what about smoking?**

Part 2

Police officers PHM Jens Noor (JN) and POM Holger Matthissen (HM) are driving in their patrol car on the road from Keitum to Morsum on the island of Sylt. They notice that a small delivery van with no rear windows in front of them drives twice onto the verge on the right side of the road. At a junction the driver, Thore Beekelsen (TB), turns left without using his turn indicator. The officers see that the driver is holding his mobile phone to his left ear and is talking excitedly. When he notices the patrol car, he puts the mobile away. Shortly afterwards the officers stop him.

JN: Good morning. But sometimes the morning is not really good. When you use your mobile phone while driving, bad accidents can happen.

TB: I've just had a short talk with Frida Sörkens's shop and informed her that I'm late. She was very angry because some customers are already waiting for their milk and fresh rolls. And now I'm losing even more time with you stopping me.

JN: You drove onto the right verge twice and turned left without signalling. When driving, you should have both hands on the wheel and concentrate on the road and traffic. If you don't, you're a possible danger to other road users, and that's exactly why using the mobile phone while driving is forbidden. Your driving licence and vehicle registration certificate, please.

TB: I didn't even notice that. Can't you make an exception and let me off? I won't do it again.

HM: That would be nice. But we'll have to make a charge out against you, because of the manner you were driving and because using the phone at the wheel is forbidden. You'll get a fixed-penalty notice of € 40, and one penalty point will be entered into the Central Register of Traffic Offenders.

TB: And I'll have to listen to Frida Sörkens's roasting. That's even worse.

9.9 The tachograph

In EU countries, motor vehicles for goods transport with a total weight of over 3.5 t as well as vehicles used for the carriage of more than eight passengers must be fitted with an "EU recording unit".

Besides vehicle movement, the EU tachograph records daily working and rest times of the driver on the tachograph chart. This ensures that the driver can effectively use the statutory rest times, and that he or she does not exceed permitted driving times.

Since the year 2000 new digital tachographs have been used to meet the requirements of the latest EU regulations.

Digital tachograph

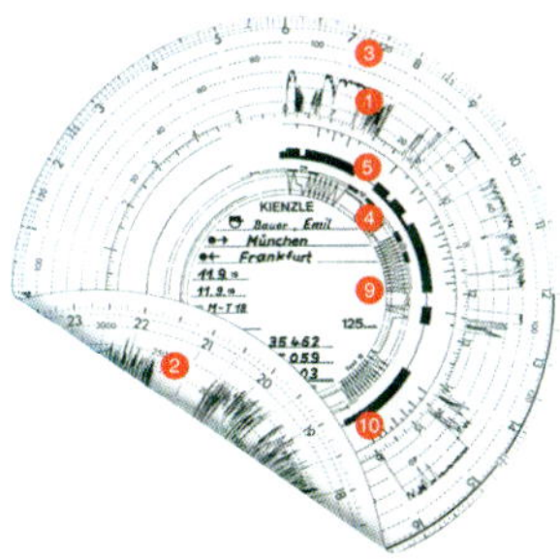

Tachograph disk/shart

9.10 Checking a lorry

Part 1 Checking the documents and the tachograph

PK Max Trutz (MT) and PK Stefan Nolt (SN) are members of a team specializing in checking lorries. Today they are on patrol with their specially equipped vehicle.

On motorway A 8 near Pforzheim an articulated lorry attracts their attention. They notice that the tarpaulin of the semitrailer is bulging on both sides. From their experience they know that the load has shifted and now presses against the tarp hoops, which stabilize the tarpaulin and therefore can in no way substitute sideboards. Police officers have nicknamed these vehicles "pregnant lorries". Officers Trutz and Nolt signal the artic to follow them to the next rest area. Both the tractor and the semitrailer have German licence plates.

The driver is Britsh national Henry Finnegan (HF).

MT: Good afternoon. Traffic check. My name is Trutz, and this is my colleague Nolt. We've stopped you because we think that your load has shifted. Would you please get out of your vehicle?

HF: Good afternoon. I didn't notice anything while driving. If there are ruts, the semitrailer sometimes swerves a little bit, but that's quite normal.

MT: We'll have a look at that in a minute. But first let me have your driving licence, please.

MT: I see you're from Great Britain.

HF: Yes, I'm from Ipswich, in the county of Suffolk in East Anglia. But I've been living in Germany for more than 20 years. In England I drove lorries for the Greene King Brewery, and met my German wife in the company.

MT: Do you already have the new digital tachograph?

HF: Yes, this artic is quite new, less than half a year old. The tachograph is built into the centre console.

SN: I'll get into the passenger seat.

A short time later, PK Nolt has checked if the driver card is inserted in slot 1 and that no other card is in slot 2.

SN: Please print today's and yesterday's driver sheet.

Henry Finnegan has no problems with the tachograph. The sheets for both days are printed out.

HF: You know, there are a number of black sheep in our trade who try to evade the regulations even with a digital tachograph. And other colleagues don't even know how to operate it correctly. It's different with our company. I attended a course which my company paid for. That was important, as with this new tachograph many things are different compared to the tachograph discs and the old tachographs.

SN: A new vehicle, and a well-trained driver. That's fine. I'll now put my checking card into slot 2 and log in with the police. And I'll remove your driver card from slot 1.

A short time later.

SN: Mr Finnegan, I'll now have a look at the printouts and check the validity of your driver card. But first we'll check the tachograph number. Please read to me the last six letters and numbers. Down there, at the bottom, is the official sticker, and the letters and numbers must be identical. Just a second, I have to get out of the vehicle first.

HF: I know. You frequently get into such spot checks, and you, the police, certainly always have the same check lists about what to check. So, let's compare the letters and numbers, and you'll quickly find out that everything is all right.

A short time later. PK Nolt has looked at the printouts. The driving times were not exceeded, and the digital tachograph was operated according to the rules. The vehicle is registered, all entries are in order. By radio PK Nolt has asked his colleagues at the police station to find out if the driver card is valid, and now he compares the names on the driver card and the driving licence. Everything is in order.

SN: Mr Finnegan, here are your driver card and your driving licence. I'll keep the printouts together with my papers. This check has been entered into the digital tachograph through my checking card, so I need not give you a certificate about this check. I'm leaving my card inserted while we're checking your load. Then I'll withdraw it, and you insert your card again. Remember that you press "working time" and not "driving time" as long as you aren't driving your vehicle.

HF: Congratulations! You really know how to do your job.

SN: We too attend training courses. That's necessary.

As you have acted very self-confidently during this check so far, I trust you and won't ask you for the printouts for the last 15 days, and I won't have to go through them. You know about the driving times, and you also know how to split them. I need not tell you anything in this respect, as the printouts for today and yesterday clearly show that you didn't break the law. And please, don't exceed the speed limits. If I took a little more time, I could also check these data.

HF: You can see the speed of the governor on the "technology" section of the printout.

SN: You really know how to do your job. That's a change.

HF: Thank you.

Part 2 Checking the load

SN: Well, now let's have a look at your load. Please give me your loading documents. What's your load?

HF: This is a 40-tonne artic. I'm transporting about 32 tonnes of wooden parquet. The parquet sheets are in stacks, welded into plastic foil. The lowest stack is placed on europallets, the other stacks are on top.

SN: Well, let's go to the back. Please open the tarpaulin. We would like to see the whole loading area.

In the meantime PK Max Trutz has checked the technical condition of the articulated lorry. He even climbed under the semitrailer.

MT: The tractor and semitrailer are quite new. So they are in good technical condition. The compressed-air hoses are properly fixed, and the coupling is in order, too. I could not see any liquids leaking. All important parts are in good working order, including the tyres and the brakes. And I assume that all the lights work perfectly, too. So let's leave it at that. It's much more important now to have a look at the load.

Henry Finnegan unties the ropes and the tarpaulin. And where the bulges are, the load has actually shifted.

HF: Oh, you're right. It's apparently worse than I thought. But I have a tie-down strap with me.

MT: The strap won't be of any help. Look, the individual stacks could not be fastened properly. The top stack is to secure all the other stacks underneath it. But this isn't possible because the stacks are of different sizes, so the strap cannot fasten the whole block. The more you tie it down, the more the stack on top presses down, and the parquet sheets will be damaged. And the edges are not secured, either. As the straps are inclined, some stacks cannot be fastened at all or only partially, because there is not enough tension. Do you understand that, Mr. Finnegan?

HF: Yes, I do. But the load is so heavy that nothing can really shift.

MT: But that's exactly what happened. The sheets were certainly loaded with a forklift truck, side by side and on top of each other. Before you started your trip and had a look at the load, everything certainly seemed to be all right. But now, and see for yourself, some of the heavier stacks have shifted towards the outside and now press against the wooden tarp hoops.

SN: Here! This tarp hoop could not sustain the lateral pressure and is partly broken. It wouldn't have taken much longer until parts of your load had fallen onto the carriageway. And I'm afraid to tell you that not all the stacks have been tied down, and positioning the stacks on top of each other like this is not possible.

HF: We always do it like this in our company. I took over the truck already loaded. The tarpaulin was already fastened, and I just went to the office to get the loading papers.

MT: Mr Finnegan, I'm sorry, but under these circumstances you're not allowed to drive on. You must sort out your load and tie down each stack with a tie-down strap. This also means that some stacks cannot be loaded again because, as I told you, they cannot be safely stacked one above the other.

I suggest that you now call your company and talk to them about how to proceed.

Part 3 Talking to the boss

HF: You don't allow me to drive on? My boss will be very angry. When I get him on my mobile, would you please speak to him?

During the phone call the company's boss threatens to contact a lawyer and tells PK Trutz that he will sue him for all the costs which will arise because the artic has been stopped. He tells him that he really should think it over. The boss is not open to any arguments. Only with difficulties can the officers explain the further procedure to him.

MT: The truck won't be allowed to continue like this! Your driver can uncouple the semi-trailer, then he can drive on with the tractor unit. If you agree to that. But then the load will not be guarded..... We cannot take care of that. That's why I am talking to you..... All right, the tractor won't be uncoupled. How do you intend to sort out and secure the load again?.... Your driver can't do that. And he doesn't have a forklift either. We could close the rest area so that the semitrailer can be unloaded. But you would have to pay extra for the closure..... Listen! Let me me finish what I'm trying to tell you, and don't you shout at me..... Can someone from your firm come and reload the cargo? .... Yes, I know that your transport firm is nearly 300 km from here..... No, that won't work.

PK Nolt comes back. Together with Henry Finnegan he checked if he had more tie-down straps on board, but this isn't the case. He informs his colleague.

PK Trutz continues his telephone conversation with the company's boss.

MT: There are not enough tie-down straps. Do you know a firm that you could ask to come here? .... No? Then I can give you a phone number, and you will be told about a firm from this area which has a contract with the police..... That's a firm which can also tow large goods vehicles. But it's you who's got to instruct them. From experience I know that the staff of that firm check here, at the scene, if the load can be secured, at least for the time being..... That's possible in most cases..... In that case we'll escort your vehicle to the premises of that firm. We'll secure the truck at the back with a police vehicle, and at the front this will be done by a vehicle of the towing firm..... Yes, you'll have to pay police costs. On the premises, the load will be redistributed, and the semitrailer loaded again. You can also buy additional tie-down straps there and store part of the load..... We're going to keep the loading papers and the vehicle registration certificate for the semitrailer. When everything has been done, we'll come and check..... Then you'll get your papers back. And when you've paid the costs, your truck can carry on..... I don't know how much that will be. You'll have to ask the towing firm.

PK Trutz gives him thc number and finishes the call. Some time later the boss calls his driver again on his mobile and asks to speak to the police officer.

MT: Yes, I understand. You've instructed a company to come here..... Then everything is going to be done as I suggested to you.... I beg your pardon. You're still threatening me that you'll hire a lawyer to sue for damages, and you want to lodge a complaint against me so that I won't be happy again for the rest of my life? Well, I'm no longer going to listen to your aggressive remarks..... Your driver, Mr Finnegan, is the decent sort. I'm going to give him my card. On it you'll find my name and the address of my police station. I'm going to press charges against you as the boss of the company, as you've instructed Mr Finnegan to do the trip and failed to have the load properly secured. And I'll also press charges against the driver of your forklift truck, as he is also responsible for properly loading and securing the cargo. Mr Finnegan took over the truck with the tarpaulin already closed. He relied on proper loading and securing the cargo. This trust has now been breached, as we'll also have to press charges against Mr Finnegan, as he is the driver in charge. He should have inspected the load and should not have set out on his journey under the given circumstances. We have taken photos as evidence. And I'll ask an expert (of DEKRA) to assess the situation, for you and for us. ....That won't be cheap..... You can take all the judicial steps you want. All the documents will be sent to you. Do you have any further questions?.... No?.... Then I'll discuss everything else with Mr Finnegan. Good-bye.

MT: Mr Finnegan, you've heard what I said. I'm now going to hear you about the fixed-penalty proceedings, but first I'm going to inform you about your rights.

HF: I understand. But please understand that I won't say anything, and I won't sign anything either. My boss told me that I should act like this, because he wants to inform the company lawyer.

MT: Could you please tell me who loaded the semitrailer? Who was the driver of the forklift?

HF: There are several drivers. You'd better ask the company. I wasn't present during the loading, so I don't know who it was.

MT: All right. We'll take that into consideration when investigating the matter. Here's my card. We'll now wait for the other company to arrive. And I'll also call for an expert to come and make a report. For the moment I'll keep the loading papers and the registration certificate for the semitrailer.

SN: Here's your driver card. I'll withdraw our checking card from the digital tachograph, and you insert yours in slot 1.

HF: All right. This is definitely not a good day for my company.

9.11 Bail

The Schwegenheim "Autohof" services are situated between the towns of Speyer and Germersheim on federal road number 9; this road is a busy trunk road to the French border near Lauterbourg, and is frequented by many trucks from various nations.

José Salvo Arabí (JS) from the Spanish town of Teruel has spent the night at the parking area of the Autohof. Now it is Sunday. In Germany trucks of more than 7.5 tonnes and trucks with trailers are not allowed to travel between midnight and 22.00 hours on Sundays and on holidays.

José has just woken up and watches a police patrol car and a truck arriving at the parking area. José knows about police checks, and so he is not surprised to see two police officers talking to the driver. He sees forms being filled in and the driver handing cash over to one of the officers. About half an hour later the matter seems settled, and the other driver, Adam Bogdanowicz (AB) from Warsaw, parks his articulated truck right beside José's truck. José addresses him.

JS: Good morning. I'm José Salvo from Teruel in Spain. You're from Poland, aren't you?

AB: Good morning. Yes, I'm from Warsaw. I'm Adam Bogdanowicz. Nice to meet you.

JS: I've just got up and made coffeee. Would you like a cup, too?

AB: Thank you. I'll certainly join you.

JS: Then come with me into my cab. Did the police catch you because you were driving today?

AB: I've been on the road for nearly five hours now, with various short breaks, and I wanted to proceed to Strasbourg in France where I'll get new freight, wines from Alsace for a number of posh hotels in Warsaw. And now the police tell me that I can't drive on until ten p.m tonight. Trucks are not allowed on Sundays in Germany. I don't know about it, and it seems that up to now I've been quite lucky.

JS: Did the officers explain all this to you?

AB: They asked me if I spoke or understood German. But my German isn't good enough for a conversation. I'm glad that we could understand each other in English. Well, and then they explained to me what the law in Germany is.

JS: And did you have to pay a fine, too?

AB: I paid € 60, and I got this paper. It's a receipt for the bail I paid as I'm a foreigner and I'm going to leave Germany again. But I was surprised that they have this form not only in German but also in English and Polish. So it's easy for me to understand what it is all about.

JS: Let me have a look. I didn't know that. I also had to pay once, but then the police only had a form in German.

JM: At the top left there is the police station, and beside it the date and the name of the acting police officer. And then there are my personal data and my residential address.

About in the centre of the form there's a note that I committed an offence, and immediately below the amount of security I had to pay.

On the line below the amount of € 60 has been entered, and also the fact that I paid cash. In reality my offence only entails a fine of € 40, but they added € 20 administrative costs. And then there is the address of the fixed-penalty office. The officer told me that they would send me a fixed-penalty notice to my home address, but that's only a formality. In fact, everything has been settled.

JS: Have you read what's underneath?

AB: Of course. There the officer entered the name of the person who does the administrative and postal formalities for me in Germany and who will be the person to contact first.

I signed a statement to the effect that I'm aware that I committed an offence. Why should I start long discussions? Perhaps I'm lucky and my firm will pay the fine.

JS: What else did they give you?

AB: A flyer about driving bans for trucks during the holiday season in July and August.

JS: Does it say anything about exceptions, too?

AB: There are exceptions, mainly for transporting fresh and perishable goods. But you'd better check on the internet.

JS: Well, let's have another cup.

9.12 Overcrowded rest and service areas

Tuesday evening. One truck follows another in the right lane of the motorway. Every driver is under pressure to move as fast as possible, so they use every chance to overtake a slightly slower colleague, even in no-overtaking areas.

Often the difference in speed is minimal, so overtaking takes a long time, blocking the left lane for cars. In colloquial German, this is called "Elefantenrennen" (= elephants' race). If a truck takes more than 45 seconds to overtake another, the driver commits a traffic offence which is punished with a fine of € 80 and one point in the Central Register of Traffic Offenders. Trucks have built-in governors, which limit their speed to 89 kph. Slight differences in speed are due to topography and/or their loads.

The drivers are constantly pressed for time, so they only stop for their mandatory breaks when absolutely necessary. Often they exceed their permitted driving times. A transport company derives an advantage vis-à-vis its competitors if its vehicles are faster.

Rest and service areas are overcrowded. Drivers have to stop for a rest, because they are tired and exhausted after having driven for many hours. The police are increasing the number of checks, and if a driver is caught, it will be rather expensive for him and his company. And any profit gained as a result of driving longer than permitted will be lost.

Entering the rest area. It's still possible to slow down in the deceleration lane, but two hours later trucks will also park there because they cannot enter the rest area. Other trucks park not only in the spaces provided for them, but also on the carriageway, two or three abreast, or block their colleagues, and often there is just enough space for cars to pass.

Very "clever" truckers drive through the rest area and park on the acceleration lane. There they cannot be blocked and do not lose any time when they start again. But this is dangerous for other drivers and not tolerated by the police. In such cases, the police order them to proceed, even if they haven't rested long enough.

But where to? The next rest area is full, as is the following one. Truckers don't like leaving the motorway and park in industrial areas, as this means longer trips, loss of time and using up more fuel. So they just park wherever possible, switch on their parking lights or even the emergency flashers – and hope the motorway police won't wake them up and that everything will be all right.

But it isn't, as serious and even fatal accidents have happened at the entrances of rest areas when the driver of an arriving truck overlooked a parked truck and crashed into it.

7 p.m. The rest area is full. Nobody can move forward. Only some narrow spaces are left for an ambulance or fire engine to pass, but this is not the case everywhere. Rest periods end at varying times, so some truckers want to get going again, but they are stuck and have to move to and fro, often bumping into other vehicles, thus causing minor road traffic accidents, which would normally be avoidable.

At about 4 a.m. most trucks have left. The situation is the same all over the Federal Republic. And it gets even worse during the summer months when more cars, caravans and coaches are on the road. It's quite astonishing that this system works somehow or other. There are a lot of problems, but in the end the truckers get going, and there are only a few cases where serious difficulties arise.

All this is monitored by the motorway police. Sometimes they are tolerant, often they aren't. There are stubborn truckers who refuse to leave their cabin and only see reason when the officers threaten them that they will be towed away – the high cost of which they'll have to pay. There are truckers who shout insults at the officers, threatening them and do not understand why they are getting a charge and penalty points at Flensburg.

Some drivers don't even react when the police knock at the door of their cabin. In that case the only remedy is the loud siren, but then all the other drivers are awakened as well. That's constant stress for the officers. And there are the language problems with drivers from abroad – often sign language is the last means.

It's more quiet at weekends. And the rest areas are almost empty during the Christmas holidays.

More rest areas are being built, but not enough, as there are more and more trucks on the roads.

Describe your own experience

9.13 Word comb

Complete the word comb using the clues below

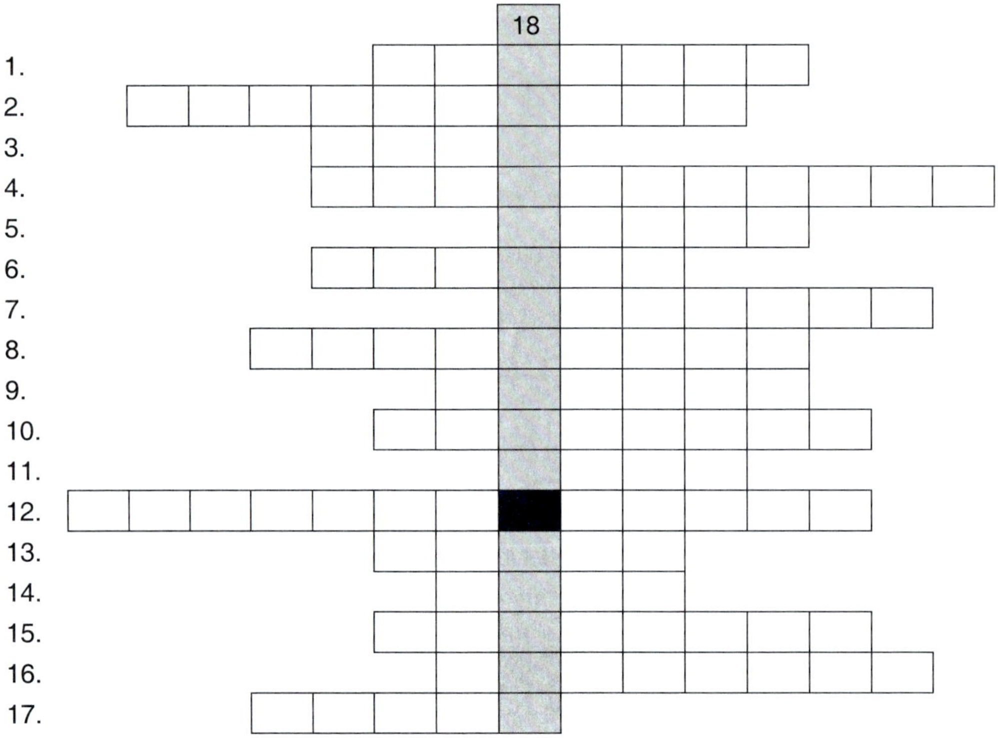

1. a large motor vehicle which is used for pulling ploughs, trailers etc
2. a device which records speed, stopping periods and distance travelled
3. a long narrow hole for putting cards and coins in
4. a trailer having wheels only at the rear end
5. the freight carried by a truck, ship or plane
6. to make something safe, to fasten
7. official permission
8. heavy waterproof sheet to cover something
9. narrow pieces of strong material to fasten something
10. force which causes people to do something
11. a round device on which information is stored
12. the times a driver spent behind the steering wheel
13. swollen or sticking out
14. the amount of weight carried by a vehicle
15. a lifting device with two steel bars that can be raised
16. a written document produced by a computer
17. British English for truck
18. a large vehicle consisting of two separate sections, with the front section as the power unit

9.14 Adverb 1

Funktion

Ein Adverb bestimmt näher: ein Verb, ein Adjektiv oder ein anderes Adverb
*this car runs **nicely** – this is a **really** nice car – this car runs **really** nicely*

Formen
„ursprüngliche Adverbien",
zusammengesetzte Adverbien und adverbiale Bestimmungen
sie sind auf Grund ihrer äußeren Form allein nicht als solche zu erkennen
quite, just, here; always, anyhow, however; at school, with pleasure
„abgeleitete Adverbien"
Bildung in der Regel durch Anhängen von ***-ly*** an das entsprechende Adjektiv
*great – great**ly**, surprising – surprising**ly***

Schreibregeln bei abgeleiteten Adverbien
-y nach Konsonant am Wortende wird zu ***i***
*easy – eas**ily***
-ic oder *-ical* am Wortende wird zu ***-ically***
systematic – systematically; ethical – ethically
-le fällt weg
*impossible – impossib**ly***

Besonderheiten
good – well

Adjektiv und Adverb haben gleiche Form und gleiche Bedeutung
daily, early, enough, fast, much

Adjektiv und Adverb haben gleiche Form, aber unterschiedliche Bedeutung

only	– 1. einzig	2. nur
still	– 1. still	2. (immer) noch
well	– 1. wohl	2. gut (Gesundheit)

ein Adjektiv – zwei Adverbien

hard	– *1. hard* (= hart, schwer)	2. *hardly* (= kaum)
just	– *1. just* (= gerade, gerade jetzt)	2. *justly* (= gerecht)

Steigerung
mit *-er* und *-est* – alle einsilbigen Adverbien *fast – fast**er** – fast**est***
mit *more* und *most* – alle abgeleiteten Adverbien
*beautifully – **more** beautifully – **most** beautifully*

Besonderheiten
allmähliche Steigerung; im Deutschen meist immer + Komparativ
faster and faster; worse and worse; more and more carefully

Beachten Sie
immer wieder = *again and again*
je ..... desto = *the .... the: the sooner the better*
um so + Komparativ = *all the + Komparativ: all the better*

9.15 Adverb in German – verb in English

angeblich	to be said to	anscheinend	to seem to
gerne	to like to, to be glad to	hoffentlich	to hope
leider	to be afraid, to be sorry	lieber	to prefer to
sicher(lich)	to be sure	wahrscheinlich	to be likely to
weiter	to go on, to continue to		

Translate into English

1. Der Fahrer, der den Unfall verursacht hat, war angeblich betrunken.

   ....

2. Anscheinend war der Sattelanhänger stark überladen.

   ....

3. Felix Stockmann fährt mit seinem LKW nicht gerne nach Spanien, weil er dort auch schon bei geringfügigen Geschwindigkeitsüberschreitungen eine hohe Geldbuße bezahlen muss.

   ....

   ....

4. Ehefrau zu Ehemann am Steuer bei einer Verkehrskontrolle: „Hoffentlich bemerken die Polizisten nicht, dass unsere Hinterreifen schon stark abgefahren sind.“

   ....

   ....

5. Ich muss Ihnen leider sagen, dass Sie nicht weiterfahren dürfen, weil die Ladung nicht richtig gesichert ist.

   ....

6. Ich fahre lieber mit öffentlichen Verkehrsmitteln ins Stadtzentrum als mit dem Auto.

   ....

7. Es macht Ihnen doch sicherlich nichts aus, wenn ich mit meiner Firma telefoniere?

   ....

8. Wahrscheinlich wird der Güterverkehr auf der Straße in den nächsten Jahren noch zunehmen.

   ....

9. Fahren Sie langsam auf der Standspur weiter bis zum nächsten Parkplatz. Wir bleiben bei eingeschaltetem Blaulicht hinter Ihnen und sichern Sie ab.

   ....

   ....

9.16 Fill-in exercise

Fill in the correct form; choose from the following:

bad – badly, close – closely, deep – deeply, drastic – drastically, fair – fairly, fluent – fluently, full – fully, hard – hardly, high – highly, incredible – incredibly, innocent – innocently, late – lately, near – nearly, right – rightly, strong – strongly, unconscious – unconsciously, urgent – urgently, wrong – wrongly

1. We .... agree with you.
2. Sometimes police officers must work ...., but at other times there is .... any work for them to do.
3. There has been another .... accident in Eich; three pedestrians were .... injured.
4. The weather continues to be ...., so it will be .... safe to go by car.
5. "You've already had a number of .... drinks, so I .... advise you not to use your car."
6. We have a colleague who speaks French ....
7. They were .... lucky to escape unhurt.
8. The new vehicles are .... needed.
9. It is .... improbable that he will be arrested, as he has friends in .... places.
10. Spending on equipment has been .... reduced.
11. His wife hasn't been very well ....; that's why she got up .... this morning.
12. In the accident a woman was hit by a speeding car, two children were .... run over, and nothing happened to two men who were standing .... the wall.
13. Mr Tennent was .... accused of handling stolen goods.
14. The driver of the delivery van was .... blamed for the accident.
15. A police spokesperson said that the force .... regretted that mistake.
16. The policeman tried to interfere and was knocked ....
17. According to law, a man is presumed .... until proven guilty.
18. Prisoners are .... guarded these days.

9.17 Useful phrases

Erklären Sie einem irischen Kollegen, dass

1. in Deutschland überhöhte oder nicht angepasste Geschwindigkeit die Hauptursache für Verkehrsunfälle ist.

   ....

2. die Polizei bei geringfügigen Verkehrsverstößen ein Verwarnungsgeld von bis zu € 35 an Ort und Stelle erheben kann.

   ....

   ....

3. es in Deutschland eine Verkehrssünderkartei gibt, in der die Punkte für Verkehrsvergehen zentral eingetragen werden.

   ....

   ....

4. bei 18 Punkten die Fahrerlaubnis entzogen wird.

   ....

5. viele Leute glauben, dass Geschwindigkeitsüberwachungskameras nur dazu dienen, die Autofahrer abzuzocken.

   ....

6. die Benutzung eines Handys am Steuer eine große Gefahr für den Fahrer und andere Verkehrsteilnehmer darstellt.

   ....

7. die Polizei regelmäßig Kontrollpunkte einrichtet, um Handybenutzer zu überführen, die dann ein Bußgeld von € 40 zahlen müssen und einen Punkt im Verkehrszentralregister in Flensburg eingetragen bekommen.

   ....

   ....

   ....

8. bei LKW-Kontrollen häufig Fahrer erwischt werden, die viel zu lange gefahren sind.

   ....

9. alle Fahrzeuge für den Transport von Waren über 3,5 t mit einem Fahrtenschreiber ausgerüstet sein müssen, der bei Neufahrzeugen seit Januar 2000 digital sein muss.

   ....

   ....

10. Polizeibeamte eine Kontrollkarte haben, mit der sie Zugang zu allen Daten eines digitalen Tachographen haben.

....

11. Fahrern, deren Ladung nicht richtig gesichert ist, die Weiterfahrt untersagt wird.

....

12. bei fehlerhaft oder nicht gesicherter Ladung nicht nur gegen den Fahrer, sondern auch gegen die dafür verantwortliche Person Anzeige erstattet wird.

....

....

9.18 Key words and phrases

accident black spot – accident-prone – bypass – Central Register of Traffic Offenders – checking card – crawler lane – digital tachograph – driver card – driving ban – exceed the speed limit – excessive speed – Federal Motor Transport Authority – governor – heavy traffic – insert – mobile phone – perishable goods – receipt – road licensing regulations – roadworks area – ruts – slot – speed camera – swerve – tachograph chart/disk – tarpaulin – tie-down strap – visibility

Unit 10

Serious traffic offences 1

This unit deals with

- serious traffic offences
- the seven deadly sins in road traffic
- two cases of road rage and
- the position of adverbs.

10.1 Traffic offences in Germany

According to German law, a driver who has committed a minor traffic offence may get off with a verbal cautioning by the police officer, or he or she will have to pay an on-the-spot warning fine to the police officer (cf unit 7).

In case of more serious offences, he or she may get off with a fixed-penalty notice, penalty points in the Central Register of Traffic Offenders at the Federal Motor Transport Authority in Flensburg and a driving ban of up to three months. Such offences are, for example, exceeding the speed limit by more than 60 kph, jumping the lights, or overtaking where it is not allowed.

If the offence is really serious, it will be dealt with in court. The driver either gets a substantial fine or a prison sentence, usually on probation. In addition, he or she will get up to 7 penalty points and may be disqualified for a longer period. Such offences include, for instance, failure to stop after an accident, causing a fatal or bodily injury accident, or driving without proper insurance.

However, it must be pointed out that each case must be judged on an individual basis. For example, exceeding the speed limit will be punished with a fixed-penalty fine. If, however, another traffic participant is endangered in the process, the matter will go to court.

10.2 The seven deadly sins

The seven deadly sins in road traffic are

1. not stopping at a stop sign or not giving way at a give-way sign or not giving way to traffic coming from the right
2. incorrect overtaking
3. not stopping at a pedestrian crossing
4. speeding when the road is not sufficiently clear ahead, at junctions, crossroads or railway crossings
5. not keeping to the right when the road is not sufficiently clear ahead
6. turning, reversing or driving in the wrong direction on motorways or dual carriageways, or trying to do so
7. not warning other drivers at a safe distance if a vehicle has stopped or broken down.

In all these cases the life and limb of other persons or items of considerable value are bound to be endangered. It does not matter if the above offences were caused by drink or drugs (this also applies to cyclists) or by physical or mental deficiencies on the part of the driver. These offences are punished with a substantial fine or prison sentence and disqualification, either for a certain period or even for life.

10.3 Road rage – facts

Extremely aggressive driving, like tailgating at high speed in conjunction with flashing one's headlights, overtaking on the right or weaving in and out of lanes in dense traffic, is nowadays referred to as "road rage". This sort of behaviour is not confined to Germany, the only country in the world without a general speed limit on its motorways. Everywhere in the world there are road hogs who drive at extremely high speeds and ignore all traffic rules, thus endangering themselves as well as other motorists and pedestrians.

About 2,000 young adults between 18 and 24 years die on German roads every year. This age group is most frequently involved in accidents (and therefore pay the highest insurance premiums). Every fifth seriously or fatally injured person is aged between 18 and 24.

Lack of inhibition and overestimating one's abilities seem to be the causes of many accidents. Alcohol and drugs are also a problem.

Find out the wrong translation(s) of the following words

1. driver	=	Fahrer(in), Fahrzeugführer(in), Motorradfahrer(in), Treiber (Computer)
2. minor	=	Minderjährige(r), Minderheit, geringfügig, Bergmann
3. police officer	=	Polizist(in), unterster Dienstgrad bei vielen Polizeien, FBI-Beamter, Polizeioffizier
4. offence	=	Anstoß (*Fußball*), Offensive, Angriff, strafbare Handlung
5. court	=	Gericht, Bauernhof, Hof, Spielplatz
6. probation	=	Zustimmung, Approbation (*Arzt*), Probezeit, Bewährungsfrist
7. insurance	=	Verletzung, Versicherung, Sicherheit, Sicherstellung
8. however	=	jedoch, allerdings, wie immer, wann immer, wer immer
9. overtake	=	überholen, übernehmen, überstechen (*Kartenspiel*), überbringen
8. junction	=	Autobahnanschlussstelle, Weiche, Verteiler (*Auto*), Einmündung
9. deficiency	=	Defizit, Demenz, Mangel, Unzulänglichkeit
10. tailgate	=	Heckklappe, Fuchsschwanz, (zu) dicht auffahren, Schwanzspitze
11. lack	=	Lack, Lackaffe, Mangel, entbehren

Match the words and definitions

1. road hog	a. not stop when traffic lights are red
2. jump the lights	b. follow (too) close
3. substantial fine	c. there is enough room
4. tailgate	d. person who behaves inconsiderately in road traffic
5. sufficiently clear	e. driving licence taken away from you
6. disqualification	f. great amount of money to be paid as penalty

10.4 Road rage – a typical case

Part 1

Holidaymakers Andrew Alderney, 62, and his wife Maud, 58, from St. Peter Port, Guernsey, are on motorway A 20 near Rostock. Traffic is very heavy, and in the right lane one truck follows the other. Andrew Alderney drives in the left lane at about 120 kph, keeping a safe distance to the car in front of him.

In his rear-view mirror he suddenly notices a sports car approaching at a much higher speed. The driver has set the left turn indicator and flashes his headlights repeatedly. Because of the many trucks Mr Alderney cannot get into the right lane. The sports car gets very close, then slows down a little bit, accelerates again, and continuously flashes its headlights. Andrew Alderney now looks more into the inside and outside rear-view mirrors than ahead. He isn't used to such behaviour, and he's helpless as he can't either get into the right lane nor accelerate since there is another vehicle in front of him.

All this has been going on for more than one kilometre. So he decides to squeeze into the small gap between two trucks. The sports car rushes past, but has to slow down again behind the next vehicle in the left lane. Andrew Alderney is afraid to get into the left lane again, and he stops at the next rest area.

The police have been informed by a truck driver about the incident and talk to him and his wife at the rest area. Unfortunately, both are only able to say what make of car it was.

Part 2

POK Gunnar Müller (GM) and PK Torsten Pauler (TP) of the motorway police have escorted a driver, for whom an alert was out, to a rest area on the motorway. He is suspected of aggressive driving. Police have received various reports about his driving. The driver of the other vehicle, Guernsey resident Andrew Alderney and his wife Maud, were met by a second patrol crew at another rest area. The driver and keeper of the vehicle is 31-year-old Ernesto Klett (EK).

GM: Mr Klett, various reliable witnesses have informed us that, a few minutes ago, you seriously endangered another vehicle. My colleagues are just talking to the driver and his wife. They're not well. I'll press charges against you for endangering road traffic and causing bodily harm. Before you answer any of my questions, I have to inform you that you are not obliged to make any statement or that you can hire a lawyer; but if you make a statement, we could clear up the matter right here.

EK: I can't remember anything. What am I supposed to have done? Endangered another driver? Are you sure that it was me with my car?

GM: Yes, we're sure, because your aggressive driving was also noted by other motorists. We have received various reports at our station about your vehicle and your licence plate number. And there can't be any mistake as all these messages give a description of your vehicle, its type, its colour and its number plate.

EK: Where do you say that was supposed to have happened?

GM: On this motorway, about 10 to 15 kilometres back. Do you remember a silver-grey VW Passat in the left lane? Witnesses claim that you tailgated that car.

EK: I remember that traffic was very heavy. All the trucks in the right lane, and occasionally a passenger car in the left lane. But I do not remember a VW Passat.

GM: We were also informed that you continually flashed your headlights and that your left-turn signal was switched on all the time.

EK: Rubbish! Why should I have done that?

GM: Are you in a hurry?

EK: When I'm on the road I'm always in a hurry. I'm a dealer in sports cars, and right now I'm on my way to see a prospective customer. I'm already late. I'll have to call him on my mobile phone.

GM: Well, that might be a reason for the aggressive driving that was reported. You wanted to get there in time, and the Passat driver prevented you from doing so.

EK: That's what you say. I already told you that I can't remember anything like that. What you're accusing me of isn't true.

GM: Mr Klett, has it ever happened to you that another motorist behind you tailgated you at a distance of about one metre, then dropped back and tailgated you again, that he kept flashing his headlights and also swerved to the left and right to indicate that he wanted to pass and that you should make room for him?

EK: What's that got to do with me? There's always a lot going on on the motorway; just watch TV.

GM: What I just described was the way you were driving. At least, that's what the witnesses say.

EK: Well, who are those witnesses? They can tell you anything!

TP: OK, calm down. At the other rest area we have the other driver and his wife. They don't feel well, and our colleagues are thinking of calling an ambulance. The husband is unable to drive on. They told us that they were fearing for their lives. You know, Mr Klett, even if you deny all this here and now, you should think over what might have happened..... Yes, yes, I know that you already told us that nothing had happened. But I don't believe you. Why should the witnesses lie? We had to start a major police operation to find you and to make sure that you won't repeat such aggressive driving, and, if necessary, to prevent you from driving in the future. With your statements you just want to protect yourself.

EK: Don't talk to me like that! I'm going to inform my lawyer about that.

TP: At the moment I'm trying to explain to you that you have to drive less aggressively. You can't drive like that and endanger other drivers. Don't you have any scruples? Just think, for a moment, of the two persons who almost had a nervous breakdown..... Yes, tell your attorney about the manner I was talking to you. He'll tell you that I'm right.

EK: I'm not saying anything else. Do I get my documents back now?

GM: I have to note all the necessary details. Are you alone in your vehicle?

EK: Yes, I'm on my own. Have been all the time.

GM: Do you still live at the address stated here on the vehicle registration certificate?

EK: Now, what's that? That's what it says on my vehicle registration.

GM: Neverthelss, you might have moved to another place without having had this recorded in this document.

EK: I still live there.

GM: Mr Klett, that's it for the moment. Here are your documents. If it turns out that what I told you is true, I'll recommend that the prosecution office start proceedings to disqualify you for an extended period. You may drive on now. But you've been warned. If this happens again, we'll secure your vehicle and ask the prosecutor to secure your licence immediately. You'll be hearing from us.

EK: And you're going to hear from my lawyer.

10.5 Exercise

You have been asked to give a talk to high school students about aggressive driving.

Prepare the talk.

What questions are likely to be asked by the students?

Draw up a list of possible measures, sanctions etc.

Here are some points to start with:

disqualification, tightening up the law, road safety training in schools

10.6 The law

The law is the system of rules which a particular country or community recognizes as regulating the actions of its members and which it enforces by the imposition of penalties. In any modern society there are many different types of law.

1. **Translate into German and give a short definition**

2. **Find out all the terms for "Rechtsanwalt" and explain the difference**

10.7 Adverb 2

Stellung im Satz

Die Stellung von Adverbien/adverbialen Bestimmungen im Satz wird durch drei Kriterien bestimmt: Typ, Länge, Betonung.

Adverbien der Art und Weise stehen in der Satzmitte, d.h. vor dem Verb oder nach dem (ersten) Hilfsverb

The accused angrily denied having strangled his estranged wife.

The careless driver could easily have caused a serious accident.

Beachten Sie abweichende Stellung bei langen und betonten Adverbien

He paid the warning fine reluctantly.

He speaks French well.

Adverbien des Ortes und der Zeit stehen am Satzanfang oder Satzende; stehen sie unmittelbar hintereinander, gilt die Reihenfolge Ort vor Zeit

Tomorrow operation "Bumblebee" ill be completed.

I can't find my driving licence anywhere.

The suspect was seen here yesterday.

Adverbiale Bestimmungen stehen aufgrund ihrer Länge entweder am Satzanfang oder Satzende

In the circumstances we decided to put the drunk driver into the sobering cell.

The stolen items were found in the river at five o'clock yesterday afternoon.

10.8 Word order exercise

Form correct sentences

1. the CID officers – have – generally – in their office – breakfast

2. the dog – her handler's commands – obeys – promptly – always

3. such nonsense – heard – have – in my career – I – as a plain-clothes officer – never

4. at home – the suspect – is – at weekends – seldom

5. viciously – with a blunt instrument – the coroner – that the old man – established – had been struck – on the head – soon

6. probably – this – ten-euro note – a – forgery – is – most – crisp – clever

7. often – aware – elderly – are – of dangers – near-sighted – people – therefore – not – always

8. after midnight – by forcing – entered – the burglar – in this affluent neighbourhood – by anybody – a house – shortly – with a jemmy – the basement door – without being noticed

9. her work – our – looks – new – female – good – well – colleague – and does – in our division

10. and – in their home town – the red lights – occasionally – drive – jump – taxi drivers – even – usually – fast – rather

11. rather – after school – carelessly – cross – many youngsters – frequently – the street

12. severe – burns – in the fire – and – Mr Burns – died – sustained – eventually

10.9 Useful phrases

Erklären Sie ausländischen Freunden, dass

1. – geringfügige Verkehrsverstöße in Deutschland mit einer Verwarnung geahndet werden.

2. – deutsche Autofahrer, je nach Verstoß, auch Strafpunkte im Verkehrszentralregister bekommen und sogar mit einem Fahrverbot für einen bestimmten Zeitraum belegt werden.

3. – zu dichtes Auffahren bei hoher Geschwindigkeit und Betätigen der Lichthupe ein häufiges Vergehen auf deutschen Autobahnen ist.

4. – junge Erwachsene zwischen 18 und 24 Jahren die meisten Verkehrsunfälle verursachen und deshalb auch die höchsten Versicherungsprämien bezahlen müssen.

5. – falsches Überholen, Nichtbeachten der Vorfahrt und Fahren in der falschen Richtung auf der Autobahn zu den sieben Todsünden im Straßenverkehr gehören.

6. – liegengebliebene Fahrzeuge in ausreichender Entfernung kenntlich gemacht werden müssen.

7. – Ausländer manchmal schnelle Autos in Deutschland mieten, damit sie auf Autobahnstrecken ohne Geschwindigkeitsbegrenzung sehr schnell fahren können.

8. – oft mehrere Zeugen bestätigen können, dass ein Autofahrer sehr aggressiv gefahren ist.

9. – die Polizei dem Staatsanwalt empfehlen kann, einem Autofahrer den Führerschein zu entziehen.

10.10 Key words and phrases

endangering road traffic – failure to stop after an accident – fatal – flash one's headlights – gap – jump the lights – road hog – road rage – tailgate – weave in and out

Unit 11 Serious traffic offences 2

This unit deals with

- the dangers of driving under the influence
- alcohol-related accidents
- checking a driver for alcohol and drugs and
- conditional clauses.

11.1 Friends don't let friends drive drunk

Only the first and last sentences are where they belong – can you tell what happened?

Some months ago there was a party at a friend's house.	She was hysterical, sobbing and crying and telling me that there had been an accident.	Two girls got into the back, and they left.
They assured us that they would leave their car in the driveway and a friend would pick them up.	We had no idea that the friend had been drinking, too, and was heavily intoxicated.	It was rather late when two girls said they were going home.
All of us had too much to drink, but that was no problem as we did not want to drive anyway.	Twenty minutes later one of the girls called me on my mobile phone.	The front passenger and the girl behind him suffered only minor injuries.
Their car slid under the lorry, whose high bumper sheared off the roof.	That driver's younger brother was sitting in the front.	The driver, who was not wearing his seatbelt, was thrown out of the car and died immediately.
The girl who was sitting behind him died in hospital two days later.	Later we learnt that they were driving around a bend, and since they were going too fast the driver did not see the articulated lorry ahead of them.	From that night on – I'm telling you – I've never had and will never have a sip of alcohol when I drive.

11.2 Driving under the influence of alcohol and/or drugs

Unit 11

Part 1 – Alcohol

Driving under the influence (of alcohol) – a trivial offence only?

Certainly not. Alcohol is a drug, albeit a legal one; its effects in road traffic are often underestimated.

Alcohol is instantly absorbed in the blood, and people react in different ways when consuming it.

Therefore certain deficiency symptoms, which constitute great risks, can be noticed sooner or later.

Reaction time, perception and concentration decrease, the inhibition threshold decreases, and wrong assessment of situations, readiness to take risks and an exaggerated opinion of one's abilities increase.

This already begins with an alcohol concentration of 20 milligrams of alcohol in 100 millilitres of blood.

With 50 milligrams of alcohol in 100 millilitres of blood the risk of causing an accident doubles.The ability to see red diminishes, so red brake lights and red traffic lights are only perceived belatedly. A driver with 80 milligrams of alcohol in 100 millilitres of blood reacts, on average, one second later than a sober driver.

With 100 milligrams of alcohol in 100 millilitres of blood, visual perception is either blurred or doubled. Speech is slurred and becomes unclear. Tunnel vision sets in. With 160 milligrams of alcohol in 100 millilitres of blood, there are unmistakable deficiency symptoms like staggering and slurred speech.

A level of more than 200 milligrams of alcohol in 100 millilitres of blood means that drivers are in a state of intoxication, more than 300 milligrams of alcohol in 100 millilitres of blood can be lethal.

Driving while intoxicated is, and has always been, a danger in road traffic, the degree of which cannot be assessed in advance.

Fill in the table

Milligramms of alcohol in millitres of blood	Deficiency symptoms
20	Reaction time, perception + concentration decrease,
50	to see red diminishes, risk of causing accidents doubles
80	one second later than a sober driver → Reaction
100	~~perception~~ visual perception blurred doubled, tunnel vision
160	staggering + slurred speech
200	
< 300	

Complete the words

Driving under the i.................. is classified as either a misdemeanour or a criminal o.................., depending on the blood alcohol or breath alcohol con.................. .

We distinguish between minor traffic infractions due to alcohol ....ption, diminished fitness to drive and unfitness to drive.

The consequences of driving under the influence of alcohol may be: the driver has to park his/her car and the k.................. are secured, a blood s.................. is taken and the driving licence is secured or conf.................., or he or she has to undergo a medical and psychological examination to establish if he or she is f.................. to drive a motor ....le.

Financial consequences may be: fixed-.................. fine, order of summary punishment or trial, a court-imposed f.................., or the insurance company refuses to pay for the d.................. caused.

In case of dis.................., additional cost may result, e.g. fares for public .... sport in extreme cases a drunk driver may even lose his/her job.

Part 2 – Drugs

The influence of drugs on driving cannot be predicted as every person reacts differently to drugs. The danger potential is very high, especially if a combination of various drugs is taken or a drug is taken together with alcohol.

A person under the influence of drugs endangers road traffic to a high degree. Many drug users are not aware of the fact that not only alcohol, but also drugs and medication have a considerable effect on their fitness to drive, an effect which can last quite long.

Detailed knowledge about drivers under the influence of drugs is relatively recent. In the past, it often happened that a driver acted like being drunk, although he/she had not drunk any alcohol, and this fact was hard to explain. It was only gradually realized that a new kind of traffic offence had become more and more frequent: aggressive and uncontrolled driving, very agitated or totally calm behaviour, no awareness of the situation and surroundings, not showing any reaction(s) and therefore a danger to himself/herself and other traffic participants.

In the past, drug users apparently took their illegal drugs at the scene of an event or at a party and got intoxicated there, but today they also drive a car or ride a motorcycle.

Most drug users don't know the real effects of the drug they have taken. They take part in road traffic under the mistaken assumption that they took the drug three days ago and thus their fitness to drive is no longer impaired. But also persons who have taken drugs a short time before no longer abstain from driving. They don't realize that they are committing an offence. It is apparently smart, cool, and absolutely not dangerous. Parliament had to act, and so it did. And the police reacted, too.

Drivers who have been found to be under the influence of drugs did not necessarily take hard drugs. That's the exception rather than the rule.

Most drivers take drugs which are easy to obtain and consume and not too expensive. Most offenders are young adults of up to 25 years. It should also be noted that these drug addicts normally do not cause any difficulties when confronted by the police. Most of them immediately admit that they have taken drugs and consent to a urine or other test. The situation only gets serious when a blood sample has to be taken and the driving licence is secured or confiscated.

11.3 Alcohol-related accidents

Nearly half of all fatal road traffic accidents in Germany are alcohol-related. These accidents mostly happen during the night and at weekends, and in most cases the drivers are young males. Male drivers involved in fatal crashes are nearly twice as likely to have been intoxicated as females. On Friday and Saturday nights, between 10 p.m. and 4 a.m., two thirds of all motorists killed have had alcohol levels above the legal limit. Even if no lives are lost, these accidents often result in severe injuries for the drivers and passengers involved and in badly damaged vehicles.

1. **Why are male drivers more likely to drive under the influence than females?**
2. **Should there be curfew laws for young drivers? What are the pros and cons?**
3. **Do you know anybody who has been involved in an alcohol-related accident? What happened?**

11.4 Visual clues for drunk-driving

A driver is likely to be drunk when he or she

- grips the wheel tightly with his or her face close to the windscreen
- makes wide turns
- crosses or straddles the central line
- zigzags, swerves and weaves from one lane to another
- drives on the shoulder or in the wrong lane
- drives very slowly
- stops without cause.

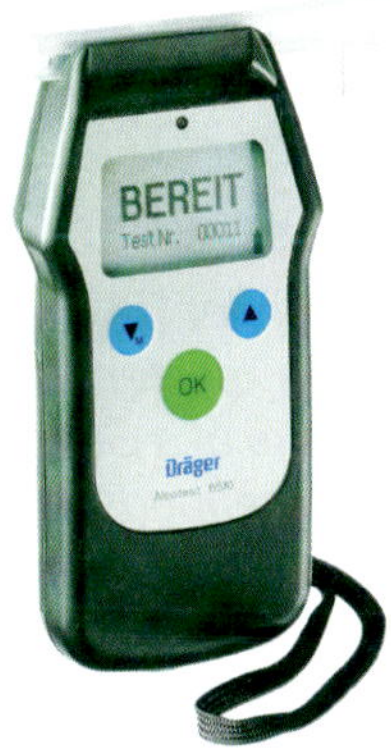

Reproduced by kind permission of Dräger Safety AG & Co. KgaA

11.5 Role play/discussion/essay

1. **People do not always act sensibly when stopped after drinking alcohol and sometimes they offer rather strange excuses. How would you react in the following situations?**

   a) You stop a middle-aged driver in the late afternoon because he has been weaving in and out and driving at a very slow speed. He tells you that he has not drunk any alcohol but inhaled it as he works in a distillery.

   b) You stop a lady after dark because she has been driving on a country road without headlights. She tells you she did so because of deer crossing the road.

   c) You stop a car, and when the driver winds down the window you notice a strong smell of alcohol. The driver tells you that the day before he had transported some bottles of "Federweißer" on the back seat, and one bottle had fallen off the seat, the cork had popped out and the wine had soaked the carpet.

2. **What do you know about the effects of alcohol on drivers?**

3. **Should there be large-scale sobriety checks during local festivals? What would be the effect?**

4. **Do you think the penalties for drinking and driving are adequate?**

5. **Should insurance companies be informed of cases of drink-driving?**

6. **Should the names and addresses of drunk drivers be published in the local newspapers?**

11.6 Drunk and under the influence of drugs

PK Ilka Anger (IA), driving the police car, is on patrol, together with PK Frederik Schott (FS), in a residential area in the small town of Bad Waldsee in Upper Swabia. In the early hours of a Sunday morning in summer, they notice a car with its fog lights switched on, and the loudspeakers blaring. The driver, a young man, drives rather slowly, then accelerates, swerves to the centre of the street, then swerves to the right, almost hitting the kerb. In other words, he is driving erratically. He hasn't noticed the police car. Following their professional instinct, the officers immediately decide to stop the car. They follow it.

Part 1

Stopping the vehicle

IA: That driver is either drunk or under the influence of drugs.

FS: You're right. He's zigzagging. We've got to stop him immediately, before he causes an accident. Many cars are parked here. Let's hope no car comes from the opposite direction. Can you see how many people there are in the car?

Ilka Anger switches on the blue lights and also the flashing "STOP POLIZEI" sign. The driver does not react immediately, but stops after she has flashed her headlights at him repeatedly.

Part 2

Breathalyzer test

When checking the driver, 22-year-old British citizen Percy Haines (PH), who is alone in his car and who lives in Germany, the officers notice that he smells of alcohol. On the floor in front of the passenger seat and on the back seats there are empty alcopop bottles. The breathalyzer test shows 170 milligrams of alcohol in 100 millilitres of blood. Percy Haines's car is parked at once in the residential area, PH is arrested and taken to the police station. A doctor is called to take a blood sample.

IA: Mr Haines, we're waiting for the doctor. He'll take a blood sample. I'm preparing the necessary forms. I'd like to ask you a few questions about the food and drink you consumed. Before that, I have to inform you about your rights. You're under the influence of alcohol, and the way you've been driving shows that you're not fit to drive. The breath specimen showed 170 milligrams of alcohol in 100 millilitres of blood. In other words, you've committed a serious traffic offence. According to German law, it's up to you whether to make a statement or not. You've got the right to contact a lawyer at any time, and to request that investigations be made which might result in your favour. Did you understand all that?

PH: Yes, I did. I'm going to make a statement, and I haven't decided yet whether to contact a lawyer or not.

Part 3

Drug test

While IA is talking to Mr Haines, FS has checked on the computer if the personal data are correct, if he still lives at the address he gave, and if he is wanted for some reason. He finds out that PH has been registered with the police as a drug user, and that he has been photographed and fingerprinted. According to these data, the latest drug offence was committed four months ago. With this information, FS addresses Mr Haines:

FS: Mr Haines, have you taken any drugs lately? We, the police, know that you did in the past. But you certainly know better. So I'm asking you directly: Did you take any drugs today? Did you smoke hashish, or did you take anything else? I already informed you about your rights. That also refers to this question.

PH: You seem to know everything. Yes, I smoked a joint. But I won't tell you where I got the stuff.

FS: My colleague will write all that down in our report, but before that I'd like to do a pupil test with you. Do you agree?

PH: Yes, I already know.

Percy Haines looks straight ahead, and the officer flashes his torch into both eyes. Normally the pupils contract when they are exposed to light. After the consumption of cannabis the reaction is different: the pupils contract briefly, then widen immediately and afterwards start pulsating. This is called the "rebound effect", and that's exactly Percy Haines's reaction.

Part 4

Urine test

FS: Many thanks. Do you also consent to having your urine tested?

PH: Why, you've already arranged for a blood sample to be taken. So you can have everything examined, can't you?

FS: Analyzing your blood sample for alcohol and drugs isn't cheap. You'll have to pay for it. With a urine test, it's easier for me to determine what you really consumed and leave it to the prosecutor to decide on whether or not a more detailed analysis is really necessary.

The officer knows that a blood sample is easier to analyze for alcohol than for drugs. A blood analysis for drugs is much more complicated and only done on orders of the prosecution service, after the results of a preliminary test have been submitted. But, depending on the individual case, the complicated test may not be necessary.

PH: OK, I'll try.

FS: Here's a small plastic cup. Don't fill it to the brim. There, at the end of the corridor, is the toilet. I'll be coming with you and will be staying with you all the time.

PH: Yes, yes, I know.

Part 5

Interview

After a short while the officer takes the bottle. PH is interviewed by IA.

IA: Mr Haines, what and how much did you drink during the last 24 hours? Also tell me, please, what and what quantity you drank at what time.

PH: Last night, at about 20.00, I had a few alcopops. Until about 23.30, I had the odd small bottle, and in between I had a wheat beer.

IA: How many bottles was that, what do you think?

PH: Probably five small bottles and one wheat beer.

IA: And when did you smoke the marihuana?

PH: Already in the afternooon, yesterday. At home. At about 6 p.m.

IA: And what did you eat?

PH: I was at a party. There were only potato crisps and salted nuts. In the afternoon I had a pizza.

IA: Where did you drink the alcohol?

PH: At a friend's place. But I'm not going to tell you who he is and where he lives.

IA: And where did you get the marihuana? Or was it hashish?

PH: Do you really think I'm going to tell you that? I've got a small quantity for myself. It was marihuana, prime quality.

Part 6

Tests and result

IA has filled in the report form in accordance with Mr. Haines's statement.

IA: Would you please sign this report? Here, at the top, is the note that you were informed about your rights, and below we have your statement. Please sign here, and there, too.

In the meantime FS has conducted a "Mahsan test". Using a pipette, he put a drop of urine onto the test section of a test strip. The result: cannabis. The urine sample, together wih the blood sample, is sent to the forensic institute. The results of the analyses will be used in the court proceedings.

Part 7

Blood sample and medical report

In the meantime, the doctor has arrived. In his medical report he describes Mr Haines's (bodily) constitution, specifying his height, weight, and sex. Then he takes a blood sample from the upper arm vein. Of course, date and time are also entered in the form.

The doctor signs various labels with identical numbers, personal data and docket numbers. These labels are also put onto the police and medical forms, the small glass tube with the blood sample and the bottle with the urine sample. This is done to make sure that there are no errors.

Afterwards the doctor asks PH if he agrees to answer his questions and to do the tests.

Case history: medical measures and occurrences (e.g. shock, vomiting), taking of medication/drugs, diseases.

Findings: indication of drug influence, conjunctiva, size of pupils, language/pronunciation, behaviour, mood, results of various tests.

Diagnosis: indication of influence of drugs (clearly of alcohol), overall impression.

Copies of the medical report, signed by the doctor, and of the police report with the statement regarding Mr Haines's consumption of alcohol and drugs will be forwarded to the forensic service.

The doctor makes out his bill. The amount will be paid for by the police administration, but later Mr Haines will have to reimburse them. The doctor leaves the police station.

Part 8

Securing/confiscating the driving licence

IA: Mr Haines, you stated that you've been living and working in Germany for nearly two years. We checked your residential address and the date of your registration with the registration office on the computer. When we stopped you, you gave us a German driving licence. Do you still have your British licence?

PH: I got my German driving licence only a short time ago, because I've been living here for such a long time. I've still got my British licence.

IA: May I have that as well?

PH: Why? And I want my German licence back.

IA: I'm afraid that's not possible. I'm going to secure your licence and forward it to the prosecution service. Let me explain. According to German law, the driving licence is to be secured in such cases. We asssume that you're not fit to operate any motor vehicle for which a licence is required. In the course of the further proceedings, and when all results of the analyses are available, our assumption will be corroborated, or mitigated. A judge will decide about that. If you were allowed to keep your licence, you might commit the same offence again. Alcohol and drugs, consumed at the same time or one shortly after the other, cause a state of inebriation which endangers you and other motorists. That's why we believe that the judge will disqualify you. We'll secure your driving licence in order to prevent you from endangering others until then. As from now, you're not allowed to use a motor vehicle for which a driving licence is required. Which means: no car, and no motorcycle, either. Do you understand that?

PH: From now on I'm not allowed to drive a car any more? But I need my car. How am I supposed to go to work, how am I supposed to live without a car? That's impossible.

IA: I'm afraid that's how it is. Most people don't think about the consequences. But now you see how important it is to have a driving licence. You'll have to learn how to live without a licence. If you consent, I'll secure your licence. If you don't agree, I'll confiscate it. But in either case, I won't give it back to you.

PH: What's the difference? Secure, confiscate?

IA: If your licence is secured, it will be included in the case files until the prosecution service or a court decides and a sentence is pronounced. If your licence is confiscated, it will also be included in the case files. But in that case, a judge will have to decide within three days about how long you'll have to do without your licence. Now, what are we going to do?

PH: That's getting worse and worse. I need to have my licence. As a British citizen I wasn't aware of the fact that you would take my licence from me. I won't have it.

IA: Mr Haines, this objection does not delay our procedure. I herewith confiscate your driving licence, and I'll make a note of it on this form here.

Part 9

Foreign driving licence

IA: And where's your British licence?

PH: I won't give it to you. That's got nothing to do with my German licence.

FS: Yes, it certainly has. Your British licence must be submitted to the state prosecutor, who will endorse it accordingly. You must hand it over. Please do so, otherwise I'll be forced to search your clothes and your car.

PH: What next? OK. All my papers are in this leather bag. Also my British driving licence.

Part 10

Search

FS: Thank you. Nevertheless I'm going to search you now to make sure that you don't have any more drugs on you.

PH: Go ahead. I haven't got anything else on me. By the way, I could have thrown it away in the meantime. But I only had a small quantity for myself. Maybe there are some crumbs left in my pocket.

FS searches Mr Haines's clothes and the leather bag. He doesn't find anything.

IA: Mr Haines, please sign the report form about the confiscation of both your driving licences. On the form you also find the information that you don't have a driving licence any more and are not allowed to operate a vehicle for which a licence is required. If, in spite of this, you were to drive such a vehicle, you'd commit the serious traffic offence of driving without a licence.

FS: We're now taking you to your car. We must search that, too. And afterwards we'll take you home. That's not a problem, as you live in our beat area. Do you consent that we not only search your car for drugs, but also your flat? If you don't, I'll get a search warrant from the duty prosecutor.

PH: That's not necessary. I consent. I hope you'll mention in your report that I'm being cooperative. I don't have any drugs, neither in my car nor in my flat.

FS: Well, we'll check that. I'm going to inquire if a dog handler with a drug-sniffing dog is available and can assist. Of course you'll get a copy of the report about the search.

When I've got all the results you'll get a summons. In case your lawyer has power of attorney you probably won't be present. Your lawyer will demand access to all the files, and afterwards issue a statement.

I also have to press charges against you for purchasing and consuming drugs. What you did is an offence against the drugs act. But you certainly know from last time. The court will decide about the sentence.

By the way, we're going to deposit your car keys at our station. You can pick them up after a period of 24 hours. But, as I told you, you're not allowed to drive any more.

11.7 Drunk horse-rider

In Exeter in southwest England, a man was fined £ 150 for being drunk when riding a horse. The man admitted that he was drunk when riding the horse, without a saddle, in the street in an Exeter suburb when police stopped him. The penalty was based on an act dating from 1872 which forbids being drunk when in charge of horses, cattle and ...... steam engines.

1. What do you think of this story?

2. What happens to drunk horse riders in Germany?

11.8 Conditional clause

Nebensatz – conditional clause	Hauptsatz – main clause
Typ I – Erfüllung der Bedingung ist realistisch	
Präsens	Futur I
If you take the 9 o'clock train,	*you will be there at 9.55.*

Anmerkung

Das Hilfsverb *"will"* (für Futur I) kann durch *"be going to"* oder durch ein anderes Hilfsverb wie z.B. *"can"* oder *"may"* ersetzt werden.

If they arrive on time,	*we are going to have dinner in a good restaurant.*
If the weather is nice,	*we can go for a swim.*
Typ II – Erfüllung der Bedingung ist nicht realistisch oder unwahrscheinlich	
Imperfekt	Konditional I
If he had more money,	*he would buy a new car.*
If it were fine this afternoon,	*we would still be able to go for a walk today.*
Beachten Sie:	
If I were/was you,	*I would tell the truth.*
Typ III – Bedingung (realistisch oder nicht realistisch) ist vorbei	
Plusquamperfekt	Konditional II/Konditional I
If you had locked the door,	*the burglars would not have been able to enter the house.*
If you had't come to my rescue,	*I would not be alive today.*

11.9 Fill-in exercise

Fill in the correct form of the verb

Part 1

If you (live) .... in Florida and (be) .... 15, 16, or 17 years old, you (need) .... to know the following:

At the age of 15, you may drive with a Florida Learner Driver's License if a licensed driver aged 21 or older (accompany) .... you. If a 15-year-old person (have)........................ this license, he/she is not allowed to drive at night. If he/she (want) .... to drive between 11 p.m. and 6 a.m., he/she would have to be 16 years old. But if he/she only (drive) .... to and from work or school, he/she would be allowed to do so at night. If you (be)........................ 17 years old, you (obtain) .... a different license. Even in this case you (need) .... an older licensed driver sitting next to you if you wanted to drive between 1 a.m. and 5 a.m. You (lose) .... your driving privilege if you receive four points on your driving record within a year. If this (happen) ...., your driving would be restricted to business purposes only. If you received additional points during this period, the restriction (be) .... extended.

Part 2

1. If many accidents happen within a certain area, the police (concentrate) .... on patrolling such black spots.
2. The blood alcohol concentration would have been evident if the driver (take) .... the breathalyzer test.
3. If he took the test, he (must) .... blow into the mouthpiece of the drunkometer.
4. If motorists (not, exceed) .... the speed limit constantly, the authorities would not have been using cameras and other technical devices so often over the years.
5. If a driver (cause) .... a danger to other drivers, he/she must be prosecuted.
6. If Mr Branson (not, cause) .... an accident under the influence of alcohol, he (not, be, disqualify) .... for a year, and, as a consequence, (not, lose) .... his job.
7. Mrs Cameron (not, allow) .... her son to use her car if she (know) .... that he used to drink heavily at parties.
8. What (you, wear) .... if you (be, invite) .... to a stag party in a pub?
9. If Mr Keanes, the landlord of the Irish Pub in Luckenwalde, (notice) .... that one of his regulars has had one too many, he (take) .... his car keys and (call) .... a taxi for him.
10. Erica to her boyfriend: "I (not, drive) .... any more if I (be) .... you; if you (insist)........................ on driving home, I (not, come) .... with you but (call) .... my father to pick me up."

11.10 Useful phrases

Sagen/erklären Sie einem Autofahrer, dass

1. – Sie ihn wegen seiner unsicheren Fahrweise und weil er in Schlangenlinien fuhr, angehalten haben.

2. – er stark nach Alkohol riecht und Sie glauben, dass er nicht mehr fahrtüchtig ist.

3. – er aussteigen und seine Papiere sowie den Wagenschlüssel aushändigen soll.

4. – er Ihnen mitteilen soll, was und wieviel er in welchem Zeitraum getrunken hat.

5. – er seinen Wagen stehen lassen und mit dem Taxi oder der Straßenbahn nach Hause fahren soll.

6. – Sie ihm einen Alcotest anbieten und dass dieser Test nicht verpflichtend ist.

7. – im Falle der Ablehnung des Alcotests eine Blutprobe entnommen wird, dass er Letztere nach deutschem Recht nicht ablehnen kann und dass sie notfalls unter Anwendung unmittelbaren Zwangs erfolgt.

8. – bereits geringe Mengen Alkohl die Fahrtüchtigkeit erheblich beeinträchtigen.

9. – alkoholisierte Auto- und Motorradfahrer Verkehrssituationen häufig nicht richtig einschätzen können.

10. – in der Nacht von Samstag auf Sonntag besonders in ländlichen Bereichen viele sogenannte Disko-Unfälle passieren, bei denen Alkohol und Drogen im Spiel sind.

11. – überall in der Welt die Polizei durch spezielle Maßnahmen versucht, das Fahren unter Alkoholeinfluss zu unterbinden.

....

....

12. – das Alcotestgerät einen Wert von 1,78 Promille anzeigt, was deutlich über der gesetzlich zulässigen Grenze liegt.

....

....

13. – die Sicherstellung des Führerscheins mit seiner Zustimmung und die Beschlagnahme ohne seine Zustimmung geschieht.

....

....

14. – er ab sofort in Deutschland kein führerscheinpflichtiges Fahrzeug führen darf.

....

15. – er keine Aussagen zu machen braucht und jederzeit einen Anwalt hinzuziehen kann.

....

....

11.11 Key words and phrases

blood sample – breath specimen – deficiency symptoms – drive erratically – driving under the influence (of alcohol) (DUI) – intoxicated – secure/confiscate the driving licence – sobriety check – zigzag – 50 milligrams of alcohol in 100 millilitres of blood

Unit 12

Road traffic accidents

This unit deals with

- the reasons for road traffic accidents
- categories of accidents
- some examples of typical road traffic accidents
- measures taken at the scene of an accident
- first aid (including parts of the body, injuries and types of sickness)
- failing to stop after an accident and
- reported speech.

12.1 Road traffic accident – definition

A road traffic accident (RTA) is any sudden happening in road traffic on public highways, caused unintentionally, and resulting in damage and/or bodily injury.

Some road users are involved in an accident on their way to work, others while going to an event in their leisure time, and others on their way to a holiday destination.

There are about ten thousand accidents per day, often with severe consequences. Something happens all of a sudden, affecting people's lives, making them appear helpless, and yet they are required to do something.

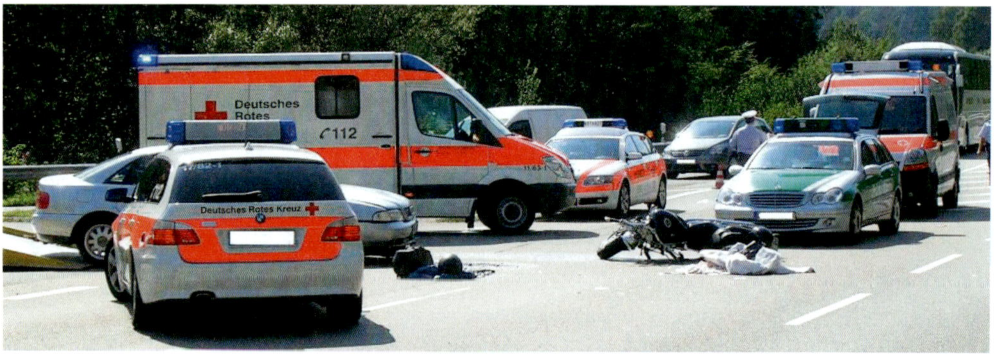

Name other types of accident; example: aircraft accident

12.2 Reasons for road traffic accidents

The seven main reasons for traffic accidents in the USA ("the unlucky seven") are: excessive speed, failure to give way, following too closely, driving left of centre, improper turning, improper overtaking and ignoring a traffic signal.

The seven main reasons for traffic accidents in North Rhine-Westphalia are: drunk driving, excessive speed, following too closely, improper overtaking, failure to give way, improper turning and offences committed against and by pedestrians.

Compare the reasons for accidents in the United States and North Rhine-Westphalia

12.3 Categories of accidents in Rhineland-Palatinate

category 1	fatal road traffic accident
category 2	road traffic accident with seriously injured person(s)
category 3	road traffic accident with slightly injured person(s)
category 4.1	road traffic accident due to serious traffic offence, vehicle(s) no longer roadworthy
category 4.2	road traffic accident due to minor traffic offence, vehicle(s) no longer roadworthy
category 5.1	minor road traffic accident, with/without on-the-spot fine
category 5.2	road traffic accident due to minor traffic offence, with fixed-penalty notice, vehicle(s) still roadworthy
category 5.3	road traffic accident due to serious traffic offence, vehicle(s) still roadworthy
category 6	road traffic accident due to serious traffic offence, vehicle(s) still roadworthy, alcohol

1. **Why do you think road traffic accidents are divided into categories?**
2. **Are these categories the same in all federal states in Germany?**

12.4 Minor road traffic accident and on-the-spot fine

Causing a minor traffic accident or "fender bender" is regarded a minor infraction, as the driver was "only" inattentive. An on-the-spot warning fine of € 35 will be imposed.

Police report of a minor accident

Mr John Davies from Fareham, England, drives behind another vehicle, driven by Mrs Antje Reinicke, from Hamburg, in a residential area in Hamburg-Altona with priority from the right at junctions. At one junction Mrs Reinicke slows down, accelerates, and suddenly steps hard on the brake as a vehicle approaches from the right. Mr Davies slows down, too, accelerates as well, but notices too late that Mrs Reinicke has braked hard, and bumps into the rear of her car.

1. **Write down what Mr Davies tells his wife when he is back home**
2. **Write down what Mrs Reinicke tells her husband**
3. **Write down the conversation between Mr Davies and Mrs Reinicke**

Unit 12

12.5 Minor road traffic accident and fixed-penalty notice

Causing a minor road traffic accident which cannot be punished with an on-the-spot fine but which is not (yet) serious will be punished with a fixed penalty, usually ranging from € 40 to € 75 plus administrative costs. Depending on the circumstances, one to three penalty points will be entered in the Central Register of Traffic Offenders. Foreign nationals have to pay the fixed-penalty fine on the spot (if necessary they have to put up bail), but do not get any penalty points.

Police report

In heavy rain Indian businessman Chandrakant Singh drives down the long downhill section on the B 85 between Lengefeld and Blankenhain in Thuringia. Being too fast, he loses control of his rental car in a right-hand bend, gets into the left lane and bumps into the crash barrier. From there the car is thrown back onto the carriageway, drifts across it and ends up in the ditch on the right side.

What does Mr Singh tell the rental agency on the telephone?

12.6 Serious road traffic accidents

If one or more persons are injured in a traffic accident, the driver who caused it is normally guilty of negligent bodily harm. The injured person(s) can press charges against the guilty driver. An order of summary punishment or court trial may result, often the driver is disqualified, and seven penalty points are entered in the Central Register of Traffic Offenders. Foreign nationals have to put up bail, but don't get any penalty points.

Part 1

Police report

Antony Perkins from Wangarei, Northland, New Zealand, drives in his rental car on Schubertstraße in Weimar and fails to give way to motorcyclist Wilfried Schreiner coming from the right. The two vehicles collide. Wilfried Schreiner falls and both he and his motorcycle skid and hit Herbert Teusch's parked van. Wilfried Schreiner is seriously injured by the impact and taken to hospital. Mrs Perkins in the passenger seat is in a state of shock. The motorcycle is a write-off. Antony Perkins' car and Herbert Teusch's van are slightly damaged. As petrol was leaking from the tank, the fire brigade was called. There were delays.

Mr Perkins sends an SMS to his daughter and son-in-law in Rotorua, informing them about the accident. What could he write?

Part 2

An injury accident

Police officers Diana Södermann (DS) and Felix Gabrecht (FG) arrive on the scene of an accident on the B 109 near Anklam in Mecklenburg – Western Pomerania on a rainy morning. A British car is upside down in the field beside the road. The driver, Elwyn Wynne (EW), is tending his wife Irene (IW), who is lying beside the overturned vehicle.

EW: She's unconscious. Can you help?

FG: The ambulance is on its way and should be here any minute.

DS: We must put her in the recovery position. The ambulance crew will find out what kind of injuries there are. What about you? Are you all right?

EW: I think so. I'm just a bit shaken.

At that moment the ambulance arrives and takes Mr and Mrs Wynne to the local hospital. Officer Södermann takes photos of the scene and makes some notes. Officer Gabrecht speaks to a witness, a Danish lorry driver, Jens Jespersen (JJ) from Ribe.

FG: Good morning, sir. Please tell me exactly what happened.

JJ: This car was coming towards me on the wrong side of the road, then suddenly swerved to the right and ended up in the field.

FG: Were there any other cars?

JJ: No, there weren't. That car was simply travelling on the wrong side of the road. Maybe the driver wasn't concentrating and thought he was at home.

FG: What happened next?

JJ: I stopped, ran into the field and helped the driver and his passenger out of the vehicle. I don't think the woman is seriously injured.

FG: Were their seatbelts fastened?

JJ: Yes, they were. That was lucky, mind you, I had some trouble getting them out because the doors wouldn't open. The man was able to get out by himself after I had smashed the window, and then the two of us managed to pull her out.

FG: Let me take down your personal details ..... Thank you. Have a safe journey.

Having completed their work at the scene of the accident, the officers drive to the hospital where they are informed that the couple are Mr and Mrs Wynne from Ystradgynlais, Wales.

DS: How's your wife? Has she come to?

EW: Yes, she has. Thank God she's quite all right. The doctor says it's mild concussion, and she's broken her left arm.

DS: I'm glad it's not so bad.

FG: Mr Wynne, how did the accident happen?

EW: I'm afraid it was all my fault. Somehow or other I was driving on the left side of the road. When I saw the oncoming lorry I realized I was on the Continent and panicked. The next moment the car overturned and we found ourselves in the field.

FG: Then what happened?

EW: A man smashed the window and helped me get out of the car, and then the two of us pulled my wife out.

FG: In other words, you are responsible for the accident.

EW: Yes, I am.

FG: Mr Wynne, I'm afraid we'll have to forward our accident report to the prosecutor's office. The prosecutor will decide whether to prefer charges against you or not since it's an injury accident. However, in your case, a charge will probably only be made if the injured person demands it, and why should your wife do that?

EW: Oh dear, whatever next? By the way, have you got the name and address of the gentleman who helped us? There was no time to ask him and I'd like to thank him for his kind assistance.

The officers give him Jens Jespersen's name and address and do all the necessary paperwork.

1. **Should a driver be punished for causing an accident in which only he/she is involved?**
2. **Should right-hand driving be introduced throughout the European Union?**
3. **Find out why the British and Irish drive on the left**
4. **Where else do they drive on the left?**

12.7 Measures at the scene of an accident

Write down what measures the police have to take at the accident scenes described in 12. 4, 12. 5 and 12. 6

12.8 First aid

First aid is the skilled application of accepted principles of treatment after an accident or in the case of sudden illness, using facilities or materials available at the time.

Treatment and aids

adhesive dressing	bandage	emergency resuscitation
give/render first aid	kiss of life	mouth-to-mouth resuscitation
recovery position	relieve pain	roller bandage
sling	splint	stitch
stretcher	syringe	tourniquet

1. **Find out the meanings of the above medical terms (use your dictionary)**

2. **The above list is by no means complete. Add words and phrases which you consider necessary**

3. **Form sentences by using words and phrases from the above list Example: A splint is used if the upper arm is fractured.**

12.9 Parts of the body

abdomen	airway	ankle	artery
backbone	bone	blood vessel	calf
chest	collar bone	forearm	heart
hip	jaw	joint	kidney
liver	lungs	pelvis	rib
shin bone	shoulder blade	skin	skull
spine	tendon	thigh	tissue
trunk	upper arm	vein	windpipe
wrist			

Form sentences by using words and phrases from the above list

Example: The ankle is the joint which connects the foot with the leg.

12.10 Injuries and types of sickness

abrasion	asphyxia	bite	bleeding
breathing difficulties	bruise	burn	concussion
cramp	crush	cut	dislocation
drowning	fainting	foreign body in the eye	fracture
gunshot wound	heart attack	hypothermia	incision
internal bleeding	laceration	poisoning	puncture
scald	stab wound	sting	stroke
suffocation	tachycardia	unconsciousness	vomiting
whiplash injury			

Form sentences by using words and phrases from the above list

Example: A fracture is a break or crack in the bone.

12.11 Failing to stop after an accident

An accident has happened. However, the driver who caused it did not stop. POK Patrick Hörner (PH) is talking to Roger Burkitt (RB) and his wife Linda (LB).

PH: Mr Burkitt, what kind of car was that? Can you tell me the make?

RB: That's my first accident after 40 years of driving. I'm so old already, and now this has had to happen. Back there, in the roadworks section where the lanes are rather narrow and where the carriageway is slightly inclined, that bloke drove too far to the right and tore off my outside mirror when overtaking. There, have a look! That's an electric mirror, it's still hanging on the cables.

PH: Mr Burkitt, you told me that already. Now, please try to remember the other vehicle.

RB: Ah, yes, the other car. I thought the driver had noticed. I even honked my horn.

PH: So it was a man who drove the other car?

RB: Yes, an elderly man, with a full beard.

PH: To be able to send out an alert as soon as possible (asap), please tell me what kind of car it was.

RB: Well, everything went so fast. I think it was a Ford. A fastback. And not the latest model.

LB: I'm not quite sure about that. It could also have been a Renault. And it was an estate car.

RB: Linda, I think it was a Ford. It was right beside me. And the driver was very close, strange, quite unusual.

PH: Were you able to read part of the number plate?

RB: No. Here, on the motorway, at the beginning of a roadworks section, I paid attention to the carriageway.

LB: The licence plate began with GB.

PH: The colour of the car?

LB: Light blue.

RB: It was ivory, yellowish, and had black decorative stripes at the side.

PH: Let's get back to the driver. An elderly man, you say. How old approximately?

RB: About 50. He had a dark full beard, and still thick hair. Judging from the way he was sitting in his car he is quite heavy. And he wore a dark, checkered shirt.

LB: Yes, that's correct. I saw that as well.

PH: Here, there are only some scratches in the plastic. But just a moment! Here, on the wing, there are some traces of colour. Have a look, light blue! Your wife was right. The wings of the two vehicles touched. In that case you must have heard the scratching.

RB: I didn't notice anything.

PH: But you're lucky. I'm going to scratch the paint off with a knife and put it into this small bag, and afterwards I'm going to stick adhesive plaster on that part of the wing. Paint parts and paint dust will stick to the plaster, and we can keep it for further examination. I'll also measure the site of the impact exactly and make a sketch. But, before that, once again: a light blue Ford or Renault, elderly, big driver, the licence plate begins with GB.

At that moment another motorist (A), who had been standing beside his car, having a break, addresses the group.

A: Excuse me, please, for interfering. But I heard part of your conversation. You're looking for the blue Ford Focus from England?

PH: I beg your pardon?

A: The Englishman? He had the GB nationality sign on the left side of his rear bumper, clearly to be seen. But I can't remember the licence plate number. I noticed him because he had the steering wheel on the right and was sitting on the wrong side.

RB: That's it! That's why I thought something was strange. Why didn't I remember...?

12.12 Informing relatives

There was a fatal head-on collision on federal road 112 between Frankfurt/Oder and Küstrin. An articulated lorry was too fast in a sharp turn to the right and swerved to the left side of the road, hitting the oncoming car of Mr Bill Burrow and his wife Deirdre from Scarborough, England. Mr and Mrs Burrow were both severely injured and were rushed to hospital where they died despite all the efforts of the staff on the emergency ward.

Police officers Sebastian Metzen (SM) and Tanja Kappes (TK) now have the very unpleasant task of informing the Burrows' relatives. In Mrs Burrow's handbag they find an address book with the name of a Peter Burrow of 152 Springfield Drive, Scarborough, phone number 567756. They phone the Scarborough police and talk to superintendent Vernon Williams (VW) and police sergeant Charles Adcock (CA).

Sebastian and Tanja have a phone with a loudspeaker in their office, so both can talk and both can hear what is being said at the other end of the line.

SM: Well, I suppose we have to inform some relatives in England about the tragedy. Peter Burrow might be the father or brother.

TK: He might also be Bill Burrow's son.

SM: Of course. Anyway, we'll have to make the call, and then we'll certainly find out. I've only got the number 567756. I suppose that's a number in Scarborough. What's the area code for Scarborough? I know the international code for England, it's 0044.

TK: We have the book with the telephone codes in our control room. Scarborough should be in the book. If not, we'll have to call directory inquiries.

SM: Let's try control first.

He dials ....

SM: Hello, Helmut, can you find out the telephone code for Scarborough in England?

Helmut Reuter (HR), who is working the desk that day, answers:

HR: I'll have to look it up, hold on for a moment, oh yes, here it is, it's 01723.

SM: Thanks.

He dials 0044–1723–567756.

SM: Mm, the phone is ringing, but nobody's answering.

He puts the receiver down.

SM: Tanja, what are we going to do now? There's nobody there.

TK: As usual, you're a little bit too fast. Think before you act! It is difficult and awkward enough to tell somebody in German that a family member has been fatally injured, and you want to do it in English!

SM: What do you suggest then?

TK: Let's call the police in Scarborough, they'll certainly help us. So let's find their number first.

Directory inquiries tells them the number, which is 500300. So he dials 0044–1723–500300.

CA: Scarborough police, can I help you?

SM: Hello, my name is Sebastian Metzen of the police headquarters in Frankfurt/Oder, Germany. I'd like to talk to a senior police officer. You see, we've had a road traffic accident in our area in which two citizens from Scarborough were killed.

CA: Oh my God. Wait a second, I'll put you through to Superintendent Williams. Hold the line, please. I'm sorry, his line is engaged at the moment. But I'll try again, please hold on a little longer.

VW: Police Superintendent Vernon Williams speaking, can I help you?

SM: I'm police constable Sebastian Metzen of the police headquarters in Frankfurt/Oder, Germany. We had an RTA a few hours ago in which, unfortunately, a Mr and Mrs Burrow from Scarborough were fatally injured.

VW: Oh dear!

SM: What can my colleagues and I do about it? We have to inform some relatives. We've found the name and address of a Peter Burrow, 152 Springfield Drive, Scarborough, phone number 567756. We don't know if he is the father, the brother or the son or just a friend with the same name. I tried to call him myself a few minutes ago, but nobody answered. Perhaps it might be better if somebody from your station got in touch with him.

VW: What was the name?

SM: Peter Burrow. I'll spell Burrow: B for Benjamin, U for Uncle, double R for Robert, O for Oliver and W for William.

VW: And could you repeat the phone number, please?

SM: It's five-six-double seven-five-six.

VW: So I've got the name and address of a relative. What can you tell me about the victims?

SM: They are Bill and Deirdre Burrow, both born in 1949, their address is 14, Alton Close, Scarborough.

VW: Thank you. How did the accident happen?

SM: An articulated lorry was too fast in a bend, swerved to the wrong side of the road and caused a head-on collision.

VW: So they didn't cause the accident?

SM: No, it seems as if it was the lorry driver's fault. He wasn't hurt, but suffered severe shock and is still in hospital. We haven't been able to talk to him yet. I've already informed the British Consulate, and you'll receive a fax from them soon.

VW: Well, we'll do our best to contact any relatives as fast as possible. I'll call you back as soon as we have found someone. On what number can I reach you?

SM: I'm Police Constable Sebastian Metzen, S – E – B – A – S – T – I – A – N M – E – T – Z – E – N from the police headquarters in Frankfurt/Oder, Germany. The country code for Germany is 0049, the code for Frankfurt is 335, and the number of police headquarters is 5610. My extension is 234. Make sure you ask for Sebastian Metzen, as we also have a Herbert Metzen. But you can also ask for WPC Tanja Kappes. She was with me at the scene of the accident.

VW: Thank you for calling, Goodbye.

SM: Goodbye.

1. Did Sebastian Metzen and Tanja Kappes follow the correct procedure by trying to contact Peter Burrow in Scarborough?

2. Who is Peter Burrow?

3. Has the exact cause of the accident been established?

12.13 Reported speech

Die indirekte Rede wird immer mit einem Verb, dem sogenannten Einführungsverb, eingeleitet. Von diesem Einführungsverb hängt die Zeitenfolge in der indirekten Rede ab.

Regel 1

Einführungsverb im Präsens und Perfekt → indirekte Rede gleiche Zeit wie direkte Rede

He says (has said):	*He says (has said) (that)*
"Overtaking is a dangerous manoeuvre."	*... overtaking is a dangerous manoeuvre.*
"Last night we went to a soccer match."	*... last night they went to a soccer match.*
"I've been living in this town since 1989."	*... he's been living in this town since 1989.*
"We will go to Scotland next year."	*... they will go to Scotland next year.*

Regel 2

Einführungsverb im Imperfekt → Umstellung auf entsprechende Vergangenheitsform

Präsens	→ Imperfekt	Futur I	→ Konditional I
Imperfekt	→ Plusquamperfekt	Futur II	→ Konditional II
Perfekt	→ Plusquamperfekt	Konditional I	→ Konditional I
Plusquamperfekt	→ Plusquamperfekt	Konditional II	→ Konditional II

He said:	*He said (that)*
"Sexual abuse is a crime."	*... sexual abuse was a crime.*
"Three persons were killed."	*... three persons had been killed.* (auch: *...three persons were killed).*
"The operation has been a success."	*... the operation had been a success.*
"This will never happen again."	*... this would never happen again.*

Indirekter Fragesatz – Zeiten wie bei Regeln 1 und 2

He asks: "Do you work at Aachen?"	*He asks if/whether I work at Aachen.*
He asked me: "Where do you live?"	*He asked me where I lived.*

Bei Fragen ohne Fragewort wird *if* oder *whether* eingefügt; bei Fragen mit Fragewort wird das Fragewort übernommen.

Die Umstellung von Zeit- und Ortsangaben

(z. B. *tomorrow → the following day; here → there*)

und Pronomen (z. B. *you → I*) erfolgt ebenso wie im Deutschen.

12.14 Exercise

Convert into reported speech

Part 1

1. "I like your new uniform."
   She said ....
2. "I was looking for witnesses to the accident."
   He inquired...
3. "How long have you been working here?"
   He asked me ....
4. "You should inform your insurance company."
   I suggested that ....
5. "I saw the old lady."
   The suspect admitted ....
6. "What are you going to do after the meeting?"
   He wanted to know ....
7. "Why didn't you call me yesterday?"
   She wondered ....
8. "Have you checked your tyres?"
   I tried to find out ....
9. "When will the tow truck arrive?"
   He asked me ....
10. "I would prefer to write the report tomorrow."
    I told him ....
11. "Where have you been?"
    I was asked ....
12. "Do you know that jumping the lights is a severe offence?"
    The policeman asked my wife ....
13. "Can you give first aid?"
    He asked her ....

Part 2

On Monday morning when police officer Turner starts his shift, his colleague John Seller tells him about three terrible accidents during the night shift.

"First a red Ford hit a young lady in Lime Street. She was seriously injured and the driver left the scene. We haven't found him yet. Fortunately two witnesses remembered parts of the licence plate number, so it shouldn't be a problem to find him soon.

Only a few minutes later we were called to another accident. On Hopton Road a young man had been driving too fast while it was raining and lost control of his minivan. He collided head-on with another vehicle. Both drivers were severely hurt and a passenger died on the scene. The young man will have to spend the rest of his life in a wheelchair.

On Grand Avenue a 29-year-old driver crashed against a tree in a bend and was thrown out of his car. He died on the spot. His 18-year-old passenger was badly injured and was taken to St. Mary's Hospital. Peter will try to ask him a few questions this afternoon."

In the evening officer Turner told his wife that ....

12.15 Useful phrases

1. Informieren Sie eine Autobahnstreife, dass ein LKW Ihr Fahrzeug beschädigt hat.

   ....

2. Sagen Sie, dass der grüne Kombi mit Anhänger die Vorfahrt des Motorradfahrers nicht beachtet hat.

   ....

3. Erklären Sie dem Fahrer des Lieferwagens, dass Sie ihn angehalten haben, weil er einen Schaden an einem anderen Fahrzeug verursacht hat.

   ....

4. Fragen Sie den Fahrer, warum er nicht rechtzeitig gebremst hat.

   ....

5. Fragen Sie ihn, ob er nicht bemerkt hat, dass der Fahrer des vorausfahrenden Fahrzeugs nach links abbiegen wollte.

   ....

6. Fragen Sie den Fahrer, wie der Unfall passiert ist.

   ....

7. Sagen Sie dem Zeugen, dass Sie noch seine Personalien aufschreiben müssen, bevor er weiterfahren kann.

   ....

8. Erklären Sie dem Fahrer, dass Sie alle Unterlagen an die Staatsanwaltschaft weiterleiten werden.

....

9. Erklären Sie ihm, dass es wegen seiner vermutlichen Fahrerflucht zu einer Gerichtsverhandlung kommen wird.

....

10. Erklären Sie einem Raser, dass es in der ganzen Welt häufig zu schwersten Verkehrsunfällen mit Dutzenden von Toten und Verletzten kommt.

....

....

11. Sagen Sie ihm, dass überhöhte Geschwindigkeit die häufigste Ursache für Unfälle ist.

....

12. Fragen Sie, ob jemand verletzt ist und wer erste Hilfe geleistet hat.

....

13. Erklären Sie, dass alle Unfallbeteiligten ins Krankenhaus gebracht werden.

....

14. Fragen Sie einen Zeugen, ob die Sicherheitsgurte angelegt waren.

....

15. Erklären Sie einem britischen Polizeibeamten am Telefon, dass das Ehepaar Straw in Deutschland tödlich verunglückt ist und bitten Sie, dass die Angehörigen informiert werden.

....

....

16. Teilen Sie ihm mit, dass die offizielle Bestätigung per Fax über das Konsulat unterwegs ist.

....

17. Sagen Sie ihm, dass Sie unter der Telefonnummer 0049–335–561–234 zu erreichen sind.

....

....

12.16 Key words and phrases

area code – first aid – bodily injury – delay – failure to give way – hold the line – order of summary punishment – recovery position – road traffic accident (RTA) – roadworthy – trace – yield

Unit 13 Theft of and from vehicles

This unit deals with

– the parts of a car and motorcycle
– stolen cars
– home-jacking and
– the definite article.

13.1 Definitions

"Theft **of** a vehicle" means that the vehicle itself is stolen; "theft **from** a vehicle" means that either parts of a vehicle are stolen, for example the wheels, or that items are stolen from inside the vehicle, for example a radio or built-in navigation system or a laptop computer which has been left inside the vehicle.

13.2 Parts of a car

Which is which?

aerial*(GB)*, antenna *(US)*, bonnet *(GB)*, boot*(GB)*, brake lights, bumper, door handle, exhaust, fender *(US)*, foglights, fuel cap, headlights, hood *(US)*, hub cap, indicators, licence/number plate, rear/tail lights, side mirror, sliding roof, sunroof, tires *(US)*, trunk *(US)*, tyres *(GB)*, windscreen *(GB)*, windshield *(US)*, wing mirror, wipers

Which is which?

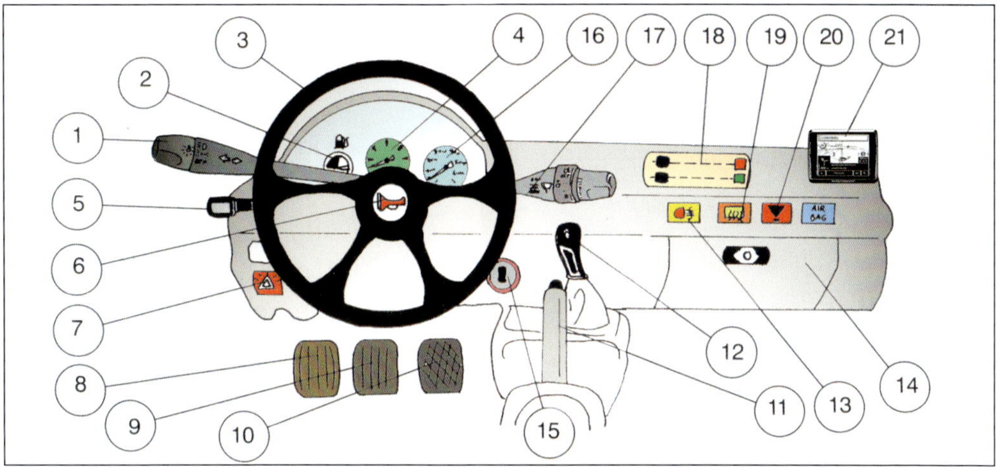

accelerator (pedal), brake (pedal), clutch (pedal), cruise control, fuel gauge, gas (pedal), gear lever, glove compartment, handbrake, hazard warning flashers, heater, horn, indicators, light switch, navigation system, odometer, rear window demister, rev(olution) counter, speed control, speedometer, steering and ignition lock, steering wheel, wipe-wash

Which is which?

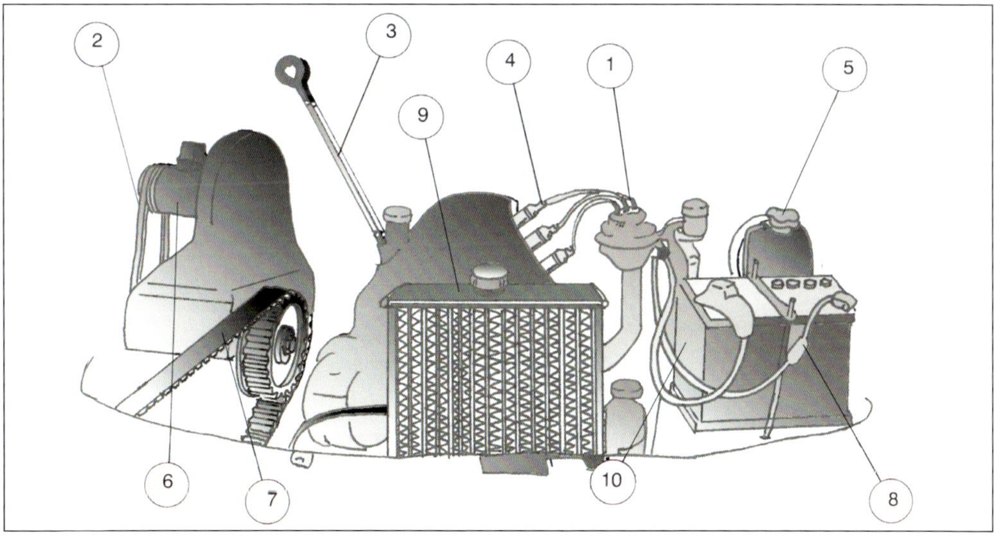

alternator, battery, battery lead, brake fluid reservoir, dipstick, distributor, fan belt, ignition lead, radiator, spark(ing) plug, timing belt (= cambelt)

What functions do they serve?

13.3 Two advertisements

1939 Citroën 11 Légère Traction

Paris-built – Very original throughout – Pilote wheels; 10" front drums; 6V electrics, 1911cc "Perfo" engine/35FA1 carburettor. Standard 3-speed box with high ratio (10 x 31) cwp. Full (bare metal) respray in 2006. Complete engine rebuild in 2007 – inc. white metalling, balancing and lead-free conversion. Stainless steel bumpers and exhaust system. Tidy interior (original head lining). Reliable touring car – will cruise tirelessly all day at 100-110 k.p.h. Current tax disc and MoT to December.

Price: £12,500.00 o.v.n.o.

Contact: ....

FOR SALE

2009 Volkswagen Golf Variant Trendline, reflex silver metallic paint, TDI 4Motion with diesel particulate filter, black roof rails, Xenon headlights, electronic immobilizer, cruise control, air conditioning, daytime driving lights, heated front seats, radio navigation system with DVD for Western Europe, electric windows, park pilot, tyre monitoring display, fully garaged, 18 months MoT, 10,000 miles. Phone 01234-567890.

1. You want to buy a classic car in Britain. Draw up an advertisement for a car magazine

2. Describe your car – and your dream car

3. You have witnessed a hit-and-run accident. Describe the offender's vehicle

13.4 Word square

Find the hidden words from the field "motor car". Go in all directions (horizontal, vertical, diagonal).

Write down the words, indicating where they begin, e.g. 14 C: foglight.

There are 21 words altogether

	A	B	C	D	E	F	G	H	I	J	K	L	M	N	O
1	R	O	I	A	M	M	E	T	E	R	M	D	H	A	T
2	H	E	N	F	E	H	C	B	L	L	I	I	R	S	E
3	S	X	D	U	O	E	O	O	A	B	R	T	V	V	E
4	H	H	I	E	L	A	E	O	B	T	A	Y	I	N	I
5	O	A	C	L	O	D	W	T	G	T	T	R	N	A	M
6	C	U	A	G	C	R	E	R	L	O	D	E	T	V	N
7	K	S	T	A	A	E	C	E	S	T	L	L	R	I	E
8	A	T	O	U	R	S	B	R	A	K	E	A	V	Y	E
9	B	P	R	G	R	T	Z	A	P	T	L	Y	E	R	R
10	S	I	A	E	A	B	L	O	W	E	R	F	A	N	C
11	O	P	M	E	D	E	S	T	A	T	E	C	A	R	S
12	R	E	S	H	I	R	L	F	O	E	L	F	C	A	D
13	B	E	D	A	O	T	Z	I	R	B	R	I	H	L	N
14	E	L	F	O	G	L	I	G	H	T	N	C	C	E	I
15	R	I	D	A	S	H	B	O	A	R	D	F	R	P	W

13.5 The motorbike

Which is which?

brake lever, clutch lever, disk brake, exhaust pipe, footrest, gear pedal, handlebar, mudguard, pillion, saddle, spoke, spring, stand, struts

13.6 Thief strikes in the night

The Boston family from Fareham in southern England had packed their car in order to spend their four-week holiday in their summer house in the Dordogne, France, and left it in the garage. They intended to set off first thing in the morning. At 3.30 a.m. they were alerted by their neighbour, Mr Sharman, who informed them that their garage door was open and their car had been broken into.

Simulate the following dialogues: the Bostons and Mr Sharman, the Bostons and the police, Mr Sharman and the police, Mr and Mrs Boston, the Bostons and their insurance agent

Give a detailed list of all the items in the trunk of their car

13.7 Home-jacking

Part 1 – Definition

Home-jacking is defined as domestic burglary in the course of which the burglar(s) obtain(s) the original car keys by entering the house while the residents are present, usually at night when they are asleep. Often there is a direct contact and/or confrontation between the offender(s) and the victim(s), with the offenders threatening their victim or even resorting to violent behaviour.

Part 2 – A case of home-jacking

Alan Carter (AC) is chief engineer of an international airplane manufacturer. Since the language within the company is English, it is not necessary for him to learn German, and so far he has not had the opportunity to do so. His wife Mary speaks a little German. They have lived in Germany for 18 months, close to Cologne, in a detached house provided by the company. At about 03.00 a.m. Alan Carter hears a slight noise in the house. He immediately thinks it is a burglar. He wakes his wife, but she seems to be under shock, so he calls the police, dialling 110.

Dispatcher Pedro Salaguer (PS), shift leader PHK David Gerk (DG)

PS: Police, what can I do for you?

AC: I think we're being burgled.

PS: Please don't hang up. Give me your name and address.

AC: My name is Alan Carter. I live in 36, Gutenbergstraße, Hürth. It's a detached house.

PS: Please give me your telephone number, just in case we're disconnected.

AC: 719493.

PS: Don't put down the receiver under any circumstances. I want to stay in touch with you. Can you hear anything?

AC: It seems as if a window is being forced open.......... Now I can hear a noise from the hall.

PS: I'm dispatching some patrol cars. Can you lock the door of your bedroom?

AC: Yes, the key is in the lock, from the inside.

PS: OK. Lock the door and pick up the receiver again.

AC: Done. What's going to happen now?

PS: The shift leader, who is in one of the patrol cars, will inform me as soon as he's arrived and the patrol cars are in position. You'll probably see headlights and the lights of torches. That'll be the police. Now please tell me how many people there are in the house.

AC: Just my wife and me.

PS: And I'd also like to know what you look like and what you're wearing, so the officers will be able to recognize you.

AC: I'm wearing striped blue pyjamas and a blue bathrobe. I'm 61 and have full grey hair. My wife is wearing a white robe. She's also 61, and she has blond hair.

PS: Thank you. I'll pass on these descriptions to the officers deployed.

AC: Just a moment, I can hear something...... I think the garage door is being opened...... They're starting the engine – they're stealing my car!

PS: Keep calm and stay where you are, don't go out. Please tell me the licence plate number of your car.

AC: It's a white Audi A 8, the vehicle number plate is BM – AC 1234. The car is only three months old.

PS: I'll put out an alert for the car immediately, and inform the officers deployed. I've just been told that they've arrived. Don't do anything yet, the officers will first search the house and then contact you.

AC: OK, we'll be waiting in the bedroom.

PS: The officers have taken up their positions. I hear that the front door and the garage door are open. Where exactly is your bedroom?

AC: On the first floor, straight ahead from the staircase.

PS: The shift leader will contact you in a minute.

AC: Good, I'll be waiting.

A few minutes later officer Gerk knocks on the bedroom door.

DG: Hello, Mr Carter, this is the police. My name is David Gerk. You can open the door now.

PS: Mr Carter, shift leader Gerk is in front of your bedroom door. Your house has been searched, no intruder has been found. You can open the door now and talk to the officers.

AC: All right, thank you.

Alan Carter opens the door.

DG: Good morning, Mr Carter, we've searched the house and not found any intruder. The alert for your car is out. Please come with me now so we can find out exactly what happened.

They go downstairs and walk to the window beside the front door.

AC: Apparently this window was prised open and somebody climbed in. It's always closed.

DG: The intruder or intruders probably only looked for the car keys.

AC: Obviously I made it quite easy for them. See, I always put the house keys, the car keys and also my wallet on the shelf here, and now everything is gone. What are you going to do now?

DG: That modus operandi isn't a new one on us. We have to deal with cases like this occasionally. Probably one offender watched you and your habits.

AC: That's terrible, what else are we going to be in for?

DG: Possibly it was a planned theft. Such a new car can easily be sold abroad. Good business for professional gangs.

AC: Do you think they'll come back?

DG: You never know, but probably not. The offenders have your car, and they'll certainly assume that you'll upgrade your security measures.

AC: You can be sure of that. What happens next? What about the chances of getting my car back?

DG: If it was stolen by a professional gang, chances are rather slim. We're doing everything possible to find the thieves. The CID department has already been informed, and a CID officer will come to secure traces. There's a nationwide alert out for your car. And my colleagues at headquarters will collate this case with others to find out if we possibly have some intelligence about the offenders.

AC: What do I have to do now?

DG: The officer who secures the traces will give you a phone number. Please call that number tomorrow, not before noon, and arrange for an interview. He'll then have all the intelligence about the case. Also inform your insurance company in the morning. And please also call the vehicle registration office so that your number plate can be blocked. And talk to the CID officer about all other possible measures.

AC: Is there anything else I should do?

DG: No, that should be everything – except, you might pay a visit to our information department. There they'll advise you on how to better secure your home. Perhaps you might be able to get some sleep now.

AC: That'll be rather difficult. But many thanks for your instant help.

Part 3 – Home-jacker's arrest

The search for the car is successful soon after the alert went out. The car is detected close to the Belgian border. After a short pursuit the vehicle is stopped.

At the wheel is Renato Rotondu (RR), a young man from south-eastern Europe, who does not speak German, but his English is fairly good. He is taken to the detective on duty, KHK Willi Dolenc (WD), who questions him.

WD: Good morning. Certainly not a good time for a talk. But you were arrested driving a stolen car, and that's why I have to talk to you now.

RR: But I don't want to talk to you, and I'm not obliged to talk to you, either.

WD: Of course you don't have to. By the way, it would make my job easier, and I could go home at 7.00 a. m. Whether it will help you in your situation remains to be seen. It's for you to decide. First of all, we'll note your personal data, and we'll take your fingerprints. Then we'll see if you've been arrested in Germany before. And afterwards you'll be brought before a magistrate.

RR: You'll do that anyway, it won't matter if I tell you anything or not.

WD: That's very probable, but you can't be sure. That depends on various details, for example why you were arrested, if you have a permanent residential address, and other things. But maybe you've already got some experience in that field.

AC: If I tell you the truth, what will I get? Will you let me go then?

WD: I can't make any promises, as it is up to the state prosecutor to decide.

RR: Well, better to be in remand custody in Germany than in prison at home.

WD: Are you going to tell me now how you got the car?

RR: If you put in a good word for me with the prosecutor.

After the personal data have been noted and RR has been photographed and fingerprinted:

RR: Two men took me to that house tonight. I was to break in, take the car keys from the hall and steal the car from the garage. And that's what I did.

WD: Who are the other two men, and where were they?

RR: I only know them as Nico and Conni. They live in Belgium, and from there they smuggle cars which some others and I steal in Germany. They were nearby to make sure we were not disturbed. Afterwards they immediately went back to Belgium.

WD: Were there any problems during the break-in?

RR: No, it was very easy to force the window, and I was in the house and out again as fast as greased lightning.

WD: Did you expect any resistance?

RR: Sometimes these blokes have the car keys in their pyjamas, and then you have to wrestle with them to get the keys out. But I was on my own and had been told not to take any risks.

WD: What happened then?

RR: The house was quiet. Everybody was fast asleep. I grabbed the keys and left. The garage door creaked a little. But that wasn't a problem. I drove the car out of the garage, and was off in a second.

WD: How did you know where the keys were?

RR: They are always on the shelf in the hall, in most cases beside the telephone. And very often the wallet is beside it. But I didn't take it.

WD: How did you know that the owner of the house has such a car?

RR: That isn't difficult to find out. Sometimes we get the information from a garage, sometimes we watch a car at a petrol station and follow it to the house. It all depends on whether the car is a model which can easily be stolen and sold.

True or not true?	true	not true
1. The Carters' house is connected to their neighbours'.		
2. The dispatcher asks Mr Carter for his phone number to check him out.		
3. He asks him not to put the phone down.		
4. Mr Carter gives a description of the clothes he and his wife are wearing to the shift leader.		
5. Mr Carter is afraid that his car is being stolen when he sees the lights.		
6. The bedroom door is opened by Mr Gerk, the shift leader.		
7. The burglar must have climbed through a window to enter the house.		
8. The keys and wallet were easy to grab for an intruder.		
9. PHK Gerk thinks that the chances to get the car back are pretty good.		
10. PHK Gerk promises to check whether the police have more intelligence about the thieves.		
11. There is nothing an owner has to do after his vehicle has been stolen.		
12. The stolen vehicle was found and the driver arrested after a short chase.		
13. KHK Dolenc agrees that Mr Rotondu is not required by law to make any statement.		
14. Mr Rotondu was told to break into the house and steal the car keys.		
15. Two other criminals watched the burglary and then left for Belgium.		
16. Mr Rotondu did not take any risks as he was working alone.		
17. The theft had been carefully planned.		

13.8 Revision: questions

The car of a Canadian couple was broken into at Wolfslake-Ost motorway services in Brandenburg. You are at the scene of the crime and interview the tourists. Translate the questions and give the corresponding answers

War das Fahrzeug abgeschlossen?	Was the .....
Erinnern Sie sich, wo Sie die Kamera hingelegt haben?	Do you .....
Wo war Ihre Geldbörse?	Where was .....
Vermisst Ihre Frau etwas aus ihrer Tasche?	Does .....
Haben Sie etwas Verdächtiges bemerkt?	Did you .....
Gibt es Zeugen?	Are .....
Wie lange haben Sie hier Pause gemacht?	How long did .....
Wohin wollen Sie fahren?	Where do .....
Haben Sie dort eine Adresse?	Do you .....
Wollen Sie Anzeige erstatten?	Do you .....
Können Sie uns zur Polizeiautobahnstation folgen?	Can you .....
Würden Sie hier bitte unterschreiben?	Would you .....

13.9 Car theft – some statistics

Stolen cars in Germany

Year	Stolen cars	Not recovered
1996	170,000	9,000
1997	138,000	9,000
1998	112,000	9,000
1999	93,000	8,000
2000	83,000	7,000
2001	75,000	7,000
2002	70,000	7,000
2003	63,000	7,000
2004	58,000	7,000
2005	50,000	6,000

1. **What do you make of the above statistics?**
2. **How does modern technology (e.g. immobilizers) fit in?**
3. **Find out about the latest theft statistics. Use the media and the Internet**

13.10 The definite article

Der bestimmte Artikel *the* wird verwendet

vor Nomen, die eine einzigartige Sache bezeichnen

the earth, the sun, the moon, the sky

vor Nomen, die vorher bereits erwähnt wurden

A woman was run over by a sports car last night; she was killed, but the car was not damaged.

vor näher bezeichneten Nomen

the biscuit-coloured estate car, the man in the street, the driver of the double-decker bus

vor Nomen, deren Bezug eindeutig ist

in the sitting room, under the pillow, the postman

vor Komparativen und Superlativen

the better of the two, the best thing to do

vor Nomen, die eine Gattung oder einen Typ bezeichnen

The car has changed the world. The motorist will be milked again.

vor vielen geographischen Namen

the Rhine, the Alps, the North Sea, The Hague, the United States

Der bestimmte Artikel entfällt

vor den meisten Länder- und Ortsnamen sowie Straßennamen

Austria, Poland, Switzerland, London, Rome, in Garden Street, in Goethestrasse, in Marktplatz, in Victoria Square

vor Ortsangaben, die nicht näher konkretisiert werden

at home, in bed, in court, at school, at work

13.11 Fill-in exercise

Fill in the definite article where necessary

1. .... Mrs Green came to report a theft. – Do you mean .... Mrs Green who works in the post office?
2. The policeman tried to help .... poor Jack.
3. How can we help .... poor man?
4. Our neighbours lived in .... Turkey for ten years. Now they are back.

5. In which part of .... France do they live? – In .... Normandy or on .... Côte d'Azur?
6. . ... USA is one of the great world powers.
7. .... Zugspitze is the highest mountain in .... Bavarian Alps.
8. .... Danube rises in .... Black Forest and flows into .... Black Sea.
9. .... Kennedy Airport is New York's principal airport for international flights.
10. We walked along .... 42nd Street and .... Broadway until we came to .... Times Square.

13.12 Useful phrases

Fragen Sie(,)

1. – wann die Familie den Diebstahl bemerkt hat.

   ....

2. – wann das Auto im Parkhaus abgestellt wurde.

   ....

3. – nach Fabrikat, Modell, Farbe und Baujahr des gestohlenen Fahrzeugs.

   ....

4. – nach besonderen Merkmalen des Fahrzeugs.

   ....

5. – welche Gegenstände sich in dem Fahrzeug befanden.

   ....

6. – ob der Wagen vollgetankt war.

   ....

7. – ob Jugendliche oder verdächtige Personen im Parkhaus gesehen wurden.

   ....

8. – ob der Wagen werksseitig mit einer Wegfahrsperre ausgerüstet ist.

   ....

9. – nach der Art der Versicherung (Haftpflicht, Teilkasko, Vollkasko).

   ....

10. – ob Sie anderweitig behilflich sein können (Weiterreise, Heimreise, Unterkunft, Kontakt mit Versicherung usw.).

   ....

13.13 Key words and phrases

classic car – force open – home-jacking – intruder – precaution – rightful owner – roof rails – theft – torch – vintage car – ..... and all the words of 13. 2 and 13.5

Unit 14 Shoplifters, pickpockets, thieves, description of persons

This unit deals with

- shoplifting and shoplifters
- pickpockets and thieves
- lost and stolen documents
- the description of persons and
- the indefinite article.

14.1 Shoplifting

In 2006, 428,553 cases of shoplifting were reported in Germany, which means a decrease of 5.4 % compared to 2005. 92.8 % of the shoplifting cases were cleared up. The high clear-up rate is due to the fact that the shoplifters are usually detained by staff until the police arrive and charges are preferred. On the other hand, it must be assumed that the number of undetected cases is pretty high.

Shoplifting would not be detected at all – and thus would not appear in the crime statistics – if store detectives and other personnel weren't so attentive. Many shoplifters are children who have not yet reached the age of criminal responsibility and can therefore not be prosecuted at all, or youths who can only partly be held responsible.

There is also a connection between juvenile shoplifters and truancy; often youths go shoplifting at times when they should be at school.

14.2 Shoplifters

FIll in the right word; choose from the following:

beggar, foreigner, fraud, illiterate, impostor, largest, locking, mirrors, offence, posing, plain-clothes, supermarket, theft

A shoplifter is a person who steals goods from a retail outlet while .... as a customer. In many countries it is a specific ...., whereas in other countries, for example in Germany and in the United Kingdom, it falls into the category of ...., i.e. a crime.

There is no typical shoplifter: he or she may be young or old, male or female, rich or poor, ... or have a university degree, a .... or a citizen of the country concerned, an atheist or a religious person. However, children and young people tend to be the .... group of shoplifters.

Of course, shops try to fight shoplifting, for example by employing .... detectives and security guards, by .... away expensive goods like jewellery, expensive liquor and perfumes in cabinets, by using convex ...., or by special staff training. Nevertheless, shoplifters have developed many techniques to steal goods.

14.3 Businessman and shoplifters

Heinz Schmitz is a businessman. For more than 30 years he has been running a sports goods and sportswear shop in the centre of Wittlich. He has one full-time and two part-time employees, and his wife helps out whenever she can. He is interviewed by a group of police trainees.

Here are his answers. What questions do they ask?

Answer 1

First of all I must tell you that I can only talk about my experience, so my answers are certainly not representative of the retail trade in general. And I must also tell you that my shop is not so large that I can afford sophisticated prevention measures like surveillance cameras or electronic tags for my goods.

Answer 2

Not really, but I have to "spot" possible shoplifters as soon as they enter my shop, and I have to keep an eye on them all the time. And I lock away expensive small items like sports and stop watches or darts.

Answer 3

The preferred objects are sportswear of all kinds, including shoes, with brand names which are very popular among young people, and things which can be hidden easily. Shoplifters do not take large items like exercise cycles or Nordic Walking sticks.

Answer 4

They nearly always come in groups, and they watch from outside to see how many staff are inside. If I'm alone or only one of my staff is with me, and it is very busy, they will enter, one of them will try to distract me, for example by asking some rather stupid questions about a pair of soccer boots, and one of the others will try to steal an article. They are very active on special occasions like open Sundays, when we are very, very busy. Then it's almost impossible for me and my staff to watch everything.

Answer 5

Most of them are between 10 and 20, many still go to school. And there are many unemployed persons, and, I must say, many of migrant backgrounds.

Answer 6

Well, often they do not steal because they really need the T-shirt or jacket or scarf with the logo of one of the first division soccer clubs, it's rather a test of courage for them.

Answer 7

In former times the youngsters were usually crestfallen, and, of course, promised never to do it again and I often let them off with a stern warning. Nowadays they are quite "cool", they don't seem to be concerned. They couldn't care less and think they can get away with it.

And when they are minors and I call their parents, the parents don't even bother to show up here and pick their children up. In other words, they aren't interested in their children's misdemeanours. I regard that as an open invitation to steal again. And it's a proven fact that many criminal careers start with petty offences like shoplifting.

Answer 8

Well, when I call them, it usually takes a very long time until they arrive. And that's very bad for me, because during that time I have to close my shop as I cannot hold a shop-lifter and serve other clients at the same time. So often I just don't call them and don't prefer charges against a shoplifter.

Answer 9

The younger ones don't have their ID cards on them, and the older ones just refuse to show me theirs. And when they want to leave the shop and I stop them by force, I run the risk that they or their parents sue me for having "injured" them.

Answer 10

To put it very bluntly: the government does next to nothing to protect shopkeepers.

1. **How should shoplifters be punished?**

2. **Have you ever come across cases of shoplifting?**

14.4 Some hints to prevent shoplifting

Watch out for:

- packages, rucksacks, bags, purses; sometimes they have hidden compartments or false bottoms
- newspapers or magazines; they are sometimes used to conceal small or flat items
- bulky clothes; pants, coats; they are often used to conceal stolen goods of all kinds
- groups of customers; do not get distracted by them
- nervous people or anyone loitering or lingering in remote areas of the store.

14.5 Role play

Simulate various situations of shoplifting. Include not only a store detective and a police officer, but also sales staff and other customers as well as the parents of a minor who have come to the store after their daughter/son has been caught.

14.6 Intention or mistake?

Motorists fill their tank and drive away without paying

Stealing fuel at petrol stations is a "modern" offence. The inhibition threshold is quite low. Ever-rising fuel prices are a motive to leave a petrol station without having paid for the fuel.

Fuel stations have installed surveillance cameras to monitor the filling islands and the interior of the shop. However, fuel thieves use false, forged or covered number plates, or have no number plates at all. The typical fuel thief avoids looking into the camera, his main aim is not to be recognized. Driving on after the tank has been filled is no problem at all. The petrol station personnel cannot describe the offender(s) and are only able to give some vague information about the vehicle concerned. How could they, with the large number of customers at the filling islands and in the shop? It's just not possible to receive payment for fuel, to sell goods from the shop and to monitor the filling islands at the same time. Thus petrol station operators lose a lot of money every month, and no insurance company covers these losses.

But there are also motorists who actually forget to pay their bill, either because they have simply forgotten to do so, or because they think one of their passengers has paid. On motorways these motorists are easy to find as they just continue their journey; they don't try to get away. They are not really offenders. Usually they are surprised and embarrassed, and, of course, they immediately pay their bill. Sometimes they return to the petrol station after they have realized that they drove off without payment.

1. **Why is the number of fuel thefts at filling stations on the increase?**

2. **How do filling stations protect themselves?**

3. **How do fuel thieves try to "protect" themselves?**

4. **Why is it difficult for the personnel to watch cars and drivers?**

5. **Why is it easy to find drivers on the motorway who were just distracted and "forgot" to pay?**

6. **Have you ever forgotten to pay your fuel bill?**

14.7 Theft of fuel?

Flann Shannon (FS), his brother Patrick (PS) and their friend Darragh Donegal (DD) from Tullamore in Ireland are exploring Germany in their motorhome. Right now they are travelling southbound on the A7 and are stopping at the Aalbeck-West services to refuel. PK Asmus Bergen (AB) and PHM Olaf Marn (OM) of the Neumünster motorway police are on patrol.

FS: Here, at this island there's diesel. I'm going to fill up.

DD: Patrick and I are going to the shop. We'll have a look at what they've got.

FS: Then you can also pay for the fuel.

While Flann Shannon is filling up the tank, his companions are looking around in the shop; they pick up some souvenirs, look at them and put them back, but then take some bottles with soft drinks and go to the checkout. Some other customers are in front of them, so Darragh Donegal decides spontaneously to take a road map from the shelf. In the meantime, Flann Shannon has finished filling up and gets into the car, waiting for his companions. They have paid for their shopping and also get into the motorhome.

FS: All right, let's go on. Are all the doors closed?

They've hardly left when the cashier in the shop notices that the bill at island 4 hasn't been paid yet, but there is no vehicle any more. She immediately calls her colleague Tine Geest (TG), who looks at the video of the surveillance camera and calls the motorway police.

TG: Tine Geest of Aalbeck-West services. About seven minutes ago somebody filled his tank and left. I've had a look at the CCTV tape. It's a Ford Transit. A motorhome. Foreign number plates 08OY791. My colleague says that there were two men in the shop who spoke English..... No, she doesn't have an exact description. Could you send somebody?..... Thank you.

Control asks the patrol car crew to look out for the motorhome. About 25 minutes later the wanted vehicle is spotted and directed to the Bimöhlen rest area.

OM: Good afternoon. Motorway police. We've been looking for you. About half an hour ago you stopped at the Aalbeck services and filled up your tank. Correct?

FS: Yes, but what's the problem?

OM: You didn't pay for the fuel.

FS: But I told my brother to pay. He was in the shop with our friend.

PS: Oh God! You know, we bought a few things there, and looked at some other items. And then we paid. But I didn't think of the fuel. Darragh, I think we've got a problem now.

DD: We are very sorry. What's going to happen now?

FS: That's really embarrassing. Sorry. Of course, we want to pay for the fuel.

AB: According to German law, you've committed a crime. We'll have to press charges. Can I have your passports, please?

After he has got the passports, he talks to his colleague at the station and asks him to contact the prosecutor's office to get instructions about bail.

AB: First, we're going back to the service station, where you can pay for the fuel. Then I'll tell you how we're going to proceed. Please follow us.

FS: Of course. We won't cause any problem.

At the service station the officers and the three Irishmen enter the shop.

TG: These two were at the checkout. I don't know the third person.

They continue to talk in the operator's office. AD writes down the personal data, addresses and passport numbers. His colleague OM checks them with control. There are no entries for the three Irishmen.

FS: We are sorry. It was just a mistake. We've got enough money on us, and we can withdraw money at an ATM any time. Here, have a look at my purse! There's more than € 300, and the bill amounts to € 87. Could I pay, please?

The prosecutor in charge has decided that charges have to be preferred, and that the exact addresses of the three Irishmen have to be established, but bail can be waived if the statements are trustworthy.

The officers inform and interview the Irishmen, fill in all the necessary forms by hand and note that the amount of the bill has been paid. The addresses are substantiated by other documents. The officers explain the further procedure. The operator is not interested in any kind of prosecution and accepts the Irishmen's excuse. Afterwards all of them have a cup of coffee together.

FS: We're going to continue our journey. Thanks a lot for your understanding.

PS and DD: Goodbye. Thank you very much.

AB: Have a nice trip and enjoy your stay in Germany.

Do you think it was really necessary to prefer charges against the three Irishmen?

14.8 Pickpockets

Picking other people's wallets is not "the", but one of the oldest crimes in the world. Pickpockets operate worldwide, especially in places where many people are to be found, for example at train or underground stations or at mass events, like Olympic Games, soccer championships or carnival processions, and in tourist areas, as tourists often carry substantial sums of money and often are not familiar with the place and don't speak the language. A skilled pickpocket can "earn" quite a lot of money within a short time, and does not run the risk of being severely punished in case he/she is caught.

Pickpockets often work in teams of two or three and use many techniques to rob their victims. Probably the most frequent method is diverting someone's attention. One person does so, for example by suddenly stopping in front of the victim who is walking behind him so that the victim bumps into him. At that moment the second pickpocket, who is walking behind the victim, steals the wallet and quickly hands it to the third person who walks away with it.

As pickpockets don't know where people carry their wallets, they use another trick. In a crowded underground train, for example, one pickpocket shouts loudly: "Somebody has just stolen my wallet!" Most of the people around him automatically make sure their wallet is still there, so that the pickpocket's accomplices know exactly where the other passengers keep their money, and the gang can steal a wallet or two a few minutes later.

Read the article above and choose the most suitable heading:

A special incident – Successful schemes – How to make money – How to find wallets – Popular places for pickpockets

14.9 Victim of a professional team of pickpockets

Köln Hauptbahnhof © Raimond Speakking/Wikimedia Commons/CC-BY-SA-3.0 & GDFL

My wife and I were standing on platform 6 at Cologne main station, together with many other travellers. We were all waiting for the ICE from Berlin that would take us to Munich. It was a hot summer day, nevertheless each of us was wearing a light jacket, not because it was not warm enough, but because we didn't want to carry it.

I noticed two men on the platform, both about 30 years old, apparently of southern European origin. Looking back, I clearly remember them: one was wearing rather shabby jeans, but a brand-new jacket, the other one a long coat, despite the heat. He was reading a newspaper. They did not have any luggage, and they pretended not to know each other. The man in the jacket was pacing up and down the platform, sometimes in front of me, sometimes behind me. And I remember that once he looked at the other man who slightly nodded his head. The pickpockets had found their victim: me. But I didn't give a thought about what would happen a few minutes later.

My jacket has an inside pocket which can be closed with a zip, and I was thinking of taking my purse out of the back pocket of my trousers and put it in there, as I had often done before. However, for some reason I decided against it that day.

The train arrived, many people got off, and then everybody wanted to enter at the same time. My wife was in front of me, I followed her, and we managed to enter the carriage. I was carrying our two small travel bags. The man in the coat was ahead of me; suddenly he turned around and grabbed my travel bags as if he wanted to help me carry them. I told him to stop that. He did not speak a word, just looked at me, and let go of the bags because for a few seconds nobody was able to move on. And when we were able to proceed again towards our seats, he grabbed my bags again. Rather angrily, I told him again to stop it, and he let go of my bags. When sitting down at our reserved seats about a minute later, I noticed that my purse wasn't in my back pocket any more. I thought I might have lost it and walked back to the entrance, looking for it, but, of course, I couldn't find it.

The purse contained, among other things, not only a considerable amount in cash, but also my bank card, my credit card, my identity card, my driving licence and my IPA membership card.

The train departed. My first thought was to have my credit card and my bank card stopped. I still didn't think that I had been robbed, I only wanted to make sure that nobody could withdraw money with one of my cards. So I went to find someone of the train staff. The lady was very helpful. She asked me if I had seen any children on the platform as there were many cases of under-age pickpockets operating in Cologne station, but I hadn't. She gave me her mobile phone (I didn't have one at the time) so that I could have my bank card and my credit card stopped immediately. She had the respective numbers saved. Making the phone calls was quite complicated as I did not reach human beings but machines, and because of the noise of the train and also the fact that we were passing several tunnels where communication was not possible, but I finally managed.

I walked back to my seat, talked to my wife, and slowly wound down. And then I suddenly remembered the two men on the platform. So I contacted the lady again, and I phoned her colleagues at Cologne station and described the two men, but, of course, they were not there any more.

Four and a half hours later we arrived in Munich, and I walked into the Federal Police station where I reported the theft and gave all the details. However, the young female officer was not too optimistic that I would get my purse back. Nor was I.

Four days later we were back home. The thought of all the paperwork necessary to get a new driving licence and a new ID card was dreadful. Getting a new driving licence was most important as we were going to the USA a few weeks later, and I would need the licence to hire a car there. However, I was lucky: there was an e-mail message from a post office in Vienna, Austria. All the contents of my purse, except the cash, had been found in a letterbox there. I called the post office, and a few days later I got my papers back. I was quite happy as there was no need any more to get a new ID card and driving licence.

The envelope also contained a number of credit card receipts and the address of a man in Vienna. I phoned him, and yes, his wallet had been stolen on a train from Budapest to Vienna a few days before, apparently by the same gang.

About four months later, I was invited to have a look at the rogues' gallery of pickpockets at Cologne police headquarters, but there were, of course, no photographs of those two men; in fact, all the pickpockets registered there were minors.

What about my feelings? At first I was filled with anger, I could have killed those two men. But gradually I realized that I had acted very carelessly by leaving my purse in the back pocket of my trousers. So, in future I'll be much more careful not only when travelling by train but every time when I go to crowded places. One of my precautionary measures will be to have my purse hidden in some inside pocket and put a dummy purse in my back pocket. If a pickpocket steals it, it will contain nothing but a short note: "See, I'm smarter than you!"

1. Questions

1. Where were the victim and his wife going to?
2. What can you tell about their clothes?
3. Why did the victim notice the two men?
4. What should the victim have done to prevent possible theft?
5. What did one of the pickpockets do to divert his attention?
6. Was it easy to stop the various cards?
7. What did the victim do as soon as he arrived in Munich?
8. Why was he lucky when we think of his cards?
9. How did he get his ID and his driving licence back?
10. What are we told about children at Cologne Central Station?
11. What precautionary measure will the writer take in future?

2. Find the words in the text whose definitions are given here

1. in poor condition through long use ....
2. suitcases and/or bags used when travelling ....
3. leave, especially when starting a journey ....
4. all the people employed by an organization ....
5. an artificial underground passage ....
6. small pouch used for carrying money ....
7. flat paper container with a sealable flap ....
8. collection of photographs of known criminals ....
9. model or replica of a human being or object ....

14.10 Stolen papers and documents

In 1947, my father was going by train from Munich to Hanover. He was from the Sudetenland. He had survived WW II, and he had found his wife and children, who had had to leave their home region and now lived in Bavaria, near Munich. 39 years old, he was going to Hanover to apply for a job. He found a seat in a crowded compartment of the train, and put his small suitcase on the floor between his legs. The suitcase contained, apart from some clothes, all his papers, his university degree certificates from the universities of Prague and Brno, and many documents of the firm he had owned before he was drafted early in 1941.

In those days, the steam trains were rather slow, and at about midnight everybody in the compartment was fast asleep. Some time in the early morning father woke up with a start and found that his suitcase had gone. Somebody had stolen it.

Can you imagine all the paperwork that followed? There were no photocopies at that time. It took father more than three years to get all the statements from witnesses – all of whom had to leave the Sudetenland as well – to verify that he really had a university degree, that he really had owned a firm. At the time no evidence could be obtained from the Czech authorities.

Without any papers he didn't get the job in Hanover, and he had to walk and hitch-hike back to Bavaria as he did not have the money for a train ticket.

14.11 Stopping bank and credit cards as well as access to bank accounts, obtaining substitute documents

Clifford Stevens (CS) and his wife Holly (HS) live in Nassau, capital of the Bahamas. Both are high-ranking officials at the office of the British Governor General. The University of Mannheim has invited them to give some talks to representatives of the Rhine-Neckar metropolitan area. They are staying in a hotel in the centre of Mannheim. From there it is only a short walk to the Elector's Palace, which now houses the university. The "Planken" shopping mile is also quite close. From Paradeplatz towards the old water tower of 1889, this former boulevard has been pedestrianised, and there are many posh shops and cafés. The whole town centre with the "Nationaltheater", the town houses, fountains and squares is considered to be Germany`s largest art deco area.

All this prompts the Stevenses to discover the town on foot. They enjoy the day, enter shops and boutiques, admire the architecture and watch the people. They decide to sit in a nice open-air café. In the early evening they get back to their hotel. Only now does Holly Stevens notice that her small shoulder bag is missing. After a moment of shock, she remembers exactly that she paid with her credit card in a boutique. She had put her shoulder bag on a small table to take her purse out of it, in which she also carried her credit card. When paying, she had signed the receipt, taken the bag and just put her purse into her pocket without thinking of her shoulder bag.

Clifford Stevens had not noticed that, as he had left the shop and waited for his wife outside in the busy pedestrian precinct. But now he decides immediately to contact reception. As they have the receipt slip, the clerk can phone the boutique, but the staff there cannot find a shoulder bag. The clerk calls a taxi for the Stevenses who want to go back to the shop to find out for themselves. HS had her passport and a small purse in her shoulder bag, and in her purse were two more credit cards. She does not worry about the other items in her purse.

Very disappointed that the search in the shop ended without any result, the couple ask where the nearest police station is. The boutique staff inform them about the police station within the premises of Mannheim police headquarters in square L 6, 1. Mannheim is known as the "squares town", as the town centre is divided into equal squares, and the streets are named accordingly. As it is not far, they walk there.

PK Eckhard Petermann (EP) is in charge of the case.

EP: And you're sure that it was in this boutique? Not in a café or another shop?

Holly Stevens is absolutely certain.

HS: No, it wasn't elsewhere. It happened in the boutique.

EP: Right, I'll make a note of your statement. I'll make out a charge, and I regard it as a case of appropriation of a find. Of course, it might be that somebody found your bag and handed it in. We don't know where the potential finder lives. Perhaps this person goes directly to the lost property office or the city administration. Apart from that we have several police stations. I'll check with the city centre police station as it is located close to the pedestrian area. Just a moment, please.

A short time later.

EP: My colleagues haven't found a bag. It is much more probable that your bag was taken because the thief thought it contained cash. He will go through its contents, take out money and valuable objects, and then throw it away. To make sure, a police crew will have a look at the litter bins in the surroundings. But now let's start the paperwork. Please tell me, giving as many details as possible, …

A short time later.

EP: I'll have your passport and credit cards put on the wanted list. Thus we can make sure, in case of a check or when the documents are found, that we know who they belong to. It would be very helpful if I could have all the details.

Clifford Stevens interrupts him.

CS: Oh, that's no problem at all. I've made copies of our passports, they are in the hotel with our other things. I've also noted down the numbers of our credit cards. I always take these precautionary measures when I travel. I'll call you immediately.

EP: That's very good. But you don't have to call. I'll take you to your hotel afterwards and also make copies for our files, and write down everything.

After all the paperwork has been completed and all documents are ready to be signed, PK Petermann checks with the Internet.

EP: Here you are, this is a certificate about the charge; it contains, among other things, the address of our police station and the docket number. With this paper you can apply for an emergency passport. I don't think that you can leave Germany and enter the Bahamas with it. You'll probably need an official letter from your embassy. I've just checked on the Internet. I'll write down the addresses for you. There is an honorary consul for the Bahamas in Germany, Flottenstraße 14-20, 13407 Berlin. And the nearest Bahamian Embassy is in Great Britain, 10, Chesterfield Street, London W1J 5J1.

CS: Thank you. I know the Chesterfield phone number. I'll call there as soon as possible. And they can probably tell me how I can stop the credit cards and my bank account. And my wife will contact our bank at home immediately.

EP: In Germany we have the emergency number 116 116. When calling it, you can have various electronic media stopped, credit cards included. However, this only applies for accounts in Germany. They need to know the numbers of the respective credit cards and bank accounts, and also the names and addresses of the banks concerned. Do you have something like that in the Bahamas?

CS: I don't know. But we'll check that, too. The sooner the bank account is closed, the sooner one can prevent the abuse of credit cards.

PK Petermann also notes how long the Stevenses will stay in Mannheim. In case the passport and the credit cards are handed in, or found by the patrol, they will be taken to the hotel, otherwise they will be sent to the honorary consul or the embassy. The police and the Stevenses agree to inform each other. Clifford Stevens is even thinking of extending his stay in Mannheim.

14.12 Police description of a missing person

Part 1

Sarah Beckford was last seen leaving the coffee shop in Volusia Mall in Sanford, Florida, in the afternoon of June 17, 2009. She has not been seen or heard of since.

She is described as follows: height: 165 cm, weight: approximately 70 kg, hair: grey, short, curly,

complexion: pale, colour of eyes: brown, short-sighted, wearing glasses, distinctive mark: scar on right knee. She was wearing a light summer dress and sandals. The 74-year-old is a diabetic and has to take medication daily.

Anyone who has any information as to the whereabouts of Sarah Beckford please call your police station.

After his shift PC Turner tells his wife about the wanted person. She asks him:

How tall is she? How much does she weigh? .....

Part 2

Wanted by the FBI – Unknown bank robber

Description

Age:	25 to 30 years old	Build:	medium
Sex:	male	Hair:	dark brown
Height:	6'0" to 6'2"	Eyes:	unknown
Weight:	200 to 210 pounds	Race:	Caucasian

The unknown male suspect is wanted in connection with a robbery of the Citibank in Macomb, Illinois, on December 13, 2009. Three people were shot during the robbery, one of whom died immediately. The suspect entered the bank and told the employees that he was a member of the federal police checking the security system of the bank. After being shown the bank's security and alarms, he pulled a weapon and ordered one of the employees to get him money. One bank employee was shot and killed, while two customers were shot and survived. After receiving the money, the suspect escaped.

He was wearing a dark blue, nylon jacket with white "police" letters on the sleeves and the back. He also wore dark jeans and stud earrings in both of his ears.

14.13 Vocabulary exercise

Which word does not belong? Cross it out and write the correct word in the last column

ankle	~~facial hair~~	shin	leg	*knee*
heavy	foot	heel	sole	
pupil	eyelid	bald	eyelashes	
hand	palm	finger	blond	
cheek	chin	toe	face	
eyebrow	thumb	moustache	beard	
stocky	stout	slim	wrist	
knee	short	straight	curly	
fair	brunette	forehead	dark	
elbow	eye	forearm	arm	

14.14 Description of a person – vocabulary

Persons who are wanted or missing or found dead without any identification papers can often be traced with the help of a description or a composite picture.

Name
first name(s), family name(s), nickname(s), alias(es), maiden name, name at birth

Age
date of birth, either exact or approximate, also place of birth

Occupation
present, past, possible, present and/or former employer(s)

Appearance

height	exact, approximate
build	thin, slim, well built, stout, corpulent, heavy, obese
head	large, small, narrow, square
face	round, oval, long, wrinkled, flabby, fat, high cheekbones
complexion	fresh, ruddy, pale, fair, sallow, blotchy, pimply, uses cosmetics
hair	colour, turning grey, bald, straight, wavy, curly, (un)parted, long, short, bleached, dyed, greasy, unkempt, wears wig/toupee, sideburns
hair on face	size, shape and colour of beard or moustache
forehead	high, low, broad, narrow, wrinkled, bulging, receding
eyebrows	colour, thick, thin, bushy, meet in centre, arched, plucked, pencilled, sparse
eyes	colour, red-rimmed, long lashes, glass eye (colour), wears glasses (type, colour) habitually or for reading, sunglasses
nose	large, small, long, short, hooked, broken, broad base, wide/narrow nostrils
mouth	large, small
lips	thick, thin, well shaped, protruding upper/lower lips
teeth	clean, discoloured, decayed, irregular, dentures, implants, fillings, gold-crowned, gaps
chin	dimpled, cleft, double, round, protruding, receding
ears	large, small, small/large lobes
hands	long, short, large, small, long/short fingers, well kept, rough, callous
fingernails	long, short, bitten, manicured, varnished (colour)

Voice and language
deep, high-pitched, loud, melodious, effeminate, affected, lisp, stammer or other impediment, difficulty in pronouncing certain words or letters, accent, dialect, foreign language(s)

Distinctive marks
scars, birthmarks, moles, freckles, deformities, colour(s) and picture(s) of tattoos, piercing(s)

Characteristics and habits
drinking – beer, wine, spirits, brand(s) of drinks, places used
smoking – cigarettes, cigars, pipe, brand(s) of cigarettes/cigars/tobacco
drugs – hashish, marihuana, opium, heroin, ecstasy, LSD
associates – male/female, members of certain groups, nationality, prostitutes
places – pubs, bars, restaurants, night clubs

Dress
preference for certain types of clothing

14.15 Clothing

belt	blouse	boot	bra(ssiere)	braces	briefs
button	cap	cardigan	chemise	coat	collar
costume	dress	hat	hood	jacket	jumper
leggings	overall	panties	pants	pantyhose	pocket
pullover	rain-cape	shirt	shorts	skirt	slacks
sleeve	slip	socks	stockings	suit	suspenders
sweater	tie	trousers	underclothes	underwear	vest
wind jacket	zip, zipper (*US*)				

What do people wear?
in warm weather
in cold weather
on the job
for sports

14.16 Exercises and role play

1. **Together with other English-speaking tourists an elderly British gentleman is standing in front of the palace in Karlsruhe. The lady next to him is jostled by two youngsters. She makes a big fuss and during this time the man's wallet is taken from his hip pocket. As all his money as well as his credit cards are missing, he reports the incident at the nearest police station. He is asked to give a precise description of the youngsters.**

2. **One student describes a person all the others know, but he does not tell the name. The student who first recognizes the person concerned gets a reward. The person might be a sportsman, a film star, the home secretary or another politician, etc.**

3. **Imagine you are offered a job as an undercover agent. How would you change your appearance and clothing?**

4. **Have one of your fellow students sit/stand in front of the class. Describe him/her. Fill in the form used in your jurisdiction**

14.17 The indefinite article

Der unbestimmte Artikel hat zwei Formen

a vor Konsonanten und konsonantisch anlautenden Vokalen
a bus, a street; a European, a uniform

an vor Vokalen und vokalisch anlautenden Konsonanten sowie vor stummen h

an idea, an order; an SOS, an "x"; an hour

Der unbestimmte Artikel *a/an* wird gebraucht vor

Singularformen zählbarer Nomen *a motorbike, an answer*

Mengenangaben *a couple, a dozen, a great deal of, a little, four times a day*

Nomen, die eine Gruppenzugehörigkeit (einschl. Beruf) anzeigen
a teacher, an instructor

Namen nicht weiter bekannter Personen *a Mrs Brown*

Der unbestimmte Artikel wird nachgestellt bei

such, many, what, half, quite
such a nuisance, many a mile, what a surprise, half a litre, quite a lot of work

14.18 Fill-in exercise

Fill in the indefinite article where necessary

John is .... police inspector. He works as .... detective with the Kent Constabulary and is based in Folkestone. Folkestone is .... small town and also the English terminal of the Eurotunnel. This tunnel is .... great technological achievement. Strictly speaking, there are three tunnels, two main tunnels for the trains and .... service tunnel, which is used in case of .... emergency. The shuttle trains run up to six times .... hour during peak times. There is .... locomotive at either end of the train, and each train has .... crew of eight: .... driver, ... chef de train (stationed in the rear locomotive), and six patrolling crew members. .... trip from .... platform to .... platform takes 35 minutes, and .... ticket costs about the same as .... ferry ticket.

14.19 Useful phrases

Fragen/Sagen Sie einen/einem Ladendieb,

1. – dass Sie gesehen haben, wie er etwas in seinem Mantel versteckt hat.

2. – ob er diese Ware bezahlt hat.

3. – dass Sie gerne die Quittung für diese Ware sehen möchten.

4. – ob er bereit ist, seine Taschen zu leeren.

5. – ob er einer Durchsuchung zustimmt.

6. – ob Sie die Polizei rufen sollen.

7. – ob er sich ausweisen kann.

8. – ob er sich von einem Anwalt vertreten lassen möchte.

9. – ob er allein oder in Begleitung im Geschäft ist.

10. – dass er zur Sache nichts auszusagen braucht.

14.20 Key words and phrases

appropriation of a find – bank card – fuel theft – lost property office – misdemeanour – pickpocket – prefer/press charges – prosecutor – purse – rogues`gallery – shoplifter – stop a bank/credit card – substitute document – surveillance camera – wallet – and all the words from 14.13, 14.14 and 14.15

Unit 15

Robbery, mugging

This unit deals with

- cases of robbery
- how to interview victims of robbery
- bodily injuries and
- auxiliary verbs.

15.1 Definitions

A person who commits theft using physical force or threatens to use force against a person commits the offence of robbery. If this happens in a public place, it is usually called mugging.

15.2 Some types of robbery

The German equivalent of the word "robbery" is a collective term and is used in many different cases.
Here are some examples of robbery.

Bank robbery

Bank robbers, often armed with real or fake firearms, usually "work" alone, and in most cases they have not planned their offence carefully; the decision to commit the offence was taken, in most cases, only 24 hours before. While the robber might have planned exactly how to enter the bank and what to say there, he often has not planned how to escape. Bank robberies by gangs are very rare; probably they happen more often in TV programmes than in reality.

Robbery in amusement arcades

In many cases, an unaccompanied offender enters an amusement arcade shortly before closing time and forces the employee, usually only one and mostly elderly person, to open the slot machines and hand over the money.

Handbag snatching

A handbag snatcher very quickly grabs and snatches the handbag from the hand or shoulder of a woman. This often happens in isolated areas or at cemeteries, and the assailant is often alone, in many cases under the influence of drugs, and the victims are usually elderly ladies. He commits this crime to finance his drug habit. And in many cases the handbag is found quite close to the scene of the attack, and the only item missing is the amount of cash it contained.

In tourist areas, gangs often do it professionally. Two men on a scooter drive past a strolling tourist, the pillion rider grabs and snatches the handbag and they rush away. As incidents of this nature happened very frequently in the city of Naples, scooters and small motorbikes are now banned from the city centre.

Robbing drunk persons

Frequently a person who is getting drunk in a pub is invited to more drinks, and later robbed in the street of all his cash and other valuables.

Street robbery – mugging

Robbery in public places is mostly committed by youngsters, and usually the offender(s) and the victim(s) belong to the same age group.

In schools the muggers often take the mobile phone or other gadgets from their victims, using force or threatening to use force; in many cases the robbers are under age and cannot be held responsible for their crime.

Robbery in homes

In most cases the robber(s) and the victim(s) know each other.

According to police statistics, women very seldom commit the offence of robbery or mugging. In most cases, with the exception of handbag snatching, the offenders are not yet of age. Peer pressure often plays an important part.

15.3 Man shot as he tries to foil a robbery

A young man was shot in the chest at point-blank range yesterday as he tried to tackle two armed robbers who had attacked two security guards who were delivering money to a cash dispenser in a shopping centre in Berlin. The robbers, who were wearing hoodies and had concealed their faces with scarves, left him lying in a pool of blood and ran away towards the underground car park. Shortly afterwards they were seen speeding off on a motorcycle.

The man was taken to hospital and had to have emergency surgery. He is in a stable condition.

The robbers escaped with a substantial amount of cash. However, they won't be able to spend it as the container was booby-trapped with a red dye bomb, and some witnesses noticed red smoke coming out of the robbers' bag.

Explain the following words

foil ....

point-blank range ....

tackle ....

cash dispenser ....

hoody ....

scarf ....

pool of blood ....

booby-trap ....

dye-bomb ....

witness ....

stable ....

15.4 Interviewing robbery victims

When police officers interview the victim(s) of a robbery or mugging, they have to take into consideration that

- in more than 80 % of the cases the victim(s) prefer(s) charges and thus start(s) proceedings
- the victim(s) often is (are) the only source of information for the police
- there are still significant traces of evidence (e.g. skin injuries) on the victim or his/her clothes.

The result of a victim's statement depends on the police officer's interviewing skills. Does the officer notice traumata? Does he/she correctly judge if a statement is true or not? Does he/she help in case of blackouts? Does he/she have enough knowledge of the consequences of the offence for the victim(s), as this is absolutely necessary to take the appropriate steps, etc.?

15.5 Bodily injury

There are various degrees of bodily harm; thus, there are also various degrees of punishment.

The basic offence is "bodily harm": a person who injures another will be punished. If the injury is inflicted by means of poison or other dangerous substances, or with malice aforethought, or together with other persons, it is a case of "dangerous bodily harm".

If the victim's hearing or sight or an important limb is lost or severely impaired or impaired for the rest of the victim's life, the term "grievous bodily harm" applies. If the assailant has intended to inflict grievous bodily harm, punishment will be severer.

15.6 A bank robbery

Part 1

Characters: dispatcher POK Erwin Lehmann (EL), branch manager Gerald Heller (GH), trainee Alina Seglovskaja (AS), shift leader PHK'in Doris Keller (DK), PK Peter Fahrer (PF), POK Oswald Schreiner (OS), suspect Theo Vokafor (TV)

At "Düssel" control, a silent alarm of the Urdenbach branch of Stadtsparkasse Düsseldorf in Kammerrathsfeldstraße is triggered at 15.45.

EL: D 13/22 from Düssel.

DK: D 13/22.

EL: Alarm at Sparkasse branch Kammerrathsfeldstraße, who's going to respond?

DK: D 13/42 and D 13/43, I'll be in charge on the scene.

DK: D 13/42 and D 14/43, alarm at Sparkasse branch in Kammerrathsfeldstraße. 13/42, approach via Tübinger Straße and secure Kammerrathsfeldstraße junction. 13/43, drive through Göppinger Straße and secure the back of the building. 13/44 on standby. I'll drive through Südallee and will establish contact.

DK arrives in the vicinity of the branch at 15.50.

DK: Control from 13/22. Have arrived. Nothing suspicious.

EL: Ok. I'm going to contact the branch.

After a few moments:

EL: 13/22, the branch manager is coming out with a white handkerchief in his hand, he is wearing a beige jacket and blue trousers....... His name is Heller.

DK: I can see him, I'm going to talk to him.

DK: Good afternoon. I'm PHK'in Keller, what's happened?

GH: I'm the branch manager, my name is Heller, we've just been robbed.

DK: Please tell me what happened. We need some details to be able to find the robber. Is anybody hurt? Who else was in the branch?

GH: Only our trainee, Ms Seglovskaja. She's all right, so far she's coped quite well with the robbery. Nobody was hurt.

At about 15.45 a masked man entered the branch. He was wearing a black leather jacket and a balaclava. He was about 1.85 m tall, spoke broken German with an English accent. Under his balaclava I could see some reddish blond hair.

He threatened our trainee, Ms Seglovskaja, with his weapon.

DK: How exactly did he threaten her?

GH: He held the gun to her head and said something like: "All the money in there, quick, quick, or I'll shoot!" He gave her a white and blue Aldi shopping bag. Ms Seglovskaja was shocked and did not move at all. He then went to the till and helped himself. He put all the money into the plastic bag and ran away. I managed to trigger the alarm and then tried to pursue the robber. He jumped on a bicycle and rode away towards Kohlhagenstraße. Back there lies his cap, he lost it when he collided with an overhanging branch.

And he shot at me. When I pursued him he turned around and shot at me. So I gave up the pursuit. But he didn't hit me, the bullet went into the wall of that house over there, I could hear it.

DK: Thank you, that'll do for the moment. I'll pass on the description to all officers deployed. I assume that control has already informed the robbery department or the CID watch, and our colleagues are already on their way. They'll secure traces here in the street and on the premises.

GH: I'm going to close the branch for customers and inform my superiors.

Part 2

Continuing the case

D 13/44 is on patrol and routinely checks a car park on the edge of Hellerhofer Forst. The officers talk about the bank robbery that took place a short time before.

OS: Let's go to the car park, there is only one car.

PF: Somebody is just getting into the car, and there is a bike leaning against the fence.

POK Schreiner addresses the man, while PK Fahrer ensures the officer's safety.

OS: Good afternoon, please wait a moment, I'd like to talk to you.

TV: What do you want from me? I'm about to go home.

OS: There was a bank robbery nearby a short time ago. The description of the robber might fit you.

TV: Fit me? I just went for a walk in the forest. What's the robber supposed to look like?

OS: You're wearing dark clothes like the robber, and you've got reddish blond hair. These clues prompted us to check you. First I'll have to search you. Please stand in front of the vehicle, legs wide apart, and lean forward.

The suspect does so and is searched. Only a purse and his driving licence are found.

OS: Thank you. Now I have to search the car. Please move to the side.

The vehicle is searched, and POK Schreiner finds a .65 Walter PKK.

OS: What have we got here then? That's a Walter PKK pistol, a type which the police used many years ago. Have you got a firearms licence or a permit to possess a gun?

TV: I don't think so. The weapon belongs to my father.

OS: Why do you have the gun in your vehicle?

TV: After my father's death I put the weapon into my car for my personal protection.

OS: That bicycle over there, by the fence, is it yours?

TV: No. Why?

OS: It isn't locked, and there are fresh traces of mud on the tyres, as if somebody had just been riding it.

TV: I can't tell you anything about that.

OS: We'll see. Right now I'm arresting you on suspicion of having committed a bank robbery. We're going to establish your identity by having your fingerprints checked and by other means, and the crime scene officers will take care of the car, the weapon and the bicycle.

1. True or not true?

	true	not true
1. D 13/22 did not notice anything suspicious at the scene.		
2. The branch manager's name is Keller.		
3. Ms Seglovskaja is a veteran bank official.		
4. The bank robber spoke with a French accent.		
5. Ms Seglovskaja gave the bank robber € 12,000.		
6. The bank robber escaped on a bicycle.		
7. There were a dozen cars at the car park.		
8. The man at the car park said he wanted to drive home.		
9. The man at the car park refused to be searched.		
10. The man admitted that he was the owner of the bicycle.		

2. Judge the facts according to criminal law

3. Is the arrested man the bank robber? Which details indicate that he is the bank robber, and which details don't?

15.7 Word square

Find 16 words from this unit

A	Y	C	K	E	L	M	V	Q	Y	M	X	U	V	J	Y	E	F	S	X
H	B	Z	F	D	D	U	N	H	Y	R	L	W	K	X	I	D	T	A	R
A	O	C	A	B	T	C	C	Z	W	E	E	L	V	K	U	H	Q	R	I
N	X	G	D	S	B	N	A	A	V	X	M	B	F	U	P	J	G	C	P
D	H	H	W	E	A	B	B	C	Q	N	Y	Z	B	O	T	G	I	A	F
B	T	O	T	R	I	G	G	E	R	K	D	Z	N	O	Y	S	E	D	H
A	O	Y	B	E	C	F	M	A	H	S	C	E	A	I	R	D	R	E	X
G	L	W	D	S	P	L	G	G	Z	Z	J	A	F	B	C	C	W	Q	T
I	S	E	T	N	E	L	I	S	Q	Y	B	A	T	G	C	V	G	U	P
F	J	K	V	E	K	U	P	V	H	A	X	R	B	T	H	D	F	O	E
F	G	K	R	P	T	J	L	A	V	A	L	C	A	L	A	B	N	E	I
S	I	H	L	S	U	C	I	M	W	T	T	W	L	W	Z	M	C	J	H
B	T	R	I	I	S	T	O	H	Z	G	G	N	V	U	L	D	K	G	C
Y	A	U	E	D	B	R	S	Y	E	R	F	J	U	M	E	L	H	O	T
E	Z	I	M	A	V	F	W	R	I	P	Q	M	U	K	T	I	E	I	A
Q	G	Q	R	N	R	V	W	E	Q	Z	N	G	J	K	J	S	U	O	N
H	U	G	J	R	O	M	V	X	O	P	G	I	N	L	L	S	R	D	S
T	P	I	X	K	P	O	P	N	Y	I	T	M	M	C	R	M	S	Q	A
O	D	S	J	Q	U	L	L	Q	N	S	Z	N	B	U	B	W	N	T	P
F	G	J	R	S	K	N	M	G	R	S	O	A	P	C	A	B	V	O	U

15.8 Auxiliary verbs

be und *have* werden nicht nur zur Bildung von Zeitformen verwendet, sondern auch um eine besondere Bedeutung auszudrücken

be to drückt eine formelle Verpflichtung aus *We are to assemble at 7 p.m.*

have to wird bei sozialen Zwängen verwendet (Erwartungsdruck)
I'm afraid we'll have to attend the staff party.

Außerdem wird *have to* an Stelle von *must* bei Vergangenheits- und Zukunftsformen verwendet *We had/will have to help these people.*

Unvollständige Hilfsverben – defective auxiliaries

Im Gegensatz zu *be* and *have* sowie *do* (s. Unit 4) können diese Hilfsverben nur eine begrenzte Anzahl von Zeitformen bilden.

must drückt aus

– einen vom Sprecher oder von einer Behörde stammenden Zwang
You must be more careful in future. Pedestrians must cross at this point.

– einen als dringend empfundenen Wunsch bzw. eine dringende Empfehlung
I must tell you about the accident. You must buy yourself a proper dictionary.

– eine Erwartung bzw. Schlussfolgerung
They must be here by now. It must have rained.

must not drückt aus

– ein Verbot: *Passengers must not cross the line.*

can drückt aus

– eine Fähigkeit *I can't remember; can you do it?*

In dieser Bedeutung wird es, insbesondere bei anderen Zeitformen, durch *be able to* ersetzt *I was/will be able to sort things out.*

– eine Erlaubnis *You can go now.*
– eine Bitte *Can you help me?*
– eine Wahrscheinlichkeit *That can't be true.*

could drückt aus

– eine Bitte *Could you (perhaps) give me a hand?*
– eine Möglichkeit *It could happen/have happened to anybody.*
– einen Vorschlag *We could, of course, go elsewhere.*

may drückt aus

– eine Erlaubnis *May I come in? – Yes, you may.*
– eine Möglichkeit (vielleicht) *He may have missed the bus.*

might drückt aus

– eine eher unwahrscheinliche bzw. taktvoll formulierte Möglichkeit	*You might get there if there are no hold-ups.*
– einen indirekt ausgedrückten Vorschlag	*I thought we might eat out tonight.*
– einen höflichen Tadel	*You might have told me.*
– eine verspätete Einsicht	*I might have guessed it was him.*

will drückt aus

– eine Erwartung/Prognose	*Tomorrow will be fine with occasional showers.*
– einen Willen	*I will not (won't) do it.*
– eine Anordnung (Befehl)	*Members of the riot squad will assemble at 5 p.m.*
– eine Vermutung	*That'll be your taxi.*
– eine Gewohnheit bzw. ein typisches Ereignis	*Boys will be boys. Pigs will eat anything.* *Accidents will happen in this sort of weather.*
– eine Möglichkeit	*The car will do 100 mph at a pinch.*
– eine Bitte	*Will you do this for me?*
– eine Aufforderung	*Will/won't you come in?*

would drückt aus

– eine Gewohnheit (i.d.V.)	*He would get up at 5 a.m.*
– eine Bitte	*Would you please pass me the file?*
– ein Angebot	*Would you like a cup of coffee?*

shall drückt aus

– einen Vorschlag	*Shall we open the window?*

should drückt aus

– eine (nachdrückliche) Empfehlung	*You should see a specialist.*
– eine Annahme	*The motorway should be less crowded today.*

ought to drückt aus

– eine (nachdrückliche) Empfehlung	*You ought to apologize.*

need drückt aus

– eine (zumeist verneinte) Notwendigkeit	*You need not worry.*

used to drückt aus

– eine Gewohnheit in der Vergangenheit	*She used to smoke before she had the child.*

15.9 Fill-in exercise

Part 1

Fill in the gaps with an auxiliary verb from the following list

can, can't, couldn't, may, might, must, mustn't, needn't, shall, should, ought to, will, would

1. Chief Constable Roger Hoskins has broken his leg. That means he .... take part in this afternoon's meeting about lateral entry into the police service.
2. If you want my advice, I think you .... buy a new car.
3. I .... see a light in the sergeant's office on the fifth floor, so he .... be working overtime again.
4. I've got some important news for inspector Burke. Do you think he .... be in this afternoon?
5. I'm not sure where your portable radio is. I .... have put it on the shelf.
6. PC Sue Watson is very good at languages, she .... speak French, German, Spanish and Italian. So we .... employ an interpreter in many cases.
7. No, you .... stay here a second longer, the bomb .... go off any moment.
8. I've already found three people to help me, so you .... come if you are busy.
9. I looked for the Williams file everywhere, but I .... find it. Someone .... have taken it out of the drawer.
10. .... I get you some cigarettes when I'm out for lunch?
11. .... you like another piece of Battenberg cake?
12. I .... do any overtime tonight, I'm afraid. It's my wife's birthday, so I .... be late home today.
13. You .... wait for me. Tom is going to give me a lift.
14. He's been told that he .... be here at two o'clock.
15. Don't worry, I'm sure they .... be back soon.

Part 2

Fill in the right auxiliary or substitute verb

1. PHK Michael Franz and his family (müssen) .... move to the state capital as he was transferred to the ministry of the interior there.
2. Riot police officer's wife to her husband: "I hope you (nicht müssen) .... to go to work next weekend."

3. Police lieutenant Gavin Church from the Tulsa Police Department hopes that his men (können) .... arrest the robbers during tomorrow's raid.
4. In former times police trainees (nicht dürfen) .... leave the police academy except at weekends.
5. PC Geoffrey Walker (nicht brauchen) .... go out on patrol last week as he was on desk duty.
6. The officers (vielleicht, können) .... arrest the muggers if they had been informed earlier.
7. You (nicht, solltest) .... work overtime every night.
8. The phone is ringing. That (wahrscheinlich) .... be the arrested woman's lawyer.
9. The ambulance (sollte) .... be at the scene of the accident right now.
10. Motorists (nicht dürfen) .... overtake when there are the corresponding signs.

15.10 Useful phrases

Erklären Sie einer Gruppe von älteren Bürgern

1. Unter Raub versteht man Diebstahl unter Anwendung oder Androhung von Gewalt.

   ....

2. Bankräuber benutzen oft echte oder täuschend echt aussehende Waffen.

   ....

3. Handtaschenräuber entreißen älteren Damen die Handtasche häufig auf Friedhöfen.

   ....

4. Wehren Sie sich nicht, wenn Sie Opfer eines Raubüberfalls werden; prägen Sie sich das Aussehen des Täters, seine Kleidung usw. ein.

   ....

   ....

5. Wenn Paare nebeneinander gehen, sollte die Frau die Handtasche immer auf der Seite ihres Partners tragen.

   ....

6. Meiden Sie bei Dunkelheit Parks und unbeleuchtete Gegenden.

   ....

7. Lassen Sie sich auf dem Nachhauseweg von Ihnen vertrauten Personen begleiten.

   ....

8. Nehmen Sie lieber ein Taxi als allein nach Hause zu gehen, und bitten Sie den Taxifahrer zu warten, bis Sie ins Haus gegangen sind und die Tür verschlossen haben.

....

....

9. Achten Sie auf Personen, die Ihnen verdächtig vorkommen. Folgt Ihnen jemand? Werden Sie von mehreren Personen eingekreist?

....

....

10. Halten Sie Abstand zu Personen, die Sie beunruhigen. Gehen Sie in ein Hotel oder Lokal oder zu einem Taxistand.

....

....

11. Weisen Sie besonders jugendliche oder alkoholisierte Personen nicht auf ihr Fehlverhalten hin (z.B. Rauchen in öffentlichen Verkehrsmitteln), sondern versuchen Sie, sich möglichst weit von diesen Personen zu entfernen.

....

....

....

15.11 Key words and phrases

amusement arcade – balaclava – cash dispenser – clue – grievous bodily harm – fake firearm – handbag snatcher – mugging – pursuit – robbery – silent alarm – slot machine – statement – threaten – trigger the alarm

Burglary

Unit 16

This unit deals with

- the definition of the word "burglary"
- houses, rooms and furniture
- selected burglary cases
- information about how you can protect your home to prevent a burglary and
- reflexive pronouns.

16.1 Definition

In the United Kingdom, according to the Theft Act 1968, a person is guilty of theft if he/she "dishonestly appropriates property belonging to another with the intention of permanently depriving the other of it"; i.e. it is immaterial whether taking the property is for one's own gain or benefit or not. This same act repealed the Larceny Acts of 1861 and 1916, in which "larceny" involved "carrying away" of property with the intent of stealing. Since 1968, therefore, "larceny" has not been used as a legal term.

"Robbery" is basically stealing by using force, actual or threatened.

"Burglary", once the crime of "housebreaking at night" (i.e. between 9 p.m. and 6 a.m.), was also redefined by the 1968 Theft Act. "Burglary" is now defined as "entering any building or part of a building as a trespasser with intent to commit certain offences (such as stealing or inflicting grievous bodily harm) or, having entered, committing, or attempting to commit, such offences".

"Aggravated burglary" involves a firearm – even an imitation one – or any offensive weapon, or explosives.

16.2 Some statistics

In 2006, 6,304,223 criminal offences were reported in Germany. 2,603,644 (41.3 %) were thefts. 47.6 % of these (1,239,335) were cases of aggravated theft.

In the 1960s, the number of burglaries in shops and enterprises was more than twice that committed in private homes; nowadays burglaries in private homes are widespread all over Germany.

Burglaries in private homes have been decreasing for a number of years. Apparently, this is due to better preventive measures.

Most theft crimes are reported by the victim. Burglaries in detached houses are mostly committed from the back of the house, where the burglar cannot be seen, by forcing terrace or balcony doors.

In 2001, in 52.05 % of burglaries of detached houses in Cologne, the terrace door was prised open.

In 26.4 % of cases, a window, in 13.88 % of cases the front door, and in 6.93 % of cases the basement door or window was prised open.

The burglars can operate more easily in blocks of flats where the inhabitants often do not know each other and are not interested in their neighbours. Entering blocks of flats is rather easy for burglars. They usually enter ground-floor or rooftop flats.

16.3 The house

Part 1 – Where do people live?

apartment house	block of flats	bungalow
cottage	country house	detached house
farmhouse	flat	frame house (US)
half-timbered house	houseboat	housing estate
hut	mobile home	row house (US)
semi-detached house	skyscraper	terraced house
thatched cottage	timber house	trailer park
villa	weekend house	

Explain the functions and features of the above dwellings

Part 2 – A nice house

attic – awning – balcony – balcony door, French door – basement flat – bay – carport – chimney – downpipe, drainpipe – front door – front garden – garden fence – garden gate – garage with up-and-over door – gutter – inclined skylight – loft with sloping walls – porch – satellite dish – terrace – (window) shutter

Part 3 – Floor plan –

bathroom – broom cupboard – children's room – dining area – guest room – hall – kitchen – living room – master bedroom – staircase – study – toilet

What's in the house

(entrance) hall

wardrobe with chest of drawers for shoes – on top purse/wallet, keys, car keys – coat rack – umbrella stand – spyhole

kitchen

wall cupboard – refrigerator and freezer – electric cooker – gas cooker – dishwasher – drawer – bin – sink – sink unit – movable water tap, movable faucet (*US*) – working top – oven with hiding place for housekeeping money – cooker/extractor hood

sitting room, living room

couch, sofa – coffee table – armchair – wall unit – shelves – carpet – wall safe – pictures, paintings – curtains – TV set – stereo system – DVD set – indoor plants, house plants – flat-screen TV set

parents' bedroom

double bed – wardrobe, clothes closet (*US*) – bedside cabinet – duvet – pillow – mattress – laundry basket – photo/video equipment – wife's jewellery – bed frame – bedside rug – dressing table

children's room

sofa – shelves – desk with chair – computer and computer games, CDs and DVDs

bathroom

(bath) tub – shower (cubicle) – wash basins

16.4 Seven raids in four days in one street. So what do police do?

They put up this sign:

In a London street, seven houses were burgled in four days. The victims were:

1. Fred Green – BMW stolen – on Tuesday
2. Charles Mewell – attempted break-in
3. John Douglas and his wife Natasha – burglar alarm – on Wednesday 6.30 a.m.
4. Malcolm King – retired academic – first victim – money and keys stolen from house
5. Dorothy Marple – private eye – last incident
6. Robin McMaccles – financial adviser – golfer – Monday's victim
7. Charlotte Jones – Pilates teacher – expensive vehicle stolen – Sunday morning

Who makes the following statements? What happened when? What was stolen?

Interview the witnesses and ask detailed questions

"I know it is just personal belongings but I haven't slept since, I'm petrified. They stole my golf clubs, a plasma TV and designer coats. The police did not coordinate operations at all. It was only when we heard of the crimes they had committed in our street already and pointed out the similarities that the police linked them."

"I'm furious. Our family homes are just 150 yards apart in a normal London suburb. We've had burglaries when they tried to get into my house. I had to watch out and scare them off with my dog. The police response was to install notices on lamp posts saying: 'Burglars operate in this area. Can you imagine?"

"My son's girlfriend had left the house in the early Sunday morning. There were burglars in the house but they were hiding somewhere. It was only when I came down an hour and a half later that I found the window and front door open and our wallets and car keys gone. Someone could easily have been hurt."

"As a mother of two and as a businesswoman I have a very light sleep. When I heard a noise I knew that burglars were trying to open our front window, which is stuck shut by too much fresh paint. Then the alarm went off, scaring them away. I called the police while my husband tried to catch them."

"The police have been utterly useless! Had we been told of the Sunday and Monday burglaries, we would not have left the car in the driveway."

"It's dreadful! It was 7.30 a.m. and I was fast asleep. A neighbour saw a guy driving my car away and when he came to tell me he found my front door wide open. We have surveillance cameras all over London. Every decent Londoner is video-taped three hundred times a day, that guy must be on the pictures driving my new convertible Mercedes – it seems the police just couldn't give a damn."

"The burglars were real professionals, striking when they knew police shifts ended and homeowners would be asleep. Several police stations were dealing with the break-ins, but their investigations were not coordinated. Once a pattern emerged it was easy to guess where they would strike next. My friend and I were literally waiting for them. We heard them working their way up the street. You'd think they would be worried about increased police surveillance, but they were obviously confident that nothing would happen. I'm glad that we were able to apprehend them and, to be fair, the police were there in five minutes. Now they are arrested on suspicion of having committed several burglaries."

16.5 Some cases of burglary

Case 1

In the town of Aschersleben in Saxony-Anhalt an ironmonger's was burgled on Friday. The thieves forced the door to the shop. They stole electrical tools worth more than € 15,000. According to the police, the burglary must have been committed by at least three persons who emptied all the shelves in the shop, only leaving small items behind. They must have used a small truck to carry off the loot, consisting to a large extent of cordless drills, angle grinders and other tools. The shopkeeper thinks that the theft was committed on someone's orders, probably by one of his competitors, as all the tools were unpacked and cannot be sold in their original boxes.

Case 2

The shopping arcade in Northeim with its 60 shops closes every night at 20.00, when all the doors are locked. Only cleaning personnel and the security service have access afterwards. At about 2.30 a.m. the security service called the owner of a jeweller's shop and told him that thieves had entered his shop and stolen golden jewellery worth more than € 100,000. It is not yet known how the two masked thieves, who were caught on CCTV, had entered the arcade and the shop as no traces of forced entry were found. Apparently the thieves also knew that the shopping arcade has about a dozen security doors which can easily be opened from the inside in case of an emergency, and they escaped through one of them.

Case 3

On Wednesday night a supermarket in Quakenbrück was burgled for the third time within a year by the same gang of burglars. The first two times the burglars were apparently disturbed and got away without any loot. This time two burglars climbed onto the roof, removed a few tiles and lowered themselves into the office. They cut all telephone wires and also the wires of the alarm system, but even so the alarm went off in the office of the security firm at exactly 11 p.m. When employees of the security firm and police arrived on the scene 20 minutes later, they found that the thieves had managed to open the safe and got away with more than € 20,000. Accomplices were waiting in a stolen car about 300 m from the supermarket.

Case 4

In broad daylight, between 8 and 10 a.m., burglars prised a window of a detached house open while the husband was at work and the wife was shopping. The thieves rummaged through the house and escaped with a single-lens reflex camera, a small amount of cash and jewellery worth about € 27,000.

Find the words in the text whose explanation is given here

1. flat length of wood or other material attached to a wall or forming part of a piece of furniture, which provides room for the storage or display of goods

   ....

2. person or company that makes and/or sells watches and jewellery.

   ....

3. stolen goods

   ....

4. thin slab of baked clay or other material, used to cover roofs

   ....

5. device with a rotating abrasive disc, used to grind or polish all kinds of materials

   ....

6. strong cabinet with a complex lock used to store valuables

   ....

7. person who helps another to commit a crime

   ....

8. house which is not joined to another on any side

   ....

9. married man

   ....

10. elude, break free, run away

    ....

11. container with a flat base and flat sides, square or rectangular or round, with a lid

....

12. mark or object which proves the existence or passing of something/somebody

....

13. search unsystematically

....

16.6 How to secure your home

Part 1

Roger Lincoln (RL) is a British businessman who lives in Düsseldorf with his family and who works in a British bank. Last week his house was burgled. The burglar or burglars entered the house through the kitchen window at the back in the late morning, and stole Roger Lincoln's wife's jewellery as well as expensive electronic gadgets belonging to husband and son, who still goes to school. The officers who investigated the burglary strongly advised Mr Lincoln to contact the police advisory centre and get information about additional security measures. Mr Lincoln has taken them up on their suggestions and talks to PHK Hubert Carstens (HC).

HC: Good morning, Mr Lincoln, nice to meet you. Did you find a space to park your car?

RL: Yes, no problem. There are two multi-storey car parks close by. It's much more convenient than at police headquarters, where you almost never find a space for your car.

HC: Please have a seat. How can I help you?

RL: Thank you, I already told you on the phone that my house was burgled. And now I'd like to get some information about possible measures to secure the house.

HC: What exactly happened?

RL: Apparently the burglar or burglars entered the house between 08.00 and 11.00 a.m. My wife wasn't at home. She'd taken our son to school and then had breakfast with some friends. The burglar or burglars probably noticed this and entered the house while nobody was at home. But we made it quite easy for him, the kitchen window was tilted. So it was quite easy to enter the house.

HC: That doesn't sound good. What does your insurance company say?

RL: That's the problem. The insurance company refuses to pay as the kitchen window was not closed.

HC: I'm sorry. But that's part of many policies. How is your house secured?

RL: We bought the house two years ago, and the only security measure was to fit window and door handles with locks. What can I do? What are burglars interested in?

HC: Burglars are not very demanding. They not only go for isolated houses or houses where they cannot be seen by others, but also for terraced and semi-detached houses. In most cases the burglar watches the house for a while. If he thinks that nobody is at home, he burgles it.

RL: Where and how do burglars enter?

HC: Burglars usually enter where they cannot be seen, i.e. normally through back doors or back windows. Burglars enter more often through basement doors than through the main doors where they can easily be seen.

RL: What can one do about that?

HC: It's advisable to secure these areas properly. Burglars with the usual tools can be stopped with rather cheap measures. And if you take more sophisticated measures, burglars are usually deterred. Of course, there is no such thing as perfect security. But a burglar doesn't want to be detected and caught. And he wants to succeed in no time. Therefore, if in doubt, he tries a house which is not well secured.

RL: Then I should especially secure doors and windows?

HC: Yes, securing windows and French doors is very important, because that also protects you against daytime burglaries.

RL: Isn't it sufficient when the shutters are down?

HC: That depends on the quality of your shutters. And I strongly recommend securing your shutters especially against them being pushed up. But you've got to bear in mind that, during the day, closed shutters indicate that nobody is at home.

RL: Then I'd better buy a burglar alarm. What do you think of that?

HC: There are silent and audible alarms. An audible alarm system produces the blaring sound of a siren and perhaps also triggers a flashing yellow warning light. A silent alarm activates the signal in a security company, and this company then sends a team to check. Both systems have advantages and disadvantages. A serious disadvantage of an audible alarm system is the noise. And this is especially unpleasant in cases of occasional false alarms. And in such cases you also have to pay for the police to arrive. And you also have to consider that the alarm system only registers unlawful entry.

RL: Should I install exterior lights or leave the lights switched on inside the house?

HC: Switched-on lights inside the house can make a burglar believe that somebody is in the house. Exterior lights are also very good. They can deter a burglar when they suddenly come on.

RL: Are burglars really disturbed by visible security measures?

HC: Yes, certainly. Additional door locks, solid shutters, bars in front of the windows and other visible measures show the burglar that he needs more time to break in. And a burglar doesn't have time. The more time he needs to get into the house, the higher the risk that he might be surprised by a resident returning home or a neighbour.

RL: Isn't it dangerous to confront a burglar?

HC: Normally a burglar wants to steal things without being interrupted. He doesn't want to attack people. So he will run away. You can switch on the light or address him in a loud voice. In most cases that's enough. In no case should you try to block his way. Better call the police. And make a note of what the perpetrator looked like. Write down which direction he took, and perhaps also what his vehicle looked like, if possible.

RL: What would you advise me to do now?

HC: First I'll have to have a look at your house and see whether it is easy to burgle. That depends on the location, the neighbourhood and to what extent it can be seen from the road. Then I'll be able to make some relevant suggestions.

RL: Sounds good. I'm glad that I've called.

Part 2

"Delay him and he'll go away."

- Make sure your house looks occupied – use time switches for lighting and close the curtains.
- Don't advertise that you are going on holiday – ask a neighbour to keep an eye on your property and empty the letterbox every day.
- Make sure your home has security locks – these will deter the opportunist thief.
- Fit window locks – they make it difficult for the thief to break in without making a lot of attention-drawing noise.
- Make sure that your front door is robust, capable of withstanding being kicked or pushed.

Part 3

"If in doubt, keep them out."

Never let anyone in unless you are absolutely sure they are genuine. Crooks come in many disguises, for example as "bogus officials", who may be smartly dressed and claim to come from the council, gas board or other organization, as "bogus dealers", who may offer to buy antiques, furniture or jewellery at what seems to be a good price or as "bogus workmen", who say that they need to come in to check something or make urgent repairs. In all these cases they just want to come in and steal things.

Part 4 – Word comb

Fill in words from the above text

16.7 Reflexive pronouns

Reflexivpronomen werden gebraucht, wenn das Subjekt eine Handlung an sich selbst vollzieht und eine Rückbeziehung vorliegt. Es findet nur Verwendung, wenn Subjekt und Objekt identisch sind.

Formen

myself	*ourselves*
yourself	*yourselves*
himself	
herself	*themselves*
itself	

Bei allgemeinen Aussagen benutzt man oneself.

Beachten Sie

Es gibt einige englische Verben, die im Gegensatz zu ihren deutschen Entsprechungen ohne Reflexivpronomen verwendet werden:

change	sich ändern	*concentrate*	sich konzentrieren
differ	sich unterscheiden	*happen*	sich ereignen
join	sich anschließen	*refuse*	sich weigern
remember	sich erinnern	*wonder*	sich fragen

16.8 Exercise

Fill in the reflexive pronoun, if necessary

1. I introduced ....
2. As the sergeant was absent, the constable had to answer the phone ....
3. They decided to do the job ....
4. A policeman to his colleague: "I'm afraid you'll have to write the report ....".
5. I remember .... the graduation ceremony at the police academy.
6. Did you speak to the officer in charge .... or to his secretary?
7. I refuse .... to answer that question.
8. How can I possibly concentrate .... in all that noise?
9. We should like to speak to the driver .... if he is still around.
10. If you get .... in trouble, there's little we can do.
11. I'm afraid we can't commit .... at this stage.
12. We'd better begin concentrating .... on the theft.
13. All our efforts to trace the stolen vehicle have proved .... rather difficult.
14. You two have to decide for .... whether or not to stay in town for the night.
15. Tourists should guard .... against people who accost them in such places.
16. Have you satisfied .... that you locked the car properly?
17. The code of your car radio is something you should keep to ....
18. Apparently the offender prised open the door with a jemmy and helped .... to what he considered worth taking.
19. The local Irish consulate will help you extricate .... from this situation.

16.9 Useful phrases

Erklären Sie einem Haus- oder Wohnungsbesitzer, dass

1. Einbrecher häufig von der Rückseite des Hauses her in das Haus eindringen.

   ....

2. fast die Hälfte aller Straftaten in Deutschland in die Kategorie „Diebstahl" fallen.

   ....

3. die Einbrecher in Einfamilienhäusern in über 50 % der Fälle eine Balkon- oder Terrassentür aufbrechen.

   ....

4. Einbrecher in Wohnblocks das Erdgeschoss oder das oberste Stockwerk bevorzugen.

....

5. viele Einbrüche am helllichten Tag stattfinden.

....

6. man alle Fenster durch Schlösser sichern sollte.

....

7. Einbrecher ihr Ziel oft über längere Zeit beobachten.

....

8. man Rollläden gegen das Hochschieben von außen sichern sollte.

....

9. eine Außenbeleuchtung, die sich durch einen Bewegungsmelder einschaltet, mögliche Einbrecher oft dazu bringt, von ihrer Tat abzulassen.

....

....

10. man die Innenbeleuchtung mit Zeitschaltern versehen sollte, so dass es so aussieht, als ob jemand zu Hause wäre.

....

....

11. man sich einem Einbrecher nie in den Weg stellen, sondern sich so viele Einzelheiten wie möglich über ihn notieren und die Polizei informieren sollte.

....

....

12. man Nachbarn bitten sollte, während des Urlaubs jeden Tag den Briefkasten zu leeren.

....

13. man nie unbekannte Personen in das Haus oder die Wohnung lassen sollte, wenn sie sich nicht entsprechend ausgewiesen haben.

....

....

16.10 Key words and phrases

aggravated burglary – bogus official – break-in – broad daylight – burglar alarm – detached house – larceny – prise open – security lock – tilted window – time switch – window shutters

Punch-ups, riots, hooliganism, criminal damage to property

This unit deals with

- entrance checks at soccer matches
- the central register of offenders in connection with sports events
- a case of criminal damage to property
- a pub brawl
- a violent demonstration
- "ladette" offences and
- relative pronouns and relative clauses

17.1 No admission for lager louts

TSG 1899 Hoffenheim are playing Manchester United in the Champions' League. A coach from Manchester arrives at a parking area a few hundred yards from the stadium. The English fans, including about a dozen women, all in their early twenties, seem to have been drinking quite heavily. Police officers Siegfried Maurer (SM), Christiane Holdorf (CH) and Andreas Itzig (AI) check the fans as they are getting off the bus. Two of them, Frank Webster (FW) and John Grant (JG), have a carryall with dozens of bottles of beer.

Hoffenheim Stadium Reproduced by kind permission of TSG 1899 Hoffenheim

SM: Good afternoon. What have you got in that bag?

FW: Only some beer. Kind of ammunition to support our team. They've got to win. Where's the entrance to the stadium?

SM: Well, first I have to tell you that you aren't allowed to take any alcoholic drinks into the stadium.

FW: What? Aren't I allowed to have a pint of beer in this fucking country? Blimey!

SM: In this country you can have as many pints of beer or whatever other drink you like as long as you don't cause a disturbance or danger to others. As a result of previous experience, the organizers of the match have prohibited the sale and consumption of any kind of alcoholic drinks in the stadium.

JG: Hey, copper, why don't you just shut up and let us go?

SM: As I told you, no alcohol in the stadium. And that means you'll have to leave that bag here in the bus. There's no chance you'll be allowed in with so many bottles of booze.

CH: I see you've got about two dozen bottles of 'Speckled Hen' strong ale and 'Flying Scotsman' ruby ale. Those are very good beers. I know them from my last trip to Britain.

JG: You're right. And that's why we want to have a couple of them in the stadium. You see, cheering and singing makes us very thirsty.

SM: Yes, and it also makes you prone to irrational behaviour and possibly violence, especially if your team do not win. And that's why no alcoholic beverages are allowed in the stadium.

FW: I like my beer and enjoy having a pint with the lads at the 'Red Lion'. Don't you drink beer?

SM: No, I don't. I never drink alcohol.

FW: Oh shit, the Salvation Army! Bloody non-drinkers! Peelers. Blue bells. Fuzz. Babies. Teetotallers.

SM: Sir, I'm a police officer, and the fact that I don't drink does not give you the right to insult me.

FW: Shut up. I'm going into the stadium, and my friend and I are taking these few bottles with us, and you aren't going to stop us.

The other passengers of the bus are standing around, but they do not interfere.

SM: Well, I've had enough now. You're drunk, and so you can't go into the stadium.

JG: What, you want to stop him going in?

SM: That's right. And that goes for you, too. You're both drunk, and you won't be allowed to enter the stadium, as there's a great chance that you'll cause a disturbance or start a fight.

JG: Here are our tickets. We've paid quite a lot of money for them. And you bloody motherfuckers tell us we can't watch the match?

AI: Didn't you understand what my colleague told you? You're drunk, and you're not allowed in the stadium.

JG: If I can't go in, who's going to give me my money back? You stupid cop certainly won't.

AI: There are plenty of people around who haven't got a ticket yet. Maybe you can sell it to one of them. By the way, when you bought the ticket, you accepted all the rules that apply in and around the stadium.

JG: Ah, just forget about it, bloody pig.

SM: Watch it. Or else we'll arrest you for insulting police officers on duty. Take the bag into the coach. I'm sure the driver will make sure nobody steals it. Drink that beer on the way back home.

CH: I hope you won't get seasick on the ferry.

FW: Okay, okay. But what are we going to do with the German money that we get for our tickets?

CH: Go into that pub over there and have some more drinks. You seem to need it. The publican is a former boxer, he'll make sure that you behave, even after you've had one too many.

JG: Bloody pig!

SM: Goodbye. And have a nice time.

1. Do you think the German police officers behaved correctly by not taking action as a result of the insults?

2. Should the sale and consumption of alcoholic drinks be prohibited in sports stadiums?

17.2 Police officers hurt keeping rival groups apart

Fill in the following words

appear – arrests – batons – closely – contact – custody – departure – dispersed – footage – gathered – injuries – missiles – mounted – operation – pitch – public – regained – treatment – violent

600 angry Cardiff fans had (hedrgtae) .... outside the stadium as 800 visiting Stoke fans left to make their way home to the Midlands. Although an extensive police (onoreptia) .... was put in place to ensure the safe (tedruearp) .... of the fans, three officers needed hospital (ntttereeam) .... and a number of others suffered minor (nijeiurs) ....

The police, including (tednmuo) .... police, were using their (aontbs) .... to keep the two sets of fans apart when (elisssim) .... – bottles, rocks, bricks and even fence posts – were thrown by the Cardiff fans. At 10.30 p.m. police (agreiedn) .... control and most of the fans (edsidpsre) ....

A number of (srsrtea) .... has been made, but the police say they will be looking .... (clylseo) at the CCTV (fotoega) .... to identify more people attacking police officers. They have also asked anyone with information to (cttnaoc) .... the police.

The people arrested were a 17-year-old, arrested for (voitlen) .... disorder, two 20-year-olds, charged with (cupibl) .... order offences, and a 39-year-old, arrested for throwing missiles onto the (tpcih) ....

The two men arrested for public order offences were kept in (oytscdu) .... , the others were bailed to (rpapea) .... before a magistrate.

17.3 Central register of offenders at sports events

In 19991 the state ministers of the interior decided to establish a central register of offenders before, during and after sports events. Its task is to collect intelligence on soccer hooligans all over Germany, establish situation reports and exchange data with other federal states and other nations. The aim is to prevent soccer hooligans from entering the stadiums.

As most clubs of the Bundesliga are in North Rhine-Westphalia, the central register was established at the North Rhine-Westphalia State Criminal Police Office in Düsseldorf.

Intelligence about persons who have been charged with or sentenced for offences committed before, during and after sports events, is input by "Zentrale Informationsstelle Gewalttäter Sport" (ZIS) and "Landesinformationsstelle Gewalttäter Sport" (LIS) into the "Gewalttäter Sport" (violent offenders) database at the Federal Criminal Police Office. The consequences can be: prohibition to enter any stadium in the Federal Republic of Germany, temporary confiscation of one's passport or restrictions with regard to leaving the country.

The soccer clubs have no access to this central register.

There are three categories of soccer fans:

- category A = peaceful fans
- category B = violence-prone fans
- category C = violence-seeking fans

During the 2006/2007 soccer season, about 6,000 B fans and about 2,500 C fans were entered into the register.

Find out the different meanings of the following words:

state, minister, intelligence, report, office

17.4 Criminal damage to property

David Mayes (DM) from Fresno, California, and his German wife Ulla (UM) live in Werder (Havel). David Mayes works for an international bank in Berlin, his wife is a teacher at one of the local primary schools.

They have three children, Joshua, 17, Audrey, 13, and Keith, 7. Audrey and Keith still go to school, Joshua is an apprentice at a posh hotel in the neighbouring town of Brandenburg. As he often has to work until 10 p.m. or longer and as there is no public transport that late, the hotel has provided an apartment for him on its premises. But he goes home whenever he can or public transport permits, or one of his parents acts as chauffeur.

One day Ulla and David Mayes receive a letter from the mayor's office at a neighbouring village, about 10 km from Werder.

Dear Mr Mayes,

On Saturday, February 5, we had a carnival event in our village hall, at which your son Joshua was present, together with Axel Gellert, 17, also an apprentice at the hotel in Brandenburg. At about 1.30 a.m. on Sunday, February 6, Axel Gellert and Joshua Mayes were caught throwing snowballs and stones at the lanterns in the small park in front of the village hall, smashing six of them. The total damage they caused amounts to € 845.60. As both boys admitted their foolish deed, we will not press charges if the amount of € 845.60 is paid within a fortnight.

We therefore ask you to transfer the amount of € 422.80 to our account number 12345678, Sparkasse Michendorf, sort code 87654321.

We must inform you that it is a case of joint liability, in other words, if the other party involved does not pay his share, you will be held liable for the total amount of € 845.60. If you do not pay at all, we will press charges against your son and sue you for the money.

Yours truly,

Heinz Schmücke

Mayor

The Mayeses are rather surprised, as Joshua has not told them about this incident. They talk to him in the late afternoon after he has returned from his weekly attendance at the vocational school. And they have informed their neighbour Alfred Salzmann (AS) about their son's misbehaviour and asked him to support them. Alfred Salzmann is a detective with the CID at Potsdam.

David Mayes hands the letter to his son.

DM: Now, Josh, what have you got to say?

JM: Hm, hm, well, yes, it's true. Axel and I did it. I'm sorry.

UM: It's not the first time that you're causing trouble. Will you ever grow up?

JM: I'm sorry. Axel and I had been drinking, we weren't sober any more, and the lanterns were good targets for our snowballs.

DM: It's highly unlikely that you can smash a street lamp with a snowball. And the letter says that you also threw stones.

JM: I didn't throw any stones, only snowballs. It was Axel who had the idea, and he threw all the stones and smashed the lamps. I didn't.

AS: To make things clear: it doesn't matter who actually caused the damage; Axel and you did it jointly, so you have to pay jointly. And you can be lucky that the mayor won't press charges if you – or your parents – pay to have the street lights repaired. If he did, a magistrate would not only make you pay for the damage but would certainly punish you.

JM: What sentence could we expect?

AS: As it is the first time that you did something foolish like that, you'd probably be sentenced to do a number of hours of community work in your free time.

JM: What kind of work?

AS: There are many possibilities. You might have to work, let's say, 50 hours in a kindergarten or old people's home.

JM: I certainly wouldn't like that.

DM: Well, you won't have to do that. Mother and I will pay the € 422, but you'll have to pay back that amount in monthly instalments of € 50 from your salary. And you'll do 50 hours of "community work" at home. You can start right now. Go outside, clean and vacuum the car and then wash it.

JM: I thought the age of slavery had gone.

17.5 Man found dead after confronting youths

A 65-year-old man apparently collapsed and died when he confronted a group of youngsters in a vacant house next door. He had gone there to find out about shouting and yelling coming from the house. Half an hour later, his wife found him lying in the living room, unconscious but still breathing. She called an ambulance, but he was dead when they arrived.

The police found about twenty empty beer bottles, two empty bottles of whisky and dozens of cigarette butts in the living room. Apparently the youngsters had broken into the house, and the man had surprised them. The prosecution service arranged for a post mortem.

Police later arrested five teenagers in connection with the death.

1. **What would you do if you were in the same situation as the 65-year-old man?**
2. **Simulate a discussion between the teenagers and the man**
3. **How did the teenagers react when the man collapsed?**
4. **Why do you think the man collapsed?**

17.6 A pub brawl

Instead of watching the match, Frank Webster (FW) and John Grant (JG) enter the pub where Hoffenheim fans Elmar Peters(EP) and Torsten Niemann (TN), together with three companions, have already had quite a few beers. The Englishmen join them, and what started as a joint drinking bout soon turns into a brawl.

FW: Come on, admit it, your blue and white bastards have no chance of winning this match, not a fucking chance in hell! We're the champions.

EP: Rubbish, ours is by far the better team.

FW: You don't know bloody nothing! Don't you know that we English invented football?

TN: So what? That was many years ago, at a time when you had just crawled out of your caves.

JG: We, the English, were the world champs in 1966. And in that year we not only beat you Huns, we also invented the miniskirt. Nice to look at lovely girls' legs.

You prudish Germans would never have come up with something like that, and anyway, our lasses have nicer legs than German girls.

TN: Bugger your miniskirt and your girls' legs! We're talking about soccer players' legs, and that's where ours are much better. You only won in 66 because you bribed the Russian linesman. And you gave the referee eye drops, so his vision was blurred and he couldn't distinguish between the soccer ball and a ping-pong ball.

FW: Bloody lies! That goal was perfect. Modern computer simulations clearly prove that the ball was behind the line.

EP: With a computer you can prove anything. That was no goal!

FW: Shut up, you bloody idiot. Just shut up, shut up, shut up! We're the champions, and our team will win tonight.

TN: You'd better belt up. If you don't I'll punch you in your fucking face.

JG: You just try if you want to spend three weeks in intensive care. Big mouth! Windbag!

Suddenly one of the Germans empties his beer in Frank Webster's face, and a fight begins. Glasses and ashtrays fly through the room, bottles are knocked off the shelves, furniture is damaged. It is only after the publican, Christian Dahm (CD), has threatened to knock them all out that the fighting stops. Because of the considerable damage he calls the police. Officers Sascha Urbanowitsch (SU) and Volker Reichert (VR) arrive.

SU: Now, what happened?

CD: These youngsters started a fight for no reason.

FW: No reason! Ha. We won in 1966, and we will win tonight.

TN: No way!

VR: You just calm down. Let's try to sort things out.

CD: Who's going to pay for the damage? Just look what you've done.

FW: It was them Krauts that started. That idiot over there emptied his beer on me, so I had to hit him in the face.

TN: I had to shut him up cause he was telling bloody lies. I wasn't having any of that. We are the true champions. Bugger the damage, and bugger your team, they're just a bunch of cry-babies and divers.

SU: Now that's enough. *(To the landlord)* Can we use the adjoining room to take statements from each of them?

CD: Yes, go ahead. I'll keep an eye on the others. Whoever is to blame for the damage will have to foot the bill.

VR: Do you wish to prefer criminal charges? Claiming damages is a matter of civil law and no concern of ours.

CD: No, no charges. I just want damages.

In the presence of the officers the publican takes down the personal data of all of them, and also the names and addresses of the respective insurance companies, so that he can be compensated for the damage.

17.7 Graffiti

Illegal graffiti are, according to law, damage to property. The sprayer, if caught, has to pay damages and faces criminal prosecution. Young sprayers are often not aware of the consequences of their misdemeanour. The civil limitation period is 30 years, so a 17-year-old who sprays graffiti in 2010 can be sued for damages until 2040.

In Germany, the total damage caused by graffiti sprayers was about € 200 million in 2008.

Divide the following words into groups in any way you like (e.g. tools to draw) or draw a mindmap with the topic "graffiti" – feel free to add your own ideas

aerosol spray-can, artist, blackbooks, buses, carriage windows, damage to property, danger, detergents, drill bits, freeway overpasses, gangs, graffiti kids, high costs for the community, high-pressure hoses, indelible marker pens, inscriptions, interlocking letters, legal alternatives, paint, pride, public art, slogans, tags, trains, underpasses, vandalism, walls, wire brushes, zero tolerance

Role play

One of you is a graffiti sprayer, the other is a police officer who catches him red-handed

17.8 Violent demonstrations

The following text contains ten typing errors; find them

Whatever happens – on 1st May Berlin police officers are attacked and injured

Of course, life in Berlin is mostly peaceful. And, of course, most demonstrations on 1st May are peaceful, too. And there have been fewer and fewer injured officers and demonstrators in the past few years, due to the Berlin police strategy of de-escalation. But what can you do if your oponents don't accept this strategy?

It happened again on 1st May 2009. After some years which were relatively calm, the so-called "Black block" had aparently decided to brutally attack the police this year. The result: 273 injured police officers, 289 demonstrators arrested for causing grievious bodily harm and breech of the public piece, and 5,800 police officers deployed who almost couldn't cope with the situation.

The attacks began shortly after dark in the Kreuzberg district. Militant agressive rioters hurled petrol bombs, rocks and bottles at the officers, who used taer gas and their batons, but managed to suppress the riots for a short time only. The centre of the riots was – as happened frequently – Cottbuser Tor square, in other streets high barricades were erected and set on fire when the police arrived.

The riots peaked when police dispersed a "demonstration" of masked left-wing groups with about 5,000 participants because of their violent rioting.

Berlin's Kreuzberg district certainly is the main attraction for the so-called "Autonome" (left-wing radicals). But there are also violent riots regularly in the Schanzenviertel area of Hamburg, in Ulm and other cities. The rioters are not necessarily left-wing radicals. The number of violent demonstrations on 1st May organized by Neo-Nazis is on the increase, and it often comes to counter-demonstrations and street fights, or direct attacks on the police, as happened in Freiberg, Saxony, in 2009, when some Neo-Nazis wanted to free one of their collegues who had been arrested.

But nobody knows what the results of the criminal proceedings will be. And nobody knows if they have any influense on the May Day demonstrations in the following year.

Certainly, the reasons for these violent events are to be found in society and cannot be dealt with by the police. If the police manage, with large units of well-trained riot officers, to disperse violent rioters, they are considered to be sucessful. Others will have to take care of the social reasons.

17.9 "Ladette" offences on the increase

In Britain, young people aged ten to seventeen commit about 280,000 offences a year, which roughly means that an act of juvenile crime is committed every two minutes. Most of the offences are cases of violence against the person, public order offences, theft and handling and criminal damage.

What is quite interesting is the fact that the number of "ladette" offences, i.e. crimes committed by young women, are on the increase whereas the number of crimes committed by boys is falling. Politicians blame the marked increase in violence among girls on binge drinking.

Find out more about juvenile delinquency in various countries

17.10 Relative pronouns and relative clauses

Relativpronomen

who (der, die, das, welcher, welche, welches) bezieht sich nur auf Personen

The man who gave me this information has disappeared.

whose (dessen, deren) bezieht sich auf Personen und Sachen

The suspect, whose name is not known, is said to be about 50. The house in Jermyn Street, whose front door is painted red, is a known crack den.

whom (dem, der, welchem, welcher; den, die, das, welchen, welche, welches) wird häufig durch *who* ersetzt

The driver who(m) we stopped last night is a regular customer of ours.

which bezieht sich auf Sachen oder den vorhergehenden Satz

The equipment which we use is very sophisticated. The politician did not tell the truth, which shows that you should be wary of politicians.

that bezieht sich auf Personen oder Sachen im notwendigen Relativsatz (s. unten), besonders nach betonten Substantiven (*only ..., most important ...*)

The only thing that matters is to apprehend the serial killer.

what bezieht sich auf das, was folgt

Nobody knows what will happen tomorrow.

Nicht notwendige Relativsätze

Sie können auch weggelassen werden, da sie für das Verständnis des Hauptsatzes nicht erforderlich sind; sie werden durch Komma vom Hauptsatz abgetrennt

My brother, who is 16 years old, has gone to London. The hooligans, some of whom were arrested, were Arsenal fans.

Notwendige Relativsätze

Sie sind zum Verständnis des Hauptsatzes notwendig und werden nicht durch Komma abgetrennt

People who drive too fast should be fined.

Das Relativpronomen kann weggelassen werden, wenn es Objekt ist

The policeman (who, whom, that) we met is my uncle.

Nachstellung der Präposition

Im notwendigen Relativsatz mit oder ohne Relativpronomen wird die Präposition vielfach nachgestellt

The taxi (that) you sent for has arrived.

17.11 Fill-in exercise

Fill in a relative pronoun and add commas, if necessary

1, Those .... are under age are not allowed to purchase and consume alcohol.
2. This is .... happens if you drive under the influence.
3. Miss Hardcastle .... has been living in Germany for more than a year still uses her British driving licence.
4. Overseas visitors many of .... come from America insist on seeing Neuschwanstein.
5. The red Jaguar .... left front wing was badly dented in the head-on collision last night belongs to a James A. Rigby of 253 Blackburn Road, Chorley, Lancs.
6. The worst thing .... could possibly happen at this time of the day would be a mugging.
7. There have been seven more cases of robbery in this part of town .... goes to show that tourists had better give it a wide berth.
8. The landlord of the beer garden .... I have known since I was a child usually informs us of any suspicious-looking strangers.
9. Anyone .... has had some papers stolen knows what a hassle it is to get new ones.
10. The passport .... was found in the mailbox belongs to a Sri Lankan asylum seeker.

17.12 Useful phrases

Sagen Sie einem / fragen Sie einen Fußballfan,

1. – was er in der großen und schweren Reisetasche hat.

   ....

2. – dass es nicht gestattet ist, alkoholische Getränke mit ins Stadion zu nehmen.

   ....

3. – dass aufgrund von schlechten Erfahrungen in der Vergangenheit jeglicher Ausschank und Genuss von Alkohol im Stadion verboten ist.

   ....

4. – dass er mit seinen Beleidigungen und Schimpfwörtern aufhören soll und dass er, wenn er dies nicht tut, wegen Beamtenbeleidigung angezeigt wird.

   ....

5. – dass er mit dem Kauf der Eintrittskarte alle Bedingungen akzeptiert hat, die im und um das Stadion gelten.

   ....

6. – dass er die Tasche mit dem Bier in den Bus zurückbringen soll und der Fahrer schon darauf aufpassen wird.

   ....

7. – dass er versuchen soll, seine Eintrittskarte zurückzugeben.

   ....

8. – wer mit der Schlägerei angefangen hat.

   ....

9. – dass er für den von ihm verursachten Schaden aufkommen muss.

   ....

10. – ob er haftpflichtversichert ist.

    ....

17.13 Key words and phrases

blurred – brawl – claim damages – closed circuit television (CCTV) – criminal damage to property – disturbance – innocent – intelligence – interfere – irrational behaviour – juvenile delinquency – missile – petrol bomb – sober

Drugs

This unit deals with

- types of drugs
- drug prevention
- drug smuggling
- joint border and immigration checks
- joint drug investigation teams
- arresting a drug dealer
- a drug-sniffing sheep
- drug lingo and
- numerals.

18.1 Types of drugs

Drugs are probably as old as mankind. There have been drugs in practically all civilizations.

A distinction must be made between legal and illegal drugs, depending on the country and culture concerned. Alcohol, for instance, while popular in most parts of the world, is prohibited in many Muslim countries.

Legal drugs in Germany – and most Western countries – are caffeine (coffee), nicotine (tobacco) and alcohol (beer, wine, spirits) as well as certain medical tablets which can be obtained without prescription. Certain glues and solvents are likewise misused as drugs, especially among 12 to 16-year-olds.

There are four large groups of illegal drugs, three of which are based on plants (hemp, poppy and coca), with the fourth group being synthetic drugs.

Hemp (cannabis) is the raw material for hashish and marihuana. These drugs are mainly smoked mixed with tobacco as "joints". Consumption produces, among other things, hallucination and mental disorders, and, like alcohol, impairs fitness to drive.

The opium poppy is the base for opium and heroin. Both drugs have been used as painkillers, but they are extremely addictive. Opium is usually smoked while heroin is injected. Many heroin addicts contract AIDS because they share syringes. Long-term heroin abuse leads to physical breakdown and, eventually, death.

Cocaine is extracted from the leaves of the coca bush and is usually snorted. After a brief moment of euphoria, cocaine users suffer, among other things, from hallucination, panic and persecution mania, which, in turn, often produce aggressiveness. Crack (cocaine heated together with baking powder) causes addiction right from the beginning.

There are many synthetic drugs, like LSD and ecstasy, and nobody knows what drugs chemists will come up with next. The so-called designer drugs are specially designed variations of illegal drugs. The clandestine manufacturers seek to escape the provisions of the controlled substances acts in the consumers' countries.

Drug addicts, who want to kick the habit, often suffer from severe and painful withdrawal symptoms. This is why many rehabilitation schemes are not very successful.

As drugs are extremely expensive, "junkies" often turn to crime like theft and burglary to pay for their habit. Female addicts frequently "earn" the necessary money through prostitution.

1. **You have to prepare a talk to teenage students about drugs. Find more detailed information about the commonest types of drugs**

2. **Why do people take drugs? The following words may help you:**

   availability, boredom, curiosity, experiment, frustration, lack of confidence, peer-group pressure, sociability, stress

3. **Should soft drugs be legalized?**

18.2 Why are drugs prohibited?

Drugs are prohibited because

a) they are expensive and addicts often commit crimes to obtain them

b) unlike alcohol and nicotine, they are not taxed and thus the government does not make any money

c) they are substances which affect people's health in a dangerous way and because they can make addictive.

Which answer is correct?

18.3 Drug prevention

Drug prevention is a task for society as a whole. Therefore various institutions deal with it at different levels.

First of all, it should be a task for the parents as they set an example for their children. Drug prevention is also a task for the schools, where it is taught in class. And various local and church institutions engage in drug prevention by means of their drug advice centres.

The police also play an important part in drug prevention. All German state criminal police offices have drug prevention departments. The Rhineland-Palatinate State Criminal Police Office has established the "easi" programme (= Erlebnis, Aktion, Spass und Infos), which is aimed at children aged about 10 to 11; the police liaise with schools and all kinds of sports and other clubs.

Apart from that, police headquarters do preventive work in all fields. At each headquarters, one officer deals with drug prevention at schools, which includes joint activities with teachers, educators and parents.

The uniformed police also deal with drug prevention; their emphasis is on drugs in road traffic, and also in high and vocational schools.

Within the Neustadt/Weinstrasse police directorate, prevention meetings are organized on demand for parents, teachers, educators and tutors.

The Rhineland-Palatinate State Criminal Police Office, the "Weiße Ring" (an organization that helps victims of crimes), and health insurance companies publish flyers and brochures.

There is no cooperation between drug prevention organizations and the police.

Prevention is always to be welcomed; however, the effect of drug prevention measures cannot be measured.

18.4 Methods of importing and trafficking

According to the 2007 United Nations Drug Report, the world's drug problems are being contained, which means there is no longer an increase in the cultivation, production or consumption of the main illegal drugs.

Where drugs are hidden

Due to a computer error the letters of ten words in this text were put in alphabetical order. Find them and put in the right word

Drug traffickers are very egiinnosu when it comes to concealing the stuff. Swallowing drug-filled cdmnoos or balloons is quite an old trick, sometimes resulting in death for the courier. There is no cavity in vehicles which has not been used as a hiding place.

In the famous James Bond film "Goldfinger", gold was smuggled from Britain to Switzerland in a car whose wings were made of gold. In 2009 police in Mexico discovered a car whose wings consisted of a mixture of fibre glass and cocaine – the aceffikrrst had planned to smuggle 75 kg of cocaine into the USA.

Police and customs officials have found drugs concealed in specially prepared aabbells bats, books, cameras, dolls, tubes of aehoopstt or shaving cream, or dissolved in wine, to name but a few. Commercial cegimnnnosst have also been used: drugs were found, for example, in cans of olive oil and peanut butter jars, in containers with frozen fruit pulp, in hollowed-out aacfirrt propellers and elephants' tusks. Drugs from Latin America are frequently flown into the USA in small aircraft and dropped at aadeegnprrr sites.

In Zossen, a small town south of Berlin, plain-clothes officers stopped a cyclist at dghiimnt as his bike had no lights. As the man was known to police because of various drug offences, they searched him and found about 20 grams of hashish in his trouser pockets, and 25 grams of heroin inside a chocolate egg.

In England, a woman received a long prison sentence; the lady ran a horse-importing business and often went to Holland to buy horses, and smuggled heroin, packed in adhlllos hidden in the horseboxes, to Britain.

18.5 Joint border and immigration check by federal police, state police and customs officers within 30 kms of the border

Bad Bergzabern, southern Palatinate, close to the French border, Friday evening, 19.00 hours.

Briefing at the Federal Police barracks for officers of the traffic directorate of police headquarters Ludwigshafen, of the Border Customs Service and the Federal Police. During the night several mixed crews will be on patrol; they will by joined by dog handlers with drug-sniffing dogs.

20.00 hours. A state police officer, a customs officer and a woman federal police officer get into an unmarked BMW 530 which is equipped with a front and rear camera to record incidents. Their task: patrolling the area close to the border and check vehicles. There are large forests in the area as well as fields and vineyards; the area is also called the "green border". The crew drive on narrow rural roads, through vineyards, but also on state and federal roads and through the nearby villages. Until 05.00 a.m. they check 23 suspicious vehicles and their passengers, hide in dark areas to look for possible wrongdoers, follow suspicious vehicles, also walk some distances and arrest one young man for possession of drugs. And they also detect various customs offences.

18.6 Joint drug investigation teams

The joint drug investigation teams were established within the framework of the national drug-combating initiative after German reunification in 1990. The permanent joint drug investigation teams consist of customs officers and police officers.

Their task is to investigate and combat drug crime when police and customs are involved.

In North Rhine-Westphalia the joint investigation teams deal with all cases of organized drug crime. Thus considerable synergy effects can be achieved. The joint teams' task is not to arrest small dealers, but dealers and traffickers who smuggle drugs on a large scale.

In North Rhine-Westphalia there are joint drug investigation teams in Essen, Cologne, Düsseldorf and Münster.

At present there are 28 joint drug investigation teams in Germany, with the police officers mostly being members of the respective state criminal office. The size of the teams varies, for example there are 8/8 officers at Cologne, 4/4 at Münster, 15/15 in Southern Bavaria, and 3/3 at Itzehoe.

Some highlights

Joint drug investigation team of the organized crime department of the Hamburg state criminal police office smash drug ring

Karlsruhe: state prosecution service and joint drug investigation team again successful in their fight against international drug trade

Joint press release of Itzehoe and Hamburg police and Itzehoe and Hamburg state prosecution services: Drug dealing and trafficking ring in Schleswig-Holstein and Hamburg smashed

Kiel: joint drug investigation team successful again: three suspects arrested, 185 kg of heroin secured

Irschenberg: Italian drug courier arrested with 100 kg of hashish

Joint drug investigation teams Berlin and Brandenburg arrest two drug dealers and secure 4 kg of drugs

GER Mecklenburg-Western Pomerania and Hamburg and Rostock prosecution service discover another illegal cannabis farm; the number of farms detected has risen continually during the last few years.

18.7 Arresting a drug trafficker

Federal Police Officer Anton Hager (AH) and customs inspector Manfred Zackig (MZ) of the Düsseldorf Airport Customs Station are checking incoming travellers. Turkish citizen Yilmaz Süley (YS) has been asked to hand over his passport. His identity is then checked with the Schengen Information System via computer.

AH: Mr. Süley, do you speak German?

YS: Yes, but only a little. I would feel more comfortable if we could speak English, please. What are you doing with my passport?

AH: I'm checking your personal data. I've to make sure that you are eligible to enter Germany. There are some requirements you have to meet as you are a traveller from outside the Schengen area.

YS: What are the requirements?

AH: As a Turkish citizen, you are not a citizen of the European Union. Therefore you have to meet the following requirements: You need to produce a valid cross-border paper such as a passport or an ID card. And in your case you also need a visa. In addition to that, you need to prove that you have enough money to pay for your stay in Germany and there must be no warrant in the system barring you from entering Germany. Where have you come from, Mr Süley?

YS: I've come direct from Istanbul.

AH: Is this your first visit to Germany?

YS: Yes, it is. It's the first time I've ever been to Germany.

AH: And what's the reason for your trip?

YS: I want to meet friends in Cologne and I want to see the city.

AH: How long do you intend to stay?

YS: Just three days, I have to go back to Turkey on Monday.

AH: Where will you be staying during your visit?

YS: At the Ibis hotel in downtown Cologne.

AH: Do you have a reservation?

YS: Yes, here it is.

AH: How do you intend to get to the hotel from here?

YS: I'll take the train to Cologne.

AH: How much money have you got on you, Mr Süley?

YS: Some € 500 in cash, and plastic money. Is anything wrong?

The computer check shows that there is no warrant out for Mr Süley, and he has a valid visa. Then the officer notices some irregularities in the print of the personal data in the passport.

AH: Mr Süley, your passport shows some irregularities. Please follow me to my office. I need to check your passport thoroughly. Bring your hand luggage along.

YS: Am I under arrest now?

AH: No, not at all. I'll just take you to my office to check your eligibility to enter the country.

YS: My passport is okay, but of course I'll come with you. Can I leave my hand luggage here?

AH: No, please bring it with you.

Mr Süley follows Officer Hager into his duty room.

AH: Is there any more luggage?

YS: No, I only have hand luggage.

Officer Hager now checks the passport with a document tester and finds out that the print shows some irregularities. It is partly blurred and shows razor marks. He then asks Mr Süley to allow his clothing and his luggage to be searched. Officer Hager has become suspicious and believes that the search will produce material which will help him to establish the traveller's identity.

AH: Please open your bag, Mr Süley. I need to search it.

YS: Well, if you have to....., I've nothing to hide.

Officer Hager puts the bag on the table and finds it unusually heavy. After having opened it, he finds various ID papers, among them a Turkish ID card, an Egyptian passport and a Lebanese driving licence in a side pocket. Then he detects a hidden compartment at the bottom of the bag.

AH: What's this?

YS: What do you mean?

Officer Hager opens the compartment and finds several plates, wrapped and vacuum-sealed.

AH: Looks like drugs, doesn't it?

YS: I don't know anything about that. I refuse to answer any more questions.

AH: It is your right to remain silent. I will hand you over to customs, they will deal with you now.

Officer Hager calls a customs officer, who is busy with luggage checks. He explains that he has a Turkish citizen here, trying to smuggle in about eight kilos of drugs.

AH: Hello Manfred. Have a look at this stuff. I'm sure it'll interest you.

MZ: Sure, looks pretty much like drugs. I'll take over now. Please write your report and I'll take this gentleman to our office.

18.8 Drug-sniffing dog and drug-sniffing sheep

New ways of fighting drugs at Ruchheim motorway police station

For more than three years the members of Ruchheim motorway police station have kept sheep as four-legged lawn mowers on the vast area surrounding their police station building, and have thus helped to keep budget costs down.

Purely by chance POK Bernd Müller happened to notice a special skill of his "colleague" Sammy, a one-year old ram.

Bernd Müller:

"Since I've had dogs for many years, I know all about their olfactory sense. At work, our police dogs again and again surprise us with their outstanding sniffing skills.

Being a gourmet, I also know about truffle-sniffing pigs, but I was almost speechless when I discovered by chance that Sammy is crazy for "grass".

It happened last year. I was watching Sammy sniffing at a car right next to its enclosure. The car belonged to a "customer" who had been arrested for drug use before. Sammy's behaviour prompted me to have a closer look at the vehicle. And indeed, in the boot I found 30 grams of grass with a high content of intoxicating substances. First I thought it was pure chance.

But when Sammy reacted in the same way several times afterwards, I no longer had any doubts: Sammy would become the first drug-sniffing police sheep.

At first, my superiors didn't think I was serious, but after a demonstration they were quickly convinced and approved Sammy's becoming a drug-sniffing sheep, specialized in detecting "grass".

After intensive training at the dog handlers' training facility at Enkenbach, POK Müller and his drug-sniffing ram have been used for drug-sniffing tasks.

If Sammy continues to be as effective as he has been so far, he might also play a role in the public relations activities of the police."

What do you think of this story?

18.9 Drug lingo

Drug users have their own lingo to conceal their addiction from outsiders and to avoid being detected by law enforcement officers. Their terms change frequently.

Here are some examples:

acid	=	LSD
beat the gong (*US*)	=	smoke opium
black smoke/pills/stuff	=	opium
blast	=	illegal narcotic
bomb, bomber, bombita	=	marijuana cigarette, dose of cocaine
C	=	cocaine, crack
camel	=	smuggler of illegal narcotics
candy	=	illegal narcotics
nose candy	=	illegal narcotics in powdered form
China white	=	heroin
Chinese tobacco	=	opium
coke	=	cocaine
cold turkey	=	the effect of sudden and sustained deprivation of narcotics
Colombian gold	=	high-quality marijuana
connection	=	source of illegal narcotics
controlled substance	=	a narcotic
cook	=	addict who ingests heated illegal narcotic
cool	=	not carrying illegal narcotics
opposite	=	hot
cruise	=	be under the influence of illegal drugs
crystal	=	cocaine
deck (*US*)	=	packet of illegal narcotics
do a line	=	ingest narcotics illegally through the nose
doll	=	narcotic in pill form
dragon	=	habitual illegal use of narcotics
dream dust	=	heroin
Eastern substances	=	illegal narcotics
get off	=	ingest narcotics illegally
girl (*US*)	=	cocaine
God's own medicine	=	a narcotic or hallucinogen
gone	=	drunk or under the influence of drugs
goof (*US*)	=	habitual user of illegal drugs
(green) grass	=	marijuana
happy dust (*US*)	=	cocaine
herb	=	marijuana
hot shot (*US*)	=	fatal dose of illegal narcotics
ice	=	illegal narcotic, cocaine
Indian hemp	=	cannabis
joy	=	heroin

junk	=	illegal narcotics
lid	=	an ounce of marijuana
line	=	nasal ingestion of narcotics
Lucy in the sky with diamonds	=	LSD
Mary	=	marijuana
Mexican brown (*US*)	=	marijuana
(the) monkey (*US*)	=	addiction to illegal narcotics
mule, yak (*US*)	=	carrier of illegal narcotics
pot	=	marijuana
powder	=	narcotic taken illegally
punk	=	low-quality marijuana
racked, ripped (*US*)	=	under the influence of narcotics
recreational drug	=	illegal narcotic
red cross	=	morphine
reefer	=	marijuana cigarette
runny nose	=	cocaine addiction
sent, shattered, smashed, stoned, strung out, tanked (up), up, way out, wired, wrecked, zoned out, zonked	=	under the influence of narcotics
slang (*US*)	=	sell illegal narcotics
smack	=	heroin
snow	=	cocaine
speedball	=	cocktail of illegal narcotics
stash	=	supply of illegal narcotics or the place where it is hidden
stick	=	marijuana cigarette
sugar	=	illegal narcotic
suspect cigarette	=	marijuana cigarette
sweet tooth	=	addiction to illegal narcotics
tea	=	marijuana
Thai stick	=	marijuana or heroin cigarette
travel agent	=	illegal dealer in narcotics
weed	=	marijuana
white girl/lady	=	heroin or cocaine

Find out about other terms. Here are some examples

angel dust – Angola black – Aunt Emma – Aunt Hazel – Aunt Mary – backdoor artist – Bernies – Big Harry – Big John – black bomb – black shit – blue cheese – broccoli – candy man – carry the M-monkey – have a Chinaman on the back – Corina – crying weed – double dimples – dynamiter – eight – flea powder – fu – great tobacco – haircut – heater dealer – iron house – Jane Boy – jojee – kukuge – lettuce – Madeleine – Mexican horse – number seven – Prince-of-Wales feathers – pumpkin seed – red oil – ride the witch's broom – San Francisco rainbow – silver bike – snow flake – Texas tea – yellow football

18.10 Numerals

Grundzahlen

Die Grundzahlen kennen Sie alle, beachten Sie aber folgende Besonderheiten

Die Null ist entweder

nought – als Zahlenwert

zero – als Nullpunkt einer Skala und

o – beim „Buchstabieren", also z.B. bei der Durchsage von Telefonnummern

Zwischen Zehner und Einer steht ein Bindestrich, sonst auseinander

twenty-two, two thousand five hundred and fifty-five

Bei Zahlen über 100 steht vor Zehner und Einer das *"and"*

Two hundred and forty-seven, five thousand and three.

Vor *hundred, thousand* und *million* steht entweder *a* (ungefähr), *one* (genau) oder ein Zahlwort

a hundred, one thousand, five million.

Bei großen Zahlen (ab vier Stellen) werden jeweils drei Stellen durch Komma oder Lücke abgetrennt, Ausnahme sind die Jahreszahlen

12,954, 34 678, the year 1999.

Ordnungszahlen

first – 1st, second – 2nd, third – 3rd, fourth – 4th, fifth – 5th etc.

Ab 21 werden die letzten beiden Buchstaben angehängt, also *21st, 32nd, 43rd, 69th* etc.

Bei Dezimalzahlen steht im Englischen ein Punkt und nicht wie im Deutschen ein Komma. Die Ziffern hinter dem Punkt werden einzeln gelesen, eine Null vor dem Punkt wird in der Regel weggelassen, also

34.567 wird gesprochen *thirty-four point five six seven*

.38 = point thirty-eight

Datum

Folgende Schreibweisen sind möglich

16th May, 1999 – May 16th, 1999 – 16 May, 1999 – May 16, 1999

Die Aussprache ist in allen vier Fällen gleich *"on the sixteenth of May 1999"*

Kurzformen sind *16/05/99* oder (besonders im Amerikanischen) *05/16/99* – traurige Berühmtheit hat *9/11* erlangt, der 11. September 2001, als Terroristen das World Trade Center in New York zum Einsturz brachten.

Bei Verwechslungsmöglichkeiten wie z.B. 3. April nachfragen, ob 03/04/1999 den 3. April oder den 4. März bedeutet.

18.11 Useful phrases

Übersetzen Sie

1. Man unterscheidet zwischen legalen Drogen (Koffein, Nikotin, Alkohol) und illegalen Drogen (Haschisch, Marihuana, Heroin, Kokain, synthetische Drogen).

   ....

2. Es gibt viele Gründe, weshalb Leute Drogen nehmen, z.B. Langeweile, Neugier, mangelndes Selbstvertrauen, Druck von Gleichaltrigen usw.

   ....

3. Weiche Drogen sollten nicht legalisiert werden.

   ....

4. Verschiedene Institutionen befassen sich mit der Drogenprävention.

   ....

5. Drogenschmuggler sind sehr einfallsreich beim Verstecken der Drogen.

   ....

6. Um nach Deutschland einzureisen, brauchen Sie einen Reisepass und ein Visum.

   ....

7. Was ist der Grund für Ihre Reise?

   ....

8. Wo wohnen Sie während Ihres Aufenthalts in Deutschland, und wieviel Geld führen Sie mit sich?

   ....

9. Ich übergebe Sie einem Zollbeamten, der sich weiter um Sie kümmern wird.

   ....

10. Drogensüchtige haben ihre eigene Sprache, um ihre Sucht vor Außenstehenden zu verbergen.

    ....

11. Drogensüchtige kann man z.B. an sehr kleinen oder sehr großen Pupillen erkennen.

    ....

12. Schweißausbrüche, unkoordinierte Sprache und extreme Nervosität deuten auf Drogenmissbrauch hin.

    ....

18.12 Key words and phrases

addictive – controlled substances act – courier – designer drug – drug-sniffing dog – euphoria – hemp – (il)legal drug – intoxicating substance – joint – lingo – persecution mania – poppy – snort – syringe – trafficker – visa – withdrawal symptom

Unit 19

Incident on a train

This unit deals with

- fare dodging
- assault and arrest and
- the infinitive and participle.

19.1 Fare dodging

Fare dodging can either be intentional or negligent. Intentional fare dodging means that a person enters a bus or other means of public transport knowing full well that he/she does not have a valid ticket. In the case of negligent fare dodging, the person concerned has, for example, a season ticket, but does not carry it on him/her when caught by an inspector.

In most German cities you have to pay a fine of € 40 (officially referred to as "erhöhtes Beförderungsentgelt" = "increased fare") when caught without a ticket. If you have a season ticket and present it at the transport company's office within seven days, you only pay an administrative fee of € 5 to € 7.

In many cases not carrying a ticket is a result of thoughtlessness, although sometimes certain systems can make it difficult. In Munich, for example, in buses and trams you have to validate your ticket in the vehicle, whereas on the underground and S-Bahn trains you have to do it on the platform. So it might easily happen that you enter an S-Bahn thinking you can validate your ticket in the carriage, and you find out that this isn't possible.

If a person is caught in Germany without a valid ticket and cannot be or refuses to be identified, the inspectors will call the police. The inspectors often work in plain clothes so that potential fare dodgers cannot identify them before boarding a train or bus. And these officers usually work in teams of two or three.

In January 2009, the fine for fare dodging on the underground or on a bus in London was increased from £ 20 to £ 50; however, if you pay within three weeks, the fine is reduced to £ 25. The public transport system in London employs about 500 inspectors. By the way, former British Prime Minister Tony Blair was once caught on the train from Heathrow Airport to London without a ticket.

Have you ever been caught on public transport without a valid ticket?

19.2 Two stories

Story 1

For many years, the cities of Frankfurt and Offenbach did not have an integrated public transport network. So if you travelled by tram from Frankfurt to Offenbach, you had to get a ticket to the city boundary, and from there another ticket to the centre of Offenbach. Once it happened that a group of Japanese businessmen who went to the International Leather Goods Fair in Offenbach only had tickets to the Frankfurt city boundary and had to pay the corresponding fine.

The Japanese businessmen are back home. What do they tell their friends?

Story 2

A mother with three children aged 4, 6 and 7, had forgotten to validate the tickets on the platform before entering an S-Bahn train. When she was asked to show her tickets, the officer did not insist on a fine but told her that at the next stop she should quickly get off the train, validate the tickets on the platform and get on again. She did so. However, she was not fast enough, and the train with her children inside left without her.

Continue the story

19.3 Assault and arrest

Characters: train conductor Zebedeus Saarner (ZS), Maltese citizen Pietru Debrincat (PD), federal police officers POM Thomas Berbig (TB), and PK Michael Eschert (ME), KHK Rainer Gürtler (RG), custody officer Gunnar Wiedemann (GW), judge Dr. Oberfell (RO), state prosecutor Gerhard Faber (GF)

Train conductor Zebedeus Saarner thinks he has got a quiet Sunday ahead. He starts work in the morning in Berlin; he is in charge of ICE 599 Berlin – Stuttgart. The train leaves Berlin on time, at 11.37, and is due to arrive at Stuttgart at 17.08.

ZS takes his time and gets the latest pieces of information from the engine driver by telephone. In the meantime the train has left Berlin and is on its way to Brunswick. ZS begins checking the passengers' tickets in a first-class open-plan carriage. Nearly all seats are occupied. The passenger on seat 76 is asleep. ZS does not wake him and continues checking the tickets of the other passengers.

Then he goes back to seat 76 and gently nudges the sleeping man. The man slowly wakes up and first does not know what ZS wants from him. Then he answers in English that he has to look for his ticket. He starts rummaging in his pockets, but does not find anything.

ZS thinks that all this is taking too long and now asks for an ID. The man does not respond and continues rummaging in his pockets, and in a low voice he makes some derogatory remarks, which are apparently aimed at the conductor.

ZS: Good afternoon, your ticket, please.

PD: Just a moment, I must have it somewhere here. Shit, waking me up. Stupid conductor, hasn't got anything else to do....

ZS (putting his hand on the man's shoulder and trying to calm him): Calm down, we've got enough time. You do have a ticket, don't you?

PD jumps up and shouts:

PD: Don't you touch me. What kind of behaviour is that?
And he murmurs: Idiot, I didn't think that they would check tickets here.

ZS: I'm sorry. I only wanted to tell you that you don't have to hurry.

PD: Are you crazy, waking me up? Haven't you got anything better to do? Get lost before I hit you in the face.

ZS: Mind your tongue. Either you show me your ticket now, or you'll have to pay for a ticket and also pay a fine.

PD: Just you try.....

He gets up from his seat and punches the conductor who cannot step back fast enough and is hit in the face twice. At once two passengers get up and help the conductor restrain PD, who is kicking and punching around. PD is locked into the conductor's compartment with one of the witnesses volunteering to keep an eye on him until the police arrive. ZS thanks the passengers.

ZS: Thank you very much for your prompt help. It doesn't happen very often that I'm attacked or that I'm being helped so promptly. At our next stop at Brunswick a federal police patrol will board the train and take care of everything. Please be prepared to make a statement as witnesses, and please give me your personal data.

The two witnesses give the conductor their calling cards, which is sufficient for the moment. Then ZS goes back to his compartment and watches PD, who continues to shout threats against ZS.

The train reaches Brunswick, where a two-man patrol of the federal police are already waiting on the platform. They enter the train and stay on it to Göttingen. They first record the statements of the conductor and of the two witnesses, and then they turn to PD.

TB: You're under arrest on suspicion of fare dodging as well as assault and battery. We're going to search you now for our own safety. Please lean against the wall.

PD does so, and ME searches him. In PD's jacket ME finds not only his passport, but also a sharp 16 cm-long knife.

ME: What have we got here? That's a dagger, it's far too long, you're not allowed to have it on you.

PD: Why not? In Malta, my home country, everybody has such a weapon for self-defence.

ME: But not in Germany. Here, carrying such a weapon in public places is prohibited. That's "only" a minor offence, but it can entail a fine of up to € 10,000 and confiscation of the weapon. I'm going to secure it now. Do you consent?

PD: What can I do? What happens if I don't consent?

ME: Then I have to confiscate the weapon. That means more paperwork, and a judge has to confirm the confiscation.

PD: ... fuck, do what you want to do; apparently I've got no chance to do anything about it.

ME: This passport in the name of Pietru Debrincat, is it yours?

PD: Yes, of course, what you think?

The other federal police officer checks PD's passport and learns that there is a warrant for PD of Amtsgericht (magistrates' court) Darmstadt for failing to appear in court in a case of grievous bodily harm.

TB: Mr Debrincat, I must inform you that there is a warrant out for you of Amtsgericht Darmstadt for a bodily harm offence. In Göttingen you'll be taken to CID officers who'll deal with you.

PD: Shit......

The train stops at Göttingen, and PD is taken to a detention cell at the station. Officers TB and ME make out the charge and write all the necessary reports. At about 16.00, PD is taken, together with the charge, to Göttingen CID station, where KHK Rainer Gürtler handles the matter; PD is taken to his office.

RG: Good afternoon, Mr Debrincat, I'm detective inspector Gürtler. How well do you speak German?

PD: Not all that well, but I see your English is quite good, so let's continue in that language.

RG: Here I've got an arrest note of the Wolfsburg federal police. You were arrested on the train from Berlin to Brunswick as you were in the first class section without a valid ticket and because you attacked the conductor. That's quite a lot. Apart from that, there is an arrest warrant of Amtsgericht Darmstadt for you. That's why you'll be brought before an investigating magistrate tomorrow. I'll have to question you about what happened, and get your personal data. Are you willing to make a statement about the facts?

PD: I don't care. What am I to do, you won't let me off anyway.

RG: True. First of all I have to inform you about your rights. You've got the right to make or to refuse to make a statement. You can retain a lawyer at any time. If you want to, I can give you a list with lawyers whom you may phone. If you don't have enough money, a duty solicitor will be appointed. If you don't speak German well enough, we'll call an interpreter who will translate everything. You can ask for evidence be secured, and we'll inform the Maltese consulate in Berlin about your arrest.

PD: Yes, I know all that, and later you'll fingerprint me. It doesn't matter, let's just go on.

RG: Then let's get down to the facts. Please tell me what happened today.

PD: I wanted to go to Stuttgart by train today, as a friend had promised me a job there. I was fed up with Berlin.

RG: Did you have a ticket?

PD: Of course not. How am I supposed to get a ticket without any money? I was broke, and that's why I had to go to Stuttgart.

FG: Where did you live in Berlin?

PD: At a girlfriend's. But she's got a new boyfriend and threw me out.

RG: What about your friend in Stuttgart? What's his name? How can I reach him? What kind of job were you to get there?

PD: He's an Englishman, John Walker. I haven't got his phone number, but he's always at the station.

RG: Where does he live?

PD: I don't know, he's always at the station.

RG: Well, what kind of job would you have got?

PD: We haven't talked about the details yet. But he promised me.

RG: What happened when the conductor wanted to check you?

PD: I can't remember. I just went bananas as he didn't leave me in peace. I never thought that they would check tickets in first class.

RG: Do you remember where you hit the conductor?

PD: Of course, right in the face. I had told him. And he would have got more if the other two hadn't held me.

RG: What about the dagger?

PD: That's a souvenir from my home country. There everybody has such a dagger for self-defence. I didn't know that you aren't allowed to have one on you here.

RG: What about the warrant from Darmstadt?

PD: Ah, that was last year. I hit a store detective who caught me shoplifting. I was remanded in custody for a short time, and then they let me go. They told me I would get a summons for the trial, but I never got it.

RG: How could you have got it without a fixed address?

PD: They could have sent it to Malta, and my mother would have informed me.

RG: I rather think you hoped that you would never be checked again.

PD: *(grinning)* What next?

RG: Have you committed any other offences?

PD: No, no, that's all.

RG: Then please read what I wrote down here in English. If everything is correct, please sign here.

PD: Ok.

RG: Ok, you already said it yourself that we have to establish your identity. Part of that is taking your fingerprints and photograph. The fingerprints are then checked with our files. Tonight you'll sleep in our detention cell. When we've established that you are the person identified in your passport and when we've got the warrant you'll be brought before a magistrate tomorrow.

In the photograph and fingerprinting office, PD has to sit on a swivel chair where he is photographed. Afterwards the prints of all ten fingers are taken and transferred onto a special sheet which will later be faxed to the Federal Criminal Police Office.

PD: What are you doing with my fingerprints?

RG: They will be sent to the Federal Criminal Police Office, where they will be compared with others. So we can find out if you've perhaps committed other offences.

PD: You won't find anything.

RG: I'm not sure about that, but we'll see. Now that all the paperwork has been done, I'm taking you to the custody officer.

In the custody officer`s office.

GW: Please put all your valuables on the table. Also your watch, your belt and the laces from your shoes.

PD: Is all that really necessary?

GW: Yes, we don't want your valuables to disappear. And we also must make sure that you won't hurt or even kill yourself with the belt or the shoelaces.

PD: If I wanted to kill myself, I would have done so a long time ago.

GW: You never can tell. That's why we have our rules. You'll soon get something to eat in your cell, and I wish you a good night.

After the warrant has arrived, KHK Gürtler includes it in the arrest file. Afterwards he adds the statements of the conductor, the two witnesses, the federal police officers and PD and makes a final report which contains the most important facts and pieces of evidence. In this report he suggests, because of the incident on the train and the risk of escape, issuing an arrest warrant and to note "Überhaft" (extended detention) because of the Darmstadt warrant.

The accused's statement is translated the following morning by an interpreter and added to the file. This file is then sent to the prosecution office, together with the arrest file from Darmstadt.

In the morning DB is brought before the magistrate; the prosecutor is already there.

RO: Good morning, Mr Debrincat. You've been brought here because there's a warrant out for you by Darmstadt magistrates because of a criminal offence. You've got a copy of the warrant in the meantime. Are you the person named in the warrant?

PD: Yes, that's obvious.

RO: I have to question you about yesterday's incident on the train. Do you wish to make a statement?

PD: What can I say? I already told the CID officer everything yesterday.

RO: Yes, I've seen that you signed a confession. But I have to ask you again. Why did you assault the conductor?

PD: Because he acted stupidly. Apart from that I didn't think that tickets would be checked in first class. I was so frustrated as I didn't have any money.

RO: Where do you live?

PD: Nowhere at the moment. In Berlin my girlfriend threw me out, I can't go back. I was to get a job in Stuttgart, but I haven't got there yet.

RO: What's the name of your friend in Stuttgart, and how can he be reached?

PD: We had planned to meet at the station, he's always there.

RO: Don't you have an address? Or phone number?

PD: No, I don't, but he is well known in Stuttgart.

RO: Mr prosecutor, over to you.

GF: Well, I think the facts are clear. Mr Debrincat is of no fixed abode and has no permanent job. Apparently he has no ties within the Federal Republic of Germany, and he didn't appear at the trial in Darmstadt. I therefore request that Maltese citizen Pietru Debrincat be arrested. I also request his being arrested because of the incident on the Berlin – Stuttgart train, to make sure he'll be present at the trial.

RO: Mr Debrincat, have you got anything else to say?

PD: What else am I to say, everything is clear, you're going to arrest me anyway.

RO: I herewith rule as follows:

The warrant issued by AG Darmstadt will be executed, Mr Pietru Debrincat will be held in remand custody. Mr Pietru Debrincat will also be held in remand custody because of risk of absconding, in the proceedings of STA/AG Göttingen.

19.4 Outsmarting a criminal

Kevin Junglen (KV) prepares the food and drinks for his 35th birthday party. He has invited about a dozen of his closest friends.

Suddenly the phone rings. It's his girlfriend Laura Brandt (LB).

KV: Kevin Junglen speaking.

LB: Hi, darling. Anything new from Freddy?

KV: No, that bloke certainly won't press charges against me. He's a coward, and he's afraid of me. I think I taught him a lesson when I knocked him out. He won't ever dare insult me in the future.

LB: Well, let's hope so. I'll be with you in about an hour. I love you.

KV: So do I.

A week before KV had knocked down and injured another guest rather badly at his favourite pub. That man has pressed charges, there is a warrant out for KV, and, as a result, officers Alexandra Matisiak (AM) and Rouven Eichhorn (RE) have come to arrest him. They ring the bell. KV walks to the door and sees the two officers through the spyhole. So he does not open the door, trying to make the officers believe that he is not at home.

Outside the door:

AM: He isn't at home. We'll have to come back another time.

RE: I'm sure he's in.

AM: Even if he's in we can't force the door. So let's go back and come another time.

They go back to their patrol car, where, before they leave, they have another look at KV's file.

AM: Rouven, it's his birthday today. I'm sure he was inside and didn't open when he saw us. Maybe he was preparing a birthday party. I think I have an idea. Let's pretend we're guests for his party and bring him a present. He might watch us from the window, so let's drive our patrol car round the corner.

They do so, walk back to the flat and ring the bell again. But they not only ring the bell, they also sing loudly "Happy birthday to you!"

KV opens the door and is handcuffed immediately.

19.5 Infinitive and participles

Der Infinitiv ohne *to* sowie die Partizipien (*-ing, -ed,* 3. Form bei unregelmäßigen Verben) werden nach Verben der Sinneswahrnehmung, nach *have* sowie nach einer Reihe weiterer Verben verwendet. Nach *have* wird eine Erfahrung bzw. eine Veranlassung oder Genehmigung ausgedrückt

The federal police saw/watched five illegal immigrants wade/wading through the Neisse river last night.

They noticed some strangers approaching the west bank of the river and arrested them.

The immigrants were taken to the nearest detention centre, because the federal police did not want to keep them waiting in the freezing cold. This was not the first time they had caught illegal immigrants crossing the Neisse.

The officers found a car equipped with all sorts of devices.

The suspects had their fingerprints taken.

We can't have people entering the country without valid documents.

When we were in Italy, we had our car stolen.

Relativsätze können sowohl mit Hilfe des Partizips als auch des Infinitivs mit *to* verkürzt werden. Dabei wird der Infinitiv vor allem nach betonten Substantiven verwendet.

The prices paid for forged passports can be considerable.

Those applying for political asylum must have valid reasons.

The first illegal immigrant to be arrested was a Russian drug smuggler.

19.6 Abridgement exercise

Shorten the following sentences

1. Crossing an unguarded border is one of the easiest things **you can do**.

2. The ID card, **which was issued** by his local authority, was stolen so that it could be used by forgers.

3. There was nothing **which suggested** that he was someone else.

4. We saw **how they crossed** the border near the bridge.

5. I expect **that the fugitives will be caught** within the next few hours.

6. Of course, the public want to see **that offenders are punished**.

7. Did you hear **that the door was being closed** behind you?

8. We observed **how a young man climbed** over the fence and made a bee-line for a blue pickup, which was waiting for him on the other side.

9. The sums **which are demanded by those who smuggle** people across the border are incredibly high.

10. The person **who was arrested** last night is wanted for various offences.

19.7 Useful phrases

Übersetzen Sie

1. Fahren ohne Fahrschein in einem öffentlichen Verkehrsmittel kann absichtlich oder unabsichtlich geschehen.

   ....

2. Sie müssen Ihren Fahrschein in der Straßenbahn entwerten.

   ....

3. Wenn Sie sich nicht ausweisen können oder wollen, müssen wir die Polizei rufen.

   ....

4. Fahrkartenkontrolleure arbeiten meist in Zivilkleidung und oft zu zweit oder zu dritt.

   ....

5. Wer ohne gültige Fahrkarte angetroffen wird, muss ein sog. „erhöhtes Beförderungsentgelt" (= Geldstrafe) bezahlen.

   ....

   ....

6. Wer seine gültige Monatskarte vergessen hat, muss sie innerhalb einer Woche in der Geschäftsstelle vorzeigen und braucht dann nur eine Verwaltungsgebühr von € 5 zu bezahlen.

   ....

   ....

7. Fahrkartenkontrolleure werden oft beschimpft und beleidigt, manchmal sogar tätlich angegriffen.

   ....

8. In der Londoner U-Bahn müssen Schwarzfahrer eine Geldstrafe von £ 50 zahlen.

   ....

9. Bei Bezahlung innerhalb von drei Wochen verringert sich die Geldstrafe auf £ 25.

   ....

19.8 Key words and phrases

assault (and battery) – be broke – calling card – conductor – custody officer – dagger – fare – fare dodging – fixed abode – platform – public transport network – remand custody – season ticket – summons – ticket inspector – valid ticket – validate

Unit 20

Domestic violence, stalking

This Unit deals with

- domestic violence
- stalking
- child abuse, child neglect and
- participle constructions to abridge certain types of dependent clauses.

20.1 Definitions

Domestic Violence

The German Federal Ministry for Family, Seniors, Women and Juveniles defines violence in the family as "violence between adults who are living or have been living in an intimate relationship. The decisive factor is the place where violence took place, i. e. the home."

The US Office on Violence against Women (OVW) defines domestic violence as a "pattern of abusive behavior in any relationship that is used by one partner to gain or maintain power and control over another intimate partner."

Stalking

Stalking is defined as "behaviour where an individual wilfully and repeatedly engages in harassing conduct directed at another person which reasonably and seriously alarms, torments, or terrorizes that person".

Find out more about domestic violence and stalking in the EU countries. Use the internet

20.2 Two cases of stalking

Case 1

A suspect chased his ex-girlfriend through the streets of a small town in his car. He had previously been convicted of strangling her unconscious and beating her, then looking for her immediately after being released from jail. Five weeks later he attempted to cut the phone line to her house. He smashed the window to her bedroom with a lump of heavy rock. She was able to escape through a bathroom window and run to a neighbour's house. He shot and killed her boyfriend and wounded her daughter. He then set fire to the house and committed suicide in an upstairs bedroom.

What offences/crimes, according to German law, were committed in this case?

Case 2

For some time Sylvia Schön, a 26-year-old medical student, has been molested by an unknown stalker who has been sending her unwanted letters and flower bouquets. She has repeatedly seen an unknown man stalking around the house where she lives in a ground floor flat. Since she has become more and more worried, and also has some psychic problems, she has reported the stalking incidents to the police. In the evening she hears someone trying to force the door of her flat and immediately calls the police, who arrest the intruder at the door. The offender is 33-year-old casual worker Freddy Faul (FF), who, after having been fingerprinted and photographed, is taken to detective inspector Herbert Hurtig (HH). After he has been informed about his rights, he declares that he is willing to make a statement and does not want a lawyer. So he is questioned about the facts.

HH: Mr Faul, I've just told you that you've been arrested because you're suspected of attempted burglary and stalking, as defined in § 238 of the penal code. Please tell me why you've moved to our city.

FF: Well, you already know that I'm from northern Germany. I grew up as the youngest of six children, and I was always badly treated. There was never any money. My brothers and sisters were always preferred to me. Both my parents had a job, father was an alcoholic and often involved in brawls.

HH: What about your mother?

FF: She always did what my father wanted her to do. According to the principle "Noch'n Spruch – Kieferbruch" ("If you don't shut up, I'll break your jaw"). Father was always the winner. I left school and only got odd jobs afterwards.

HH: Let's have a look at your criminal record.

FF: There isn't much. A few times because I smoked hash, and things like that.

HH: And coercion and bodily harm?

FF: Yes, every time I get the sack I get really mad. And when a girlfriend leaves me, it's even worse, and then it may happen that I beat her up. Last time they even sent me to a psychiatric hospital.

HH: That was because of your suicide attempt. And you got two years on probation for serious bodily harm committed against your girlfriend.

FF: Yes, true, but that was unjust. When dealing with women you must be insistent and dominant. And if you have a strong hand, they'll do what you want them to do.

HH: Why did you move to our town?

FF: I was fed up to the back teeth with the birds at home. They do nothing but cause problems. I usually make friends easily, but after a short period the girls leave me. I was fed up of living alone. Here in the Rhineland the girls are much less reserved, and I thought everything would be all right.

HH: How did you think it would work?

FF: I chose Sylvia, as I saw her quite often in the pub and when she went shopping. And the more trouble I had at work, the better I felt when I saw her. When I see her, at the window of her flat, in the street or in the pub, I get quite crazy. Only then do I feel well. It's quite clear that we belong to each other.

HH: Have you ever told her?

FF: No, not at all, I've not yet spoken to her. I must be sure that this time everything is going to be all right, and I have to prepare everything very carefully, with letters, small gifts etc. I need her very much. When I can see her often enough, she'll certainly understand.

HH: How was all that to go on?

FF: Well, sooner or later she'll understand that we belong to each other.

HH: Please tell me what happened tonight.

FF: Okay, okay, I tried to break into Sylvia's home, as I thought she wasn't at home. Today, I was once again mad about everything. My boss gave me a second warning, and I'll probably be sacked this week. I really had to let off steam.

HH: What did you want to do at Sylvia's place?

FF: I had bought some roses and planned to distribute them in her flat. I also wanted to take some souvenirs. But apparently that was pretty stupid.

HH: Souvenirs? What for?

FF: I wanted to take some of her underwear, because then I can always think of her.

HH: Mr Faul, that's the end of the interview. Tomorrow morning, after our meeting with the state prosecutor, you'll be taken before the examining magistrate.

20.3 Child abuse, child neglect

In September 2009, five-year-old Marie Anna painfully died as a result of neglect in her parents' home. Shortly before, she had been taken to hospital, but could not be saved there.

According to the post mortem report, the little girl only weighed seven kilogrammes; 15 to 20 kilogrammes is the normal weight for girls of that age. The girl died of hunger and thirst, and, as was proved by numerous injuries, had apparently been beaten and maltreated.

The 26- and 23-year-old parents, both unemployed, were remanded on suspicion of causing death by neglect.

In 2007, 1,452 cases of child abuse were reported in the federal crime statistics. 80 children were killed, 245 were raped. As is nearly always the case, there is a link between the criminal and the victim. The clear-up rate is almost 98 %.

20.4 Participle constructions to abridge certain types of dependent clauses

Mit Hilfe von Partizipien (*-ing, -ed*) können verschiedene Arten von Nebensätzen verkürzt werden. In bestimmten Fällen sind Konjunktionen (Bindewörter) unbedingt erforderlich, weil sonst die Zuordnung nicht immer eindeutig ist.

Temporalsätze

(When) looking at the CCTV screen, the officers spotted a group of Liverpool fans crossing the pitch.

Founded by Sir Robert Peel in 1829, the Met developed into an effective police force.

Kausalsätze

Having been denied admission, the Rangers supporters turned on innocent bystanders and started a fight.

Begleitumstandssätze ('wobei') bzw. mit *and* angeschlossene Sätze

The supporters of the home team walked past, keeping their hands in their pockets.

Folgesätze (immer mit *thus* eingeleitet)

The away team scored one goal after the other, thus infuriating the home team supporters.

Konditionalsätze

This explosion would have caused hundreds of casualties happening in a crowded street.

Konzessivsätze (immer mit *though*)

The phenomenon of hooliganism, though associated with football, must be seen in a wider context.

20.5 Abridgement exercise

Shorten the following sentences

1. When they returned to the train station, the hooligans went on the rampage in the city centre.

2. They would make a better impression if they were sober rather than punch-drunk.

3. The officers were standing at the turnstiles and frisked every spectator.

4. Since they knew full well how violent some of the Arsenal fans can be, the members of the special squad made sure that all offensive weapons were confiscated.

5. Some Tottenham fans climbed over the fence and, as a result, joined the crowd without being checked.

6. Although they had been warned beforehand, five Amsterdam supporters insisted on carrying flick-knives and knuckle-dusters.

7. Unruly behaviour can be stopped in its tracks if it is met with firmness right from the beginning.

8. As they were not allowed in at the northern entrance, the crowd surged forward and trampled sixteen people to death.

9. After they had waited in vain for an opportunity to get tickets, the lager louts started to throw bricks and other missiles.

10. As/When they were confronted with hundreds of violent youths, the police decided to use water cannon.

20.6 Useful phrases

Fragen/Sagen Sie ein(em) Opfer von Stalking und häuslicher Gewalt,

1. was es getan hat, um die unerwünschten Aufmerksamkeiten des Stalkers zu beenden.

   ....

2. ob sie von anderen Stalkinghandlungen weiß.

   ....

3. wie lange die Stalkinghandlungen schon gehen.

   ....

4. wie beeinträchtigend die Belästigungen sind.

   ....

5. welche rechtlichen Schritte es unternommen hat.

   ....

6. wie oft es schon die Polizei gerufen hat.

   ....

7. dass ihm Hilfen gegeben werden können.

   ....

8. dass man häusliche Gewalt nicht dulden muss.

   ....

9. dass der Täter aus dem Haus gewiesen werden kann.

   ....

10. dass ein schlagender Täter sich selten ändert.

   ....

20.7 Key words and phrases

child abuse – child neglect – coercion – domestic violence – harass – maltreat – molest – post mortem – rape – stalk

Unit 21

Sex crimes

This unit deals with

- the definitions of rape and child pornography
- some details about child pornography, paedophilia, cybercrime and prostitution
- various cases of rape
- DNA and
- the infinitive and the gerund.

21.1 Rape: definition

Rape or sexual assault, is unwanted forced intercourse. It can happen to women and men of any age, although male rape is much less frequent. A rapist uses force or violence, or the threat of it, to have intercourse with his/her victim. Rape is a crime; the person committing it may be a stranger, a date, an acquaintance or friend, or a family member.

21.2 A rape trial

Today the Greifswald magistrates' court will commence proceedings against Jürgen S. and Alexander F. The two men, aged 25 and 26, are charged with brutally raping the then 17-year-old twin sisters Kathleen and Elizabeth T. from Norwich last May. The girls were in Greifswald on a school exchange. The accused had allegedly met the girls in a disco, had bought them many alcoholic drinks and had apparently spiked their drinks. Afterwards they carried the unconscious girls to their car and drove them to S.'s house where they repeatedly raped the two girls after the latter had come to again. The accused claim that the girls had agreed to everything, and that they had been drunk but not unconscious.

21.3 Taxi driver rapist

The New York City Police Department are investigating a series of sexual attacks on women in yellow cabs. At least half a dozen women reported having been raped by a taxi driver. They all had flagged down a taxi in Manhattan in the late evening. The taxi driver invited them to a glass of champagne, telling them he had won in the lottery, and showed them large amounts of money. A short time after they had accepted the drink they became unconscious, and the driver drove to a secluded spot, climbed into the back and raped them. Afterwards he took them home and even charged them for the ride. None of the women were able to give a detailed description of the taxi driver.

1. **Should the women have accepted the champagne?**
2. **Should they have got out of the taxi when they were offered alcohol?**
3. **Why should a man with a lottery win still drive a taxi and show large sums to his passengers?**
4. **Are taxi drivers allowed to carry alcohol in "open containers" in their vehicles?**

21.4 A case of rape

English student Audrey Davies (AD) is brought to a police station in Hamburg by two officers. Her clothes are torn and soiled, and she is obviously very distressed. Detective Karin Fischer (KF) talks to her.

KF: Can I get you a cup of coffee or anything else before we start?

AD: That would be nice, thank you.

KF: Now, please tell me exactly what happened.

AD: I was walking through the park near Dammtor station when I noticed that someone was following me.

KF: Sorry to interrupt, what time was that?

AD: I got off the train which normally arrives at half past ten. And I think it was more or less on time.

KF: Then what happened?

AD: I don't know why, but I had the feeling that the man was up to no good. So I walked faster and even broke into a run, but he grabbed me from behind. I tried to resist, but he was too strong. He threatened me with a knife and dragged me behind some bushes.

KF: Did he say anything?

AD: My German isn't good enough to make out exactly what he was saying, but there was no mistaking his gestures.

KF: What did he do then?

AD: He threw me to the ground and started to rip off my clothes. I daren't scream because he was holding the knife to my throat all the time.

KF: So you didn't resist?

AD: How could I? What with the knife on my throat? I was afraid that he was going to kill me, so I let him have his way.

KF: I'm very sorry, but we need all the details, however painful this may be for you.

AD: First he ripped open my blouse and cut my bra, then he pushed up my skirt and tore my panties. And then he forced my legs apart and did it.

KF: In other words, his penis penetrated you?

AD: Yes. It seemed to take ages. I was so frightened.

KF: Did he ejaculate?

AD: I think so. Suddenly he let go of me and ran away.

KF: Do you remember in what direction he ran?

AD: No, I don't. It was dark, and I was too scared.

KF: We'll come to the man later. First we'll have to take care of you. I'm afraid you'll have to be examined by a doctor, and then we'll have to get you some new clothes. We'll have to examine the clothes you are wearing, as they might provide important evidence.

AD: Oh my God, whatever next?

KF: I'm sorry, but we have to go through these procedures if we are to catch the rapist.

21.5 DNA analysis

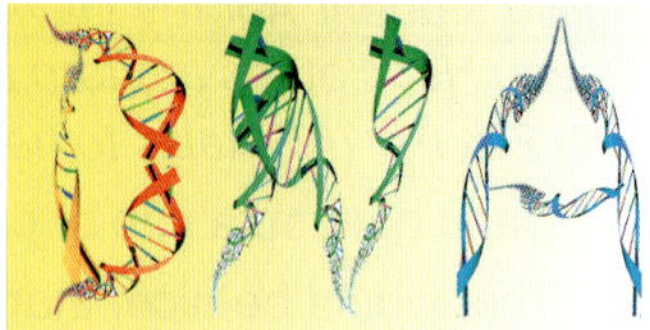

In recent years DNA typing has become a powerful investigative tool for law enforcement authorities to link suspects to a crime. Also in immigration affairs, ancestry testing or identification of unknown, otherwise unidentifiable dead or living persons – often also associated with crime – DNA analysis is mostly the last chance to solve these cases.

Deoxyribonucleic acid = DNA is a long polymer built from four different so-called bases = molecules. The DNA is called the "code of life", because the DNA encodes all necessary information needed for life and the development of cells and individuals. Each regular human cell contains the 3 billion ($3x10^9$) bases organized in chromosomes. Many parts of the DNA are variable; however, the variations are specific for each individual and inherited by the next generation (a child inherits half of the DNA from the father and the other half from the mother).

The results of DNA analyses are highly accurate and reproducible. Moreover, DNA is relatively stable over long periods of time. Therefore, the results of forensic DNA testing are mostly regarded as beyond any doubt and are accepted as proof in identifying a person as the source of biological stains and, as a result, its presence at a crime scene. This accuracy and reproducibility made possible the installation of DNA database, where individual DNA profiles are stored and matched. Also many "old" cases, which took place decades ago, were solved by DNA methods.

However, nothing in this world is perfect, and this includes DNA. In 2007, a young female police officer was shot at Heilbronn, and DNA traces of a female, called the Heilbronn phantom, were found on the scene. The same DNA traces were later found at more than 40 crime scenes in southern Germany and Austria, but the phantom could not be found. Two years later it was established that the cotton swabs used to obtain the DNA samples had been contaminated by a female worker at the manufacturing company.

Find the respective nouns and adjectives

Example

verb	noun	adjective
enforce	enforceability enforcement enforcer	enforceable

identify		
inform		
investigate		
produce		

21.6 Caught by DNA 32 years later

In Edinburgh, a man was sentenced to life imprisonment in 2008 for the rape and murder of a ten-year-old girl in 1976. The girl had been sent shopping by her mother, but never returned. Her body was found five days later. She had been sexually assaulted and stabbed 15 times.

Another man was found guilty of the crime and spent 16 years in prison – it was one of Britain's most outrageous miscarriages of justice and also a case of sloppy police work. In 1992 it was found that he could not have been the murderer. He was infertile, but semen found on the girl's underwear contained sperm.

The real murderer was not found until 2008, when the man was arrested on another matter, and a DNA profile proved to be a direct hit.

Find out about famous miscarriages of justice and also sloppy police work; use the internet

21.7 Cybercrime

Cybercrime is the use of computers and the internet to commit punishable acts. Typical acts are

fraud and phishing, identity theft, hacking, piracy and plagiarism, child pornography, glorification of violence, right-wing extremism, racism, cyberstalking and SPAM.

21.8 Child pornography, paedophilia

Definition

Child pornography is the visual presentation of child abuse; it does not matter if the abuse did really take place or if it is just fictional.

Sexual abuse means that an adult or another child engages in sexual activities with a child, or that a child engages in sexual activities with an adult. Sexual activities with a child acting sexually with himself/herself are included.

Part 1

Paedophiles convicted

In Auckland, New Zealand, six paedophiles were convicted of child abuse and producing indecent images of children.

The men had abused infants from two years old, and nearly 100,000 images of child pornography were found on their computers.

The men had posed as babysitters and won the confidence of the children's parents and thus had an opportunity to abuse the children over a period of several months.

Their crimes were discovered when one of them handed in his computer for repair and a number of indecent images were found on his hard disk.

Part 2

Nursery worker arrested

In Newry, Northern Ireland, Theresa O'Sullivan, 43, was arrested and charged with making, possessing and distributing indecent images of children. Also arrested was her common-law husband, Roger Atkinson, 55; he is charged with possessing and distributing indecent images of children.

Ms Sullivan, a nurse at the local day care unit, had apparently taken the photos, some of which are considered to be of a serious nature, on a camera phone inside the nursery school; the children there are aged between two and five. Her common-law husband had apparently distributed the pictures on the internet.

So far police have not been able to identify any of the children, because most of the images only show the torsos of the children.

The day care unit caters for nearly 100 children, and police now have the painstaking task of contacting all the parents in their effort to provide possible evidence.

21.9 Prostitution

Prostitution is "sexual activity", mostly by women but also by men, in exchange for money or other favours, for example a good job. It is often called "the world's oldest profession".

In many societies, prostitution is illegal and can even be punished by death; in others, like Germany, it is perfectly legal.

In some countries, for example Norway and Sweden, the client who pays for sex commits a crime, not the prostitute.

In other countries prostitution itself is legal, but many activities around it are illegal, for example pimping or soliciting in a public place.

In countries where prostitution is legal, the prostitutes can be employed in a brothel, they have unions, they are protected under industrial protection laws, and they must undergo regular health checks.

It is estimated that in Germany there are about 400,000 prostitutes, and that more than a million men visit a prostitute every day.

1. Find the definitions of the following words

adultery – age of consent – be on the game – blow job – buggery – circumcision – female genital cutting – incest – kerb crawling – massage parlour – pimp – public indecency – punter – red-light district – sexual harassment – sodomy – statutory rape – tart card

2. Find out more about the history of prostitution

21.10 Infinitive and gerund

Der Infinitiv *(to work)* und das Gerundium *(working)* können wie ein Nomen Subjekt und Objekt eines Satzes sein. Dabei drückt das Gerundium in der Regel eine – oft auf die Vergangenheit bezogene – allgemeine Feststellung aus, während sich der Infinitiv – oft mit Zukunftsbezug – auf einen speziellen Fall bezieht.

Teaching may be fun, but to teach this lot is going to be sheer hell.

We don't like searching drug suspects, but we need to search those crossing into Germany from Holland.

I remember having met this woman before. Remember to post the letter.

Nach vielen Verben und Adjektiven wird der Infinitiv als (prädikative) Ergänzung angeschlossen

Please do not hesitate to inform us of any suspicious behaviour.

Do you happen to know anybody in the drug scene?

The woman was obviously anxious to avoid being frisked.

We are unlikely to find anything in the suitcase.

Nach Präpositionen kann nur das Gerundium stehen

Our tactics are/is aimed at stopping all trafficking.

At present we are engaged in preventing further abuse.

21.11 Fill-in exercise

Fill in the correct form

1. Some people have no scruples about (use) .... children for smuggling purposes.
2. The drug problem is threatening (get) .... out of hand.
3. Be sure (check) .... all the baggage thoroughly.
4. Last week, we succeeded in (confiscate) .... two kilos of heroin.
5. Our narco squad have great experience in (deal) .... with such people.
6. If you consent to (take) .... a package across the border for someone else, you will run the risk of (be arrested) .... for drug smuggling.
7. I should like (know) .... whether this is your handbag.
8. (Watch) .... the house all day may be boring, but perhaps we'll be able to nail the drug traffickers.
9. She was guilty of (carry) .... several sachets of cocaine in her bra.

21.12 Useful phrases

1. Bitten Sie das Opfer der Vergewaltigung in ein Nebenzimmer.

2. Bieten Sie der Frau eine Tasse Kaffee oder ein anderes Getränk an.

3. Fragen Sie sie, ob sie sofort einen Arzt / eine Ärztin benötigt.

4. Fragen Sie, ob sie eine Person ihres Vertrauens hinzuziehen möchte.

5. Bitten Sie um eine detaillierte Schilderung des Tathergangs.

6. Erklären Sie ihr, dass Sie leider alle Einzelheiten benötigen, damit der Täter gefasst und verurteilt werden kann.

7. Fragen Sie die Frau, auf welche Art und Weise sie angegriffen wurde.

8. Fragen Sie, ob der Täter irgend etwas zu ihr gesagt hat.

9. Fragen Sie, welche Sprache / welchen Dialekt der Täter benutzte.

10. Bitten Sie um Information, ob der Täter eine Waffe benutzte, und wenn ja, welche.

11. Fragen Sie die Frau, ob und wie sie sich gewehrt hat.

12. Teilen Sie ihr mit, dass sie von einem Arzt untersucht werden muss.

13. Erklären Sie ihr, dass sie neue Kleidung bekommt, damit ihre Kleidungsstücke auf Spuren und anderes Beweismaterial untersucht werden können.

21.13 Key words and phrases

age of consent – convict – grab – indecent images of children – intercourse – miscarriage of justice – sexual assault – sexual harassment – spike a drink – victim – violence

Organized crime and terrorism

Unit 22

This unit deals with

- the history of organized crime in Germany
- the definition of organized crime
- organized crime in Italy
- trafficking in human beings
- organized crime groups worldwide
- terrorism and
- verbal functions of the infinitive.

22.1 From criminal gangs in Germany to organized crime

Part 1

Crime is part of our lives, and it is not possible to eradicate it. Throughout human history certain persons have acted in a deviant way and harmed others. And throughout human history criminals have joined and formed gangs as they found that "working" in teams was to their advantage and they were more successful.

From the 13th century we know Robin Hood as the "hero" who robbed the rich to give to the poor. According to many writers, he lived in Sherwood Forest near Nottingham in the East Midlands and committed his robberies there. There are many stories about him, some of which contradict each other. However, there is no proof that he really existed.

In1401, pirate captain Klaus Störtebecker was sentenced to death. For a number of years he had been disrupting the sea trade of the Hanseatic League with England and the Netherlands. According to a legend, he had been promised that all those of his men whom he could run past after he had been decapitated would be allowed their freedom. Although Störtebecker managed to walk past eleven men, the promise was not kept and the men were executed.

In the 16th century many knights lost their livelihood. The reasons were their lifestyles – they spent more than they earned – and their financial obligations to their sovereign. The growing power of the towns also played an important role. In this situation some knights, especially in the Rhine-Main area and along the Moselle and Saar rivers turned to systematically attacking and robbing merchants. For some years, Götz von Berlichingen, famous for his utterance (according to Goethe), made his living by means of robberies, and that's why he was ostracized and put under house arrest at his castle.

In the 18th century, in the Taunus and Hunsrück regions and along the rivers Moselle and Nahe, the Schinderhannes gang became famous. The young man, whose real name was Johannes Bückler (the name "Schinderhannes" is derived from his father's job, who was a knacker = "Schinder"), was arrested several times, but always managed to escape. For nearly six years he and his gang robbed travellers and rich people, until pressure for his arrest got too much for him. He tried to become a soldier in the imperial army, but was recognized and apprehended. In 1803, Schinderhannes and 29 men of his gang were sentenced to death and executed for several murders, robberies and thefts in the Mainz area.

In the 19th and 20th centuries, in Germany, starting from Berlin, a number of registered corporations were founded by criminals whose official aim was to help each other in case of financial difficulties and to promote cultural activities. But very often these corporations were a camouflage for crime. However, they established a "class system" for criminals, set up certain rules and enforced them. From those times we have had a kind of "ranking system" among criminals, where the robber is at the top of the list and the child abuser at the bottom.

These corporations were first started in Berlin, but afterwards also in other cities. As a consequence, the Berlin corporations founded an umbrella association which they called "Ring Berlin", and many corporations were named after it. In the 1920s these corporations experienced a boom. They were accepted in political and social circles, and ran illegal casinos which were not disturbed by the police. However, the first Nazi government dissolved these corporations and most of their members were sent to labour or concentration camps.

Part 2

In Germany nowadays, you don't hear much about gangs, and if you do, you hear about youth gangs. In fact, there are youth gangs in Germany. Actually, it is quite "normal" that, up to the age of about 16, criminal offences are committed within groups, only afterwards do individual offenders prevail.

It is alarming that, according to a study compiled in Berlin, "40 per cent of those caught red-handed have gas weapons, knives, blunt instruments and other dangerous items. It must also be stated, generally, that the readiness to resort to violence is on the increase, among each other as well as against the police and the members of security services."

Under penal law, as few as three persons can form a gang. According to crime theory and the rulings of the Federal Court, with at least three members there is increased danger, which is the consequence of, among other things, peer pressure. This definition is important, for example, when a gang commits acts of theft.

Many people still remember the bloody fights among Vietnamese cigarette-smuggling gangs, which in the 1990s caused great fear among the population.

Apart from the cold-blooded murders, in the 1990s Vietnamese gangs were also responsible for protection rackets, money laundering, robbery and blackmail. In 1997, four Vietnamese raided a Chinese restaurant in Bremen and got away with money. The victims were fettered. In Dresden in 1993, 22 Vietnamese were arrested and charged with operating protection rackets in Chinese restaurants. According to the Lower Saxony State Criminal Office, gang warfare has come to an end in the last few years. There have been no murders and homicides in which Vietnamese were involved. And so far we can only speculate whether the murder of seven people at Sittensen is attributable to gang warfare. Police arrested two 29 and 31-year-old Vietnamese citizens.

Police also have to deal with gangs from Eastern Europe whose members steal upmarket vehicles on demand or modern navigation systems from cars.

In this field it is especially difficult to distinguish between gang crime and organized crime. One difference is the degree of organization, as specified in the official definition.

Organized crime (OK) is the systematic commission of crimes, due to the fact the perpetrator seeks profits or power; these crimes, either separately or jointly, are rather important if two or more participants operate together for a longer or indeterminate period, by

- operating in professional structures,
- using violence or other means of intimidation,
- influencing politics, media, public administration, the legal system, and industry.

Organized crime usually has a hierarchic structure. The Italian Mafia organizations are good examples in this respect. Furthermore, organized crime groups often have an ethnic, linguistic, social and family background which distinguishes them from other organizations. A system of personal and criminally useful contacts is established, in which there are personal dependencies and possibilities of sanctions against dissenters.

In the past, criminal Italian organizations have used Germany not only as a refuge but also as a territory for criminal activities. The main activities are in the fields of drug trafficking and illegal arms trade, trafficking in human beings, protection rackets, fraud, white-collar crime, counterfeiting and all activities which appear to be profitable. The profits are laundered and re-injected into normal businesses.

Organized crime causes gigantic damage to a country's economy.

Underline the words in the text whose definition is given here

1. demanding money from someone in return for not revealing compromising information
2. disguising of military personnel and/or objects
3. deny the truth of, especially by telling the opposite
4. diverging from usual standards, especially in sexual behaviour
5. destroy completely
6. story regarded as historical but not authenticated
7. exclude someone from a group or society
8. person of the same age, status or ability
9. person who attacks and robs ships at sea
10. further the progress of something
11. evidence or argument establishing a fact
12. safe accommodation
13. device used as protection against rain
14. expensive car

22.2 What is organized crime?

Organized crime happens in every society, most frequently in the absence of a strong and protective state.

There are more than 100 different definitions of "organized crime". The German definition of 1990 is not very helpful and very difficult to work with: "Organized crime is the planned commission of criminal offences determined by the pursuit of profit and power, which, individually or as a whole, are of considerable importance and involve more than two persons, each with his/her own assigned tasks, who collaborate for a prolonged or indefinite period of time a) by using commercial or business-like structures, b) by using force or other means of intimidation or c) by exerting influence on politics, the media, public administration, judicial authorities or the business sector."

A good example of a definition is the OC definition of the United Nations: "Organized crime is understood as a large-scale and complex criminal activity carried on by groups of persons, however loosely or tightly organized, for the enrichment of those participating and at the expense of the community and its members. It is frequently accomplished through ruthless disregard of any law, including offences against the person, and frequently in connection with political corruption."

So we can say that organized crime is the illegal activity of people and organizations whose purpose is to gain profit as much and as quickly as possible through illegitimate business enterprises.

The activities of organized crime can be divided into four categories:

1. Exploiting humans – people smuggling – trafficking in women and children for sexual purposes – prostitution – debt bondage – slavery – trafficking in human organs	**2. Supplying illicit items** – illegal drugs – tobacco – weapons – diamonds, gold, precious stones – nuclear material – motor vehicles – rare animals
3. Extortion and protection – extortion and blackmail – protection money	**4. Manipulating money** – money laundering – gambling, bookmaking, casinos – illegal lotteries and numbers – loan sharking – counterfeiting and forgery of money and goods – cybercrime

What do organized crime gangs have in common? They mostly use the same techniques and methods:

- different levels of rank with a division of labour or degrees of specialization
- business-oriented intimidation and violence
- total control over a specific area or type of business
- strict discipline
- code of silence
- restricted membership
- immunity from prosecution through corruption.

Organized crime is big business; the accumulated income of European OC gangs outranks the revenues of many major industries and smaller states in Europe.

Underline the words in the text

1. explanation of the exact meaning of a word
2. financial gain
3. the main means of mass communication (newspapers, radio, TV) regarded collectively
4. benefit unjustly from the work of others, especially by overworking or underpaying them
5. sum of money that is owed
6. behaviour involving physical force intended to hurt, damage or kill someone
7. exemption from prosecution
8. have a higher rank than someone else
9. money paid to criminals to prevent them from attacking oneself or one's property

22.3 Italy's biggest business, the € 63 billion mob

The following text contains ten spelling errors; find them

Organized crime is Italy's bigest "business". Extortion, loan-sharking, drugs and prostitution have a total anual turnover of over € 63 billion, a report reveels. This is 7 per cent of the country's GNP.

The report says the Mafia's influence is continueing to spread to industry and comerce. "Italy's leading businesses, particularly those involved in civil engeneering, would rather make pacts with the Mafia than report a case of blackmail. And it's clear why: it's easier that way.

The mob's grib is strongest in southern Italy. There up to eighty per cent of businesses pay extortion money for fear of violence or arson.

The report says that € 7 billion of the € 63 billion is extortion money. But it is imposible to obtain acurate figures. The report says extortion had caused more than 150,000 businesses to close in three years. A mobile phone operator prefers not to open stores rather than pay protection money. Politicians say the growth of mafia business crime is "alarming", but what are they doing abut it?

22.4 Trafficking in human beings

Trafficking in human beings is a criminal offence with some risk at least to the people accompanying the illegal immigrants, such as drivers of large goods vehicles, although convictions and sentences after court proceedings are not handed down very often, because the drivers deny any knowledge of the "illegal freight" that is hidden between the items carried.

The temporary seizure of the vehicles, which then cannot be used for transporting other legal and/or illegal goods, e.g. smuggling of narcotics and tobacco, probably causes the greatest damage to the OC gangs.

An easier way to get illegal immigrants to their country of hope and glory, in our case the United Kingdom, is by using the normal and cheap ways of travelling. One modus operandi of the organized crime groups is quite simple: The illegal immigrants apply for tourist visas at, for example, the German embassy in their home country. Once they are in Germany the organized crime group collects their real documents. Counterfeit passports of an EU country are handed out, flight tickets are booked on the internet. Payment is made by using counterfeit credit cards, which have been obtained by committing other criminal offences.

Low-cost airlines are used, not only because the organized crime gang makes a greater (illicit) profit, but mainly because these airlines use small airports, where the risk of strict immigration checks is much smaller, and where there are fewer emigration checks on flights within the EU.

If anything goes wrong at the immigration checkpoint in the UK, the illegal immigrants declare that they are seeking asylum. As they are already in the country, the organized crime gang claims that they have completed their mission, that the persons have safely arrived in the UK, and demand the full payment for the trafficking operation, which is currently estimated at between € 7,000 and € 10,000.

Sometimes the crime gang forces the illegal immigrants to destroy their false passports during the flight and to ask for asylum on arrival in the UK. Thus any evidence of how the crime gang works and what methods have been used is destroyed.

Another way the crime gangs use is to book the illegal immigrants on weekend coach trips to the UK; they claim to be tourists and show their counterfeit EU passports. But the UK immigration officers do their work on French soil at the entrance to the Channel Tunnel and the Port of Calais. If illegal immigrants are caught, they will be arrested and prosecuted in France and won't arrive in the UK. So they book with coach companies that use ferry ports in the Netherlands and Belgium for the Channel crossing.

Whichever method the crime gangs use, from their point the advantage is that nobody working for them accompanies the illegal immigrants, and thus cannot be arrested in case anything goes wrong.

It is cheaper to smuggle the illegal immigrants into the UK that way than to do so by truck; the cost of false documents is approximately € 300, for the tickets approx. € 200, which leaves the organized crime gangs and their partners in Germany and the UK with a handsome profit.

In addition, illegal immigrants have to pay extra for their to trip to Germany or any other EU country, and they have also to pay for their stay in "safe" houses until departure. Females are often forced to raise the money by prostitution during the waiting period and in some crime gang brothel in the UK afterwards.

In order to be able to finance their trip to the UK, some illegal immigrants are offered a discount in "travel costs", if they agree to take class A drugs (heroin, cocaine) with them.

Former investigations have shown that the members of the crime gangs, and it does not matter in which country, run next to no risk; it is the illegal immigrants who may be caught and prosecuted, who do not know anything about the background and members of the crime gangs and cannot provide the investigators with any useful information.

The crime gangs' network spans the whole globe. Logistics systems are used for all sorts of illicit goods and criminal offences, netting enormous profits.

Due to the fact that the different sections of a crime group act independently, that members of one section do not know the members of another one, the possibilities for the police to destroy the whole network of such an organization are very limited. If parts of a crime gang are eliminated due to police work and criminal proceedings, it will normally be just a disruption, not a total defeat for them.

Fighting this sort of worldwide crime is a matter of international cooperation of police forces and judicial officials throughout Europe and mainly Middle Eastern and Asian countries.

22.5 Organized crime groups (overview)

The best-known organized crime group probably is the Mafia, which originated in Sicily. But there are many other groups all over the world. Here are some of them:

- Sicilian Mafia
- American Mafia
- Camorra
- Cosa Nostra
- Ndrangheta
- Jamaican yardies in Britain
- Russian Mafia
- Yakuza
- triads and tongs
- outlaw motorcycle gangs (Hell's Angels)
- Central and South American drug cartels

Find out more details about these organizations. Use the internet

22.6 Terrorism

A newspaper recently wrote that terrorism was the scourge of our times. Certainly, there is no doubt, threats have increased, but there have been terrorist attacks at all times. The perpetrators often call themselves "freedom fighters", whereas the members of the ruling classes call them "terrorists". The Spartakus rising, which was dramatically portrayed in a Hollywood movie starring Kirk Douglas, clearly shows these two points of view.

The borderline between terrorism and fighting for freedom is very hard to define, as was shown by the failed United Nations initiative after the hostage taking of Israeli sportsmen during the Olympic Games in Munich in 1972. Arab, Asian and African states voted against the initiative to ostracize terrorism, arguing that every freedom movement is called terrorism by its opponents and that any nation that is being suppressed and exploited has the right to defend itself.

Thus it becomes clear how difficult it is to define the term "terrorism". Terror organizations, try to get as much attention as possible through their attacks to change the political system according to their aims. A widely acknowledged definition is that "terrorism is the sustained and clandestine fight in all fields to realize political aims by engendering fear, using violence or threatening to use it, against civilians."

This means that terrorism is an asymmetric conflict which is conducted by its members, who have only limited resources, against a superior state or its citizens, and which causes enormous damage. Very often the terrorists work in small independent groups of so-called "hobby terrorists", who have a permanent job and live in normal circumstances.

After the events of Munich in 1972, terrorism was on the increase worldwide and also in Germany. Many Germans remember the Baader-Meinhof gang. One characteristic of modern terrorism is the use of force against representatives of the "system" for ideological reasons, with the intention to create an atmosphere of great fear among the population. Examples from those times are the IRA in Northern Ireland and ETA in Spain.

Here the borderline between terrorism and organized crime is hard to define, as the terrorists depend on financial resources. A good basis for obtaining financial means are illegal weapons smuggling and drug trafficking, but also bank robberies.

The New York attack of 11th September 2001 by the Al Qaida terrorist network aggravated the situation. Until then suicide attacks mostly took place in Israel only; since then such attacks have become a regular feature of this asymmetric conflict. For religious and fundamental reasons, Al Qaida wants a revolution of the economic and political systems in the world, and uses people who were born in the respective country and who, from their appearance, look like the natives, to commit assassinations and suicide bomb attacks.

The bomb attacks at train stations in Madrid in 2004 and underground stations in London in 2005 clearly show that. These attacks were intended to generate panic and fear among the population. The attacks were intended to make clear that the state cannot protect its citizens. The state is provoked to resort to counter-measures (e.g. against the Baader-Meinhof gang), and these measures are then declared as unreasonably disproportionate with the intention to instigate the population against the state.

Another important instrument for the terrorists to reach their aims is mobilizing the media and supporters, who describe the terrorists as freedom fighters for the exploited.

Apart from the attacks against persons, recently also targets of economic importance have been attacked, targets which are very hard to protect. The intention is to destabilize the economy. Examples are the attacks on pipelines in Iraq or in tourist areas in Turkey and Egypt.

22.7 Investigating a case in Turkey

Characters: KOK Erwin Heidkämper (EH) of Department 11 North Rhine-Westphalia State Criminal Office, KHK Klaus Wälter (KW), liaison officer of the Federal Criminal Police Office in Istanbul, Turkey

KOK EH arrives at Istanbul airport and is met by the liaison officer of the Federal Criminal Police Office, who has arranged all the details.

KW: Good morning, Mr Heidkämper, welcome to Istanbul. How was your flight? I hope you can cope with the time difference, we're two hours ahead of Düsseldorf.

EH: Good morning, Mr Wälter. Thanks for picking me up. The flight was all right, and I think I can manage with the time difference. But the weather is better here than in Düsseldorf.

KW: Yes, that's true. And Istanbul is a very interesting city. Perhaps we have an opportunity for me to show you a little bit of the town during the next few days. I suggest that I first drive you to your hotel, and afterwards you can meet our Turkish colleagues.

EH: Okay. I'd like to talk to you about how to proceed. I hope that we can interview the accused Ömer Yilmaz already tomorrow. I'd like to be back at home for the weekend in four days. On Friday there are the remand proceedings concerning the suspect, who has been remanded in custody in Düsseldorf, and I'd like to present the results of the interview there.

KW: No problem. Your files were sent to me via the German Embassy in Ankara. In Turkey we have two liaison officers from Germany. My colleague Berking is assigned to the German embassy in Ankara. He's the liaison officer with the Turkish ministry of the interior and responsible for Ankara and the eastern part of Turkey. I'm responsible for the western part of Turkey, with Istanbul being the centre. Our Turkish colleagues are eager to meet you, and so does the state prosecutor. However, I don't know if the interview will be possible already tomorrow; we'll see.

EH: I very much hope so. In the past few weeks I forwarded some requests to our Turkish colleagues. And, to be honest, I wonder why everything takes so much time, and I haven't got an answer yet to some requests.

KW: I can easily explain that. Here, some things are done differently. Our Turkish colleagues are eager to help, but we're not the only foreign police service that has requests. We tend to think that our cases are the most important. The gang you're investigating is well known in Istanbul, but it's neither the largest nor the most dangerous.

EH: I haven't looked at it from that point of view. But you're right, of course we tend to think that our investigation is the most important. And I might add that we're exclusively working on such a case.

KW: That's right, but it's also our job. And we don't get visitors from our home country every day, otherwise our workload would be too much. Some colleagues at home, however, cause some stress because they think that we should know all the details of every case by heart. It happens that a colleague from Germany calls about an e-mail only to complain if I'm unable to remember that e-mail. But I just can't, due to the large number of requests. I just haven't got the time to read all the files from beginning to end.

EH: I agree, but what about our Turkish colleagues? Why does everything take so long?

KW: One of the reasons is that the Turkish colleagues have to set priorities. They don't have enough personnel. From their point of view our requests are often too detailed. A police officer here who has to deal with terrorist attacks with killed and injured persons several times a year – and the press in Germany reported these cases – has only little sympathy for extensive retrospective investigations in a foreign country, especially if the main culprits have been arrested.

EH: I can certainly understand that. How do you get along with the Turkish colleagues here? Do you speak Turkish?

KW: Yes, speaking the language is a condition to be deployed here. Before I came to Turkey, I attended a language course for half a year. I've been here now for two years, and I'm getting along quite well. And most of my Turkish colleagues are really nice and try to be helpful. And in the course of time real friendships develop with one or another colleague.

EH: How long are you going to stay in Turkey?

KW: Probably one or two more years. Normally you stay for three to four years when deployed to a mission abroad. Deployment back to the Federal Criminal Police Office also depends on whether there is a successor at hand and if there are any private reasons which might affect the transfer.

EH: Now, I'm not quite with you.

KW: Well, maybe I didn't express myself precisely. What I meant was that the Federal Criminal Police Office considers our private situation. For example, if my children were about to change from elementary school to high school, it would be ideal to be transferred. If this change were to be a year later, it would be good to stay abroad for another year.

EH: Have you got your family here?

KW: Yes, of course. That's normal. My children go to school here, and by now their Turkish is better than mine.

EH: Sounds interesting. Is this your first mission abroad?

KW: No, it's my third. My two children were born in Thailand, and Thai was their first foreign language. Then, after a short stay at the headquarters in Berlin, I was deployed to Bolivia, and took my family along. And now I've already been in Turkey for two years, and I still like it very much. But here's your hotel, and we must interrupt our talk. We can continue tonight, and then an interpreter will be with us. We'll go to police headquarters as soon as you've unpacked your suitcase and are ready to meet our Turkish colleagues.

Istanbul

22.8 Verbal functions of the infinitive

Nach vielen Verben, besonders denen der Annahme (z.B. *expect, suppose*), wird der Infinitiv zusammen mit einem Objekt zur Verkürzung von Sätzen verwendet. Bei Passivsätzen wird das Objekt zum Subjekt

I expect you to tell the truth, the whole truth and nothing but the truth.

The victim was advised to consult a psychiatrist.

I wouldn't like anything to happen to her again after this traumatic experience.

The rapist's solicitor tried to persuade the girl to retract her statement.

Nebensätze können auch mit Hilfe der Präposition *for*, die das Subjekt des Nebensatzes anzeigt, verkürzt werden

It is not always easy for victims to talk about their experience.

We have arranged for a woman doctor to examine you.

Indirekte Fragesätze können mit Hilfe des Infinitivs verkürzt werden, insbesondere dann, wenn Haupt- und Nebensatz dasselbe Subjekt haben

She asked us who to apply to for help.

22.9 Abridgement exercise

Shorten the following sentences

1. Can you tell us whom we should contact first?

   ....

2. It is assumed that the sex fiend is hiding in the vicinity.

   ....

3. Could you give me an idea how I can identify the culprit/perpetrator?

   ....

4. We will arrange things in such a way that our female colleague will talk to you tomorrow.

   ....

5. We expect that the results of the test will be available tomorrow.

   ....

6. It is said that cases of rape and other forms of sexual assault are on the increase.

   ....

22.10 Useful phrases

Erklären Sie einem ausländischen Besucher

1. Das organisierte Verbrechen hat sich in der ganzen Welt über viele Jahre entwickelt.

   ....

2. Die vier Hauptbereiche der Tätigkeit der organisierten Kriminalität sind die Ausbeutung von Menschen, die Zurverfügungstellung illegaler Waren, Erpressung und Schutzgeld sowie illegales Glücksspiel und Geldwäsche.

3. Viele Mitglieder von Jugendbanden sind mit Messern, Gaspistolen und anderen gefährlichen Gegenständen bewaffnet.

4. Die organisierte Kriminalität ist auf allen Gebieten tätig, die profitabel sind.

5. Dazu gehören unter anderem Drogen-, Waffen- und Menschenschmuggel, Prostitution, Betrug, Wirtschaftsverbrechen und Falschgeldherstellung.

6. Man schätzt, dass in Italien die Mafia 7 % des Bruttosozialproduktes erwirtschaftet.

7. Menschenschmuggler wenden viele Tricks an, um z.B. illegale Einwanderer vom europäischen Kontinent nach Großbritannien zu bringen.

8. Terroristen bezeichnen sich selbst oft als Freiheitskämpfer.

9. Das Bundeskriminalamt hat zwei Verbindungsbeamte in der Türkei.

10. Deutsche Verbindungsbeamte bleiben gewöhnlich drei oder vier Jahre auf einem Auslandsposten.

22.11 Key words and phrases

camouflage – clandestine – counterfeit – culprit – deviant – extortion – forgery – fraud – gambling – hostage taking – intimidation – loan sharking – money laundering – perp(etrator) – protection racket – remand in custody – retract a statement – ruling – sex fiend – suicide bomb attack – trafficking in human beings

Unit 23

Weapons

This unit deals with

- weapons and forbidden items
- some incidents in which a large number of people were shot
- the German firearms act
- the National Rifle Association in the USA
- some types of guns
- the taser and
- the conversion of adjectives into nouns.

23.1 Definition

What is a weapon?

There is no precise definition, but roughly speaking we can define it as an object which is used in some way or other to hurt or kill another person, be it for offensive or defensive reasons.

In theory, any object can be used as a weapon. A wife can hit her adulterous husband on the head with a rolling pin, the driver of a car can deliberately hit a pedestrian, a young woman can stab an intruder with a pair of scissors, serial killer Ted Bundy bludgeoned many of his victims with a baseball bat, and the 9/11 terrorists used two airliners to kill thousands of people. A dog owner who urges his dog to attack another person uses his dog as a weapon.

In this unit, the word "weapon" refers to firearms and to those weapons and items which are illegal in Germany: this unit does not deal with military weapons like chemical, biological or nuclear weapons or the equipment of armed forces.

The firearms law in Germany is dealt with in 23. 3. The following weapons and items, among others, are illegal:

knuckle-duster – elastic steel rod – cosh = blackjack *(US)* – sword cane – belt buckle knife – nunchaku – slingshot – flick knife – butterfly knife

Beeper gun

Other weapons might be

- gas cigarette lighters which explode when thrown onto the floor
- replica handguns, made of bread or soap and coloured with shoe polish, or mini-bombs made of scraped-off sulphur from matches, occasionally used by prison inmates to escape
- knife-like sharpened objects of any kind, also used in prisons.

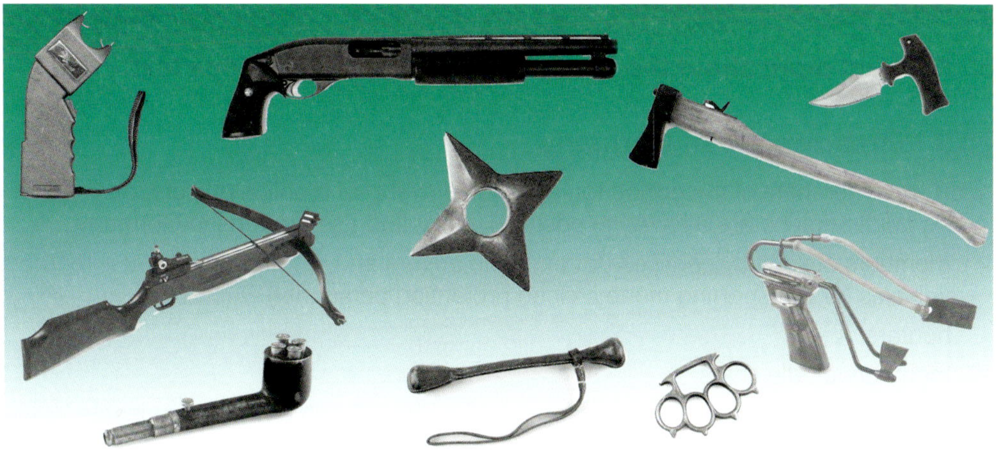

23.2 "Guns don't kill people – people kill people"?

Every once in a while there are reports in the media about killing sprees when some maniac shoots and kills a number of innocent people without any apparent reason. Such massacres have happened in many parts of the world, and place names like Dunblane, Littleton, Tasmania, Erfurt, Emsdetten and Winnenden have gained a dubious reputation.

These spectacular events conceal the fact that every day dozens of people are killed all over the world with privately owned weapons. In some American states, firearms fatalities have surpassed automobile fatalities. These deaths can be divided into firearms homicides, firearms suicides and fatal firearms accidents.

There seems to be a connection between the availability of firearms and the death toll, i.e. the easier it is to get a gun, the greater the chance that it is used to kill.

Arguments in this field are rather controversial. For example, the USA has comparatively lax firearms regulations and remarkably high rates of firearms homicides, suicides and accidental deaths. Advocates of gun control keep saying that there would be fewer fatalities if there were stricter gun laws. They frequently cite the following example: the cities of Seattle in the US state of Washington and Vancouver in the Canadian state of British Columbia are only about 200 km apart; population, lifestyles and the rates of burglary, robbery and assault are more or less the same, but the risk of being murdered with a handgun is about five times higher in Seattle. For the gun control advocates the strict Canadian gun laws are the reason.

Firearms advocates like the influential National Rifle Association (NRA) in the USA use slogans like "Crime control – not gun control" or "Guns don't kill people – people kill people", and they argue that handguns are a good means of self-defence, that ownership of firearms is a constitutional right, that without guns a rapist attacking a woman will never hear "Stop it or I'll shoot" and that some of the most detestable figures in world history like Adolf Hitler, Mao-Tse Tung, Pol Pot and Joseph Stalin were all advocates of gun control.

1. Find out what happened at the locations mentioned in the text

2. Should the possession of firearms be controlled by the state?

3. How should the sale of firearms be regulated?

4. Why do many dictators insist on strict gun control, especially in their immediate environment?

5. Find out more about the four dictators mentioned in this text

23.3 Firearms law in Germany

Apart from members of the armed forces (Bundeswehr) and police officers, only the following adult persons are allowed to possess, carry and use firearms in Germany:

- members of security services (for example drivers and other personnel of armoured vehicles for transporting money, close protection personnel)
- hunters
- members of rifle clubs
- arms collectors, provided their weapon(s) has/have been rendered unusable.

In all cases, those concerned are checked to ensure that they are reliable persons.

In Germany, a distinction is made between "Waffenschein" (permit to use a firearm) and "Waffenbesitzkarte" (permit to possess a firearm).

The permit to possess a firearm is proof of possession of the firearm, and the person concerned is allowed to purchase suitable ammunition. On the other hand, the permit to use a firearm allows the bearer to actually use it.

Hunters have a green permit to possess a firearm, which allows them to carry it all over the Federal Republic of Germany, in conjunction with a hunting licence (permit to use a firearm), which allows them to use it all over Germany.

Amateur riflemen have a yellow permit to possess a firearm; they are only allowed to carry their weapon(s) from their house to the shooting range and back. When engaged in shooting competitions, they are also allowed to transport their weapon(s) to other places and use it/them at the shooting range there. There are strict rules for transporting firearms.

Hunters and amateur riflemen are required to keep their weapon(s) safely at home; there are strict rules in this respect.

Members of security services are subject to certain restrictions. They are only allowed to carry their weapons on duty. At the end of work, they are required to leave their weapon, stored safely, on their company's premises. They are not allowed to buy ammunition, the latter being provided by their employer.

1. Find out more details about firearms laws in Germany

2. Find out about firearms laws in other countries

Exercise 23.1 – 23.3

Match the definitions with the words

1	an object used in fighting	A	to store
2	someone who kills animals for food or sports	B	armoured
3	the exact copy of a weapon, an object	C	fatality
4	a metal weapon that is fitted over the fingers to cause injury when hitting	D	inmate
5	a weapon with a handle and a long sharp metal blade	E	terrorist
6	a long stick used for hitting	F	defensive
7	a gun such as pistol or rifle	G	permit
8	a sudden and violent attack	H	close protection personnel
9	a weapon that explodes	I	replica
10	an official document, a licence	J	weapon
11	death caused by an accident or violence	K	detestable
12	bullets that can be fired from guns	L	firearm
13	a person who commits acts of violence for political purposes	M	cane
14	place where you can practise shooting	N	assault
15	to keep things	O	hunter
16	prisoner	P	knuckleduster
17	steel-plated/bullet-proof	Q	sword
18	body guards	R	bomb
19	antonym of “offensive”	S	shooting range
20	antonym of “exemplary”, ‘“ovable”	T	ammunition

23.4 The National Rifle Association (NRA) in the USA

Correct the following text

there are various versions of the text of the second amendment to the american constitution the version passed by congress in 1791 reads "a well-regulated militia being necessary to the security of a free state the right of the people to keep and bear arms shall not be infringed."

the nra promotes firearms ownership rights within the united states claiming that gun ownership is a civil liberty protected by the second amendment as quoted above.

the nra has about 4 million members and is probably the best organized lobby in the world whenever gun control legislation is proposed within the usa be it at local state or federal level its members are alerted and respond with letters faxes e-mails and other means to the elected representatives to make their views known.

the nra was formed by general george wingate and colonel william church in 1871 as both were dismayed by the marksmanship of their troops in the american civil war.

1. **Find out more about the NRA. Use the internet**
2. **Find out more about the Second Amendment to the US Constitution and the different interpretations**

23.5 Finding firearms

Officers Sergej Mandelkow (SM) and Ute Hommes (UH) have been called by control to proceed to a block of flats in Bremen immediately in order to see whether a person reported by neighbours to have entered a third floor flat is trying to burgle it. When they arrive, they find the flat door open. They enter the flat where they catch a Dutchman, Will van der Keulen (WK), prising open a drawer with a jemmy.

SM: May I ask whether you live here? According to the neighbours, you don't.

WK: I was just trying to ....

SM: .... burgle the place, weren't you?

UH: Now stand against the wall, with your arms high up and your legs apart. We're going to frisk you for our own safety.

Officer Mandelkow frisks the suspect, while officer Hommes watches from a safe distance just in case Mr van der Keulen turns and attacks officer Mandelkow.

SM: What have we here then? A knife, a screwdriver, some car keys and some vehicle documents. Did you come by car?

WK: No, I walked all the way from the station.

SM: We'll see about that in a minute. Perhaps there's a car with the right registration number in the area. You'd better come with us then.

WK: All right, all right. What's the hurry?

Officer Hommes has meanwhile called for support, and another patrol car arrives. When the backup crew learn that the suspect is Dutch, they remember a car with Dutch registration plates parked a block away. The suspect is taken there, and from the vehicle documents it is quickly established that the car is registered in Will van der Keulen's name.

UH: So you didn't walk after all. Perhaps we should have a look at your vehicle.

WK: There's nothing of any interest.

UH: We'll see. Let's have a look at the boot.

Officer Mandelkow unlocks and opens the boot.

SM: Just as I thought. The tools of the trade: a jemmy, several sets of keys, some levers .... and what have we got under this blanket? Good heavens, an entire arsenal. A sawn-off shotgun, two revolvers, a sub-machine gun and a real Kalashnikow!

WK: I don't know anything about these guns. Someone must have put them there.

SM: For a start, we'll secure the vehicle because it was used for two criminal offences, burglary and illegal possession of firearms.

WK: You can't do that.

SM: Yes, we can. You have three days to lodge an objection with the court. Meanwhile we'll check whether you are on our wanted list.

Mr van der Keulen is taken to the police station for the usual procedures.

23.6 Some types of guns

Pistol: single-chambered; the trigger must be pulled and released for each shot.

Revolver: has multi-chambered cylinder rotating around an axis when the hammer is cocked; the trigger must be pulled and released for each shot.

Shotgun: smooth-bore short-range firearm discharging shells containing numerous pellets or a single slug.

Rifle: long-barrelled firearm with spiral grooves in the bore causing bullet to rotate for greater precision.

Explain your service gun to an English friend. The following words may help you:

ammunition (ammo), barrel, grip, hammer, magazine, safety lever, trigger

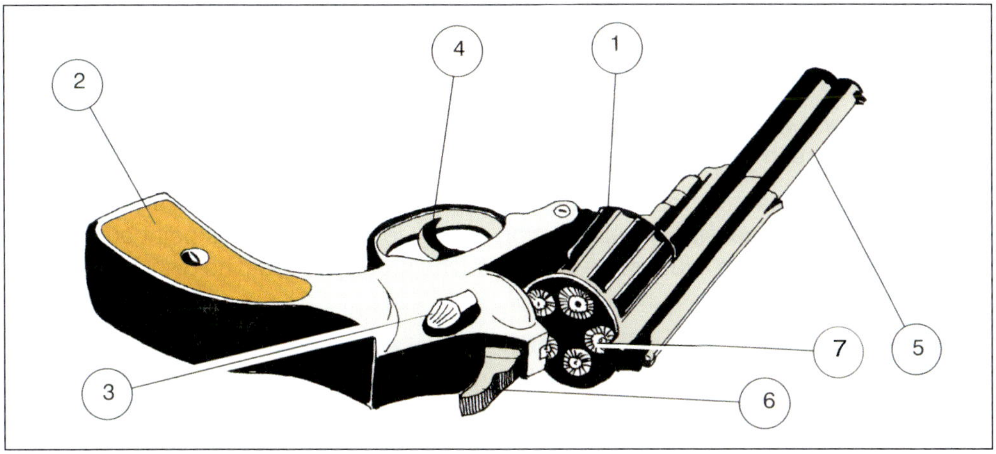

23.7 The taser

Read the list of headings and then the text. Choose the most suitable heading for each paragraph. There is one you do not need.

1. The pros and cons of the taser
2. A tragic incident
3. Professional use of any weapon must be considered carefully
4. The invention of the taser
5. The novels of Jack Cover
6. The need for a new weapon for special purposes
7. Widespread use

1. In the 1960s, there were a number of hijackings, and police and airlines were looking for measures to prevent them. One idea was to have armed "air marshals" on board who would confront the hijacker(s). However, shots fired on board an airplane might cause the plane to crash.

2. Nuclear physicist Jack Cover (1920 – 2009) had an idea when he heard of an accident in which a man was paralyzed for a short time when he was hit by a falling power line. He started experimenting in his garage, and the result was "**T**homas **A**. **S**wift's **E**lectric **R**ifle" (Thomas A. Swift is the protagonist in various popular novels whom Jack Cover admired), which paralyzes persons briefly, but does not injure or kill them as a firearm would.

3. Today the taser is used by many police services in countries all over the world, and in many U.S. states everybody can buy one for self-defence. However, its use is controversial, as a number of people have died after a taser had been used against them.

4. In New Orleans, a partially deaf 24-year-old man was involved in a street fight. A police officer ordered him to lie on the ground; the man didn't hear him, so the officer tasered him. The man fell to the ground, paralyzed; then he was told to show his hands, and as he didn't do so, the officer tasered him again. The man died in hospital three hours later.

5. Since 2008 special police units in 13 German federal states have been testing this electroshock weapon, which has been used in the USA for 20 years. Since then there have been heated discussions about its use.

   Taser advocates point out that it is very effective to take out attackers and that it offers one more possibility before using deadly force. Opponents point out that the taser can also cause injuries like fractures. The problem should be discussed rationally.

6. But also the use of truncheons, rubber bullets, even pepper spray, CS spray and other, similar sprays can cause death in unfortunate circumstances. The use of the taser should be tested carefully, and should be regulated accordingly. Not every uniformed official needs a taser, and not every officer needs a spray can.

1. **Find out more about the taser. What do you think of its use?**
2. **The word "taser" is an acronym (= an abbreviation which has become a word in its own right). Can you think of other acronyms?**

23.8 The conversion of adjectives into nouns

Englische Adjektive können in Substantive – immer mit dem bestimmten Artikel – umgewandelt werden. Dabei sind folgende Regeln zu beachten

- Adjektive, die eine gruppentypische Eigenschaft bezeichnen, können in Pluralsubstantive ohne Pluralendung umgewandelt werden. Für den Singular muss ein Substantiv hinzugefügt werden

  the rich and the poor, the wounded; aber: *a/the rich man*

- Adjektive, die eine nicht auf Personen zutreffende Eigenschaft ausdrücken, können zu abstrakten Substantiven umgewandelt werden. Als solche stehen sie nur im Singular

  the improbable, the inevitable

- eine kleine Gruppe von Adjektiven aus der Rechtssprache können sowohl in Singular als auch in Pluralsubstantive umgewandelt werden, wobei sich die jeweilige Form aus der dazugehörigen Verbform und dem Kontext ergibt

  the insured, the deceased, the accused, the undersigned

23.9 Exercise

Fill in the correct form; add a noun if necessary

1. This is asking for the (impossible) ....
2. The (injured) .... is of above-average height.
3. The (most difficult) ....will be to identify all the (dead) ....
4. The (insured) .... will forfeit their no-claims bonus if they cause accidents.
5. The description given by the witness led to the arrest of the (wrong) .... , as the latter had a perfect alibi.
6. The (murdered) .... was found in a roadside ditch, where she had apparently been dumped from a passing car.
7. Are you sure we have done the (right) ....?
8. The (accused) .... has two scars on his forehead.
9. The (last) .... to see the missing child in our street has contacted the police.
10. An (unemployed) .... of no fixed abode is helping police with their inquiries.

23.10 Useful phrases

1. Fordern Sie die Person auf, die Waffe wegzuwerfen und die Hände hochzuheben.

2. Erklären Sie ihr, dass Sie sie nach Waffen und gefährlichen Gegenständen durchsuchen müssen.

3. Fragen Sie die Person, was sie in ihrer Jackentasche hat.

4. Fordern Sie sie auf, die Jacke auszuziehen.

5. Fragen Sie sie, wozu sie die Waffe benötigt.

6. Weisen Sie darauf hin, dass es in Deutschland verboten ist, Schreckschuss- und Gaswaffen bei öffentlichen Veranstaltungen mitzuführen.

7. Erklären Sie der Person, dass nach deutschem Recht auch ein Schießkugelschreiber als Schusswaffe gilt.

8. Erklären Sie ihr, dass sie sich durch das Mitführen dieser Waffe strafbar gemacht hat.

9. Sagen Sie ihr, dass grundsätzlich nur Schreckschusswaffen erlaubt sind.

10. Erklären Sie ihr, dass Sie die Pistole als Beweismittel beschlagnahmen müssen.

23.11 Key words and phrases

advocate – argument – at gunpoint – availability – barrel – beyond reasonable doubt – cartridge – chamber – disguise – firearms regulations – gun control – illegal possession of firearms – maniac – marksman – mock – pellet – replica – shell – shotgun – slug – trigger

Murder, manslaughter

This unit deals with

- manslaughter and murder
- famous murder cases
- capital punishment and
- prepositions

24.1 Definitions

Murder is the most serious crime in any society and therefore investigated with top priority. Thus it is no wonder that in Germany around 95 % of all murder cases are cleared up.

In 2006, there were 2,500 cases of accomplished and attempted murder and manslaughter; 934 of them were committed in conjunction with robbery and in conjunction with sex crimes. The suspects and the accused are generally male adults. Recent statistics show that in robbery/murder cases almost 50 % of the accused were young males under 21 years of age.

The German criminal code differentiates between several forms of murder and manslaughter, which are dealt with in chapter 16, Crimes against Life.

Murder, which is a special form of manslaughter, is dealt with in article 211, and the general punishment is a life sentence. Manslaughter is defined in article 212.

What does "life sentence" in Germany mean? Do convicts really have to serve time until they die?

In Germany, the average custodial sentence for murder is 15 years, after which time the convict has the right to apply for parole. Only if the court has decided that the crime was especially serious is the right to apply for parole postponed.

There is certainly a north/south divide with convicted murderers serving more time in southern German states.

The German constitution prohibits the death penalty. In addition, the German Constitutional Court has stated that life imprisonment without the possibility of parole contravenes human dignity. Human dignity is the basis of the United Nations Declarations on Human Rights and it is also the basis of the German Constitution. The Constitutional Court has stated that everybody must have a chance to end his life in freedom. Therefore, most convicts are released after 15 to 23 years in jail. There are of course provisions in case the criminal still represents a danger to the public after having served his term. In such a case he can be held in preventive detention.

1. Discuss the pros and cons of capital punishment

2. Find out from the internet:

- Which states still have capital punishment?
- How is capital punishment viewed by religious leaders?
- What are the states with the greatest number of executions?
- What forms of capital punishment are still being used in several states?

24.2 Investigating a case of attempted murder by committing arson

Fire at a hotel

It's Sunday afternoon, end of September. A nice sunny day.

In the industrial town of Witten, 100,000 inhabitants, the "Ostpark Hotel" is situated 30 metres off a quiet side street, right beside a small forest and a local recreational area. The hotel is a long-established feature of the area.

The hotel, which is a massive building, was built in the 1930s. It was repeatedly refurbished, however, the last major refurbishment was done more than ten years ago.

The owners' flat is situated in the basement and has its own staircase and side entrance. The main entrance to the hotel is at the front. On the ground floor there are the restaurant, the lounge, the kitchen and several storage rooms. From one of the storage rooms you can also get to the basement on an old staircase. On the first and second floors are 14 guest rooms. The building has a pitched roof covered with roofing tiles.

At about 17.20 the residents of the next building, about 60 m away, hear a muffled noise, which they cannot define, coming from the hotel. When looking out of the windows towards the hotel, several witnesses notice that a fire must have broken out at the hotel. Flames are coming out through two burst windows on the ground floor.

When the fire brigade arrive, the whole restaurant is on fire. Apparently nobody was in the building when the fire was detected. Extinguishing the fire and securing the building take until late at night. The restaurant is completely destroyed, and the rest of the building is severely damaged. The damage is at least € 500,000.

Detectives deployed to the scene cannot yet enter the restaurant, but they notice traces which suggest that the door of the side entrance was prised open. The chief of the firemen thinks that the fire started in two different places in the restaurant. Apart from that, he is sure that there is a smell of petrol in the restaurant. He thinks that the fire was raised intentionally.

The building is cordoned off. For the rest of the night a fire watch remains at the scene.

On Monday morning the reports written by then are on the table of the chief of the arson department, who calls an experienced investigator for a meeting.

Characters: chief of arson department EKHK Manfred Dressel (MD), investigator KHK Jens Schuster (JS)

MD: Good morning, Jens. You've heard about our operation yesterday afternoon, and you're familiar with the results of our investigations so far. By the way, here I've got a notice, which has just come in, that the owner of the hotel contacted us a few minutes ago. Apparently he had, together with his wife, visited some relatives over the weekend and they came back an hour ago. Probably they already left on

Friday evening. There were no guests at the hotel over the weekend, as extensive refurbishment was planned. Fortunately nobody was injured during the fire. You are the lead investigator in the case, so let's just discuss the best way how to proceed.

JS: We haven't got much intelligence yet. Therefore, in my opinion, we'll have to investigate the bare facts as well as possible motives.

As it is very probable that the fire was raised intentionally, two arson investigators from our department should establish the facts, together with an arson expert and a scenes of crime officer. And it would be a good idea to have an arson-sniffing dog at the beginning of our investigations.

In addition, we need some officers to find and interview possible witnesses in the neighbourhood.

MD: I fully agree with you that we need quite a number of officers at the beginning of our investigation. At least in former times, the "Ostpark Hotel" was very popular, and the owner is well-known. I know the rumours that fewer and fewer guests stayed at the hotel during the last few months, and that the owner had a lot of debts. But that must not affect our investigations.

Perhaps a burglar set the hotel on fire to delete any traces. Maybe the fire was started as a kind of revenge. Of course, it can also be that the owner started the fire himself, or instigated someone to start it. Anything is possible.

By the way, we have to take into account that the public are very much interested in the case. Our press department have already called and want to know details.

JS: They'll have to wait. So far we can only speculate. The expert has to come as soon as possible. And the scenes of crime office should send us two officers and a photographer. And we can get the arson-sniffing dog only through our command office.

MD: I'm going to organize all the officers we need, and I'll give them all the necessary information. And I'll immediately inform our boss and ask him to send two investigators from other departments. Then I'll deploy one team to the scene and two teams to investigate external factors.

Jens, please phone the hotel owner and ask him to come here so that we can interview him extensively. He'll certainly understand that the police must talk to him as soon as possible.

JS: Okay, I'll do that.

I'm trying to be objective. But, to be quite honest, I don't think it was a "normal" burglary with subsequent arson.

Until the hotel owner arrives, I'm going to ask our finance investigators if they can already now give us some information about the financial situation of that man. Apart from that I'm going to call the telecommunications experts. I'd like them to find out if the perpetrator or perpetrators used a normal or mobile phone in the hotel area before or after the fire.

MD: Good idea. I've just remembered that I have to inform the prosecutor in charge. We can get decisions to prefer charges if he says so. And he can also prepare a press statement. Let's start right now. You can always reach me on my extension number, and I'll have my mobile phone switched on all the time.

I suggest that we meet in my office at 13.00 to assess the situation. If something important comes up before, we'll talk on the phone.

JS: All right. I'll contact the investigation team at the scene in the meantime. Perhaps questions arise at the scene which I can clear while interviewing the hotel owner. Of course, it may also happen that the man tells me something which can be corroborated or proved wrong at the scene.
See you later.

Two weeks later....

The officers working at the scene found out that the door of the side entrance had been prised open with an untypical tool. It didn't look like as if the hotel owners' private rooms had been rummaged. At three sites in the restaurant petrol had been poured and set on fire with rolled-up newspapers.

No witnesses could be found, despite press releases and canvassing the neighbourhood. The hotel owner had a good alibi for the time of the fire.

Investigations into the financial situation revealed that the hotel was run-down and overindebted. Potential buyers had been deterred by the level of necessary renovation work.

A few days before the fire € 5,000 had been transferred from the owner's account to an account in another country.

Checking the connections on two of the owner's mobile phones revealed that several calls had been made to and received from a known criminal. Among them were calls on Saturday before the fire and late on Sunday night.

The telephone surveillance installed because of this intelligence finally revealed the truth. The hotel owner and the arsonist instigated by him had talked about the arson, its consequences, the likely police measures and the reward for the arsonist.

Both are now in remand custody, awaiting trial.

The owner's wife was flabbergasted when her husband was arrested.

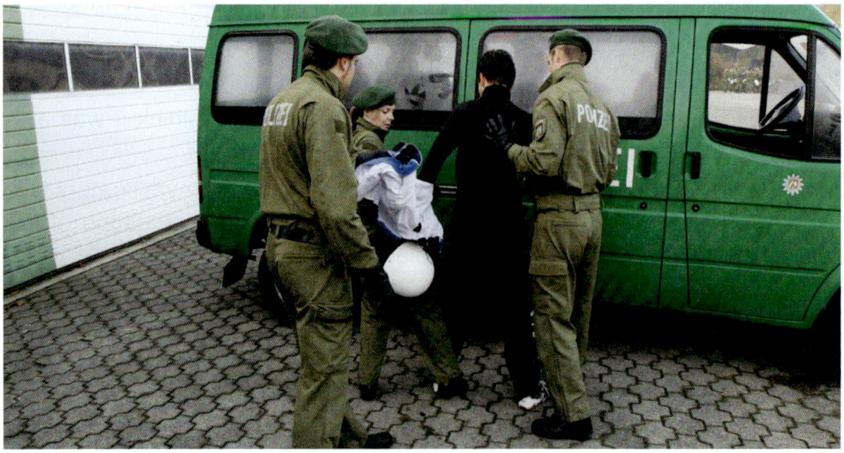

24.3 Capital punishment

Capital punishment is something which usually leads to heated discussions. Should criminals who committed really bad crimes be put to death? Does man have the right to kill other human beings?

Here are some arguments for and against

For

1. Capital punishment is a greater deterrent than any other punishment. Being threatened with execution makes some criminals think twice.
2. Capital punishment is just. Justice means an "eye for an eye."
3. If capital punishment is abolished, the crime rate will rise.
4. Terrorists are a threat to the state and society.
5. Capital punishment helps to decrease the level of drug crimes.
6. Who kills has forfeited his own life. A criminal's life isn't worth more than that of the victim.
7. A person who has been executed is no longer a danger to society.
8. Hardened criminals can live in prison without any problems, and the taxpayer has to pay for it all.
9. In a democracy the government has to respect the will of the people; in most countries there is a majority in favour of capital punishment.
10. It's much worse for a criminal to spend the rest of his/her life behind bars than to be executed.

Against

1. There is no scientific evidence that capital punishment is a deterrent. In US states without capital punishment, the murder and homicide rates are lower than in those where they still have executions.
2. There is no relation between the introduction of the death penalty and a falling crime rate. Serious crimes are often committed on the spur of or in the heat of the moment.
3. One of the ten commandments is: "Thou shalt not kill".
4. A miscarriage of justice can never be ruled out. The death penalty is irreversible.
5. Capital punishment does not deter terrorists. They are convinced of their ideas and risk or, in case of suicide bombers, even sacrifice their own lives.
6. There is no scientific evidence that murderers are repeat offenders.
7. In a society threatened by a rising number of violent crimes, the death penalty can only offer superficial protection against crimes where structures are more deeply rooted.
8. The costs of an execution (from the sentence to the actual execution) are much higher than those of life imprisonment.
9. Public opinion can be manipulated and can thus be a danger. The courts must decide only on the facts.
10. Any punishment must include the chance of atonement and making up for one's deeds. The death penalty makes it impossible for wrongdoers to mend their ways.

24.4 Some murder cases

1. A 24-year-old Afghan man, who lives in Germany, was given a life sentence for the "honour killing" of his 21-year-old sister in Hamburg last week.
2. A 40-year-old Syrian man was shot and killed in Nordpark in September. Although seriously hurt, he managed to get to the parking area where he collapsed. The murderer, a Syrian man, also 40 years old, was arrested a few days later. However, he could not be convicted – up to now the murder weapon has not been found.
3. The brutal stabbings of teenagers in London continue. On Saturday night a 16-year-old was killed. Two killers stabbed the boy after he left a cinema in the East End. He is the sixth victim within the last four months.
4. The daughter of rich parents committed a cruel crime. She drugged her parents and stabbed them, with her boyfriend helping her. Her father managed to resist while fighting for his life and bit her hand. Because of that it was established that she did the stabbing.

24.5 Famous murder cases

Fritz Haarmann

Fritz Haarmann, born in Hanover in 1879, killed at least 24 young men between 1918 and 1924. He probably killed some more men, but that has never been proved. He was executed on 15th April 1925.

Rosemarie Nitribitt

Rosemarie Nitribitt was born in Düsseldorf in 1933. She became a call girl after WW 2 in the area around the main station in Frankfurt. Some of her punters were rich and influential people, so she soon became wealthy and was able to buy a black Mercedes 190 SL with red leather upholstery. On 1st November 1957 she was found dead in her luxurious apartment. Her killer has never been found.

The Moors murders

Between 1963 and 1965, two girls and three boys aged 10 to 17, were murdered in the Manchester area. Four of the victims were buried on Saddleworth Moor, therefore these cases came to be known as the "Moors murders". The killers were Myra Hindley (born in 1942) and her lover Ian Brady (born in 1938). They both received life sentences as the death penalty had been abolished only a short time before they were tried. Myra Hindley died in prison in 2002. Ian Brady is unlikely ever to be released.

Ted Bundy

Ted Bundy was born at Burlington, Vermont, on 24th November 1946 and executed by means of the electric chair at Florida State Prison in Starke, Florida, on January 24, 1989. Between 1974 and 1978 he killed an unknown number of young women; estimates range from 29 to 100.

Find out more about famous murder cases. Use the internet

24.6 Prepositions

Präpositionen stehen vor Nomen und Pronomen und dienen u. a. der Orts- und Zeitangabe; außerdem werden sie im übertragenen Sinn verwendet.

Ortsangabe

at home, down the road, in the house, under the table, on the bed, above the city, below ground, across the street, through the door, off the road

Zeitangabe

at five o'clock, in the afternoon, from six to eight

übertragene Bedeutung

at odds, in trouble, on good terms, beyond reasonable doubt, above reproach, in/under the circumstances, of age

Beachten Sie

Englische Präpositionen unterscheiden sich in Bedeutung und Gebrauch erheblich von ihren deutschen Entsprechungen. Im Zweifelsfall sollte ein Wörterbuch konsultiert werden.

24.7 Fill-in exercise

Fill in the correct prepositions

1. Firearms regulations differ .... country .... country.
2. The availability .... all kinds .... guns .... the United States is fiercely defended .... the NRA.
3. In many countries police officers are issued .... pistols rather than revolvers.
4. .... a short distance, beeper guns can be very effective.
5. .... some neighbourhoods .... Los Angeles, shootouts .... the streets are a common occurrence.
6. There was a carjacking .... the road between Truth or Consequences and Williamsburg, NM. The driver was shot .... the leg and had to be taken .... hospital.
7. You'd better go .... the airport .... taxi.
8. The burglar entered the house .... the back door.
9. The suspect was last seen running .... the river.
10. .... German law, married women who are not yet .... age are regarded as adults.
11. Fooling around .... mock rifles is .... a joke.
12. Granting asylum is not .... the powers of the police.
13. The fastest way to go .... London .... Exeter is .... Bristol .... the M4 and M5 motorways.
14. Funny sort .... language: .... the USA you park your car .... the driveway, and you drive it .... the parkway.
15. You get breakfast .... the morning, you have lunch .... noon, you would like to have a nap .... the afternoon, you watch TV .... the evening and you go .... bed late .... night.

Unit 24

24.8 Useful phrases

Übersetzen Sie

1. Mord und Totschlagisnd die schwersten Verbrechen in jeder Gesellschaft und werden daher mit Vorrang verfolgt.

   ....

2. Mord wird oft in Zusammenhang mit Raub und Sexualdelikten begangen.

   ....

3. Die Todesstrafe schreckt Terroristen und Selbstmordattentäter nicht ab.

   ....

4. Das Feuer wurde absichtlich gelegt, und es wurden Brandbeschleuniger benutzt.

   ....

5. Schwerkriminelle, die nach Verbüßung ihrer Haftstrafe immer noch eine Gefahr für die Öffentlichkeit darstellen, werden in Sicherungsverwahrung genommen.

   ....

   ....

6. Die Polizei geht bei ihren Ermittlungen immer vom schwersten Delikt aus.

   ....

7. Mord ist ein Beziehungsdelikt. Wenn man die Beziehung kennt, kann man die Tat klären.

   ....

8. Ein großer Teil der Tötungsdelikte findet im engen Beziehungskreis der Familie oder Wohngemeinschaft statt.

   ....

   ....

9. Ein Brandstifter kann zum Mörder werden, wenn bei der Brandstiftung Menschen getötet werden.

   ....

10. Will der Täter durch Brandstiftung Menschen töten, sind diese aber zufällig nicht anwesend, so wird er dennoch des versuchten Mordes angeklagt.

    ....

    ....

24.9 Key words and phrases

arson – arson–sniffing dog – attempted murder – capital punishment – Constitutional Court – corroborate – homicide – life sentence – manslaughter – murder – murderer – murderess – parole – preventive detention – stabbing

Water police

Unit 25

This unit deals with

- the tasks and responsibilities of the water police
- two incidents on the Rhine
- motorists in a nature reserve and
- a grammar test.

25.1 Tasks and responsibilities

There are nearly 5,000 miles of navigable waterways in Germany, and about 30 % of all goods are transported on these waterways.

With the exception of Thuringia, each German federal state has its "Wasserschutzpolizei", which is responsible for its waterways.

There are some special details, however. The Hamburg "Wasserschutzpolizei" are responsible for the Elbe river also in the states of Mecklenburg-Western Pomerania, Lower Saxony and Schleswig-Holstein, and the Rhineland-Palatinate river police have joint jurisdiction with their Luxembourg colleagues on the Moselle River in Luxembourg, except for the lock areas.

They patrol inland waterways, lakes, ports and coastal waters within a 12-mile zone. Apart from general police duties, their tasks are

- to detect dangers for navigation and deal with them
- to enforce navigation rules, for example the navigation proper, equipment, crews
- to check papers and licences of the crews
- to assist environmental agencies.

In seaports they act as immigration officers and issue shore leave passes for sailors who need a visa to enter Germany.

Convert the miles into kilometres

Find out about the different names of "Wasserschutzpolizei"

25.2 Barge in distress

At 08.00 on a Sunday morning the captain of a push vessel informs the river police station at Ludwigshafen by telephone that his barge has run aground at Rhine km 447. Nobody on board is hurt, and there is no leakage, but the barge now blocks half the channel.

The station immediately inform the river police boat 17 and the NIF ("Nautischer Informationsfunk" = nautical information radio), which inform all barges and tourist ships in the area. The river police station at Gernsheim deploy police boat Hessen 10 as support.

At 08.40 WSP 17 reaches the barge. Two officers enter the barge to investigate the accident while the captain and the crew of Hessen 10, who have arrived in the meantime, direct the river traffic. Via radio all ships are informed that passing each other and overtaking are prohibited at the scene.

On board the barge the officers start their investigation. First they inspect all documents and interview the captain. Thus they establish that the barge's draught is 202 cm.

At the Worms gauge, which is relevant for this section of the Rhine, a draught of 200 cm is established. In other words, the barge is overloaded, as, according to the respective rules, a barge's draught must be adapted to the water level.

According to the navigation regulations on the Rhine, this is a minor offence. When questioned, the captain admits that he already knew at Rotterdam that the water level of the Rhine river was falling due to lack of rain. He had hoped he would still be able to get through. He also admits that about 10 km downriver his barge had shortly scraped the river bed. Because of that statement he is now suspected of having committed a serious offence. He is informed about his rights and interviewed.

In the meantime officials of the Worms waterways authority arrive and take over, as the river police are only responsible for recording the accident.

250 tonnes of the barge's freight have to be unloaded onto a smaller vessel. Thus the barge's draught is reduced by 10 cm, and it is no longer stuck and moves to Worms harbour where it will be closely inspected.

25.3 A motorboat accident

19.30 hours on a cold November evening. WSP boat 17 is going upriver on the Rhine close to km 445, with river police officers Andreas Schlüter (AS), captain, Kurt Becker (KB) and Dennis Huth (DH). There is dense fog, visibility is about 50 m. Navigation by sight is not possible. Therefore course and speed of the boat are determined by radar.

Suddenly they receive the following message by radio:

"Motorboat accident at Rhine km 435, left bank. The information was given by the captain of barge 123 by telephone. Apparently a motorboat hit a breakwater and got stuck. There is no contact with the crew. And we have no information about injured persons. The boat is not in the shipping channel, so barges are neither obstructed nor endangered. The Rhine river navigation radio has been informed and passes on this message to the barges in the area."

Officer Schlüter activates the blue light and accelerates, taking the limited visibility into consideration. Officer Huth also watches the radar screen. Oncoming and overtaken vessels are contacted by radio and their captains are informed about course, speed, passing and overtaking.

After some 15 minutes there is a small echo on the radar screen. Officer Schlüter adapts the radar system to a larger scale, and now the radar echo is much better to be seen. Due to the fact that the echo does not move, and due to their precise knowledge of the area the officers know that they have found the motorboat.

Officer Schlüter tries to establish contact with the boat by radio, but there is no answer. As visibility is slightly better, the crew decide to get alongside the boat which they illuminate with their spotlight. They get closer and closer, and officer Schlüter is constantly watching the sonic depth finder to be informed about the draught. Finally they can fasten their patrol boat to the motorboat which is marooned on a breakwater.

Officer Huth leaves the boat, and notices that a male person, who turns out to be Bertilo Bretzler (BB), climbs out of the motorboat.

BB: Thank God you're here. I don't know any more what's front and back.

DH: Good evening. I'm officer Huth from the Ludwigshafen river police. Is anybody hurt on board? Did anybody go overboard?

BB: No, no, everything's all right with me. I was alone on board. I'm quite confused, I really don't know what happened. Suddenly there was a bang and a jolt, and I fell down into the cabin. What happened?

DH: You ran aground. You drove onto the breakwater, and now you're stuck.

BB: That can't be true. I've been sailing around here for ten years, and I know the area. Tonight I wanted to go from the Waldhöfer Altrhein downstream to Worms where I've got my berth.

DH: It makes a big difference if you are on your way in good weather or in fog. Apparently you got lost. Do you have any experience in sailing in bad weather and poor visibility?

BB: I`m afraid not. I do not use my boat all that often, and when I do, I do so in good weather only. That's when boating is fun. And with the price of petrol you think twice before you go on a trip on your boat.

DH: Does your boat have the necessary technical equipment for bad weather? Do you have a radar licence and a two-way radio licence?

BB: No, I don't have either. Do I need something like that?

KB, who has listened to Dennis Huth and Bertilo Bretzler, interferes:

KB: Mr Bretzler, when you left the Waldhöfer Altrhein, it was foggy already, wasn't it?

BB: Yes, that's correct.

KB: Then I have to ask you if you're familiar with the bad weather regulations on the Rhine.

BB: No, I've never heard of them.

KB: As you've got a motorboat licence you should know about that. Let me explain. First of all, to be allowed to sail in this weather, certain conditions re crew and technical standards have to be met. On the technical side, to be able to move your boat in such conditions, when the course can only be established by radar, you must have a radar system. Visibility at present is about 20 to 50 m. Your boat doesn't have a radar system, does it?

BB: Correct.

KB: Then your boat doesn't meet the necessary requirements in this respect. I assume that you don't have a radar licence either, which is absolutely necessary to be allowed to make a radar-controlled trip.

BB: No, why should I need something like that?

KB: According to the regulations a radar-equipped boat can only be operated by persons with a radar licence. Even if your boat had such equipment, you wouldn't have been allowed to use it. A second person would have had to be on board with such a licence. You said you were alone on board?

BB: Correct. I shouldn't have left at all, should I?

KB: Yes, you've realized that all right. But I have to tell you more about radar regulations. You certainly don't have a radio on board, do you?

BB: By God, I think all these regulations are exaggerated. But no, I don't have a radio on board.

KB: This too is a precondition for sailing ucing your radar. As you can't move without or with very poor visibility, you must be able to send, listen to and answer radio messages. How do you know if there's an oncoming vessel, how do you communicate with the captain? By giving acoustic signals? Do I have to continue? Do you think you can avoid a collision with a large container barge? And what will happen if this barge runs over you? I think you're being rather careless.

Officer Huth continues to explain other regulations to Mr Bretzler, which the latter should have paid attention to. He also explains to him that he committed an offence, and a charge will be made out against him. His motorboat is towed by WSP 17 to its berth at the Worms boating club. On board the charge is made out, with Mr Bretzler's statement. In the end Mr Bretzler agrees that he acted foolishly, and he's grateful that the officers got him off the breakwater. Then the crew say good-bye and return to their base.

25.4 In the nature reserve

Part 1

During a patrol in the Pfälzische Rheinauen nature reserve, the crew of WSP 17 notice a car and various persons on the Otterstädter Altrhein bank, close to a forest.

Captain Steffen Begi (SB) docks the police boat close to the car. PK Lasse Noor (LN) and PK Heinrich Fock (HF) leave the boat to check the car and the persons.

During the talk the persons explain that they want to spend a nice day in the Altrhein area. PK Fock informs the young adults that they are in the Pfälzische Rheinauen nature reserve and that they have to comply with certain regulations.

HF: These regulations have been established to preserve and protect the nature reserve, its appearance and beauty, especially of the floodplain forest.

When asked what this means, PK Lasse Noor explains.

LN: In a nature reserve you are not allowed to drive and park except on public highways and public areas, unless you have a special permit from the nature protection authority.

Then he addresses the driver whose identity PK Fock has established in the meantime.

LN: This floodplain forest is a protected area. There are several signs which are clearly visible. Yet you drove along here. It's always the same thing: you want to be close to the river, but do not want to walk too much, and you want to be close to your car, so it's easy to unload all your stuff, and also listen to the car radio. As I can see, you intend to have a barbecue. Perhaps you also want to pitch a tent. This area is protected, because nobody should interfere with fauna and flora, and the lane on the dike must not be damaged. Ruts quickly develop.

The driver admits that he does not have a special permit and that he does not know anything about the regulations. In fact, the group wanted to swim, have a barbecue, stay the night and start a campfire.

PK Begi takes some photos of the scene from the boat. The others note the personal data of the group and also the data of the vehicle. Lasse Noor addresses the driver once more:

LN: You committed an offence, and I'll press charges against you. You'll probably get a fine of about € 70. Within the next few days you'll get a form on which you can make your statement. I think the situation here is quite clear and we need not engage in a discussion.

HF: Please take all your things and leave the nature reserve. On your way back you'll see all the prohibition signs. And remember that you are not allowed to pitch a tent, have a barbecue or start a campfire. Apart from that we don't mind if you have a swim here. But do not leave any rubbish! Good-bye.

The officers get back onto their boat, and captain Begi slowly moves away from the bank.

Part 2

Some time later the crew are on the Rhine near Hamm in Rheinhessen, after they have passed Worms, the City of the Nibelungs.

Again they notice a car parked on the main dike. In some sections its top is even tarmacked, but not everywhere, and frequently motor vehicles are driven on it. The drivers are, for example, youngsters who do not yet have a driving licence and try to get some practice, as you are almost never caught along the Rhine. Others are tourists from the nearby towns of Oppenheim, Nierstein and Ingelheim, sportsmen and anglers. Often the dike is closed to vehicles by barriers, but not everywhere, and many drivers ignore the prohibition signs.

This is a routine situation for the crew. Captain Begi decides to get close to the bank which consists of large basalt rocks. He keeps the boat in position while his colleagues leave the boat. They notice an elderly couple in the car.

LN: Good evening. River police, my name is Lasse Noor, and that's my colleague Fock. You're parked here on the main dike of the Rhine, and that's not allowed.

The officer learns that the couple wanted to enjoy a beautiful sunset by the river, and from the dike they also have a good view of the hilly Rheinhessen area. The driver hands over his driving licence and vehicle registration certificate, but does not see why he should do so and asks for an explanation.

LN: The main Rhine dike is specially protected by the Rhine dike regulations. Its purpose is flood control. Therefore everything is prohibited which might endanger the current condition and safety of the dike. When you drive and park here, the dike is weakened, and the grass is damaged. Maintenance costs are pretty high already. Animals hollow out the dike, which might well sag as a result.

All this gets worse when cars are driven on it. And in case of flood the water presses against the dike. Can you imagine the situation when back there everything is under water and the houses are flooded? When a dike bursts, the consequences are very serious. Perhaps you've heard that polders are being built to reduce the flood levels? But in such a case the dike must be in perfect order.

And you're to blame, to a very small extent, in case anything happens. Many different factors come together here. My colleague has filled in the statement form in the meantime.

HF: We've explained to you what really matters. And we have to press charges against you. You do not need to make a statement, and you can also contact a lawyer. In case we've convinced you, you should admit your wrongdoing and sign here. Then a fixed-penalty note will be sent to you. Transfer the amount, and the matter is settled. It will cost you about € 100.

River police on the beat

25.5 Grammar revision

Part 1

Rewrite the sentences beginning with the words given

1. A police officer is frisking a fan now.

   A fan ....

2. The sergeant and the inspector have known each other since 1994.

   They first ....

3. The colleagues from the detective department will arrive soon. They'll check the car for traces.

   When ....

4. You've arrived too late, that's why the burglars were able to escape.

   If ....

5. During her childhood the prostitute was raped by all men in her family.

   When ....

6. These police officers started their work five years ago.

   These police officers have ....

7. We'll discuss the aims of police co-operation after the break.

   After we ....

8. Drunken driving is a more serious offence than speeding.

   Speeding ....

9. More and more people are taking drugs and more and more crimes are being committed as a result.

   The more ....

10. All trainees must take part in first-aid courses.

    Participation ....

11. There has been a decline in the number of fatal accidents lately.

    The number ....

12. The weather was too bad for us to drive in convoy.

    Driving ....

13. What the lorry driver said was simply incomprehensible.

    We could not ....

Part 2

Find and correct the errors in the sentences. Four of them have no errors

1. Burglars would be less successful if neighbourhood solidarity would be more effective.

2. If the fans were separated last Sunday, riots wouldn't have broken out.

3. Crime prevention cannot succeed unless concerted action in the local area was guaranteed.

4. More crime prevention projects would have been presented if the deadline hadn't been so tight.

5. What measures would you concentrate on if two or three prevention workers were employed to help you?

6. If the preventive activities had been adapted to all the specific circumstances in which certain criminal offences take place, more progress would have been made in the local fight against crime.

7. Preventive activities will fail if the participants would act separately and don't coordinate their activities or only to some degree.

8. If a prevention council was formed, more representatives of the population could be integrated.

9. There will be tight security checks after the plane from Beirut will land.

10. We're having a lot of trouble with beer-swilling youngsters these days.

Fill in the correct tense

1. It was obvious that the driver of the sports car (drink) .... more than was good for him.
2. The witness said she (see) .... it all. The red estate car (enter) .... the main road without stopping.
3. If it (not, be) .... so cold last night, the surface of the road (not, be) .... so slippery now.
4. Don't worry if you (not, hear) .... from us for a while.
5. The trains to Nuremberg (run) .... every hour on the hour.
6. Your car (be) .... parked here for over two hours now.
7. (you, tell) .... me that you didn't know about the speed limit on this stretch of motorway?
8. While she (wait) .... for the lights to turn green, a delivery van (run) .... into her car.
9. I herewith (arrest) .... you for causing a public nuisance.
10. According to the disk, you (drive) .... for more than 16 hours now, Mr Todoroff.

25.6 Useful phrases

Übersetzen Sie

1. Mit Ausnahme von Thüringen hat jeder deutsche Bundesstaat eine Wasserschutzpolizei.

   ....

2. Die Wasserschutzpolizei überwacht die Einhaltung der Schifffahrtsgesetze auf Flüssen und Seen, in Häfen und innerhalb einer 12-Meilen-Zone an Nord- und Ostsee.

   ....

   ....

3. Der Schubverband „Nancy 2" ist festgefahren und blockiert die Fahrrinne.

   ....

4. An der Unfallstelle wird ein Begegnungs- und Überholverbot erlassen.

   ....

5. Ist jemand verletzt oder über Bord gegangen?

   ....

6. Nach der geltenden Rechtslage darf ein mit Radar ausgerüstetes Fahrzeug nur mit Radar geführt werden, wenn eine Person an Bord ist, die ein Radarpatent besitzt.

   ....

   ....

7. Wir schleppen Ihr Motorboot zu Ihrem Liegeplatz in Worms ab.

   ....

8. Innerhalb des Naturschutzgebietes müssen Sie die Regeln beachten.

   ....

9. Viele Autofahrer beachten die Verbotsschilder nicht.

   ....

10. Das Befahren des Hauptdeiches ist verboten.

   ....

25.7 Key words and phrases

barge – berth – breakwater – channel – coastal waters – container barge – dike – draught – environmental agency – floodplain forest – gauge – leakage – lock – nature reserve – push vessel – river police – shore leave pass – water level – water police – waterway – waterways authority

International police missions, internships

Unit 26

This unit deals with

- internships with other police forces
- preparing German police officers for missions abroad
- missions abroad
- German police officers in international organizations and
- Federal Criminal Police Office liaison officers.

26.1 Internships with other police forces

Many police officers use the opportunity to take part in internships with police forces in other countries where they get an insight into and experience in how other police services operate.

Here is an example:

My internship with the States of Jersey Police

I'm Stefan Helbing and I would like to tell you something about my practical training abroad. During my studies at the FHöV Cologne I had the opportunity to go abroad as part of my last practical training module. It was a precondition that I had to organize the secondment by myself. I also had to pay all the costs. I contacted a dozen authorities in the UK, Malta and the Channel Island of Jersey to find one which would give me the opportunity of an internship.

Fortunately I got an invitation from the States of Jersey Police for a secondment of four weeks. My liaison officer worked out a diversified programme for my stay. She also helped me to find accommodation. I stayed with a detective constable of the Special Branch and his family. That was very useful as it was a good way to have some social contact after duty.

When I arrived, I was introduced to the chief officer of the States of Jersey Police, who is head of the authority.

In the following weeks I stayed with several departments of the police force like the Scenes of Crime Department, Pro- and Reactive Investigation Team, Road Policing Unit, Dog Unit, Community Policing, Family Protection Team, Special Branch, Crime Reduction, Training Department, Shifts and several others.

In the departments I had lots of opportunities to learn about methods of policing there and the legal system of Jersey. It was very impressive how fast people are sentenced there. A drunk driver or a thief, for example, goes to court within one or two weeks to be sentenced. The sentences over there are much higher than in Germany. Especially the drug laws are very strict. For possession of a quite small amount of cannabis like 20 or 30 grams you will be sentenced to two to four years of prison without parole, even if it is your first offence.

For another three days I was flown to Guernsey, which is one of the other Channel Islands. Jersey and Guernsey are both self-governed. I was introduced to the persons in charge of the police force and I was shown around as well.

To come to a conclusion, I can say that I really enjoyed my time on Jersey and that I'm very glad that I used this unique opportunity to go abroad to get an impression of policing in another country and maybe to make some friends.

26.2 Preparing police officers for missions abroad

Since 1994 North Rhine-Westphalia has been preparing police officers for missions abroad.

Originally in Essen, department 13 of the "Landesamt für Aus- und Fortbildung und Personalwesen" (State Office for Personnel, Training and Further Training) is now situated at Brühl.

Department 13 is in charge of the selection, briefing and debriefing of male and female applicants as well as organizational details of missions abroad or in international police organizations.

Department 13 is also the communication centre for all police agencies, the officers taking part in missions abroad and their families, dealing with all related information and inquiries.

North Rhine-Westphalia deals with officers from central Germany, for Thuringia, Saxony, Rhineland-Palatinate, Saar and, of course, North Rhine-Westphalia, whereas the northern communication centre at Lübeck and the southern centre at Wertheim deal with the other parts of the federal republic, to make sure that briefing for missions abroad is of the same standard everywhere.

Apart from that, department 13 supports police agencies to re-integrate officers after their missions abroad. Officers who intend to go on a mission abroad have to take part in a two-week basic training course in English and a one-week briefing course, also in English. In addition, there are further briefing courses, depending on the tasks of the mission. Only officers who are in good health and have had all the necessary vaccinations are sent abroad.

26.3 German police officers in international organizations

Part 1

German police officers work in the following international organizations: the Department of Peacekeeping Operations (PDPKO) in New York, the Police Unit in Brussels, Europol and the International Criminal Tribunal for former Yugoslavia (ICTY) at the Hague, Interpol at Lyon. German officers also work as counsellors for the ministries of the interior in Poland, Romania and Dubai, and they work for the UN in Afghanistan.

Part 2

A German police officer as chief of the Police Unit at Brussels

In 2001 a so-called "Police Unit" was created within the General Secretariat of the Council of the European Union as part of its Directorate for Civilian Crisis Management.

The Unit was tasked to plan and implement police operations within the framework of the European Security and Defence Policy, to advise the Council working bodies on police matters and to implement the EU 2001 Police Action Plan. To fulfil these tasks, EU Member States detached experienced senior police officers to the EU for a period of up to four years. While the "Police Unit" ceased to exist in the summer of 2007, the respective functions were transferred to a new organizational structure.

Each police officer is assigned as a member of an operational desk that deals with one of the missions the EU has deployed in areas like the Balkans, Africa, the Middle East or Central Asia.

As very often in police work, there is no daily routine. Typical tasks can include communication via telephone and e-mail with the mission, liaising with member states' delegations in Brussels, drafting reports, attending meetings or giving presentations; all of this of course by using English as the common working language and mostly without the support of a translation service. Thus, apart from their specific police expertise, police officers working for the EU Council Secretariat have to be proficient in English and confident in professional discussions.

One phone call or mail requires only the simple forwarding of information to another recipient, the next one might trigger a sequence of briefings and meetings to be prepared where additional expert advice is sought to complement the initial information and to ensure an adequate decision. At sometimes very short notice, officers have to be available for duty travel abroad or for high-level political briefings on complex issues.

The topics cover a broad range, from personnel to tactics, from policy to strategy, and the police officer is very often the only expert with a police background. In principle, the work in Brussels is comparable to command staff work in the German police; however, both level and scope are significantly different.

Stefan Feller

Part 3

Serving the United Nations as a police peacekeeper

After the break-up of Yugoslavia in the early 1990s, many attempts to solve the crisis by diplomatic means failed. The cases of Bosnia and Hercegovina and, some years later, of Kosovo required the United Nations to act in accordance with the United Nations Charter. Subsequently United Nations Peacekeeping Missions were dispatched. As a side-effect, UN crisis management and peacekeeping attracted more and more attention within Europe, not the least because of the scale of the missions. More than 2,000 police officers were deployed to Bosnia and Hercegovina whilst the number deployed to Kosovo reached its peak in 1999 with approximately 4,500 international officers. European countries contributed police officers to both these missions, including a large number of officers from Germany. The number of international officers deployed to UN

Peacekeeping Missions has grown ever since and the mandated strength throughout these missions reached some 18,000 officers in 2009. This significant growth in numbers required changes within the Department of Peacekeeping Operations (DPKO) at the United Nations Headquarters in New York. In keeping with the recommendations of a report by a panel, chaired by the former Algerian Foreign Minister Lakthar Brahimi, which assessed the efficiency and effectiveness of UN Peacekeeping Missions, the Police Division was set up as an independent body.

Arno Langanke

Part 4

Working for the UN

Since September 2007, I have been working for the United Nations in the Department of Peacekeeping Operations within the Integrated Training Service (ITS).

My first encounter with the UN was in May 1999, when I became involved in the special task of exhuming bodies in Kosovo for the International Criminal Tribunal for the former Yugoslavia (ICTY) in order to prove war crimes and alleged genocide for which Slobodan Milosevic was held responsible. Since then I have been involved in the UN Interim Mission in Kosovo (UNMIK) and the UN Mission in Liberia (UNMIL). Between those missions, I was recruited by the Department for Foreign Assignments in Bruehl, North Rhine-Westphalia. Here I started to prepare police officers for the challenging task of working in a mission. I became a trainer and worked partly with generic standardized material from the UN and other material which was developed in our training unit and the two other German Peacekeeping Training Institutes (PKTIs) for Police.

Ever since I had been working in an international environment I thought it would be the peak of my career if I could work with UN Headquarters for a period of time, but never believed it would be possible because I had specialized in one field only. But here I am! And it was exactly my special working experience as a trainer for pre-deployment training and the two different experiences in the missions which brought me here.

Now I'm working for the Integrated Training Service (ITS) and am very much involved in all kinds of different training issues, which I partly took care of in Germany as well, but with completely different implications. Part of my job is to develop new standardized materials for police pre-deployment training, advice on the development of standardized training material for all participants (police, military and civilians), work with experts on these materials and consult PKTIs from all over the world in order to find out how practical and useful the material is. Additionally I visit PKTIs when they apply for recognition of their pre-deployment training courses, and I also run trainer courses in several regions of the world.

My contract expired in September 2009, but the UN applied for an extension. I was lucky enough to know that I had the support for this extension from my superiors in Germany, and I'm glad to tell you that it was extended for another year to September 2010.

As the training service in DPKO hadn't had police officers until mid-2007, I had the great opportunity to contribute to laying the foundation for police training in UN DPKO. In mid-2007, apart from me, two more police officers were recruited by ITS and we were all working closely together on the above-mentioned tasks. Now it would be great to continue working on this foundation and see what our efforts will achieve.

KHK´in Karla Witte

Part 5

Police and human rights – a programme of the Council of Europe and its manager

The Council of Europe was set up on 5 May 1949 by 10 countries and is an intergovernmental political organization to promote democracy, human rights and the rule of law throughout the whole of Europe. It also aims

- to promote awareness and encourage the development of Europe's cultural identity and diversity;
- to find common solutions to the challenges facing European society: discrimination against minorities, xenophobia, intolerance, bioethics and cloning, terrorism, trafficking in human beings, organized crime and corruption, cybercrime, violence against children, etc.;
- to consolidate democratic stability in Europe by backing political, legislative and constitutional reform.

The Council of Europe now has 46 member states and must not be confused with the European Union (EU). The two organizations are quite distinct, but the 27 EU states are all members of the Council of Europe. The headquarters of the Council of Europe as well as the European Parliament, which is an institution of the EU, are located in Strasbourg/France. The EU is a family of democratic European countries, committed to working together for peace and prosperity. The 27 member states have set up common institutions and have delegated some of their sovereignty so that decisions on specific matters of joint interest can be made democratically at a European level.

In December 1997, the programme "Police and Human Rights 1997-2000" was officially launched in Strasbourg during a working conference of the Council of Europe. The programme "Police and Human Rights Beyond 2000" emerged from a recognition of the need for a more co-ordinated and structured approach towards improving human rights awareness among police officers serving in Council of Europe member and applicant states. This programme, created specifically for and by the police, has – since the very beginning – been managed by a senior police officer on secondment. Since its inception, the programme has continued to stimulate and facilitate the co-ordination of initiatives and concrete activities in most member states of the Council of Europe. The goal of translating the theory of human rights protection into a set of tools for daily practice remains a challenge which requires considerable attention.

In May 2006 I became the Programme Manager of the Police and Human Rights Programme in the HRCAD (Human Rights Co-operation and Awareness Division – DG II) within the Council of Europe. Before that, as a chief superintendent, I was the head of the police precinct at the police headquarters in Hagen, where I was responsible for 300 police officers and for the safety and security of 200,000 citizens. Furthermore, I have already worked part-time for the Council of Europe teaching Human Rights and Ethics and also was involved in CEPOL (European Police College) seminars. During this period I gained a great deal of experience in exploring foreign (police) organizations and tackling unexpected queries. As a distance-learning student with Portsmouth University (MSc in International Police Science), I am also learning how to interpret international legislation such as the European Convention on Human Rights and international terrorism counter-measures.

Having been a police officer for 27 years now, I am familiar with most of the challenges posed by the police service of North Rhine-Westphalia. In particular this qualification and experience as a senior police officer, but also my international experience and – most important – my command of the English language enable me to meet these exciting and absorbing challenges.

Andre Konze

Part 6

Organization for Security and Cooperation in Europe (OSCE)

The OSCE is the world's largest regional security organization, whose 56 participating states span the geographical area from Vancouver to Vladivostok. OSCE's effort to support effective policing helps create an environment where sustainable development can flourish. Good policing, which serves the people rather than just the state, is central to preventing conflicts, preserving social stability in times of crisis and supporting post-conflict rehabilitation. The OSCE supports policing in all participating states to ensure the rule of law and fundamental democratic principles and to obtain expert advice and assistance, to develop accountable policing services that protect and aid their citizens. The OSCE's Strategic Police Matters Unit helps OSCE participating States and Partners for Co-operation develop police capacity and institutions, and to improve police co-operation as part of its efforts to strengthen national criminal justice systems.

Within the OSCE, e.g. in Kosovo, but also in countries far away like Tadjikistan, serving or retired German police officers work within special programmes supporting the local police forces. Serving officers are seconded, after their police unit has approved, via the Ministry of Foreign Affairs, to OSCE and hold this position for at least one year. Retired officers are also seconded by the Ministry of Foreign Affairs and can stay within the OSCE organization for up to ten years.

26.4 Federal Criminal Police Office liaison officers

One of the tasks of the Federal Criminal Police Office as the central agency of the German criminal police is to liaise with police in other countries.

Since 1983 the Federal Criminal Police Office has been posting liaison officers (LOs) to other countries. Currently there are 65 liaison officers at 52 locations in 50 countries, from Afghanistan via France and the Netherlands to Yemen.

Liaison officers are seconded to support drug law enforcement and organized crime control as well as international terrorism. Therefore the LOs are posted especially to countries where cooperation is of great importance and where they have direct access to key law enforcement officials. They also work as strategic and tactical observers of the crime situation in their host country.

They are specifically tasked to gather and exchange information through contacts with the host country authorities, the German diplomatic missions abroad and LOs from other countries.

Liaison officers are carefully selected and trained Federal Criminal Police Office detectives. They receive their language training at the Bundessprachenamt in Hürth. While the majority of these LOs are in the Kriminalhauptkommissar ranks, some of the LOs in important countries are even at Kriminaldirektor level. Some are abroad for an extended period and take their family with them. It is not unusual that children of such a family are born in Thailand or India and become multilingual as they grow up.

26.5 Useful phrases

Übersetzen Sie

1. Viele junge Polizeibeamte nutzen die Gelegenheit, ein Praktikum bei einer Polizei im Ausland zu machen.

   ....

   ....

2. Sie lernen dort andere polizeiliche Strategien kennen.

   ....

3. In vielen Ländern gibt es noch Fußstreifendienst.

   ....

4. Auf Jersey werden Straftäter meist innerhalb von ein bis zwei Wochen vor Gericht gestellt, wobei die Strafen höher als in Deutschland sind.

   ....

   ....

5. Seit 1994 bereitet das Land Nordrhein-Westfalen Polizeibeamte auf Auslandseinsätze vor.

   ....

6. Deutsche Polizeibeamte arbeiten in vielen internationalen Polizeiorganisationen mit, z.B. Europol und Interpol.

7. Weltweit sind ungefähr 260 deutsche Polizeibeamte in verschiedenen Missionen im Einsatz.

8. Das Bundeskriminalamt ist die Zentralstelle für deutsche Verbindungsbeamte im Ausland.

9. Im Missionseinsatz kommt man mit Polizisten aus vielen verschiedenen Kulturen zusammen.

10. Verbindungsbeamte haben viele unterschiedliche Aufgaben.

11. Sie sind das Bindeglied zwischen ausländischen Polizeien und der Heimatpolizei und koordinieren Auskunftswünsche und Besuchstermine.

12. Sie befassen sich zunehmend mit Drogen- und organisierter Kriminalität und internationalem Terrorismus und müssen die Situation in ihrem Einsatzland gut kennen.

13. Dienstgrade und Ausbildung der Polizei lassen sich kaum vergleichen.

26.6 Key words and phrases

briefing – counsellor – debriefing – key official – panel – peace-keeping mission – secondment – xenophobia

International police organizations

This unit deals with

- Europol
- Interpol
- the International Law Enforcement Agency
- the Central European Police College
- the International Police Association and
- the Blue Knights.

27.1 Europol – The European Police Office

Europol is the EU law enforcement organization that handles criminal intelligence. Its aim is to improve the effectiveness and cooperation between the relevant authorities of the Member States in preventing and combating serious international organized crime and terrorism. The mission of Europol is to make a significant contribution to the European Union's law enforcement efforts against organized crime and terrorism, with an emphasis on targeting criminal organizations.

The establishment of Europol was agreed in the Maastricht Treaty on European Union of 7 February 1992. Based at The Hague, Netherlands, Europol started limited operations on 3 January 1994 in the form of the European Drugs Unit fighting against drugs. Progressively, other important areas of criminality were added. As of 1 January 2002, the mandate of Europol was extended to deal with all serious forms of international crime as listed in the European Convention, which came into force on 1 October 1998. Europol commenced its full activities on 1 July 1999.

Europol supports the law enforcement activities of the Member States mainly against illicit drug trafficking, illicit immigration networks, terrorism, forgery of money and other means of payment, trafficking in human beings including child pornography, illicit vehicle trafficking, and money-laundering. Other priorities for Europol include crimes against persons, financial crime and cybercrime. This applies where an organized criminal structure is involved and two or more Member States are affected.

Europol supports law enforcement by facilitating the exchange of information, in accordance with national law, between Europol Liaison Officers (ELOs), who are seconded as representatives of their national law enforcement agencies, by providing operational analysis in support of operations, by generating strategic reports (e.g. threat assessments) and crime analysis on the basis of information and intelligence supplied by member states and third parties, and by providing expertise and technical support for investigations and operations carried out within the EU, under the supervision and legal responsibility of the Member States concerned. Europol is also engaged in promoting crime analysis and harmonization of investigative techniques.

Europol has established and is maintaining a computerized system to allow the input, access and analysis of data. The Convention laid down a strict framework for human rights and data protection control, supervision and security. The Europol Computer System has three principal components: an information system, an analysis system and an index system.

Europol is funded by contributions from the Member States according to their GNP. The Financial Controller is appointed by the Management Board and is responsible for monitoring the commitment and disbursement of expenditure as well as the establishment and funding of Europol.

The Directorate of Europol consists of the Director and three Deputy Directors. There are 590 people working at the Europol premises. Of these, 90 are ELOs representing a variety of law enforcement agencies (police, customs, gendarmerie, immigration services, etc.). The ELOs, together with the Europol officers, analysis and other experts, provide an effective, fast and multilingual service 24 hours a day.

Europol is accountable to the Council of Ministers of Justice and Home Affairs. The Council is responsible for the guidance and control of Europol. It appoints the Director and the Deputy Directors and approves the budget. The Council of Ministers comprises representatives from all Member States, and the requirement for unanimous decisions helps ensure democratic control of Europol. The Europol Management Board comprises one representative from each Member State and has the overall task of supervising the activities of the organization. The Joint Supervisory Body, comprising two data protection experts from each Member State, monitors the content and use of all personal data.

Since international organized crime does not stop at national borders, Europol has, in addition, improved its international law enforcement cooperation by negotiating bilateral operational or strategic agreements with other states and international organizations as follows: Bulgaria, Canada, Colombia, Eurojust, European Central Bank, European Commission, European Monitoring Centre for Drugs and Drug Addiction, Iceland, Interpol, Norway, Romania, Russia, Switzerland, Turkey, United Nations Office on Drugs and Crime, United States, World Customs Organization.

27.2 A Europol officer reports

Following a nine-year period working within money laundering and organized crime units in North Rhine-Westphalia, I was recruited by Europol in 2002, as Second Officer, expert on money laundering, and responsible for developing specific IT projects. In 2003, I commenced studies in International Police Science at the University of Portsmouth, achieving a Master of Science degree in 2005. In the same year, I was promoted to First Officer by Europol. As such, I am responsible for the property crime group, supervising and steering strategic and operational activities in the areas of motor vehicle crime, organized robbery/burglary, illicit trafficking in cultural goods, counterfeiting and product piracy. The strategic work includes the production of international versions of the European Vehicle Identification Database (EuVID or EuFID in German) and the Document Information System (DOCIS or DOKIS in German) together with participation in EU working groups and cooperation with the private sector. The latest "product" is a comprehensive report on (international and organized) cargo theft, describing the phenomenon and providing advice to industry and law enforcement agencies.

I am also the project manager for one of the two analysis work files (AWF) opened within the group, AWF Furtum, which covers property crime in general. Currently, this AWF includes sub-projects on Serbian and Romanian organized crime (robberies/burglaries), it supports an Interpol project on raids on jewellery shops and is also conducting an investigation into a raid on the largest Slovenian bank. As the project manager, I have full authority on all AWF activities and I am expected to solve all related problems, be they operational, legal or administrative. My current contract has been extended to 2011.

Werner Gowitzke, First Officer, Europol Financial & Property Crime Unit

27.3 Interpol

Interpol headquaters, Lyon, France

Interpol has its origins in the decisions of an international congress which was held in 1914 to discuss possibilities for simplifying and accelerating the international search for wanted suspects, the improvement of methods of identification, the harmonization of extradition procedures and the centralization of information concerning international criminals – needs which are still there and underpin the role of Interpol in the new millenium. There are 187 member countries throughout the world (2008), and activities are coordinated from an ultra-modern General Secretariat in Lyon, France.

One of Interpol's constitutional aims is to ensure and promote the widest possible mutual assistance between all criminal police authorities within the limits of the laws existing in the different countries and in the spirit of the Universal Declaration of Human Rights. Intervention is forbidden, however, in political, religious, racial or military matters. Interpol's work focuses on organized crime, terrorism, public safety, drug crimes (illegal production, trafficking), human trafficking, money laundering, weapons smuggling, child pornography, white-collar and computer crime, intellectual property crime and corruption.

Today, the vast majority of the work of Interpol is carried out through its offices, the National Central Bureaux (NCBs), established in each member country to serve as the focal point for international cooperation. In Germany, this is one of the tasks of the Federal Criminal Police Office.

The particular problem of language is overcome by Interpol by largely restricting communications to four languages – English, French, Spanish and Arabic.

The prerequisite for cooperation of any kind is an adequate means of communication. With 187 member countries, Interpol has been faced with an enormous challenge to develop a system which will operate quickly and efficiently whichever of those countries should need to speak to each other. Today Interpol boasts an efficient, secure and reliable telecommunications system which links each of the NCBs by e-mail and gives automated access to a central database of information on international crime and criminals.

Interpol is a source of criminal information and intelligence. The Interpol Criminal Information System (ICIS) is a powerful storage and retrieval system which incorporates several fields, one of which, for example, is dedicated to information relating to drug seizures.

One of the most important features of the role of Interpol as a source of information concerns its international notices, relating to persons who are wanted for extradition. The notices include all available identifying details, including photographs and fingerprints, together with all the relevant information.

Interpol also is a medium to establish a policy for international police cooperation. More than 500 conferences are organized every year. These provide members with the opportunity for their decision-makers to agree policy and set standards for international police cooperation.

As an organization, Interpol has undergone dramatic changes during the last few years. Every effort is being made to take advantage of developments in information technology, and structures are being created to ensure a service that is focused upon the needs of its member countries. There remains, however, much to be done. It has yet to be decided, for example, how best Interpol should take advantage of the progress that has been made in the field of identification of persons, such as DNA profiling and Automatic Fingerprint Identification Systems. It is not enough, for example, simply to equip the NCBs with modern telecommunications facilities when many countries lack the infrastructure to communicate efficiently internally.

27.4 International Law Enforcement Academy (ILEA) in Hungary

In 1995 the governments of the United States and Hungary created the International Law Enforcement Academy (ILEA) in Budapest. The Academy offers training programmes for about 130 participants at a time. Course duration ranges from one to eight weeks.

Seminars are designed for mid-level law enforcement officers of the former socialist countries. Some specialized seminars with topics ranging from transnational terrorism through illegal migration and trafficking in persons are open to other nations as well. Instructors come from the United States, the U.K., Sweden, the Netherlands, Austria, Germany, Italy, and from Interpol and Europol on a visiting basis.

27.5 Central European Police College (MEPA)

The Police College is a decentralized advanced training institution supported by its members Austria, Czech Republic, Germany, Hungary, Poland, Slovakia and Switzerland.

From its central coordination office in Vienna, the college plans and organizes courses in the member states that are focused on practical work and current police requirements. These courses are for officers at the intermediate level of police management. They must have completed their training as police inspectors and must also have had several years of police work experience. In MEPA's member states, the college also offers and organizes internships that have proved to be very effective learning aids. Internships in special fields, e. g. money laundering, skimming profits, dragnet investigation, smuggling, special manhunt ("targeted search"), theft of works of art, drug trafficking, contribute to promoting international cooperation.

27.6 The International Police Association (IPA)

Part 1

The IPA is the largest police organization in the world. It was founded in England in 1950 and has since spread all over the world.

Today, in the year 2010, the IPA has National Sections in 61 countries, from Argentina to the USA, with a total membership well in excess of a 360,000. Germany, with more than 60,000 and Austria, with more than 32,000 members, are the largest IPA sections. The German IPA Section is organized in "Landesgruppen" (regions), with North Rhine-Westphalia contributing most in terms of numerical strength (16,000) and having the greatest influence on the German Section, and "Verbindungsstellen" (branches), for example 27 in Baden-Wuerttemberg.

Arthur Troop House, Nottingham

The IPA was founded by police sergeant Arthur Troop of the Lincolnshire Constabulary. He wanted to create an association for friendship and international cooperation amongst police officers, an association which focused on the development of social, cultural and professional links among its members without any discrimination of colour, language, rank, race, religion or sex.

From very small beginnings, the IPA grew rapidly and supported the formation of new sections all over the world. With the political changes in Eastern Europe in the 1990s, many IPA sections from Western Europe have taken over the task of actively supporting the development of new national sections, thus developing new contacts and new friendships.

Esperanto was chosen for the IPA's motto "Servo per amikeco" (= "Service through friendship") to underline the truly international character of the organization.

The IPA is open to every serving or retired police officer irrespective of rank, sex, race, colour, language or religion.

The IPA seeks to

- cultivate friendly relations and mutual assistance between members at home and abroad
- develop cultural relations amongst members and broaden their knowledge
- encourage the exchange of police-related experience to contribute to a mutual understanding of professional problems
- endeavour to enhance the image of the police service and to improve relations between citizens and the police
- provide a better understanding among people to secure peace in the world.

The IPA's pursuits include

- establishing contacts with members in other countries for information or even hosting
- hobby groups for members to share their interests
- friendship weeks, sports events and anniversary celebrations
- international youth exchanges for sons and daughters of members
- international youth gatherings
- professional study exchanges and travel scholarships.

IPA members and their families can spend their holidays in IPA houses, which exist in many sections.

IPA's flagship is Gimborn Castle near Cologne. It is the IPA International Education Centre, where seminars, conferences and meetings are held with participants from all over the world.

IPA International Education Centre – Gimborn Castle

Part 2

EKHK Martin Reiling (MR) is the head of the white-collar crime commissariat at Cologne. He has been an IPA member for more than 30 years, and has established many contacts during that period. When going abroad, be it on holiday or on duty, he has regularly met IPA members there, and has brought home many badges, documents and other souvenirs. EKHK Reiling uses one wall of his office to display all these souvenirs.

He meets KK Klaus Wittling (KW), who has been deployed as supporting officer for a forthcoming search. They talk about these souvenirs.

KW: Good morning, Mr Reiling. That wall looks really interesting. I've never seen anything like that.

MR: Yes, I've been collecting these souvenirs for nearly 30 years. And I've set my heart on some of them.

KW: How do you get things like these? It seems that you've travelled quite a lot all over the world.

MR: That's true. I often went on interesting trips, especially to Britain and the United States, but also other European countries, and I established many contacts. I also took part in some courses at the FBI academy at Quantico/USA and the Police Staff College at Bramshill/England. But I got most of my contacts through the International Police Association IPA.

KW: I've already heard of the IPA. They are said to be the largest police association in the world.

MR: That's true. We've got more than 300,000 members in over 60 countries.

KW: Probably there are many members in Germany, but I haven't heard too much of them.

MR: That's a pity, as IPA Germany is the largest section; there is a branch office in almost every town, there's the "Landesgruppe" in each federal state, and there's the national section; that, in short, is how we are organized.

KW: HM, I really don't know yet what the IPA is and what they do.

MR: From the legal point of view, the IPA is just a club. In fact, the IPA is a "friendship club", which was founded after World War II by Arthur Troop, an English police sergeant. In the early stages the aim was to establish contacts by organizing pen friends, and very soon aspects of mutual understanding among citizens of various states were added. At the next stage, mutual visits were organized (I've just come back from a trip to our IPA twin town in the Netherlands). The next step was the exchange of expertise and professional experience and even further training; once I even got an IPA scholarship for a two-week internship with the New York City Police Department.

KW: I do understand the aspect of friendship. But I think that our in-service further training is good enough. So why further training with the IPA?

MR: Well, let's have a look at the in-service part. If I have to check someone/something with, or need a piece of information from a police agency abroad, I can act in two ways:

I can make a formal inquiry and wait if, or until, I get an answer. And the colleague in the other country certainly has to work in many other fields. Or I can phone a friend who knows me quite well and who is certainly willing to help me. This is often a faster way. I still can decide whether to make a formal inquiry for the files, and if this is worthwhile. And when I'm abroad on official trips, the IPA members take good care of me.

And secondly: Our in-service training refers to our special fields. But sometimes you'd like to get some more information on other subjects.

KW: That's right, I agree with that. And how does further training with the IPA work?

MR: We, the IPA, are lords of the castle. Members of local IPA branches in North Rhine-Westphalia rented a castle at Gimborn, close to Marienheide and the A 4 motorway, and started an information centre there. The castle was refurbished, guest rooms were built, and for nearly 50 years seminars with many different topics in various languages have been organized. That's a first-class conference centre. Many IPA members go there every year.

KW: That must be pretty expensive. How do you pay for that?

MR: Many sections, regional sections and local branch offices, as well as individual persons, are members of the supporting association and support the information centre. Therefore the fees for the seminars can be quite low. Perhaps you should give it a try. The fees for IPA members are even lower.

KW: That was very convincing. I think I'll become a member, too.

27.7 Blue Knights

The Blue Knights are the largest international organization of active and retired law enforcement officers who enjoy riding motorcycles. Non-law enforcement persons can also become members, although their number is limited.

Like many other things .....

In the spring of 1974, police officers Ed Gallant and Chuck Schumann and five others met at Bangor, Maine, USA. They had a common hobby: motorcycling. They did not join one of the existing motorcycle clubs, as these had a bad reputation because of the motorcycle rockers. So they founded a small, local club and called themselves "Blue Knights". The rest is history.

At first their activities centred on local meetings, and family parties were at the centre of their activities. The idea was that family members should share in their hobby.

Quickly the idea spread throughout the United States. Blue Knights chapters were founded in Massachusetts and New Hampshire, and many others were to follow.

When new chapters were founded in Canada and Australia, the Blue Knights became the largest law enforcement motorcycle club and one of the largest motorcycle clubs in the world.

In 1989 the idea spread to Europe.

The umbrella organization, Blue Knights® International Law Enforcement Motorcycle Club Inc., today has more than 20,000 members in 29 countries with 542 chapters (as of 27th March 2009). In Germany there are, at present, 21 chapters with about 1,200 members.

The ideas and aims of the organization have changed in the course of time. Apart from promoting the sport of motorcycling and promoting the safe use, operation and enjoyment of motorbikes, the Blue Knigts provide assistance, enjoyment, entertainment, physical, mental and social benefits not only for its members but also for the general public.

By 31st March 2009, the Blue Knights had donated $ 11,381,236.18 to numerous charities.

There are many national and international rides and functions; often spouses and children accompany the members. Thus members have an opportunity to meet other Blue Knights at home and abroad. A Blue Knight travelling on his motorbike can be sure to be welcomed with open arms by fellow members everywhere in

The Blue Knights are truly a family.

"There are no strangers, only friends you haven't met."
Ride with Pride
Albert Karbstein
Member
Germany 25 – Kurpfalz

27.8 Useful phrases

Übersetzen Sie

1. Deutsche Polizeibeamte in internationalen Organisationen repräsentieren ihre heimatliche Polizei.

....

2. Manchmal werden Polizeibeamte befördert, wenn sie von einem schwierigen Auslandseinsatz zurückkommen.

....

3 In einigen deutschen Polizeien ist die Mitarbeit in einer internationalen Funktion Teil des Personalentwicklungsplans.

....

4. Auf jeden Fall ist es sehr befriedigend, in einer internationalen Umgebung zu arbeiten.

....

5. Heute haben deutsche Polizeibeamte viel mehr Gelegenheiten, im Ausland zu arbeiten.

....

6. Gute Kenntnisse besonders des Englischen sind höchst wichtig.

....

7. Das Familienleben wird beeinflusst, wenn ein Polizeibeamter ins Ausland will. Deshalb muss die Familie zustimmen.

....

8. Auslandseinsätze dauern etwa ein Jahr, während die Mitarbeit in internationalen Organisationen bis zu drei Jahren dauert.

....

9. Vor jedem Auslandsaufenthalt wird ein gründlicher Gesundheitstest durchgeführt.

....

10. Besonders bei internationalen Missionseinsätzen muss sich der Bewerber mehreren Tests unterziehen und an mehreren Lehrgängen teilnehmen.

....

11. Gelegentlich fällt ein guter und qualifizierter Beamter beim Englischtest durch.

....

27.9 Key words and phrases

cargo theft – criminal intelligence – cybercrime – dragnet investigation – formal inquiry – illicit trafficking in cultural goods – means of payment – money laundering – product piracy – property crime – skimming profits – targeted search – third party – unanimous decision

Unit 28

Police abroad

This unit deals with

- police and police ranks in England and Wales
- a Welsh policewoman's career
- the Cambridgeshire Constabulary
- the police in Scotland
- the police in Northern Ireland and the Republic of Ireland
- the police in the USA (Fort Lauderdale, Tulsa, Michigan, FBI, the Capitol Police, Lynchburg, California).

28.1 Police in England and Wales

There are 43 police services in England and Wales. The size of the individual force depends on the area and the population.

The force areas are divided into divisions, subdivisions and local police stations.

With more than 31,000 officers, London's Metropolitan Police Service is the largest force; its headquarters is New Scotland Yard.

The total number of police officers in England and Wales is about 142,000. This figure does not include about 2,500 British Transport Police officers. The police officers are supported by 76,000 police staff, 15,000 Police Community Support Officers (PCSOs), 14,000 "specials" (volunteer, unpaid constables who work a minimum of eight hours a month), 1,600 Designated Officers (specialist officers in investigation, detention and escort roles), and 650 traffic wardens; the number of the latter is decreasing because local authorities are increasingly in charge of parking.

In addition there are various other police services, for example the Kew Constabulary, formerly Royal Botanic Gardens Constabulary, which consists of 15 officers and is responsible for safety and security at Kew Gardens, the Civil Nuclear Constabulary (CNC), formerly the UK Atomic Energy Authority Constabulary (650 officers are responsible for all nuclear power plants in the UK), the Ministry of Defence Police (about 3,500 officers) as well as a number of small services for ports, waterways, tunnels and airports.

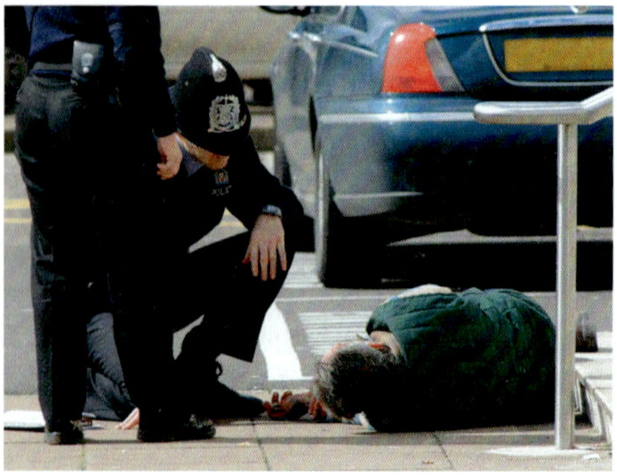

28.2 Police ranks in England and Wales

Provinces	Metropolitan Police Service
constable	constable
sergeant	sergeant
inspector	inspector
superintendent	superintendent
assistant chief constable	commander
deputy chief constable	assistant commissioner
chief constable	deputy commissioner
	commissioner

In addition, there are various grades within some ranks, e.g. "chief inspector" or "chief superintendent". The above ranks are usually prefixed by the word "police" or "detective", e.g. "police constable" (PC) or "detective inspector" (DI). The detective ranks are from constable to superintendent only. In most forces, female officers are identified by the word "woman", e.g. "woman police constable" (WPC).

28.3 A Welsh policewoman's career

Beti Jones (1930 – 2001) was a police inspector in Wales. Here are the details of her professional career:

1951	joined the (then) Denbighshire Constabulary at the age of 21
	three months training at Bruche Training Centre
1951 to 1953	two-year probationary period at Force Headquarters, Wrexham
1953 to 1958	beat officer at Colwyn Bay
1958 to 1959	one year in Cyprus (then a British colony)
1959 to 1960	beat officer at Colwyn Bay
1960 to 1967	assistant inspector in Northern Rhodesia (until 1964 a British colony, since then independent state of Zambia)
1967 to 1968	beat officer at Denbigh
1968 to 1969	beat officer at Llandudno
1969	promotion to sergeant, with a staff of six women constables
1975	promotion to inspector
1975 to 1980	divisional inspector at Llandudno
	prosecuting inspector at magistrates' court
1980 to 1985	training department at Police Headquarters, Colwyn Bay,
	training recruits and special constables
1985	retirement

28.4 Cambridgeshire Constabulary

Each police force in England and Wales is responsible for up to three counties. The Home Secretary has no powers of instruction. However, the Home Office has an influence on the police forces by appointing H.M. Inspectors of Constabulary and by allocating funds.

The Cambridgeshire Constabulary is overseen by a police authority consisting of local councillors, lay persons and magistrates. This authority appoints the chief constable as well as the deputy chief constable and the assistant chief constables. The chief constable is responsible for appointing all the other ranks.

Cambridgeshire is divided into the Northern, Central and Southern Divisions, which, in turn are sub-divided into sectors – the Northern comprises Eastern, Southern and Western; Central Division comprises Huntingdon, St. Neots, St. Ives and Ramsay, March and Wisbech. The Southern Division comprises Cambridge North, Cambridge South, Cambridge Centre, Ely, Histon and Sawston.

The Force Headquarters is situated at Huntingdon. Also based at Headquarters are the Administration Departments, the Investigation Inspectorate and the Safer Communities Inspectorate, which is responsible, amongst other things, for the Road Policing Unit, the Dog Section, the Air Support Unit and the Tactical Firearms Unit.

28.5 The long arm of the law

The underlying principles of policing in England and Wales are based upon the common law and policing by consent. The common law is very different from many European judicial systems. It is a continually evolving system of unwritten laws that reflect the common will of the people. It gives, for example, powers of arrest to all citizens including police officers, and requires that accused persons are taken before magistrates for trial. Magistrates are drawn from their local community. Each police officer is personally vested with certain powers. He or she is sworn in by a magistrate and empowered to use his or her authority throughout the country.

All uniformed constables and sergeants have identifying numbers on their uniforms, which greatly assists their accountability to the public.

Police officers do not carry guns, but they are armed with truncheons and, in some forces, with CS spray. However, specialist firearms officers support their unarmed colleagues if necessary.

In recent years, pressures on the police have increased enormously.

Any police officer walking his or her beat can now call upon a vast support network. This ranges from patrol cars, motorcycle units, motorway crews and flying squads to plain-clothes officers, frogmen and dog handlers. All these units are supported by a comprehensive system of information and control, e.g. personal radios, databases, closed circuit television (CCTV) cameras, and other sophisticated equipment.

In order to ensure absolute impartiality, police officers are not allowed to join a trade union or a political party. The following groups with statutory membership represent the interests of the various ranks:

- the Police Federation for all officers up to and including chief inspectors
- the Superintendents' Association for all superintendents and chief superintendents
- the Association of Chief Police Officers (ACPO) for all ranks from assistant chief constable.

28.6 Police in Scotland

A foreign tourist travelling through England and Scotland will not notice any differences between the respective police services. However, there are some differences.

There are eight independent police forces in Scotland:

Central Scotland Police – Dumfries & Galloway Constabulary – Fife Constabulary – Grampian Police – Lothian & Borders Police – Northern Constabulary – Strathclyde Police – Tayside Police.

In addition, there is the Scottish Police Services Authority, which provides expert policing and support services to the eight forces and which is also responsible, among other things, for the Scottish Criminal Record Office, the Scottish Drug Enforcement Agency and the Scottish Police College.

Find out more about the Scottish police services. Use the internet

28.7 Police in Northern Ireland

The Police Service of Northern Ireland, until 3rd November 2001 the Royal Ulster Constabulary, employs 7,500 full-time regular police officers and 2,700 police staff. The PSNI is responsible for an area of 13,843 square kilometres with about 1.8 million inhabitants.

Whereas more than 90 % of the members of the Royal Ulster Constabulary were Protestant officers, today half of all new recruits are Catholics. Police trainee recruitment is managed by "Deloitte", an independent professional recruitment agency. In 2006, 20 % of the PSNI officers were Catholic, and it is hoped that by 2011 30 % of the service will be Catholic.

There are no formal qualification requirements. However, applicants must be at least 18 or under 57 (!), must meet nationality requirements, must not have a conviction that will exclude them and must meet required medical criteria. A pool of qualified candidates, who have passed the initial selection test, the medical examination and who have met the assessment standards, is created, out of which trainees are selected on a 50:50 basis (Catholics and Protestants).

The colour of the PSNI uniform is "bottle green", and, unlike the police forces in England, Scotland and Wales, all PSNI officers are armed.

PSNI's headquarters is in Knock, East Belfast.

28.8 Police in the Republic of Ireland

The Republic of Ireland's national police service, official name An Garda Siochána, has about 15,000 unarmed uniformed officers, and about 1,700 plain-clothes detectives armed with handguns.

Its headquarters is in the Phoenix Park on the western side of Dublin city.

Its chief is the Commissioner, who is appointed by the Government and who is responsible to the Minister for Justice, Equality & Law Reform.

His management team consists of

- the Deputy Commissioner in charge of Operations
- the Deputy Commissioner in charge of Strategy & Change Management
- the Chief Administrative Officer (CAO)
- 12 Assistant Commissioners
- the Director of Finance
- the Executive Director of Information and Communication Technology
- the Director of Communications
- the Chief Medical Officer.

Within the Garda, there are the following ranks and numbers of officers as of 31st December 2008:

Garda	11,585
Sergeant	2,229
Inspector	344
Superintendent	187
Chief Superintendent	52
Assistant Commissioner	12
Deputy Commissioner	2
Commissioner	1

For policing purposes, the country is divided into six regions, each of which is commanded by an Assistant Commissioner.

These regions are:

- Dublin Metropolitan Region
- Northern Region (counties Donegal, Sligo/Leitrim, Cavan/Monahan, Louth)
- Western Region (counties Mayo, Galway, Clare, Roscommon/Longford)
- Eastern Region (counties Meath, Westmeath, Laois/Offaly, Carlow/Kildare, Wicklow)
- Southern Region (counties Limerick, Kerry, Cork N, Cork W, Cork City)
- South Eastern Region (counties Tipperary, Waterford/Kilkenny, Wexford).

Each region is divided into districts (commanded by a Chief Superintendent), sub-districts (commanded by a Sergeant) and stations.

Basic training is divided into five phases and lasts two years. Initially, students spend 22 weeks at the Garda College in Templemore, followed by a period of 24 weeks spent at selected stations under the direct supervision of tutorial staff. After further training at the College, students become members of the Service and are attached to stations. While they are now empowered to enforce legislation, they remain on probation for a further two-year period.

The current Garda operational uniform consists of the Garda cap, shirt, clip-on tie, epaulettes, ballistic/anti-stab vest, trousers/skirt, belt, waterproof jacket and fleece, waterproof trousers, utility belt (holds handcuffs, torch, notebook, fixed-charge forms, baton, radio, gloves), footwear (official boots) and gloves. High-visibility jackets are worn on outdoor duty especially at night time and when on traffic-related duties.

The Garda caps have chin straps to keep them in place in windy conditions.

28.9 Police in the USA

Part 1

In the USA more than 20,000 different government agencies have full or restricted police powers.

Most of these agencies are locally based (counties, cities, townships), about 1,000 are state police forces and about 50 are federal police services. Some have only restricted powers and are only allowed to investigate certain offences, others can only take action locally (university police, hospital police).

About 85 % of all police officers are members of local police forces. In the counties, the Sheriff's Department is the most important police force. More than 11,000 police agencies are locally based. More than 90 % of communities with more than 2,500 inhabitants have their own police force; two thirds of them employ less than 20 officers, and one third employ less than 5 officers.

Usually the sheriff is the leading administrative officer of a county; he is elected by the public. In the western parts of the USA he is often in charge of the federal justice system, he is in charge of security during trials, he has to prepare trials, and he is responsible for the county jail. He is the chief police officer of the county and the communities within the county.

In the eastern parts of the USA the sheriff's chief function is to provide security during trials. In counties without communities with their own local government he is often in charge of large and well equipped police forces.

The sheriff of Los Angeles County (outside the city boundaries of Los Angeles) commands a police force that is larger than many police departments of large cities. This force also has jurisdiction in the small towns in the area. In other, sparsely populated areas (parts of California, Arizona, New Mexico) the sheriff often represents the only police force and only has a few deputies to help him enforce state and federal law.

The US Marshal is the executive officer of the federal courts. He is in charge of security during trials. In this field he has the same tasks as the sheriff. The "Town Marshal" or "Constable" is the sheriff in a small town. He is elected by the public and also in charge of criminal prosecution. In some parts of the USA he is also the executive officer of the magistrates' court. These courts deal with minor offences. Depending on local tradition, the officer is also called "marshal" or "constable".

The basis of police organization are the municipal police departments, whose size varies greatly. In 2009 the New York City Police Department had 35,000 officers for more than 7 million inhabitants. Pittsburgh had 1,055 officers for 389,000 inhabitants. Brawly in California had 36, Amherst in Ohio 18, and Maize in Kansas only one.

In many towns there are, in addition, law enforcement agencies as special police forces with restricted jurisdiction and powers, for example, park rangers and park police officers, harbor police, tunnel police and bridge police.

With the exception of Hawaii, each US state has its state police, which in most cases only supervises traffic on freeways and interstates. In a small number of states they also fight crime in rural areas.

The executive branch of the Administration, whose nominal head is the President of the United States, supervise the federal police services. There are a large number of independent federal police authorities with different tasks. Among them are the US Marshal's Office, the US Customs Service, the Bureau of Alcohol, Tobacco and Firearms, and many others.

Part 2 – Police Officer – Fort Lauderdale, Florida (2006)

The Fort Lauderdale Police Department is accepting applications for the position of police officer. The agency consists of nearly 500 police officers and 240 civilian personnel and serves a community of 165,000.

Minimum Requirements

Interested candidates must be U.S. citizens at the time of application, they must be at least 19 years of age, they must be of good moral character, they must have no felony convictions or misdemeanors involving perjury or domestic violence and must have a high school diploma or equivalent education.

Salary

$40.393 to $63.897 annually, and $1.553 bi-weekly in the Police Academy (plus overtime).

Benefits

Include excellent health & dental plan, paternity/maternity leave, up to five weeks on annual vacation, 17 days paid military leave, no state or local employment taxes, 67.6 % pension after 20 years to a maximum of 81 % after 24 years, tuition reimbursement, personally assigned vehicle program, civil service protection, educational incentives, union representation, in-house fitness center, and shift differential.

Contact

You may contact us at: www.flpd.org, at recruiter@fortlauderdale.gov or telephone (954) 828 FLPD.

The City of Fort Lauderdale is an equal opportunity employer.

Part 3 – The Tulsa Police Department (2006)

The Tulsa Police Department is responsible for the safety and security of nearly half a million people who live and work in Tulsa, Oklahoma.

There are nearly 800 sworn police officers in the department, who are supported by about 120 civilians and about 80 "Volunteers in Police Service" (VIPS) as well as approximately 150 men and women of the Tulsa Auxiliary Police.

The sworn personnel hold the following ranks:

Officer	542
Corporal	82
Sergeant	77
Lieutenant	23
Major	8
Deputy Chief	3
Chief	1

Within the Tulsa Police Department there are the following divisions and units:

Administration, Air Support, Apprentice Police Officers, Bomb Squad, Citizens Crime Commission, Crime Stoppers, Detective Division (Personal Crimes and Property Crimes), Dive Team, Headquarters Division, Information & Technical Services Division, Intelligence Unit, K-9, Motorcycle Unit, Mounted Patrol, Narcotics, Office of Integrity and Compliance, Organized Gang Unit, Payroll and Finance, Psychological Services (including Police/Fire Chaplaincy Corps), Public Information Office, School Resource Officers, Special Events, Special Investigations Division, SWAT Team, Task Force (divided into three sections: Organized Crime Enforcement Task Force, High Intensity Drug Trafficking Area Task Force, Joint Terrorism Task Force), Traffic Safety Coordinator, Training Division, Tulsa Police Reserve, Uniform Division East, Uniform Division North, Uniform Division Southwest, Vice, Volunteers in Police Service.

Part 4 – The Michigan State Police

by First Lieutenant (ret.) Doctor Earl James †, J.D., Ph.D. (in October 2006)

The Michigan State Police (MSP), a semi-military organization, began on April 19, 1917. The first formal Michigan State Recruit School was conducted in 1924. This was also the year when motorcycles and automobiles replaced horses for police patrol work.

The MSP has general police powers throughout the state. It has always been quick to take advantage of modern technology to fight crime. The MSP was the first state agency to use lie detectors and radios, and were leaders in establishing a statewide computer system, an Automatic Fingerprint Identification System, and a DNA database.

In 2006, the Michigan State Police consisted of 1,984 sworn police officers. They were supported by 557 civilians; thus the total department strength was 2,541 employees. Fifty new troopers will be added to the force in 2007.

The department is organized with the Office of the Director at the top tier. The Director, who holds the rank of colonel, commands the entire department. Reporting directly to him are the Executive Division, Internal Auditor, Office of Highway Safety Planning, and the Behavioral Science Section.

Immediately below the Office of the Director, but reporting to the colonel, are the following bureaus: Uniform Services, Investigative Services, and Support Services. Each bureau is commanded by a lieutenant colonel.

The Uniform Services Bureau is comprised of seven districts, each under the command of a captain, who is assisted by an inspector. There are several posts in every district. Each post is commanded by a first lieutenant, who is assisted by sergeants, detectives, troopers and motor carrier officers. There are 64 posts throughout the state of Michigan. The bureau also has the Communications and Motor Carrier Divisions and Special Operations.

The Investigative Services Bureau is made up of the East Lansing and Southeastern Criminal Investigative Divisions, the Field Detective Division, the Fire Marshal Division, and the Forensic Science Division.

The Support Services Bureau consists of the Criminal Justice Data Center, the Michigan Law Enforcement Training Council, Central Records Division, Training Division, Management and Services Division, Emergency Services Division, the Office of Budget, and the Personnel Division. A captain supervises each division.

The recruit training program is very demanding and lasts for 20 weeks. Recruits reside at the Training Academy. Only one of every ten applicants is selected to become a trooper. The recruit's day begins at 0500 a.m., and often does not end until 2200 hours. The curriculum consists of the following subjects: Administrative, Legal, Traffic, Criminal Investigation, Patrol Techniques, General Police Duties, Police Physical Skills such as high-speed driving, boxing, shooting and swimming, Special Subjects, Departmental Police Procedures, Official Orders and Crime Scene Processing. The goal is to train the trooper to think independently and accept leadership responsibility.

Part 5 – Obituary Earl Wallace Krueger James, J.D., Ph. D., Michigan State Police

Earl Wallace Krueger James went to his Lord on Tuesday, February 26, 2008 after suffering a massive heart attack. Earl was born to Leland and Martha James in Kendalville, IN on June 8, 1931. Earl attended primary school in Constantine, MI. He quit school to work on his uncle's dairy farm in Wisconsin. He also worked in construction before his parents consented to him enlisting in the U.S. Marines. He was a non-commissioned officer in charge of security at the naval station in Maryland. He served as a gun commander and patrol leader in Korea during the Conflict. He was awarded several medals. After obtaining the rank of Sergeant, he was honorably discharged from active Marines; he served in the reserve for five years.

He began his police career in the military, followed by serving on the Sturgis, MI, and Washington, D.C. police forces and retired at the rank of First Lieutenant from the Michigan State Police. He served the Michigan State Police at Newberry, Calumet, Paw Paw, White Pigeon, Flat Rock, Detroit and Lansing. He was one of the original founders of the Michigan State Police Trooper's Ass'n. He was Commander of the MSP Polygraph Section. He was the founder and Commander of the MSP Internal Affairs Unit. He was a competitive pistol shooter, winning the Upper Peninsula Championship in 1960 and 1961 and the Governor's Trophy in 1968. Governors Milliken and Blanchard appointed him to the state polygraph board. He served eight years as Vice Chairman and Chairman. He was a Hunter Safety and Certified Pistol Instructor for the NRA. He was a Boy Scout Merit Badge Counselor for Firearms and Fingerprints.

Earl attended schools and universities while working fulltime. He has six degrees including a Ph.D. in Forensic Science. He has been an instructor or guest lecturer at Lansing Community College, Madonna University, Michigan State University and Windsor University. Earl researched serial killings of women and authored "Catching Serial Killers", which has been used as a textbook in many universities. He also authored the 50-year history of the Michigan State Police Polygraph unit.

Earl was a member of the National Society of the Sons of the American Revolution, served as President of the Lansing Chapter, State Chaplain, and assisted in founding the Sons of the American Revolution German Society. He was a life member of the Veterans of Foreign Wars, American Rifle Ass'n, and The Marine Corps League, of which he served 3 years as State Legislative Director. Earl has been an Elder in the Lutheran Church Missouri Synod, and is a present member of Trinity Lutheran Church, Lansing.

Earl is survived by his wife of 52 years Betty (Brueck), three children Deborah (Steward) Dendtler, Chesterfield, VA, Diana James, Westley Chapel, FL, and Mark (Peggy) James, Sheridan, IN. Four grandchildren Katheryne, Leland, Luke and Alison. Two sisters Barbara Colpetsire, Colon, MI, Linda (Herbert) Cox, Atlantic Beach, FL. And several nieces and nephews.

Earl requested there be no funeral. He will be cremated. The family is being served by Peters and Murray Funeral Home in Grand Ledge, Michigan. There will be a Christian committal service at a later date in Kimmell, IN. Earl requests memorial donations be made to the Michigan State Police Fallen Troopers Memorial. Send donations to Michigan State Police Trooper Association, 1715 Abbey Rd., East Lansing, MI 48823.

When Betty James, the widow, was asked if this obituary could be included in the book, she agreed at once. Her comment: "Earl would be very proud of it."

Part 6 – The Federal Bureau of Investigation (FBI)

The FBI was formed in 1908 as a force of special agents whose task was to deal with bankruptcy fraud, antitrust crime, neutrality violations, and peonage. Today the FBI has jurisdiction over violations of more than 200 categories of federal law. The Bureau closely focuses on the prevention of terrorist attacks, on countering foreign intelligence operations and on addressing cybercrime-based attacks and high-technology crimes. In addition, the FBI remains dedicated to protecting civil rights and to combating public corruption as well as organized, white-collar and significant violent crime.

Part 7 – The Capitol Police in Washington

2 p.m. I'm to meet Jürgen Hynes, whom here everybody calls Jerry. Jürgen comes from Frankonia, you can still hear it when he's talking. And Jürgen is a police officer, to be precise: a police officer of the US Capitol Police.

In the 1950s he emigrated from Nuremberg and became an American citizen. He owns a house in Alexandria, a small town close to Washington, where he takes care as a sole parent of his two daughters. He is a member of a political organization to which also Bob Dole and Newt Gingrich belong, and so he has quite some influence. Apart from that, he knows the Capitol very well.

Jerry is the president of the Washington IPA, and he promised to show me round the Capitol. We meet at his station about a block away from the Capitol. After a short tour of the station, we go down into the basement, and a small underground electric train takes us to the Capitol. Everywhere we meet Jerry's colleagues, one of them is his younger brother Hans. Security is very tight. And while Jerry shows me the Capitol, he also informs me about the Capitol Police.

Today's U.S. Capitol Police is a modern police force with almost all the installations typical of traditional government agencies. But this force of about 1,300 officers (about the size of the police force in Duisburg or Wuppertal), which has an annual budget of $ 70 million, has some special features. There are no dwellings and shops in its area. And yet, the whole world looks at this small agency.

It was a long way from the one-man police service to its present size. The first officer was John Golding, a watchman who kept peace and order, and who got an annual salary of $ 371. He started in 1801. Although he was authorized to eject persons from the building, he needed the support of a US Marshal to arrest somebody.

During the Napoleonic war, British troops set fire to the federal buildings in August 1814. After the latter had been rebuilt, the strength of the Capitol police force was increased to four. Less than a year later the officers got full police powers and were answerable to the speakers of the Senate and the House of Representatives. Even today, in judicial terms, half of the officers belong to the House of Representatives, while the other half are paid for by the Senate.

In 1854 the Capitol Police were armed with heavy hickory batons, and they already had a kind of uniform. But only when the Civil War broke out were they allowed to carry their traditional metal shield.

The better known the Capitol Police became in the following years, the more critics expressed their opinion. One of them was Mark Twain, who speculated that the Capitol Police would soon be dissolved and would not exist much longer. But no way. On the contrary, when, in 1868, the impeachment proceedings against President Andrew Johnson were going on, the Senate hearings took place, almost without any breaks, from March to May, and large crowds gathered in front of the Capitol, which had to be controlled by the Capitol Police.

Since 1882, all members of the Capitol Police wear a uniform provided by the department. At the beginning of the 20th century, the department became larger. During the

Spanish War, there were 67 police officers, and in 1904 it was mandatory for officers to be in uniform while on duty.

In 1909, the force had already more than 100 officers, and they were quite busy.

Since 1926 they have been equipped with motorcycles.

In 1915 the first bomb damaged the Capitol building. A fanatic had placed three bars of dynamite in the Senate's reception hall.

As from 1935, the Capitol Police have been supported by FBI special agents who are deployed there and who also have full police powers.

On March 1, 1954, four Puerto Ricans entered the visitors' section of the House of Representatives and fired at the assembly. Five congressmen were wounded, the perpetrators were arrested.

This was the beginning of a more professional approach to policing, which soon became absolutely necessary in an era of massive unrest among citizens in the 1960s and 1970s.

After another bomb attack in the Senate wing in 1971, security measures were tightened even more. A canine unit was established. Every person had to identify himself/herself, and air security locks were fitted. The number of officers was increased from 621 to more than one thousand, and three years later the first female officers were appointed. After another bomb attack in 1983, security measures were tightened even more.

The main task of the U.S. Capitol Police is to maintain peace and order on the 250-acre area of the Capitol premises. In addition, the officers must provide close protection to the 535 members of the Senate and House of Representatives, and the employees, high-ranking visitors, and tourists have to be protected. In 1992 Congress extended the Capitol Police powers even more; since then, its officers also have jurisdiction in the whole District of Columbia; as is typical of the United States, outside the Capitol premises they compete with a large number of other police forces.

The fact that the Capitol Police are a special police force can also be seen from the officers' training.

After a two-week introductory course, the recruits are sent to the Federal Training Center at Glynco, GA, where also ATF and the US Marshals' Service train their officers. Then they come back to the Washington Police Academy for eight weeks for further training. After having passed their examinations, the young officers are allocated to an experienced officer for 14 weeks, before they are allowed to work on their own. Three years later they can apply, for the first time, at a selection procedure for promotion to sergeant or detective.

About 900 of the officers walk the beat, work as sentries, control traffic, patrol on bicycles or check visitors. Many of them are trained to detect drugs and drugged people; drug training is done within the Capitol Police or at neighbouring police forces.

The service cars are as modern as those of other police services. They are either Chevrolet Caprice or Ford Crown Victoria. The vehicles are white with light and dark blue lines at the sides. The Capitol symbol is affixed to both doors. The vehicles are equipped with 12-round shotguns, the officers carry a 5946.9 mm SW.

In summer the officers wear a short-sleeved open shirt with a brass-colored patch and a name tag. On the left arm there is an arm patch. The trousers are dark blue. The long-sleeved winter shirt is dark blue and has a patch on both sleeves. In addition, there is a V-necked dark blue sweater. The officers are recommended to wear soft body armour, but it's up to them.

A normal shift takes eight hours. Overtime is paid time and a half, and therefore much sought after. Jerry, whom I'm visiting at the beginning of the holiday season, is working two shifts a day at the moment.

The Capitol Police headquarters are in a seven-floor building close to Union Station, Washington's train station. The building was completely refurbished in 1988 and has enough offices as well as classrooms, a fitness center and a small detention area from where arrested persons can be handed over to the Washington Metro Police.

The command center is underground, close to the Delaware and Constitution Avenue intersection. It is relatively small. Radio messages are sent and received on three separate channels, one for watch and access control, one for patrol, and one for detectives. Apart from that, other channels, some of which can be encrypted, are reserved for special situations.

Special situations occur quite frequently. Twice a year there are demonstrations with more than 50,000 persons. The "One Million March" in fall, demanding improved opportunities for Afro-Americans, attracted more than 400,000 demonstrators. On average, more than 400 demonstrations, in other words more than one per day, take place in the Capitol area. It goes without saying that close cooperation with the adjoining police forces is necessary.

After two years of shift work, officers can apply for advertised posts in close protection, in the drug unit, in the canine unit, in the motorcycle unit (Yamaha 250 cc), in the mountain bike patrol unit, in the detective unit or others.

The close protection section consists of four units, who protect endangered persons outside the Capitol. Officers have to travel a lot. And there is permanent protection inside the Capitol.

The Capitol Police were one of the first police forces in the greater Washington area with a bike unit. They developed their own training program with their own instructors, and they also train officers from neighboring forces. Bike patrols are going on all the year round, with the exception of weeks with extreme cold or snowfall.

The detective division investigates offences by federal employees and by visitors. But they also have to deal with illegal lobbying. The last investigation in this field was against an employee of the communication industry who was suspected of having given false information to congressmen, thus manipulating them. Such investigations are not easy, and officers need a lot of experience. The detective division also investigate drug offences. This seems strange at first sight, but you have to consider the fact that they have to deal with thousands of employees and visitors every day.

Once in a while, hostages are taken. The Capitol Police prepare for such situations by having a hostage negotiation team with the corresponding equipment in reserve.

A bomb team, working to preventing bomb attacks, has become rather important ever since the Oklahoma bombing. Most of the problems can be solved with special equipment, for example video-controlled robots and a truck-mounted pressure chamber.

The canine unit has 30 German shepherds, most of them trained as explosives and drug-sniffing dogs, but they are also employed in tracing and protection duties. They live with the canine officers and their families, and they must be absolutely obedient as they often have to work in an environment with many people.

The biography of the chief of this police department is just as unusual as his department. Gary L. Albrecht was born in Geneva, Switzerland, where he also went to high school. Afterwards he was a student at Yale University, and got a degree as Bachelor of Arts in Economics. For two years he was a teacher of Latin in Washington before he joined the Washington Metro Police in 1969. First he did patrol work before he worked his way up. He worked as duty officer on night shift, as station commander, as regional/district commander and as sub-department head on Capitol Hill. After a short time as equal opportunities officer and director of planning and development, he became a deputy chief and chief of the first district in Washington. On 1st May 1992 he was appointed Chief of the Capitol Police, a position which has traditionally been reserved for members of the Washington Metro Police.

Gary Albrecht is proud of his department, and he attaches importance to the fact that intensive training is absolutely necessary for community policing. He advises all possible applicants to go to college, as competition for well-paid positions is becoming more and more intensive. And he also attaches importance to working with balanced and friendly colleagues, as he knows how strenuous the job can be. And he explains: "How often can you answer the same questions again and again, for example 'Where's President Clinton'?"

Part 8 – A German police officer in the USA

Daniel Schleyer is a police officer in the sleepy town of Brawley with 22,000 inhabitants in California, close to the Mexican border. That's nothing extraordinary, isn't it? Well, five years ago, he was a police officer in Heidelberg. What took him to the United States? Love, of course. During a US holiday he met his future wife. After she had visited him in Heidelberg, it was clear that they wanted to get married, and they thought that California would offer better opportunities.

But it wasn't easy in California, at least at first. He had to improve his English, and his German police training was of no value at all. So he worked as a security guard until he became an American citizen last year. He attended police academy, and then his dream became true: he got a position with the Brawley Police Department.

In this job you must be an all-rounder, as the department has only 36 officers. As is normal in the USA, Daniel is alone in his patrol car, and if necessary other officers will support him. His patrol car cannot be compared with German ones. A computer with links to all necessary files is his tool for reports and charges. When he ends his shift, his work has come to an end, too. Emigrating to the USA has paid off for Daniel Schleyer.

In order to become a law enforcement officer in the state of California, one has to attend a certified P.O.S.T. (Peace Officer Standard and Training) training academy. Each state of the United States emphasizes certain aspects according to the state's requirements and governmental priorities with respect to public service. Therefore, every state is different with regard to training and curriculum at the respective academy site.

In California there are two ways to graduate from a police academy. Usually, if someone wants to pursue a career in law enforcement, the candidate will apply with a particular city (municipal), County Sheriff Department or the state of California for the position of peace officer. The application process entails a written examination, oral interviews, background process, polygraph examination (lie detector test) and psychological and medical examination. If the candidate is hired by the respective agency, he or she will be sent to a police academy and begins his/her training as a police cadet/recruit in a day class from Monday to Friday on a full-time basis. The day academy takes up to 6 months to graduation and the cadet is being paid a salary while attending.

The other possibility is the extended modular program, which enables someone who works during the daytime to attend the academy during evening hours. Usually those cadets are not yet hired and have to pay for the academy tuition themselves. The extended program takes up to 10 months due to shorter training hours.

The academy training is very strenuous and requires high physical as well as mental preparedness. Usually, the cadets learn a great amount of discipline, which is monitored by tactical officers. It is not uncommon that individual cadets are being yelled at or punished with physical tasks such as push-ups or class runs. The academic part of the academy consists of certain learning domains where the cadet learns about applying the law, police tactics, scenarios with practical application and firearms training. Class time takes up approximately 60 percent and entails subjects such as criminal law, crimes against children, weapons law, traffic law, etc.

After graduation, the hired cadet is sworn in as a police officer and begins his or her field training with a field training officer of the agency for at least 12 weeks. During the field training program, the rookie officer learns about the agency, specific law applications and handling of cases. If the rookie officer finishes the program, he or she will work on his own as an individual officer without direct supervision.

Daniel Schleyer, Brawley, 390 W. Trail St, Brawley, CA 92227.

Vocabulary

Das Vokabular des gesamten Buches ist alphabetisch geordnet, nicht nach den einzelnen Units. Zusammengesetzte Ausdrücke sind – im Gegensatz zu den meisten Wörterbüchern – grundsätzlich nach dem ersten Wort angeführt; so steht z.B. “flash one’s headlights” unter “flash” oder “give someone a lift” unter “give”. Lediglich bei präpositionalen Ausdrücken wird das sinngebende Wort nach vorne gezogen, z.B. steht “in accordance with” unter “accordance”; das Gleiche gilt für Ausdrücke mit “be”; so steht z.B. “be aware” unter “aware”.

Die hinter jedem Begriff stehende Zahl gibt das erste Vorkommen im Buch an. Das gilt auch für verschiedene Bedeutungen. So erscheint das Wort “foil” als Substantiv = „Folie“ bei 9.10 genauso wie unter der Bedeutung als Verb „vereiteln“, obwohl dieses Verb erst bei 15.3 vorkommt.

Bei Stichwörtern mit mehreren Bedeutungen ist in der Regel nur die im Buch vorkommende Bedeutung angegeben, also z.B. „Heroin“ für “haircut”. Weitere Bedeutungen finden sich in **“It’s All Part of the Job – Englisch für die Polizei – ein Wörterbuch”** sowie in allgemeinsprachlichen Wörterbüchern oder im Internet.

A

abdomen 12.9	Unterleib
abode, of no fixed ~ 19.3	ohne festen Wohnsitz
abolish 1.5	abschaffen
abrasion 12.10	Hautabschürfung
abrasive 16.5	abschleifend, Schleif-
abreast 5.2	nebeneinander
abreast, two ~ 5.2	(Parken) in der zweiten Reihe
abridgement 19.6	Verkürzung
abscond 19.3	fliehen
absorbing 26.3	faszinierend, interessant
abstain 11.2	sich enthalten, etwas nicht tun
abuse 12.13	Missbrauch
abusive 20.1	missbräuchlich
academic 16.4	Hochschullehrer(in), Geisteswissenschaftler(in)
accelerate 7.10	beschleunigen, Gas geben
acceleration lane 4.2	Einfädelungs-, Beschleunigungsspur
accelerator 13.2	Gas(pedal)
access 2.14	Zugang, Zutritt
access to the files 11.6	Akteneinsicht
accident black spot 9.6	Unfallschwerpunkt
accident with injured persons 2.16	Unfall mit Verletzten
accident-prone 9.6	unfallträchtig
accommodation 6.1	Quartier, Unterkunft
accomplish 22.2	vollenden
accordance, in ~ with 2.14	in Übereinstimmung mit
accost 16.8	ansprechen
account number 17.4	Kontonummer
accountable 26.3	verantwortlich
accumulate 22.2	anhäufen
accurate 21.5	genau
accused, the ~ 9.16	Angeklagte(r)
achieve 3.9	erreichen, leisten
achievement 3.3	Leistung, Errungenschaft
achievement test 3.3	Leistungs(über)prüfung
acquainted, become ~ 3.3	kennen lernen
acting 2.16	diensthabend, mit der Wahrnehmung der Geschäfte beauftragt
actor 1.10	Schauspieler
actress 1.10	Schauspielerin
adapt 2.7	anpassen
addictive 18.1	abhängig machend
additional headlights 7.7	Zusatzscheinwerfer
additional panel 4.4	Zusatzschild
additional shift service 2.16	Zusatzdienst
address someone 8.3	jemanden ansprechen
adequate 6.8	angemessen, gleichwertig
adhesive dressing 12.8	(Heft)Pflaster
adhesive plaster 12.11	(Heft)Pflaster
adjacent 6.5	nebenan, angrenzend
adjoining room 2.15	Nebenraum, Nebenzimmer
adjust 9.2	anpassen
administration 1.2	1 Verwaltung 2 (*US*) Regierung
administrative authority 5.2	Verwaltungsbehörde
administrative costs 5.6	Verwaltungsgebühren, -kosten
administrative fee 8.3	Verwaltungsgebühr
administrative law 3.3	Verwaltungsrecht
adult 8.3	1 Erwachsene(r) 2 pornographisch
adulterous 23.1	ehebrecherisch, fremdgehend
adultery 21.9	Ehebruch
advanced training 3.9	Weiterbildung
advertised post 28.9	ausgeschriebene Stelle
advocate 23.2	Befürworter(in)
aerial (*GB*) 13.2	Antenne
affix 7.13	aufkleben
affluent 10.8	reich, wohlhabend
age identifier 7.5	Angabe des Zeitpunkts der Zulassung
age of consent 21.9	Mindestalter (*für sexuelle Tätigkeiten*)
age of criminal responsibility 14.1	Strafmündigkeit

agent 6.5	1 Agent(in), Vertreter(in) 2 Polizeibeamter, -beamtin (*z.B. FBI*)
aggravate 16.1	verschlimmern
aggravated burglary 16.1	schwerer Diebstahl
agitated 11.2	aufgeregt
aid 3.4	Hilfsmittel
air ambulance 4.6	Rettungshubschrauber
air support (unit) 28.4	Hubschrauberstaffel
airway 12.9	Luftröhre
albeit 3.3	allerdings, jedoch, ungeachtet, obgleich
alert 10.4	1 Fahndung, Alarm 2 wecken, alarmieren
A levels 3.3	Abitur
alien 2.12	Ausländer(in)
aliens law 2.12	Ausländerrecht
alight 7.13	aussteigen
alleged(ly) 21.2	angeblich, vermutlich, mutmaßlich
allocate 7.5	zuteilen
all told 5.6	alles zusammen
alternately 2.16	abwechselnd
alternative service 3.2	Ersatzdienst
alternator 13.2	Generator, Lichtmaschine
amateur rifleman 23.3	Sportschütze
amber 6.6	gelb (*Verkehrsampel*)
amendment 23.4	Ergänzungsartikel zur US-Verfassung
ammunition 2.15	Munition
ample 2.4	reichlich
amusement arcade 15.2	Spielhalle
ancestry testing 21.5	Ahnenforschung
angel dust 18.9	PCP
angle grinder 16.5	Winkelschleifer
Angola black 18.9	Marihuana aus Angola
animal disease 2.12	Tierkrankheit, -seuche
ankle 12.9	Knöchel
anniversary 27.6	Jahrestag, Jubiläum
answerable, be ~ to 2.9	unterstehen, unterstellt sein
anti-stab vest 28.8	stichsichere Weste
antitrust crime 28.9	Kartellvergehen
antonym 23.3	Gegenteil
apartment (*US*)1.10	Wohnung
apartment house 16.3	Wohnblock
apologize 15.8	sich entschuldigen
apparent(ly) 1.5	anscheinend, offensichtlich
applicant 3.3	Bewerber(in)
application form 3.8	Bewerbungsbogen, -formular
apprentice 17.4	Lehrling, Auszubildende(r)
approach 4.5	sich nähern, zugehen auf, zufahren auf
appropriate 4.3	1 geeignet 2 sich aneignen
appropriation of a find 14.11	Fundunterschlagung
approved 7.3	anerkannt
approximately 3.3	etwa, ungefähr
aptitude test 3.9	Eignungstest
archbishop 5.4	Erzbischof
arched 14.14	gebogen, gewölbt
area code 7.5	1 Vorwahl (*Telefon*) 2 Gebietskennzeichen (*Kfz-Kennzeichen*)
argument 8.3	1 Argument 2 Streit
armchair 16.3	Polstersessel
armoured vehicle 23.3	gepanzertes Fahrzeug
A road (*GB*) 4.1	Bundesstraße
arson 22.3	Brandstiftung
arson investigator 24.2	Brandermittler(in)
arsonist 24.2	Brandstifter(in)
arson-sniffing dog 24.2	Brandspürhund
art deco area 14.11	Jugendstilviertel
artic (articulated lorry) 6.2	Sattelschlepper, -zug
articulate 2.15	redegewandt
articulated lorry / truck 6.2	Sattelschlepper, -zug
artificial 14.9	künstlich
asphyxia 12.10	Ersticken
assailant 15.2	Angreifer(in), Räuber(in)
assassination 2.18	Ermordung
assault 19.3	(tätlicher) Angriff
assault and battery 19.3	tätlicher Angriff
assemble 15.8	(sich) versammeln
assembly 3.4	1 Versammlung, 2 Parlament
assess 9.10	begutachten, beurteilen, abschätzen, einschätzen
assessment 2.10	Beurteilung, Einschätzung
assessment of danger 2.10	Gefahreneinschätzung, Gefahrenprognose
assign 22.2	zuteilen
assignment 2.10	Einsatz, Aufgabe
assistant chief constable 28.2	leitende(r) Polizeidirektor(in)
assistant commissioner 28.2	leitende(r) Polizeidirektor(in) (*bei Metropolitan Police Service in London*)
Ass'n (Association) 28.9	Verband, Vereinigung
Association of Chief Police Officers (ACPO) 28.5	Vereinigung leitender Polizeibeamter in GB
assume 7.13	annehmen, vermuten
assumption 11.2	Annahme
assure 11.1	versichern
astonishing 7.1	erstaunlich
ATF ((Bureau of) Alcohol, Tobacco and Firearms) (*US*) 28.9	Polizeibehörde in den USA zur Bekämpfung von Alkohol-, Drogen- und Schusswaffenvergehen
atonement 24.3	Buße
attach 7.4	befestigen
attach importance to 28.9	Wert legen auf
attempted break-in 16.4	versuchter Einbruch
attendance 17.4	Anwesenheit
attentive 14.1	aufmerksam
attic 16.3	Dachgeschoss
attorney 10.4	Rechtsanwalt, -anwältin
audible alarm 16.6	Alarmanlage mit Sirene
Aunt Emma 18.9	Morphium
Aunt Hazel 18.9	Heroin
Aunt Mary 18.9	Marihuana
automated teller machine (ATM) 6.4	Geldautomat
auxiliary police 5.3	Hilfspolizei
availability 18.1	Erhältlichkeit, Verfügbarkeit
avoidable 9.12	vermeidbar
awarded, be ~ 28.9	verliehen bekommen (*Preis, Belohnung, Orden*)

awareness 11.2	Bewusstsein
away team 20.4	Auswärtsmannschaft
awkward 12.12	unangenehm
awning 16.3	Markise
axis 23.6	Achse

B

Bachelor of Arts in Economics 28.9	Bachelorgrad in Wirtschaftswissenschaften
back 6.1	rückwärts fahren, zurücksetzen
backbone 12.9	Rückgrat
backdoor artist 18.9	Süchtige(r), die / der andere Süchtige betrügt
background process 28.9	Abklärung der Persönlichkeit (*bei Einstellungsverfahren*)
back lights 7.7	Rücklicht
backup 2.16	Unterstützung
backup lights 7.7	Rückfahrscheinwerfer
bail 8.2	Kaution, Sicherheitsleistung
bailiff 1.1	1 Gerichtsvollzieher(in) 2 (*US*) Justizwachtmeister(in), Gerichtsdiener(in)
balaclava 15.6	Skimütze (*die auch Teil des Gesichts bedeckt*)
balanced 28.9	ausgeglichen
balancing 13.3	1 Auswuchten (*Rad*) 2 hier: aufeinander abgestimmt
bald 14.13	kahl(köpfig)
ballistic vest 28.8	schuss-, kugelsichere Weste
bandage 12.8	Verband
bang 25.3	Knall
bankruptcy fraud 28.9	betrügerischer Bankrott
banner 8.3	Transparent (*über die Straße gespannt*)
bar 18.7	hier: verhindern
bar, behind ~s 1.1	hinter Gittern
barge 25.2	Binnenschiff (*für Fracht*)
barracks 3.9	Kaserne
barrel 23.6	Lauf (*Schusswaffe*)
baseball bat 23.1	Baseballschläger
basement flat 16.3	Einliegerwohnung
basic practical course 3.3	Grundpraktikum
bathrobe 13.7	Bade-, Morgenmantel
(bath) tub 16.3	Badewanne
baton 1.5	Schlagstock
Battenberg cake 15.9	Kuchen mit Marzipanglasur
battery lead 13.2	Batteriekabel
bear arms 23.4	Waffen tragen
bear in mind 3.9	berücksichtigen, in Betracht ziehen
bear with someone 7.13	Geduld haben, ertragen
bearer 23.3	Träger(in), Inhaber(in)
beat (area) 2.15	Streife(nbezirk)
beat officer 28.3	Streifenpolizist(in)
beat, on the ~ 2.15	auf Streife
bed frame 16.3	Bettgestell
bedside cabinet 16.3	Nachtkästchen
bedside rug 16.3	Bettvorleger
beeper gun 24.7	Schusswaffe in einem Beepergehäuse
beer-swilling 25.5	Bier trinkend (*in größeren Mengen*)
Behavioral Science Section 28.9	Abteilung für Verhaltensforschung (*erstellt u.a. Täterprofile*)
belated 11.2	verspätet
belongings 5.6	Sachen, Eigentum
belt buckle knife 23.1	Gürtelschnallenmesser
belt up (*slang*) 17.6	die Klappe halten
bend (*GB*) 4.2	Kurve
benefit 3.3	Zusatzleistung
Bernies 18.9	Kokain
berth 25.3	Liegeplatz
beverage 17.1	Getränk
bhp (brake horsepower) 7.13	Brems-PS
Big Harry 18.9	Heroin
Big John 18.9	Drogenfahnder(in)
bilingual 3.11	zweisprachig
Bill, The ~ 1.1	= *Spitzname für die Polizei*
bin 14.11	Mülleimer
binge drinking 17.9	Komasaufen
bird (*coll.*) 20.2	Mädchen
biscuit-coloured 13.10	keksfarben, hellbraun
bishop's see 5.4	Bischofssitz, Diözese
bite 12.10	1 Biss 2 Bisswunde
bi-weekly 28.9	14-tägig
black bomb / shit 18.9	Haschisch
blackbook 17.7	Skizzenbuch (*von Graffitisprayern*)
black eye 1.6	blaues Auge
blackjack (*US*) 23.1	Schlagring
blackmail 22.1	1 Erpressung(sdelikt) 2 erpressen
blade 23.3	Klinge
blame someone 7.13	jemanden verantwortlich machen
blare 11.6	brüllen, heulen (*Sirene*)
bleached 14.14	gebleicht
blimey! (*salopp*) 17.1	Mensch!
bloke 12.11	Kerl, Typ
blood sample 3.12	Blutprobe
blood-stained 1.10	blutbefleckt
blood vessel 12.9	Blutgefäß
bloom, in full ~ 6.1	in voller Blüte
blotchy 14.14	fleckig
bludgeon 23.1	schlagen, knüppeln
blue bell 17.1	Polizist(in)
blue cheese 18.9	Marihuana
blunt 14.3	klar, eindeutig
blunt instrument 10.8	stumpfer Gegenstand
blurred 11.2	verschwommen
board of examiners 3.9	Prüfungskommission
bodily harm / injury 2.16	Körperverletzung
bodily injury accident 10.1	Unfall mit Verletzten
bogus dealer 16.6	falsche(r)Händler(in)
bogus official 16.6	falsche Amtsperson
bold face 3.11	Fettdruck
bonnet (*GB*) 13.2	Motorhaube
booby-trap 15.3	Sprengfalle
boot (*GB*) 13.2	Kofferraum
booze 17.1	Getränke, Alkohol
Border Customs Service 2.13	Zollgrenzdienst
bore 23.6	Kaliber, Bohrung
boredom 18.1	Langeweile

boring 21.11	langweilig
borough 3.3	Stadtteil
bother 2.19	sich die Mühe machen, sich bemühen
bound, be ~ to 10.2	hier: zur Folge haben
boundary 19.2	Grenze
bra(ssiere) 14.15	Büstenhalter
brace up 7.6	sich aufraffen
braces 14.15	Hosenträger
brake fluid reservoir 13.2	Bremsflüssigkeitsbehälter
branch 2.2	1 Zweig, Ast 2 Zweigstelle 3 (Geschäfts)Bereich
branch manager 15.6	Zweigstellen-, Filialleiter(in)
branch office 2.8	Geschäfts-, Zweig-, Außen-, Nebenstelle
brand-new 14.9	nagelneu
brass 28.9	Messing
brawl 17.6	Streit, Schlägerei
breach of public order 5.3	Verstoß gegen die öffentliche Ordnung
breach of the public peace 17.8	Störung der öffentlichen Ordnung
breakwater 25.3	Mole
breath specimen 11.6	Atemalkoholprobe
breathalyze someone 2.15	jemanden einem Alkotest unterziehen
breathalyzer 2.15	Alkotest(gerät)
bribe 5.2	1 bestechen 2 Bestechung(sgeld)
bribery 5.2	Bestechung
brick 17.2	Ziegelstein
brief(ly) 3.8	kurz
briefing 2.10	(Einsatz-, Lage)Besprechung, Vorbesprechung
briefs 14.15	Unterhose
bright lights (brights) 7.7	Fernlicht
brim 11.6	Rand
British Transport Police 28.1	Bahnpolizei in GB
B road (*GB*) 4.1	Landesstraße
broad base 14.14	breite Basis
broaden 27.6	erweitern, verbreitern
broccoli 18.9	Marihuana
broke 19.3	pleite
broom cupboard 16.3	Besenkammer
brothel 21.9	Bordell
bruise 12.10	Prellung, blauer Fleck
buckle up 8.3	sich anschnallen
bugger your miniskirt 17.6	Scheiß-Minirock
buggery 21.9	Analverkehr
build 14.12	Körperbau
built-up area 4.5	1 bebautes Gebiet 2 geschlossene Ortschaft
bulb 7.7	(Glüh)Birne
bulge 9.10	ausbeulen
bulging 14.14	hervortretend
bulky 14.4	1 groß, sperrig 2 ausgebeult (*Kleidungsstück*)
bumblebee 10.7	Hummel
bumper 11.1	Stoßstange
buoyant 7.5	lebhaft
burglar 1.3	Einbrecher(in)
burglary 2.5	Einbruch(sdelikt)
burgle 13.7	einbrechen
burst 24.2	bersten
burst into tears 6.6	in Tränen ausbrechen
bus lane 5.2	Busspur
business administration 3.4	Betriebswirtschaftslehre (BWL)
butterfly knife 7.16	Klapp-, Falt-, Butterflymesser
bypass 4.2	Umgehungsstraße

C

cab 9.11	Führerhaus
cabinet 14.2	Schrank, Schränkchen
calf, calves 1.9	1 Kalb 2 Wade
call upon 28.5	zurückgreifen auf
calling card 7.13	Visitenkarte
callous 14.14	schwielig, mit Schwielen
cambelt 13.2	Zahnriemen
camera phone 21.8	Handykamera
camouflage 22.1	Tarnung
camper 7.4	Wohnmobil
candy man 18.9	(Drogen)Dealer
canine unit 28.9	Diensthundestaffel (DH-Staffel)
canvass 24.2	von Tür zu Tür gehen und Fragen stellen
cap star 2.6	Mützenstern
capital punishment 24.1	Todesstrafe
Capitol Police 28.9	Parlamentspolizei in Washington
caravan 7.4	Wohnwagen
carburettor 13.3	Vergaser
cardigan 14.15	Strickjacke, -weste
careers master 3.9	Berufsberater
cargo 9.3	Fracht, Ladung
carjacking 24.7	Kfz-Entführung
carpenter 8.1	Zimmerer, Zimmerin
car pound 5.6	Abstellplatz (*für wegen Falschparkens abgeschleppte Fahrzeuge*)
carriage 7.4	Waggon
carriageway 4.1	Straße, Fahrbahn
carryall 17.1	Reisetasche
carry the M-monkey 18.9	kokainsüchtig sein
cartoon 1.1	1 Zeichentrickfilm 2 Karikatur
carving knife 1.10	Tranchiermesser
case handling 3.3	Sachbearbeitung
casework 3.3	Fallstudie
cash dispenser / machine 6.4	Geldautomat
cashier 14.7	Kassierer(in)
CASTOR 3.2 (**Ca**sk for the **S**torage and **T**ransport **O**f **R**adioactive Material)	Behälter für Lagerung und Transport von radioaktivem Material
casual worker 20.2	Gelegenheitsarbeiter(in)
casualty 20.4	Todesopfer, Verletzte(r)
casual worker 20.2	Gelegenheitsarbeiter(in)
cater for 21.8	versorgen
Caucasian 14.12	Weiße(r)
caution 7.11	1 Verwarnung 2 verwarnen
cave 17.6	Höhle
cavity 18.4	Hohlraum, hier: Körperöffnung
CCTV (closed circuit television) camera 2.15	Überwachungskamera
cease 6.1	aufhören, (be)enden
cemetery 15.2	Friedhof

Central Register of Traffic Offenders 9.2	Verkehrssünderkartei
central reservation (*GB*) 4.2	Mittelstreifen
central station 6.7	Hauptbahnhof
centre lane (*US* center lane) 4.2	mittlerer Fahrstreifen (*von drei*)
certificate of maturity 3.9	(Berechtigungs)Zeugnis, Reifezeugnis
certified pistol instructor 28.9	offizieller Ausbilder für Pistolenschützen
cf 10.1	vergleichen Sie!
chair 26.3	den Vorsitz führen
challenge 2.8	1 Herausforderung 2 herausfordern
challenge someone 5.4	jemandem widersprechen, Einspruch einlegen
Chancellor 2.10	Bundeskanzler(in)
channel 1.1	1 (Fernseh)Kanal 2 leiten zu 3 Fahrrinne (*Schifffahrt*)
chapter 27.7	Ortsverband
character 1.6	1 Person (*Theaterstück usw.*) 2 Zeichen, Anschlag (*Computer usw.*)
charge 2.16	Anzeige
charge, in ~ 2.2	zuständig
charity 27.7	Wohlfahrtsverband
chase 13.7	(Verfolgungs)Jagd
checkered 12.11	kariert
checking card 9.10	Kontrollkarte
checkout 14.7	Kasse
chef 1.1	Koch, Köchin, Küchenchef(in) (*nicht Chef*)
chemise 14.15	Unterkleid, (Damen) Unterhemd
chemist's 6.3	Apotheke, Drogerie
chest of drawers for shoes 16.3	Schuhschrank
chief constable (*GB*) 6.6	uniformierte(r) Leiter(in) einer "police force" in GB
chiefly 2.11	hauptsächlich, in erster Linie
chief superintendent (*GB*) 3.3	Polizeidirektor(in)
chief task 1.3	Hauptaufgabe
child abuse 20.3	Kindesmisshandlung
child neglect 20.3	Kindesvernachlässigung
chin strap 28.8	Kinnriemen
chopper 7.4	1 Motorrad (*mit hohem Lenker*) 2 Hubschrauber
chuckle 9.1	kichern, in sich hineinlachen
chug along 9.1	dahinzuckeln, sehr langsam fahren
CID inspectorate 3.3	Kriminalinspektion
CID officer 1.6	Kriminalbeamter, -beamtin
CID watch 15.6	Kriminalwache (K-Wache) und Kriminaldauerdienst
cigarette butt 17.5	Zigarettenstummel
circumcision 21.9	Beschneidung
circumstance 9.10	Umstand
citizen-oriented 5.3	bürgernah

Citizens Crime Commission 28.9	(meist hochgestellte) Personen, die die Polizei unterstützen, in erster Linie Spenden für die "Crimestoppers" sammeln
city boundary 19.2	Stadtgrenze
city hall 6.3	Rathaus
city police 2.17	Stadtpolizei
city state 1.2	Stadtstaat
civil danger 2.12	Gefahr für die Öffentlichkeit
civil engineering 22.3	Bauwesen, Tiefbau
civilian 2.7	1 Zivilist(in) 2 zivil
civil law 3.3	Zivilrecht
Civil Nuclear Constabulary (CNC) 28.1	Polizei zur Bewachung von Nuklearanlagen in GB
civil rights 28.9	Grund-, Bürgerrechte
civil service law 3.3	Beamtenrecht
civil service protection 28.9	Versicherungsschutz für Beamte / Beamtinnen
civil sphere 2.13	Zivilbereich
civil status 3.8	Familienstand
claim 9.6	behaupten, anführen
claim damages 17.6	Schadensersatz beanspruchen
clairvoyant 7.10	Hellseher(in)
clandestine 18.1	heimlich, verborgen
classic car 7.4	Oldtimer (*etwa ab 1930*)
class run 28.9	Dauerlauf einer Ausbildungsgruppe (*als „Strafe" für angeblich schlechte Leistungen*)
clay 16.5	Ton
clear 10.2	frei (*Straße*)
cleft 14.14	gespalten
clip-on connection 7.13	Klemmverbindung
clip-on tie 28.8	Krawatte, die nicht um den Hals gebunden sondern am Hemdkragen festgeklemmt wird
clock 3.9	1 Uhr 2 Zeit nehmen / stoppen
cloning 26.3	Klonen
closed-formation operation 3.3	Einsatz im geschlossenen Verband
close protection 2.10	Personenschutz
clothes closet (*US*) 16.3	Schrank
clue 1.7	Spur, Anhaltspunkt, Hinweis
clutch 13.2	Kupplung
coastal waters 25.1	Küstengewässer
coat of arms 1.5	Wappen
coat rack 16.3	Garderobenwand
cock 23.6	spannen (*Schusswaffe*)
code 1.3	1 Code 2 Gesetzbuch
coercion 20.2	Nötigung
coffee shop 14.12	Café
coffee table 16.3	Couchtisch
collar bone 12.9	Schlüsselbein
collate 1.5	abgleichen, auswerten
collective term 15.2	Sammelbegriff
colloquial 9.12	umgangssprachlich
colonel 23.4	Oberst
column 14.13	Spalte

combat 2.13	bekämpfen, kämpfen gegen
combustion 7.13	Verbrennung
come into force 9.8	in Kraft treten
come to 12.6	(wieder) zu sich kommen
comfortable 8.5	bequem
command course 3.7	Ratslehrgang
command office 24.2	Führungsstelle
commander 2.10	leitende(r) Polizeidirektor(in) (*bei Metropolitan Police Service in London*)
commence 21.2	beginnen, anfangen
commercial law 10.6	Handelsrecht
commissioned police officer 2.14	voll ausgebildete(r) Polizist(in)
commissioner 28.2	Polizeipräsident(in) (*bei Metropolitan Police Service in London und vielen Stadtpolizeien in den USA*)
commit an offence 4.3	Verstoß begehen
commit oneself 16.8	auf etwas eingehen, sich verpflichten
committal service 28.9	Bestattungsfeier
committed to 26.3	bestrebt
common law 10.6	Gewohnheitsrecht
common-law husband 21.8	Lebensgefährte
community (beat) officer 2.16	Bezirksbeamter, -beamtin
community 4.7	Gemeinde
community college 28.9	Volkshochschule
community policing 2.12	Bezirksdienstarbeit, Bezirksbeamtentätigkeit, bürgernahe Polizeiarbeit
community work 17.4	gemeinnützige Arbeit
commuter 6.7	Pendler(in)
compact car 7.4	Kleinwagen
compartment 2.15	Fach, Abteil
compete 28.9	im Wettbewerb stehen
competitive pistol shooter 28.9	Sportschütze, -schützin
competitor 9.12	Konkurrent(in), Wettbewerber(in)
compile 22.1	erstellen, zusammenstellen
complaint 8.1	Beschwerde
complaints management 2.5	Beschwerdemanagement, Beschwerdestelle
complement 26.4	ergänzen
complexion 14.12	Gesichtsfarbe
compliance with 7.1	Befolgen von
comply with 25.4	befolgen
composite picture 14.14	Phantombild
comprehensive 1.2	weit, umfangreich, umfassend
compressed-air hose 9.10	Druckluftschlauch
comprise 1.3	enthalten, umfassen
computerization 2.8	Ausstattung mit Computern, „Computerisierung“
concern 1.3	betreffen
concussion 12.6	Gehirnerschütterung
conduct 3.3	1 Verhalten 2 durchführen
conduct a traffic check 7.1	Verkehrskontrolle durchführen
cone 4.2	Kegel, Hütchen
confession 19.3	Geständnis
confident 6.1	überzeugt, voll Vertrauen, zuversichtlich
confirm 5.4	bestätigen
confiscate 7.1	beschlagnahmen
Conflict 28.9	Koreakrieg (*politisch korrekte Bezeichnung, daher Großschreibung*)
conflict resolution 3.3	Konfliktbewältigung
confront 5.2	1 treffen auf 2 hier: zur Rede stellen
confused 7.6	verwirrrt, durcheinander
Congress 23.4	Parlament der USA (*bestehend aus "Senate" und "House of Representatives"*)
conjunction, in ~ with 10.3	zusammen mit, in Verbindung mit, in Zusammenhang mit, in Tateinheit mit
conjunctiva 11.6	Bindehaut
consent 11.2	1 Zustimmung 2 zustimmen
consent to 11.2	einverstanden sein mit
consignment 18.4	(Waren)Sendung
consistent 3.9	konsequent, gleichbleibend
constable (*GB*) 1. 8	unterster Dienstgrad der Polizei
constitution 2.10	Verfassung
Constitutional Court 24.1	Bundesverfassungsgericht
constitutional law 3.3	Verfassungsrecht
constitutional right 23.2	Grundrecht
construction site 9.6	Baustelle
consumption 11.6	Gebrauch, Verbrauch
contain 2.15	1 enthalten 2 eindämmen, begrenzen 3 unterdrücken (*z.B. Lachen*)
contaminate 21.5	verunreinigen
content 14.9	Inhalt
contract 11.6	sich zusammenziehen, sich verengen
contradict 22.1	widersprechen
contraflow (system) 4.2	Gegenverkehr (*auf Autobahnbaustellen*)
contravene 24.1	widersprechen, entgegenstehen
contribution 27.1	Beitrag
controlled substances act 18.1	Betäubungsmittelgesetz (BTM)
control room 2.15	(Einsatz)Leitstelle, Wache, Führungszentrale
control room officer 3.5	diensthabende(r) Beamter / Beamtin
convention centre 6.3	Kongresszentrum
convertible 7.4	Cabriolet
convey 7.4	übertragen
convict 24.1	Verurteilte(r)
cooked meat 5.5	Aufschnitt
cooker / extractor hood 16.3	Dunsthaube
cope with 2.8	fertig werden mit, bewältigen, verkraften
copper (*coll.*) 9.7	Polizist(in), Bulle
cordless drill 16.5	Akkubohrer
cordon off 3.9	absperren
Corina 18.9	Kokain
coroner 10.8	Leichenschauer(in)

corresponding 5.2	entsprechend
corroborate 11.6	bestätigen, untermauern
cosh 23.1	Totschläger
cot 1.10	Kinderbett
cotton swab 21.5	Wattestäbchen
council 3.7	1 Gemeinde(verwaltung) 2 Gemeinderat, Stadtrat
councillor 28.4	Stadtrat, -rätin, Gemeinderat, -rätin
counselling 9.4	Beratung
counsellor 26.3	Berater(in)
counter 2.7	entgegentreten
counter foreign intelligence operations 28.9	Gegenspionage betreiben
counterfeiting 22.1	Geldfälscherei, Geldfälschung
counter-measure 22.6	Gegenmaßnahme
counter-terrorism centre 2.8	Antiterrorismuszentrum
country house 16.3	Landhaus
country police 2.17	Landpolizei
country road (*US*) 4.1	Gemeindestraße
county jail 28.9	Kreisgefängnis
county road (*US*) 4.1	Kreisstraße
county town 2.17	Kreisstadt
coupling 9.10	Kupplung, Verbindung
courier 18.4	(Drogen)Kurier
court-imposed 11.2	vom Gericht auferlegt
court penalty 9.2	vom Gericht verhängte Strafe
court proceedings 11.6	Gerichtsverfahren
craft 7.6	Fahrzeug; hier Fähre
crane 2.5	Kran
crash barrier 4.2	Leitplanke, Schutzplanke
crawler lane 9.6	Kriechspur
creak 13.7	knarren, quietschen
create 22.6	schaffen
crestfallen 14.3	niedergeschlagen, am Boden zerstört
crime commissariat 27.6	Kriminalkommissariat (KK, z.B. K1, K3 usw.)
crime control 1.3	Kriminalitätsbekämpfung
crime scene 3.2	Tatort
crime scene officer 3.2	Ermittlungsbeamter, -beamtin (*am Tatort*), Spurensicherungsbeamter, -beamtin
Crime Stoppers 28.9	Einheit, die anonyme Anrufe entgegennimmt und ihnen nachgeht, oder Anrufe, bei denen der Anrufer / die Anruferin eine ausgeschriebene Belohnung anonym erhalten möchte
criminal damage 17.4	vorsätzliche Sachbeschädigung
Criminal Investigation Department (CID) 2.2	Kriminalpolizei
criminal law 3.3	Strafrecht
criminal offence 2.2	Straftat, Verbrechen
criminal record 3.9	Vorstrafe(nregister)
crisp 10.8	frisch, nagelneu
crisps 11.6	(Kartoffel)Chips
C road (*GB*) 4. 1	Kreisstraße
crook 16.6	Gauner(in)
cross-border paper 18.7	Ausweispapier, das zum Grenzübertritt berechtigt
cross-departmental lesson 3.3	fächerübergreifender Unterricht
crossroads 4.2	Kreuzung
crosswalk (*US*) 4.2	Fußgängerüberweg, Zebrastreifen
crowd management 2.2	Demonstrationsbegleitung, Großer Sicherheits- und Ordnungsdienst (*veraltet*)
cruise 13.2	1 Kreuzfahrt 2 (langsam) fahren
cruise control 13.2	Tempomat
cruiser 9.5	1 Kreuzer (*Marine*) 2 (*slang*) Straßenprostituierte 3 Streifenwagen
crumbs 11.6	Krümel
crush 12.10	Quetschung
crying weed 18.9	Marihuana
cul-de-sac (*GB*) 4.2	Sackgasse
culprit 22.7	Schuldige(r)
cure 8.3	Kur
curfew 11.3	Ausgangssperre, Zapfenstreich
curly 14.12	lockig (*Haar*)
current events 3.3	Tagesthemen, Zeitgeschehen
curriculum 28.9	Lehrplan
curve (*US*) 4.2	Kurve
custodial sentence 24.1	Freiheitsstrafe
custody 2.16	Haft
custody officer 19.3	Gewahrsamsbeamter, -beamtin
custody service 2.16	Gewahrsamsdienst
customer 9.8	Kunde, Kundin
customs 2.13	Zoll
Customs Investigation Service 2.13	Zollfahndung
customs surveillance zone 2.13	Zollgrenzbezirk
CV (curriculum vitae) 3.7	Lebenslauf
cwp (crown wheel and pinion) 13.3	Teller- und Kegelzahnrad
cybercrime 21.7	Computerkriminalität
cyclepath 4.2	Radweg
cycling route 5.4	Radwanderweg

D

daffodil 6.1	Narzisse, Osterglocke
dagger 19.3	Dolch
dairy farm 28.9	Milchviehbetrieb
damage-only accident 2.16	Unfall mit Sachschaden
damage to property 17.4	Sachbeschädigung
dampness 7.13	Feuchtigkeit
danger assessment 2.10	Gefahreneinschätzung, Gefahrenprognose
danger level 2.10	Gefahrenstufe, Gefährdungsstufe
danger to life and limb 1.3	Gefahr für / Gefährdung von Leib und Leben
danger prevention 2.4	Gefahrenabwehr
danger spot 3.5	Gefahrenstelle
dangerous bodily harm 15.5	gefährliche Körperverletzung
dash 1.10	eilen, schnell laufen
dashboard 7.13	Armaturenbrett
data processing 2.15	Datenverarbeitung
data protection 27.1	Datenschutz
day care unit 21.8	Kindertagesstätte
daylight, in broad ~ 5.6	am helllichten Tag
daytime driving lights 13.3	Tagesfahrlicht

dead body 2.12	Leiche
dead-end street (*US*) 4.2	Sackgasse
deadline 7.12	Frist
dealer 7.13	(Vertrags)Händler(in)
death toll 23.2	Zahl der Todesopfer
debriefing 26.2	Nachbesprechung
debt bondage 22.2	Schuldknechtschaft
decal 5.4	Plakette, Aufkleber, Vignette
decapitate 22.1	enthaupten
decayed 14.14	faul, kariös
deceased 23.8	(kürzlich) Verstorbene(r)
deceleration lane 4.2	Ausfädelungs-, Verzögerungsspur
decisive 20.1	entscheidend
decrease 11.2	1 Rückgang, Sinken 2 zurückgehen, sinken, abnehmen, geringer werden
deduct 9.7	abziehen, subtrahieren
deer 5.8	1 Hirsch, Reh 2 Rotwild
Defense Department (*US*) 6.2	Verteidigungsministerium
deficiency 10.2	Fehlen, Mangel, Behinderung, Unzulänglichkeit
deficiency symptom 11.2	Ausfallerscheinung
deformity 14.14	Verunstaltung
deliberately 23.1	absichtlich
delivery van 7.4	Lieferwagen
demanding 3.3	anspruchsvoll
dense 9.2	dicht (*Verkehr*)
dental plan 28.9	zahnärztliche Versicherung
denture 14.14	Gebiss, Prothese
deny 10.4	leugnen, abstreiten
deny access 2.14	Zugang / Zutritt verweigern
depart 6.6	abfahren
department for foreign assignments 26.3	Abteilung für Auslandseinsätze
department store 6.3	Kaufhaus
departmental police procedures 28.9	Richtlinien (*innerhalb einer Polizei, hier der Michigan State Police*)
departure 2.16	Abfahrt, Abreise
deploy 2.7	abordnen, einsetzen
deployment in groups 3.3	geschlossener Einsatz, Einsatz in Gruppen
deployment-related 3.3	einsatzbezogen
deployment-related self-defence 3.3	einsatzbezogene Eigensicherung
deprive 16.1	wegnehmen
deputy 9.6	1 Stellvertreter in) 2 Polizist(in) in den USA in einer von einem Sheriff geleiteten Polizei
deputy chief constable 9.6	Leitende(r) Polizeidirektor(in)
deputy commissioner 28.2	Leitende(r) Polizeidirektor(in) (*bei Metropolitan Police Service in London*)
derive from 1.2	ableiten von, stammen
derogatory 19.3	abfällig
desk duty 15.9	Innendienst
destination 6.2	(Reise)Ziel, Ankunftsort
detach 7.13	1 abreißen 2 abordnen
detachable 7.4	abnehmbar

detached house 1.6	Einfamilienhaus (*freistehend*)
detain 2.16	verhaften, (vorläufig) festnehmen, festhalten
detective 1.1	Detektiv(in); Kriminalbeamter, -beamtin
detective inspector 19.3	Kriminalkommissar(in)
detention cell 3.12	Gewahrsams-, Haftzelle
deter 1.3	abschrecken
detergent 17.7	Waschmittel
deterrent 1.3	1 abschreckend 2 abschreckende Maßnahme, Abschreckung
detestable 23.2	abscheulich
deviant 22.1	abweichend (*von der Norm*)
device 6.2	Gerät, Vorrichtung
devote to 3.3	widmen, beinhalten
dial 3.5	1 wählen (*Telefon*) 2 Anzeige (*z.B. am Armaturenbrett*)
diesel particulate filter 13.3	Rußpartikelfilter
differentiate 24.1	unterscheiden
dike 25.4	Deich, Damm
dimmed/dipped beam / headlights 7.7	Abblendlicht
dimple 14.14	Grübchen
dipstick 13.2	Ölmessstab
directorate 2.3	Direktion
directory inquiries 12.12	(Telefon)Auskunft
disagreeable 3.9	unangenehm
disaster 5.4	Unheil, Unglück, Katastrophe
disbursement 27.1	Auszahlung
discharge 23.6	abfeuern
discoloured 14.14	verfärbt
disconnect 13.7	unterbrechen, Verbindung trennen
discretion 7.11	Ermessen(sspielraum)
disguise 16.6	Verkleidung
dishonest 16.1	unehrlich
dishwasher 16.3	Geschirrspülmaschine
dislocation 12.10	Verrenkung, Auskugelung
dismay 23.4	entsetzen
disobey 4.3	nicht beachten
dispatch 2.16	einsetzen
dispatcher 9.5	1 Fahrdienstleiter(in) (*Eisenbahn*) 2 Person, die Notrufe usw. entgegennimmt
disperse 17.2	zerstreuen, zerstören, auflösen
disproportionate 22.6	unverhältnismäßig
disqualification 4.3	Führerscheinentzug, Fahrverbot
disqualify 9.4	Führerschein entziehen / einbehalten
disregard 22.2	Missachtung
disrupt 22.1	stören, unterbrechen
dissatisfaction 5.4	Unzufriedenheit
dissenter 22.1	Abweichler(in)
dissolve 18.4	auflösen
distance-learning student 26.3	Fernstudent(in)
distinct legal entity 7.9	juristische Person
distinction 5.3	1 Unterschied, Unterscheidung 2 Auszeichnung

distinctive mark 14.12	besonderes Kennzeichen
distract 6.2	ablenken, zerstreuen
distress 25.2	Not(lage)
distressed 21.4	verwirrt, durcheinander, verzweifelt, gequält
distributor 7.13	Verteiler(in), Auslieferer(in)
disturb 13.7	stören
disturbance 17.1	Störung, Belästigung
ditch 2.17	(Straßen)Graben
diver 17.6	Fußballspieler(in), der / die eine Schwalbe macht
diverge 22.1	abweichen
diversified 26.1	aufgeteilt, gegliedert
diversion 4.2	Umleitung
diversity 26.4	Verschiedenheit
divert 14.8	ablenken
divide 24.1	Wasserscheide
divided highway (*US*) 4.2	vierspurige Straße mit Mittelstreifen
divisional inspector 28.3	Leiter(in) einer Dienststelle in einer Polizeidirektion
divorced 8.1	geschieden
dock 25.4	andocken
docket number 11.6	Aktenzeichen
dog handler 1.8	Hundeführer(in)
dog unit 26.1	Hundestaffel
domestic burglary 13.7	Wohnungseinbruch
domestic law 10.6	inländisches Recht
domestic violence 20.1	häusliche Gewalt
donate 27.7	spenden
double dimples 18.9	LSD
doubt, beyond any ~ 21.5	ohne jeden Zweifel
doubt, beyond reasonable ~ 24.6	ohne Zweifel
down under 3. 7	in / nach Australien / Neuseeland
downpipe 16.3	Fallrohr
draft a report 26.3	Bericht erstellen
drafted, be ~ 14.10	eingezogen werden (*zum Wehrdienst*)
drag 21.4	zerren, ziehen
dragnet investigation 27.5	Raster-, Schleierfahndung
drainpipe 16.3	Fallrohr
dram of whisky 3.12	Glas Whisky
draught 25.2	Tiefgang
draw 1.6	1 zeichnen 2 ziehen (*Waffe*)
drawbar combination 7.4	Gliederzug
drawer 2.15	Schublade
dreadful 8.3	schrecklich, fürchterlich
dressing table 16.3	Frisierkommode
drifter 7.16	Obdachlose(r)
drill bit 17.7	Bohrerspitze
drinking bout 17.6	Trinkgelage
drive 1.6	1 Einfahrt, Auffahrt 2 Antrieb 3 (selbst) fahren
drive erratically 9.8	unsicher / unberechenbar fahren
driver's card 9.10	Fahrerkarte
driveway 4.2	Auffahrt, Einfahrt, Zufahrt
driving ban 9.11	Fahrverbot
D road (*GB*) 4.1	Gemeindestraße
drowning 12.10	Ertrinken
drug habit 15.2	Drogensucht
drug-sniffing dog 11.6	Drogenspürhund
drugstore (*US*) 6. 3	Apotheke, Drogerie
drug trafficker 18.4	Drogenschmuggler(in)
drunkometer 11.9	Alkotestgerät
dual carriageway (*GB*) 4.2	vierspurige Straße mit Mittelstreifen
dubious 23.2	zweifelhaft
dummy 14.9	Attrappe
dump 23.9	wegwerfen
dungeon 9.7	Verlies, Kerker
duty solicitor 19.3	Pflichtverteidiger(in)
duvet 16.3	Bettdecke
dwelling 16.3	Wohnung, Wohnhaus, Wohnblock
dye 1.5	1 Farbe, Farbstoff 2 färben
dynamiter 18.9	Heroinsüchtige(r)

E

early hours 11.6	frühmorgens
edge 4.2	(Straßen)Rand
educational requirements 3.3	bildungsmäßige Voraussetzungen
effectiveness 4.7	Effektivität
effeminate 14.14	effeminiert, unmännlich
efficient 2.8	wirksam, schlagkräftig
effort 3.9	Anstrengung, Bemühung
eight 18.9	Heroin
eject 28.9	hinauswerfen, Platzverweis erteilen
elastic steel rod 23.1	Stahlrute
elder 28.9	Kirchenälteste(r)
Elector's Palace 14.11	Kurfürstliches Schloss
electric cooker 16.3	Elektroherd
electric windows 13.3	elektrische Fensterheber
eligible 18.7	berechtigt
elude 16.5	fliehen, entweichen
embankment 9.8	Bankett (*Straße*)
embarrassed 9.1	erstaunt, verblüfft
embarrassing 1.6	peinlich
embassy 14.11	Botschaft
emergency 1.3	Notfall
emergency call 2.3	Notruf
emergency lane 4.2	Standstreifen
emergency passport 14.11	Ersatzpass
emergency resuscitation 12.8	Wiederbelebung
emergency surgery 15.3	Notoperation
emergency ward 12.12	Notfallstation
emergency warning lights 7.7	Warnblinkanlage
emission 2.12	Abgas
emphasis 3.3	Betonung, Ton, Wert
emphasize 28.9	betonen
employee 2.8	Arbeitnehmer(in)
employer 14.14	Arbeitgeber(in)
employment 3.2	Beschäftigung
employment examination 3.3	Anstellungsprüfung
employment tax 28.9	Beschäftigungssteuer
empower 2.14	ermächtigen
enclosure 18.8	Gehege
encode 21.5	verschlüsseln
encounter 5.4	Zusammentreffen, Begegnung, Berührung
encrypt 28.9	verschlüsseln
endeavour 27.6	bestreben, sich bemühen

endorse 9.8	eintragen (*in Führerschein*)
enforce 3.2	durchsetzen (*Gesetz usw.*)
engaged 2.10	besetzt (*Telefon*)
engender 22.6	hervorrufen
enhance 27.6	aufwerten, erhöhen, fördern
enlist 28.9	eintreten, beitreten
enrichment 22.2	Bereicherung
enrol 3.3	einschreiben
ensure 2.12	sichergehen dass, versichern, sicherstellen
entail 9.8	nach sich ziehen, zur Folge haben
entitled, be ~ to 2.10	berechtigt sein
(entrance) hall 16.3	Flur
envelope 3.1	(Brief)Umschlag
environment 23.2	Umgebung
environmental crime 2.5	Umweltkriminalität
envisage 2.10	vorsehen
epaulette 28.8	Schulterstück
equal opportunities officer 28.9	Gleichstellungsbeauftragte(r)
equal opportunity employer 28.9	Arbeitgeber, der Chancengleichheit für weibliche und männliche Bewerber garantiert
equivalent 2.12	Gegenstück, Entsprechung
eradicate 22.1	ausrotten
erect 4.7	einrichten, aufstellen, errichten
escort 2.10	1 führen, begleiten 2 Gefangenentransport
establish the facts 24.2	Fakten zusammentragen
establishment 27.1	Einrichten, Aufbau
estate agent 6.5	Immobilienmakler(in)
estate car 7.4	Kombi
estranged 10.7	entfremdet
EU recording unit 9.9	Fahrtenschreiber, EU-Kontrollgerät
evade 9.10	ausweichen, vermeiden
evaluate evidence 3.9	Beweismaterial auswerten
eventually 4.7	endlich, schließlich (*nicht: eventuell*)
evidence 1.10	Beweismaterial, Nachweis
evident 11.9	klar, erwiesen
evolve 2.8	sich entwickeln
exaggerate 11.2	übertreiben
examiners' board 7.16	Prüfungsausschuss
examining magistrate 20.2	Untersuchungsrichter(in)
exceed the deadline 7.12	Frist überschreiten
exceed the parking time 5.4	Parkzeit überschreiten
exceed the speed limit 9.2	Höchstgeschwindigkeit überschreiten
excessive speed 9.2	überhöhte / nicht angepasste Geschwindigkeit
execute a warrant 2.16	Haftbefehl ausführen / erledigen
executive division 28.9	Führungsstab
exemption 22.2	Ausnahme
exemption permit 7.2	Ausnahmegenehmigung
exercise cycle 14.3	Heimtrainer
exert 22.2	ausüben
exhaust 7.5	1 zu Ende gehen 2 Auspuff
exhausted 9.12	ermüdet, erschöpft
exhibition centre 6.3	Ausstellungszentrum, Messe(gelände)
exit 4.2	Ausgang, Ausfahrt
expansion 3.5	Ausdehnung, Erweiterung
expectation 2.4	Erwartung
expenditure 27.1	Ausgabe, Kosten
expert advice 26.4	Rat von Experten
expertise 26.3	Sachwissen, Fachwissen, Erfahrung
expert opinion 3.9	Gutachten
exploit 22.2	ausbeuten
expose 5.5	(sich) aussetzen
expressway (*US*) 4.1	Autobahn (*meist innerstädtisch, z.T. gebührenpflichtig*)
extend 10.4	ausdehnen, erweitern
extended detention 19.3	Überhaft
extended modular program 28.9	verlängertes Abendstudium, in Module unterteilt
extension (number) 12.12	Apparat, Nebenanschluss
extensive 6.2	ausgedehnt, umfangreich
extent 2.12	Ausmaß
extinguish 2.16	löschen (*Feuer*)
extortion 2.5	Erpressung(sdelikt)
extradition 27.3	Auslieferung
extricate 16.8	befreien
eyelash 14.13	Augenwimper

F

facial hair 14.13	Gesichtshaar
facilitate 4.4	erleichtern, ermöglichen
faction 2.8	Fraktion
fail 3.9	nicht bestehen
failing to appear in court 19.3	Nichterscheinen vor Gericht
failure 7.2	Fehlen, Versagen, Nichtbeachten (*z.B. eines Gesetzes*)
failure to give way 12.2	Nichtbeachten der Vorfahrt
failure to stop after an accident 10.1	Unfall-, Fahrerflucht
fake firearm 15.2	Waffenattrappe
family status 8.1	Familienstand
fan belt 13.2	Keilriemen
fare 11.2	Fahrgeld
fare dodging 19.1	Schwarzfahren
farm road (*US*) 4.1	Gemeindestraße
fastback 7.4	Schrägheckfahrzeug
fast lane 4.2	Überholspur (*bei drei Spuren in D die linke, in GB die rechte*)
fatal 9.8	tödlich
fawn 7.13	beige
FBI agent 6.5	FBI-Beamter, FBI-Beamtin (*unterster Dienstgrad*)
feature 7.5	Einrichtung
fed up, be ~ to the back teeth 20.2	die Schnauze voll haben
federal authority 6.5	Bundesbehörde
Federal Border Guard 1.5	Bundesgrenzschutz (*heute Bundespolizei*)
Federal Criminal Police Office 1.5	Bundeskriminalamt

federal law 10.6	Bundesrecht
Federal Motor Transport Authority 7.9	Kraftfahrtbundesamt (*in Flensburg*)
federal police (service) 1.5	Bundespolizei (*allgemein*)
Federal Police 2.1	Bundespolizei (*in D*)
federal politician 2.10	Bundespolitiker(in)
federal road 7.13	Bundesstraße
federal state 1.5	Bundesland
felony 28.9	Straftat
female 4.7	1 weiblich 2 weibliche Person
female genital cutting 21.9	weibliche Genitalverstümmelung
fen 7.5	Sumpf, Moor, Fenn
fence 7.16	Hehler(in)
fender (*US*) 13.2	Stoßstange
fender bender (*US, coll.*) 12.4	leichter Unfall, Bagatellunfall
ferry 7.6	Fähre
fetter 22.1	fesseln
field of knowledge 2.14	Wissensgebiet
fierce 24.7	stark, heftig
file 3.1	Akte
(filling) island 14.6	Zapfsäule
financial adviser 16.4	Finanzberater(in)
fine 4.3	1 Verwarnungsgeld 2 Bußgeld 3 Geldstrafe
fine, on-the-spot ~ 5.5	(gebührenpflichtige) Verwarnung, Verwarnung mit Verwarnungsgeld
fire lane 5.4	Feuerwehrzufahrt
firearms fatalities 23.2	Zahl der mit Schusswaffen Getöteten
firearms homicide 23.2	Mord mit Schusswaffe
firearms law 23.1	Waffengesetz
firearms licence 15.6	Waffenschein
firearms suicide 23.2	Selbstmord mit Schusswaffe
fireplace 16.3	offener Kamin
first aid 3.4	erste Hilfe
first lieutenant 28.9	Oberleutnant (*der MSP*)
first-aid kit 7.10	Erste-Hilfe-Kasten
fitness (to drive) 7.1	Fahrtüchtigkeit
fixed address 19.3	fester Wohnsitz
fixed-charge form 28.8	Formular für Verwarnungs-, -bußgeld
fixed penalty 5.2	Bußgeld
fixed-penalty authority / office 5.2	Bußgeldstelle
fixed-penalty notice 8.2	Bußgeldbescheid
fixed-penalty proceedings 8.2	Bußgeldverfahren
flabbergasted 24.2	völlig überrascht
flabby 14.14	schwabbelig
flag down 21.3	anhalten
flagship 27.6	Vorzeigeobjekt
flap 14.9	Klappe
flash 1.6	hier: kurz zeigen, kurz sehen lassen
flash one's headlights 10.3	Lichthupe betätigen
flashlight 1.7	Taschenlampe
flat-screen TV set 16.3	Flachbildfernseher
flea powder 18.9	minderwertige Drogen
fleece 28.8	Fleece, Flausch
flick-knife 20.5	Klapp-, Spring-, Schnappmesser
flood control 25.4	Hochwasserschutz
floodplain forest 25.4	Auwald
floor plan 16.3	Grundriss
flourish 26.4	blühen
fluent 3.8	fließend
fluted radiator grille 7.13	geriffelter Kühlergrill
flying squad 28.5	schnelle Eingreiftruppe
flyover 4.2	Überführung
focal point 27.3	Brennpunkt, Zentrale
focus 27.3	sich konzentrieren auf
foil 9.10	1 Folie 2 vereiteln
following too closely 12.2	zu dichtes Auffahren
fool around 24.7	herumspielen
footage 17.2	Filmmaterial
footrest 13.5	Fußstütze
force open 13.7	aufbrechen (*Tür usw.*)
forced entry 16.5	gewaltsames Eindringen
ford 6.2	Furt
forensic 11.6	gerichtsmedizinisch
forfeit 23.9	verwirken
forged 14.6	gefälscht
forger 19.6	Fälscher(in)
forgery 10.8	Fälschung
forklift truck 9.10	Gabelstapler
fortnight 4.5	zwei Wochen, 14 Tage
forward 7.13	weiterleiten, nachsenden
found 2.8	gründen
four-corner stop (*US*) 4.5	Kreuzung mit Stop-Schild an allen vier Seiten
fracture 12.8	1 (Knochen)Bruch 2 brechen (*Knochen*)
frame house (*US*) 16.3	Fachwerkhaus
frame(work) 2.4	Rahmen
fraud 2.16	Betrug
freckles 14.14	Sommersprossen
freeway (*US*) 4.1	Autobahn (*gebührenfrei*)
freezer 16.3	Gefrierschrank
French door(s) 16.3	Terrassentür
frisk 20.5	durchsuchen, abtasten
front drums 13.3	vordere Trommelbremsen
fruit pulp 18.4	Fruchtfleisch
fu 18.9	Marihuana
fucking 17.1	Scheiß-, verdammt
fuel cap 13.2	Tankdeckel
fuel gauge 13.2	Treibstoffanzeige
fugitive 3.3	1 Flüchtling, fliehende Person 2 flüchtig, fliehend
full bare metal respray 13.3	komplette Neulackierung
full / high / main beam 7.7	Fernlicht auf dem Metall
full operation 6.2	volle Anwendung
full police powers 28.9	volle Polizeigewalt
fully garaged car 13.3	Garagenfahrzeug
function 27.7	Feier, Fest, Empfang
funeral 28.9	Begräbnis, Beerdigung, Bestattung
funeral home 28.9	Beerdigungsinstitut
furnish 9.3	stellen (*Sicherheitsleistung, Kaution*)
furnish evidence 2.14	Beweismaterial vorlegen, Nachweis erbringen
fuse 7.13	Sicherung
fuss 14.16	Aufwand, Getue
fuzz, the 17.1	Polizei

G

gadget 15.2	Gerät
Gaelic 3.11	gälisch
gambling 22.2	Glücksspiel
game, be on the ~ 21.9	auf den Strich gehen
gap 2.14	Lücke
garda 28.8	Polizist(in) in Irland
gas board 16.6	Gasfirma
gas cooker 16.3	Gasherd
gather 17.2	sammeln
gauge 13.2	Anzeige, Pegel
GDR (German Democratic Republic) 2.8	DDR (Deutsche Demokratische Republik)
gear lever 13.2	Schalthebel, Ganghebel
gear pedal 13.5	Schaltpedal
general certificate of secondary education (GCSE) 3.3	Mittlere Reife, mittlerer Bildungsabschluss
genocide 26.3	Völkermord
genuine 16.6	echt
(German) shepherd 1.8	Schäferhund
get lost! 19.3	Hau ab!
get the sack 20.2	entlassen werden
ghost 9.1	Geist, Gespenst
give / render first aid 12.8	erste Hilfe leisten
give a wide berth 17.11	einen weiten Bogen machen
give someone a lift 15.9	jemanden (*mit dem Auto*) mitnehmen
give way 4.4	Vorfahrt gewähren
glass pane 2.10	Glasscheibe
glorification of violence 21.7	Gewaltverherrlichung
glove compartment 13.2	Handschuhfach
glow stick 2.15	Leuchtstab
glue 18.1	Klebstoff
GNP (gross national product) 22.3	Bruttosozialprodukt
go bananas 19.3	durchdrehen
go to one's Lord 28.9	sterben
go on the rampage 20.5	randalieren
God's medicine 18.9	Marihuana, Morphium
golf club 16.4	Golfschläger
gonner (*coll.*) 7.13	hier: durchgebrannt
good, be up to no ~ 21.4	nichts Gutes im Schilde führen
gosh! (*coll.*) 9.7	meine Güte!, Verdammt noch mal!
governor 9.10	Geschwindigkeitsbegrenzer
Governor General 14.11	Generalgouverneur(in)
grab 13.7	ergreifen, packen
grade 28.2	Abstufung
grade crossing (*US*) 4.2	Bahnübergang
graduate 3.1	abschließen (*Schule, Hochschule usw.*)
greasy 14.14	fettig
great tobacco 18.9	Opium
grievous bodily harm 15.5	gefährliche Körperverletzung
grin 9.1	grinsen
grind 16.5	schleifen
grip 5.4	1 packen, ergreifen 2 Zugriff, Einfluss, Griff
grip the road 5.4	Kontakt mit der Straße haben
groove 23.6	Rille
guard rail 4.2	Leit-, und Schutzplanke
guidance 27.1	Führung, Leitung
guilty 1.7	schuldig
gun commander 28.9	Geschützkommandant
gun control 23.2	Reglementierung von Schusswaffenbesitz
gutter 16.3	Dachrinne
gym(nasium) 6.3	Sporthalle, Turnhalle (*nicht: Gymnasium!*)

H

habitual(ly) 14.14	gewöhnlich
Hackney carriage 7.4	Taxi (*veraltete offizielle Bezeichnung in GB*)
haggle 8.3	handeln, schachern
haircut 18.9	Heroin
hairpin bend 6.1	Haarnadelkurve
half-timbered house 16.3	Fachwerkhaus
hammer 23.6	Hahn (*Schusswaffe*)
hand 6.1	(Uhr)Zeiger
handbag snatching 15.2	Handtaschenraub
handcuffs 1.6	Handschellen
hand-held radio 2.15	Handfunkgerät
handlebar 7.4	Lenker, Lenkstange
hands-free system 9.8	Freisprechanlage
handy 6.2	gelegen, nützlich (*nicht: Mobiltelefon*)
Hants 7.5	Hampshire
harass 20.1	belästigen
hardened criminal 24.3	hartgesottene(r)
hard shoulder 4.2	Standspur, befestigter Seitenstreifen Verbrecher(in)
hardtop 7.4	Hardtop
hassle 17.11	Mühe, Umstand
hatch 2.15	Luke
hatchback 7.4	Schräghecklimousine
have a Chinaman on the back 18.9	unter Entzug(serscheinungen) leiden
have one too many 11.9	einen zu viel trinken
hazardous cargo / goods 7.2	gefährliche Güter, Gefahrengut
hazard warning flashers / lights 7.7	Warnblinkanlage
heading 23.7	Überschrift
head lining 13.3	Himmel (*Kfz*)
head-on collision 12.12	Frontalzusammenstoß
health plan 28.9	Krankenversicherung
heart attack 2.17	Herzinfarkt
heat, in the ~ of the moment 24.3	in der Hitze des Gefechts
heater 13.2	Heizung
heater dealer 18.9	bewaffnete(r) Dealer(in)
heavy traffic 9.6	dichter Verkehr
hell, be sheer ~ 21.10	die reinste Hölle sein
hemispheric 7.13	halbkugelig
hemp 18.1	Hanf
hiding place for housekeeping money 16.3	Haushaltsgeldversteck
High Intensity Drug Trafficking Area Task Force 28.9	Kommission zur Bekämpfung von Drogenschwerpunkten
higher intermediate service 3.3	gehobener Dienst
high-intensity fog light(s) 7.7	Nebelschlussleuchten
high-pitched 14.14	hoch (*Stimme*)
high-pressure hose 17.7	Hochdruckschlauch
high-rise building 6.3	Hochhaus
high-visibility jacket 28.8	reflektierende Weste

highway 4.1	Straße
highway code 4.3	Straßenverkehrsordnung (StVO)
hijacking 23.7	Flugzeugentführung
hill crest 5.2	Kuppe
hit-and-run accident 2.16	Verkehrsunfall mit Fahrerflucht
hitch-hike 14.10	per Anhalter fahren, trampen
H.M. Inspector of Constabulary 28.4	Inspektionsbeamter des Innenministeriums in GB (*gibt jährlich einen Bericht über die Effektivität und Wirtschaftlichkeit jeder „police force" ab*)
hold on / the line 12.12	am Apparat bleiben (*Telefon*)
hold someone liable 17.4	jemanden verantwortlich machen
holdall 18.4	Reisetasche
hold-up 15.8	1 Stau 2 Überfall (*z.B. Bank*)
hole-in-the-wall machine 6.4	Geldautomat
home-jacking 13.7	Homejacking
home office 3.9	Innenministerium
Home Secretary 14.16	Innenminister in GB
home team 20.4	Heimmannschaft
homicide 3.9	Totschlag
homicide squad 3.9	Mordkommission
honk the horn 12.11	hupen
honorably discharged 28.9	ehrenvoll entlassen
honorary consul 14.11	Honorarkonsul
honorary function / post 8.1	Ehrenamt
honour killing 24.4	Ehrenmord
hood 13.2	1 (*US*) Motorhaube 2 Kapuze
hoody 15.3	1 Pullover mit Kapuze 2 Jugendliche(r), der / die Pullover mit Kapuze trägt (*oft kriminell*)
hooked nose 14.14	Hakennase
horsebox 18.4	Pferdebox, Pferdeanhänger
hostage 2.7	Geisel
hostage taking 22.6	Geiselnahme
host country 26.4	Gastland
hour, on the ~ 25.5	pünktlich auf die Stunde
housing estate 16.3	Wohnsiedlung
hub cap 13.2	Radkappe
human dignity 24.1	Menschenwürde
human resources management 3.3	Personalführung
hump(back) bridge 4.2	Buckelbrücke
Huns 17.6	1 Hunnen 2 Schimpfname für Deutsche
hunter safety instructor 28.9	Ausbilder(in) für Hobbyjäger(innen) (*im Umgang mit Schusswaffen*)
hurl 17.8	werfen, schleudern
hypothermia 12.10	Unterkühlung

I

ice-cream parlour 6.5	Eisdiele
ID card 7.2	Personalausweis
identification service 2.5	Erkennungsdienst (ED)
i. e. (id est) 3.6	d.h.
ignition lead 13.2	Zündkabel
ignition lock 1.4	Zündschloss
illegitimate 22.2	illegal
illicit 22.2	illegal, verboten
illiterate 14.2	Analphabet
immaterial 16.1	unerheblich
immigration check 18.5	Personenkontrolle bei Einreise
immigration restriction 3.5	Einwanderungsbeschränkung
immobilizer 13.3	Wegfahrsperre
immunity from prosecution 22.2	Straffreiheit
impact 12.4	Aufprall
impact on 2.13	sich auswirken auf
impair 7.3	beeinträchtigen
impartiality 28.5	Neutralität, Unparteilichkeit
impassable 6.2	unpassierbar
impeachment 28.9	Amtsenthebung
impediment 14.14	Sprachfehler
implement 26.3	durchführen, realisieren
implication 26.4	Folge, Auswirkung
impose 7.11	auferlegen
impostor 14.2	Schwindler(in), Hochstapler(in)
inattentive 12.4	unaufmerksam
inception 26.3	Anfang, Beginn
incest 21.9	Inzucht
incident 2.15	Vorfall, Zwischenfall
incision 12.10	Schnitt(wunde)
inclined 9.10	schräg, geneigt
incomprehensible. 25.5	unverständlich
increase 1.3	1 Anstieg, Zunahme 2 erhöhen, vergrößern, zunehmen, ansteigen
incredible 9.16	unglaublich
indebted, be ~ to someone 1.6	in jemandes Schuld stehen
indecent image 21.8	pornographische Abbildung
indelible marker pen 17.7	Permanent-Filzstift
indicators 7.7	Blinker
industrial protection laws 21.9	Arbeitnehmerschutzrechte
inebriation 11.6	Trunkenheit, Rausch
inevitable 23.8	unvermeidlich
infant 21.8	Kleinkind
infectious disease 2.12	ansteckende Krankheit
infertile 21.6	unfruchtbar
inflict 15.5	zufügen
influential 23.2	einflussreich
information panel 3.5	Hinweisschild
infraction 8.3	Verstoß
infringe 23.4	beeinträchtigen
infuriate 20.4	wütend machen
ingenious 18.4	einfallsreich, erfindungsreich
inherit 21.5	erben
inhibition 10.3	Hemmung
inhibition threshold 11.2	Hemmschwelle
injury accident 10.1	Unfall mit Verletzten
inmate 23.1	Insasse (*Gefängnis*)
innocent 9.16	unschuldig
innocent bystander 20.4	Unbeteiligte(r)
insert 9.10	einschieben
insistent 20.2	hartnäckig
inspector 2.3	Polizeikommissar(in)
instalment 17.4	Rate

instigate 22.6	aufhetzen, anstiften
institute proceedings 2.13	Anzeige erstatten, Verfahren einleiten
insult 5.2	1 Beleidigung 2 beleidigen
insurance 7.2	Versicherung
intellectual property crime 27.3	Diebstahl geistigen Eigentums
intelligence 13.7	Information(en), Kenntnis, Erkenntnis(se)
intent 16.1	Absicht
intentional(ly) 2.5	absichtlich, bewusst
intercom 2.15	Gegensprechanlage
intercourse 21.1	Geschlechtsverkehr
interface 2.12	Schnittstelle
intergovernmental 26.4	zwischenstaatlich
interlocking letters 17.7	ineinander verschlungene Buchstaben
intermediate service 3.3	mittlerer Dienst
Internal Auditor 28.9	Rechnungsprüfungsstelle
international code 12.12	internationale Vorwahl
internship 3.3	Praktikum
intersection 4.2	Kreuzung (*in US jede Kreuzung, in GB Autobahnkreuz*)
interstate (*US*) 4.1	Autobahn
interview 11.6	Vernehmung; vernehmen
intimidate 5.7	einschüchtern
intoxicated 11.1	betrunken
intruder 13.7	Eindringling
investigate 2.13	ermitteln
investigating magistrate 19.3	Untersuchungsrichter(in)
investigative technique 27.1	Ermittlungstechnik
investigator 2.2	Ermittlungsbeamter, -beamtin
iron house 18.9	Gefängnis
ironmonger 16.5	Eisenwarenhändler(in)
irritated 5.2	irritiert
issue a parking ticket 5.4	Parkzettel ausstellen
item 7.13	Gegenstand
ivory 12.11	Elfenbein

J

Jane Boy 18.9	Marihuanakonsument
jar 18.4	Glas
jaw 12.9	Kiefer
J.D. (Doctor of Law) 28.9	Doktor(in) des Rechts
jemmy 10.8	Brecheisen
jewellery, (*US*) jewelry 14.2	Schmuck
Joint Drug Investigation Group 2.13	Gemeinsame Ermittlungsgruppe Rauschgift (GER)
Joint Financial Investigation Group 2.13	Gemeinsame Finanzermittlungsgruppe
joint liability 17.4	gemeinsame Haftung
Joint Terrorism Task Force 28.9	gemeinsame Kommission (*mit FBI*) zur Terrorismusbekämpfung
Jojee 18.9	Heroin
jolt 25.3	Ruck
jostle 14.16	anrempeln
judicial 1.2	juristisch, Rechts-
jump the lights 10.1	Ampel bei Rot überfahren
jumper 14.15	Pullover
junction 4.2	1 Einmündung 2 (*GB*) Autobahnanschlussstelle
jurisdiction 14.16	Zuständigkeit
jury 1.1	Geschworene
juvenile crime 2.16	Jugendkriminalität

K

keeper 7.5	Halter(in)
kerb 11.6	Randstein
kerb crawling 21.9	Straßenprostitution
key 9.8	Zeichen (*Ziffer, Buchstabe usw.*)
key law enforcement official 26.5	leitende(r) Polizeibeamter, -beamtin
kick the habit 18.1	Gewohnheit aufgeben
kidney 12.9	Niere
killing spree 23.2	Amoklauf
kiss of life 12.8	Mund-zu-Mund-Beatmung
knight 22.1	Ritter
knuckle-duster 20.5	Schlagring
Kraut (*coll.*) 17.6	Deutsche(r)
kukuge 18.9	Marihuana

L

label 11.6	Etikett, Aufkleber
laceration 12.10	Riss-, Schnittwunde
lack of attention 5.2	Unachtsamkeit
lad 17.1	1 Bursche, Junge 2 Kumpel
ladette offence 17.9	Straftat von jungen Mädchen und Frauen
lager lout 17.1	alkoholisierter Rowdy / Hooligan (*Kennzeichen Flasche / Dose Bier in der Hand*)
landlord 11.9	1 Gastwirt 2 Vermieter
lane 4.2	1 kleine (Land)Straße, Feldweg 2 Fahrstreifen, Fahrspur
language skills 3.8	Sprachkenntnisse
larceny 16.1	Diebstahl
laser set 9.5	Lasergerät zur Geschwindigkeitskontrolle
lash 14.14	Wimper
lass 17.6	Mädchen
lateral entry 15.9	Seiteneinstieg
lateral pressure 9.10	seitlicher Druck
launch 4.7	starten, beginnen
launder money 2.13	Geld waschen
laundry basket 16.3	Korb für Schmutzwäsche
law enforcement 2.4	Durchsetzung von Recht und Gesetz
law of assembly 3.4	Versammlungsrecht
law of proprietorship 2.14	Hausrecht
law of public order offences 3.3	Ordnungswidrigkeitenrecht
law of registration 2.12	Melderecht
law, in ~ 2.14	rechtlich gesehen
lawn mower 18.8	Rasenmäher
lay 28.4	Laie
lay-by 7.13	Parkplatz
lead investigator 24.2	leitende(r) Ermittler(in)
lead-free 13.3	bleifrei

leak 9.10	lecken, auslaufen
leakage 25.2	Leck
learner driver's licence 11.9	vorläufiger Führerschein, Führerschein auf Probe
legal guardian 8.1	Vormund
leisure time 7.4	Freizeit
lethal 7.8	tödlich
lettuce 18.9	Geld
level 9.5	zielen (mit Waffe)
level crossing 4.2	(ebenerdiger) Bahnübergang
lever 13.2	Hebel
liaise 18.3	zusammenarbeiten mit
liaison officer 2.8	Verbindungsbeamter, -beamtin
licence plate / number plate light 7.7	Kennzeichenbeleuchtung
licence plate number 5.6	Kennzeichen, Nummernschild
licensed driver 11.9	Fahrer(in) mit vollem Führerschein
lid 16.5	Deckel
lieutenant 1.8	etwa: Polizeioberkommissar (*in vielen Polizeien in den USA und in anderen Staaten*)
life and limb 1.3	Leib und Leben
lifeguard badge 3.9	Rettungsschwimmerabzeichen
life member 28.9	Mitglied auf Lebenszeit
lifetime employment 3.2	Anstellung auf Lebenszeit
liftback 7.4	Schräghecklimousine
lighthouse 6.3	Leuchtturm
lighting fixture 7.13	Beleuchtungseinrichtung
lightning, as fast as greased ~. 13.7	blitzschnell, wie ein geölter Blitz
limb 1.3	(Körper)Glied
limitation period 17.7	Verjährungsfrist
limited 3.3	begrenzt
limo(usine) 7.4	1 Limousine, geschlossener PKW 2 (*US*) Taxi
linesman 17.6	Linienrichter(in)
linger 14.4	sich aufhalten, schlendern, bummeln
liquid 9.10	Flüssigkeit
liquor 14.2	Alkohol, Schnaps
lisp 14.14	lispeln
literally 16.4	wörtlich
litter bin 14.11	Abfallkorb
loan shark 22.2	Kredithai
lobe 14.14	Ohrläppchen
local authority 2.12	örtliche Behörde, Stadt, Gemeinde
local council 3.7	Stadtrat, Gemeinderat, Stadtparlament
local government 1.5	Kommune
local memory tag 7.5	Orts-, Gebietsangabe
local police authorities 2.4	örtliche Polizeibehörden
local recreational area 24.2	Naherholungsgebiet
local tradition 2.4	lokaler Brauch
location 2.8	(Stand)Ort, Lage, Position
lock oneself out 1.4	sich ausschließen
lodge a complaint 9.10	Anzeige erstatten, sich beschweren
lodge an objection 23.5	Einwand vorbringen
loft 16.3	Dachgeschoss
loiter 14.4	sich herumdrücken
loft with sloping walls 16.3	Dachgeschoss mit schrägen Wänden
lonely 5. 4	einsam
long-established 24.2	alteingesessen
loot 16.5	Beute
lost property office 14.11	Fundbüro
lump of rock 20.2	Felsbrocken, Stein

M

Madeleine 18.9	Haschisch
magistrate 13.7	Amtsrichter(in)
magistrates' court 7.16	Amtsgericht
maiden name 14.14	Mädchenname
main road / street 4.2	Hauptstraße
maintain 1.5	aufrechterhalten
maintenance costs 25.4	Unterhaltungskosten
major event 2.11	Großveranstaltung
major road / street 4.2	Hauptstraße
make 5.6	(Auto)Marke
make a bee-line 19.6	geradewegs auf jemanden / etwas zugehen
make out a charge 7.2	Anzeige erstatten
male 1.10	1 männliche Person 2 männlich
male rape 21.1	Vergewaltigung von Männern
malice, with ~ aforethought 15.5	vorsätzlich
maltreat 20.3	misshandeln
management board 27.1	Führungsstab
mandated strength 26.4	vorgesehene Stärke (*von den UN festgelegt*)
mandatory 9.12	vorgeschrieben
maniac 23.2	Verrückte(r)
manslaughter 24.1	Totschlag
marksman 3.3	Scharfschütze
marksmanship 3.3	Schießleistung(en)
marooned 25.3	festsitzend
martial arts 3.7	Kampfsportarten
massage parlour 6.5	Massagesalon, Bordell
mass event 14.8	Großveranstaltung
master bedroom 16.3	Elternschlafzimmer
Master of Science degree 27.2	Magistergrad in Naturwissenschaften
material evidence 2.8	Sachbeweis, Beweisstück
maternity leave 28.9	Mutterschaftsurlaub
maximum speed 4.5	Höchstgeschwindigkeit (*durch Schilder angezeigt*)
means of payment 27.1	Zahlungsmittel
measure 1.3	1 Maßnahme 2 messen
measures for one's own security 3.3	Eigensicherung
median (*US*) 4.2	Mittelstreifen
medical 3.9	medizinischer Test
medication 11.2	Arzneimittel, Medikament(e)
medium-level crime 2.2	mittlere Kriminalität
melodious 14.14	melodisch
member of the public 8.1	Person, Bürger(in) (*dieser Begriff wird oft allgemein gebraucht*)
mend 24.3	hier: ändern
mental disorder 18.1	Geisteskrankheit

merge 2.3	fusionieren, zusammenschließen
metal shield 28.9	Dienstmarke
Metropolitan Police Service 28.1	Polizei in London
Mexican horse 18.9	braunes Heroin aus Mexiko
middle lane 4.2	mittlere Fahrspur
Midlands 17.2	Grafschaften in der Mitte Englands
might 1.4	1 Macht, Kraft 2 können, mögen (*Gelegenheit*) (*Beachten Sie: kein Infinitiv!*)
migration 3.5	(Ein- und Aus)Wanderung
military leave 28.9	Urlaub für Wehrübungen
milk 13.10	melken, zur Kasse bitten, abzocken
millennium 27.3	Jahrtausend
mind you 2.10	denken Sie daran!, allerdings
Ministry of Defence Police 28.1	Polizei zur Bewachung militärischer Anlagen in GB
minor 10.3	minderjährig
minor offence 8.2	(geringfügige) Ordnungswidrigkeit
minor public order offence 7.11	geringfügige Ordnungswidrigkeit
misbehaviour 17.4	schlechtes / falsches Benehmen
miscarriage of justice 21.6	Fehlurteil, Justizirrtum
misdemeanour 11.2	Ordnungswidrigkeit, Fehlverhalten
misleading 6.2	irreführend
missile 17.2	1 Wurfgeschoss 2 Rakete
mission abroad 22.7	Auslandsmission
mitigate 11.6	mildern, abschwächen
mobile check 2.16	mobile Kontrolle
mobile home 16.3	Wohnmobil
mobile intervention group 3.9	Mobiles Einsatzkommando (MEK)
mobile phone 2.16	Mobiltelefon, Handy
mobile roadworks 4.2	Tages-, Wanderbaustelle
mock rifle 24.7	Imitationswaffe
module 3.3	(Ausbildungs)Abschnitt, Modul
mole 14.14	Leberfleck, Muttermal
molest 20.2	belästigen
money laundering 2.13	Geldwäsche
monitor 1.2	überwachen, beaufsichtigen
monitoring of morality 1.2	Sittenaufsicht, Sittenwacht
MoT (Ministry of Transport) 7.3	TÜV in GB
MoT testing station 7.13	TÜV-Prüfstelle
motherfucker (*slang*) 17.1	Arschloch, Drecksau, Scheißkerl
motor caravan 7.4	Wohnmobil
motor carrier officer 28.9	auf LKW-Kontrollen spezialisierte(r) Beamter /Beamtin
motorhome 5.4	Wohnmobil
(motor) scooter 7.4	Motorroller
motorway (*GB*) 2.15	Autobahn
mould 5.4	formen
mounted police 3.2	berittene Polizei, Reiterstaffel
moustache 14.13	Schnurrbart
mouth-to-mouth resuscitation 12.8	Mund-zu-Mund-Beatmung
movable water tap / faucet (*US*) 16.3	schwenkbarer Wasserhahn
mudguard 13.5	Schutzblech
muffled 24.2	dumpf, gedämpft
mugging 15.1	Straßenraub
multi-chambered 23.6	mit mehreren Kammern
multilingual 26.4	mehrsprachig
multi-storey car park 5.4	Parkhaus
municipal 1.2	städtisch
murderer 1.10	Mörder (*Beachten Sie: Mord = murder*)
murderess 1.10	Mörderin
mutual 27.3	gegenseitig

N

nail 21.11	festnehmen, verhaften
name at birth 14.14	Geburtsname
name tag 28.9	Namensschild
nap 24.7	Schläfchen, Nickerchen
narcotics 18.9	Drogen
nasty 5.4	schlimm, unangenehm
national law 10.6	inländisches Recht, nationales Recht
National Society of the Sons of the American Revolution 28.9	Vereinigung von Nachkommen derjenigen Amerikaner, die im Unabhängigkeitskrieg gekämpft haben
national speed limit 4.5	Höchstgeschwindigkeit (durch Gesetz festgelegt)
native 22.6	einheimisch, eingeboren
nature protection authority 25.4	Naturschutzbehörde
nature reserve 25.4	Naturschutzgebiet
naval station 28.9	Marinebasis
navigable 2.2	schiffbar
navigation by sight 25.3	Fahrt auf Sicht
near-sighted 10.8	kurzsichtig
negligence 5.2	Nachlässigkeit, Fahrlässigkeit
negligence, through ~ 5.7	fahrlässig
negligent 1.4	nachlässig, fahrlässig
negligent bodily harm 12.6	fahrlässige Körperverletzung
negotiate 27.1	aushandeln, verhandeln
neighbourhood 3.2	Stadtviertel
net 9.6	(netto) einbringen
newsagent 6.5	Zeitungshändler(in)
nickname 9.10	Spitzname
no-claims bonus 23.9	Schadenfreiheitsrabatt
nocturnal 1.3	nächtlich
non-commissioned officer 28.9	Unteroffizier
non-stationary traffic 5.3	fließender Verkehr
nostril 14.14	Nasenloch
nuclear power plant 28.1	Kernkraftwerk
nudge 19.3	(vorsichtig) anstoßen
number seven 18.9	tödliche Dosis
numbers (*US*) 22.2	illegale Lotterie
nursery school 21.8	Kindertagesstätte

O

obese 14.14	stark übergewichtig, sehr dick
obey the law 8.1	Gesetz befolgen
obituary 28.9	Nachruf
objection 5.2	Einwand, Widerspruch, Einlegen von Rechtsmitteln
obligation 22.1	Verpflichtung
obliged, be ~ to 9.7	verpflichtet sein, müssen
obstacle 5.5	Hindernis
obstruct 2.10	behindern
obtain 3.3	erhalten, erlangen, erwerben
obvious(ly) 9.1	anscheinend, offensichtlich
occasion, on the ~ of 1.6	anlässlich
occasional(ly) 5.4	gelegentlich
occupation zone 1.5	Besatzungszone
occupied 16.6	hier: bewohnt
occupying power 1.5	Besatzungsmacht
occur 1.3	geschehen, vorkommen
occurrence 11.6	Vorkommnis, Ereignis, Geschehen
odd job 20.2	Gelegenheitsarbeit
odometer 13.2	Kilometerzähler
offence 2.2	Verstoß
offender 1.3	Straftäter(in), Gesetzesbrecher(in)
office duty 2.6	Innendienst
Office of Integrity and Compliance 28.9	Disziplinarabteilung
officer 1.3	1 Offizier 2 Polizeibeamter, -beamtin 3 unterster Dienstgrad bei vielen Polizeien
officer in charge 2.10	(Einsatz)Leiter(in), diensthabende(r) Beamter / Beamtin
official order 28.9	Dienstanweisung
olfactory sense 18.8	Geruchssinn
oncoming 4.4	entgegenkommend
open-plan carriage 19.3	Großraumwagen
operational 9.6	in Betrieb
operational analysis 27.1	Einsatzanalyse
operational area 2.15	Einsatzgebiet
operational law 10.6	Einsatzrecht
operational theory 3.4	Eingriffsrecht
operational training 3.4	Einsatztraining
operational uniform 28.8	(Dienst)Uniform
operations 1.3	Einsatz(bewältigung)
operations management 3.3	Einsatzlehre
operator 2.15	1 Person, die Notrufe usw. entgegennimmt 2 Betreiber(in), Tankstellenpächter(in)
opponent 22.6	Gegner(in)
opportunist thief 16.6	Gelegenheitsdieb(in)
option 6.2	Wahlmöglichkeit, Option
orbit 6.2	Umlaufbahn
order of summary punishment 11.2	Strafbefehl
ordinance 5.3	Verordnung
organized crime 18.5	organisierte Kriminalität
Organized Crime Enforcement Task Force 28.9	Kommission zur Bekämpfung organisierter Kriminalität
Organized Gang Unit 28.9	Einheit zur Bekämpfung von Bandenkriminalität
oriel 16.3	Erker
ostracize 22.1	ächten
outrageous 21. 6	abscheulich, himmelschreiend
outside lane 4.2	äußerer Fahrstreifen (*links in D, rechts in GB*)
outsmart someone 19.4	jemanden überlisten, jemanden austricksen
oven 16.3	Backofen
overindebted 3.3	überschuldet
overpass 4.2	Überführung
overturn 9.7	sich überschlagen
o.v.n.o. (or very near offer) 13.3	Verhandlungsbasis

P

pace up and down 14.9	hin und her gehen, auf und ab gehen
pad 7.13	(Schreib)Block
painkiller 18.1	schmerzstillendes Mittel
painstaking 21.8	mühevoll, langwierig
Palatinate 1.5	Pfalz
palm 14.13	Handfläche
pantyhose 14.15	Strumpfhose
paralyze 23.7	lähmen
parking fee 5.4	Parkgebühr
parking lights 7.7	Standlicht
parking space 5.4	Parkraum
parking ticket 5.2	Knöllchen wegen Parkverstoß / -vergehen
park pilot 13.3	Einparkhilfe
parkway (*US*) 24.7	Hauptstraße
parole 24.1	Bewährung (*nach Verbüßung eines Teils der Strafe*)
parquet sheet 9.10	Parkettplatte
parted 14.14	gescheitelt
participant 3.1	Teilnehmer(in)
partition 7.4	Trennscheibe
pass 2.13	1 vorbeifahren, vorbeigehen 2 überholen 3 bestehen (Prüfung)
passenger 4.7	Mitfahrer(in), Beifahrer(in)
patch 2.6	Abzeichen (*aus Stoff*)
paternity leave 28.9	Vaterschaftsurlaub
patrol duty 3.7	Streifendienst
pattern 16.4	Muster
pavement 1.6	1 (Straßen)Pflaster 2 (*GB*) Gehsteig, Bürgersteig 3 (*US*) Fahrbahn
Payroll 28.9	Gehaltsabteilung
Peace Officer 28.9	Sicherheitsbeamter, -beamtin
peacekeeping 26.3	1 friedenserhaltend 2 Friedenssicherung
peak 17.8	den Höhepunkt erreichen
peak time 14.18	Hauptverkehrszeit, Stoßzeit
pedestrian 3.12	Fußgänger(in)
pedestrian crossing 4.2	Fußgängerüberweg
pedestrian precinct 3.12	Fußgängerzone
pedestrianise 14.11	in Fußgängerzone umwandeln
peek-a-boo 1.4	Guckguck-Spiel

Peeler 17.1	Polizist(in)
peer group 18.1	Gleichaltrige
peer pressure 15.2	Druck von Gleichaltrigen
pelican crossing 4.2	Fußgängerüberweg mit Ampel
pellet 23.6	Schrot(kugel)
pelvis 12.9	Becken
pen friend 27.6	Brieffreund(in)
penal code 1.3	Strafgesetzbuch
penal law 10.6	Strafrecht
penal provision 1.3	Strafbestimmung
penalty point 4.3	Punkt (*im Verkehrszentralregister / in der Verkehrssünderkartei*)
penalty ticket 3.3	Strafzettel, Verwarnung
pencilled 14.14	mit Kosmetikstift nachgezogen
penitentiary (*US*) 1.10	Justizvollzugsanstalt (JVA)
peonage 28.9	Schuldknechtschaft
perceive 11.2	bemerken, erfassen
perishable 9.11	(leicht) verderblich
perjury 28.9	Meineid
permanent job 19.3	fester Arbeitsplatz
permanent residential address 13.7	ständige Wohnadresse
permit to possess a gun 15.6	Waffenbesitzkarte
perpetrator 16.6	Straftäter(in)
persecution mania 18.1	Verfolgungswahn
Personal Crimes 28.9	Personendelikt(e)
personal data 7.9	Personalien, persönliche Daten
personal development 3.3	Persönlichkeitsbildung
personalized / cherished / individual registration number 7.5	Wunschkennzeichen
personally assigned vehicle 28.9	Streifenwagen zum ausschließlichen Gebrauch
personnel 2.7	Personal
personnel officer 3.1	Personalsachbearbeiter(in)
petrified 16.4	versteinert
petrol bomb 17.8	Molotowcocktail
petty crime 2.2	1 Kleinkriminalität 2 geringfügige Straftat
Ph.D. (Doctor of Philosophy) 28.9	Doktor der Philosophie
physical education (PE) 3.4	Sport
physicist 3.9	Physiker(in)
pick 14.8	stehlen, klauen
pickpocket 14.8	Taschendieb(in)
pillion 13.5	Sozius(sitz)
pillion rider 15.2	Sozius(fahrer), Sozia
pillow 13.10	(Kopf)Kissen
pimp 21.9	Zuhälter
pimply 14.14	pickelig, voller Pickel
pinch, at a ~ 15.8	zur Not, im Notfall
pint 6.1	Pint (*0,565 l*)
pitch 7.16	Spielfeld, Sportplatz
pitch a tent 25.4	Zelt aufschlagen
pitched roof 24.2	Spitzdach
pizza parlour 6.5	Pizzeria
plain-clothes officer 1.3	Kriminalbeamter, -beamtin
plastic money 18.7	Kreditkarte, Bankkarte
plate 18.7	Tafel
plate-glass pane 2.10	Sicherheitsglasscheibe, Panzerglasscheibe
platform truck 7.4	Pritschenwagen

plucked 14.14	ausgezupft
point-blank range, at ~ 15.3	aus nächster Nähe
pole 6.1	Pfahl, Pfosten
police academy 2.14	Polizeischule
police advisory centre 16.6	kriminalpolizeiliche Beratungsstelle
police authority 28.4	Polizeiaufsichtsbehörde in GB
police capacity 2.13	Funktion, Rolle als Polizist(in)
police community support officer (PCSO) 28.1	Angestellte der Polizei zur Unterstützung des bürgernahen Fußstreifeneinzeldiensts in GB
Police Federation 28.5	gewerkschaftsähnliche Vereinigung von Polizeibeamten in GB (*vom constable bis chief inspector, mit Zwangsmitgliedschaft*)
Police / Fire Chaplaincy Corps 28.9	zuständige Seelsorger für Polizei und Feuerwehr
Police of the German Bundestag 2.1	Polizei beim Deutschen Bundestag
police inspectorate 2.3	Polizeiinspektion
police law 3.3	Polizeirecht
police management (theory) 3.3	Führungslehre / Management
police powers 3.4	Einsatzlehre
police service 1.5	Polizei (*als selbstständige Einheit*)
police service theory 3.3	Polizeidienstkunde
police staff 28.1	Zivilpersonal bei der Polizei
police station 1.6	Polizeiwache (PW)
police union 3.7	Polizeigewerkschaft
policing 1.3	polizeiliche Tätigkeit
policing by consent 28.5	Aufgabenwahrnehmung auf der Grundlage von Übereinstimmung mit den Bürgern
policing in formations 3.4	Verbandstraining
politician 2.10	Politiker(in)
polygraph 28.9	Lügendetektor
pool of blood 15.3	Blutlache
pop out 11.5	herausspringen
poppy 18.1	Mohn
porch 16.3	Windfang
portable radio 15.9	Handfunkgerät
pose 2.8	darstellen
posh 9.11	vornehm, nobel
position (*verb*) 9.7	aufstellen, in Position bringen
post 28.9	Polizeiinspektion (*der MSP*)
post-conflict 26.3	Nachkriegs-
post mortem 17.5	Obduktion, Autopsie
postpone 24.1	verzögern, hinausschieben
pouch 14.9	Beutel
power line 23.7	Stromleitung
power of arrest 28.5	Festnahmerecht
power of attorney 11.6	Vollmacht
powers of instruction 28.4	Weisungsbefugnis
practical training course 3.3	Praktikum
pram (perambulator) 5.5	Kinderwagen
prearrange 18.4	im Voraus festlegen, im Voraus vereinbaren
precautionary measure 14.9	Vorsichtsmaßnahme

precinct 2.10	Zuständigkeitsbereich, Revier
precious 22.2	kostbar, wertvoll
precondition 25.3	Vorbedingung
pre-deployment training 26.3	Einsatzvorbereitung
predict 11.2	vorhersagen
prefer charges 12.6	Anzeige erstatten
prefix 7.5	1 Vorsilbe 2 Anfangsbuchstabe (*bei früheren britischen Kfz-Kennzeichen*)
pregnant 9.10	schwanger
preliminary test 11.6	erster / vorläufiger Test
premises 2.9	Gebäude und Grundstücke, Dienst-, Geschäftsräume, Ladenlokal
prerequisite 27.3	Grundvoraussetzung
prescription 18.1	ärztliches Rezept
press charges 9.10	Anzeige erstatten
press release 18.6	Pressemitteilung
presume 9.16	annehmen, mutmaßen
prevail 2.15	vorherrschen, die Oberhand gewinnen
prevent 1.3	verhindern, vorbeugen
prevention council 25.5	Vorbeugungsrat
preventive detention 24.1	Sicherheitsverwahrung
preventive measure 16.2	Vorbeugungsmaßnahme
previous 8.1	vorhergehend, vorherig, früher
previous conviction 8.1	Vorstrafe
primarily 5.3	in erster Linie, hauptsächlich
Prince-of-Wales Feathers 18.9	LSD Papiertrip
principle, as a matter of ~ 1.3	prinzipiell, grundsätzlich
priority 4.5	Vorfahrt
priority from the right 4.5	Vorfahrt rechts vor links
prise open 13.7	aufbrechen (*Tür usw.*)
prison sentence 10.1	Freiheits-, Gefängnisstrafe
private eye 16.4	Privatdetektiv(in)
probation, on ~ 10.1	1 auf Probe 2 auf Bewährung
probationary period 28.3	Probezeit
procedural law 3.3	Verfahrensrecht
proceed 7.7	weiterfahren, weitergehen
proceedings 2.13	Verfahren
processing of cases / charges 2.16	Fall-, Sach-, Vorgangsbearbeitung
producer 7.2	Mängelkarte
product-oriented 2.4	zielorientiert
professional body 3.8	berufliche Vereinigung
professional career 1.10	berufliche Laufbahn
professional ethics 3.3	Berufsethik
proficiency 5.4	Kenntnisse, Fertigkeiten
proficient 26.3	kompetent, sprachgewandt
promote 2.5	befördern
promotion 3.2	Beförderung
prompt 14.11	veranlassen
prone to 17.1	anfällig für
pronounce a sentence 11.6	Urteil fällen
proper authority 5.3	zuständige Behörde
property crime 27.2	Eigentums-, Vermögens-, Sachdelikt
property damage 2.16	Sachschaden, Sachbeschädigung
prosecute 5.3	zur Anzeige bringen, strafrechtlich verfolgen
prosecution office / service 10.4	Staatsanwaltschaft
prosecutor 10.4	Staatsanwalt, -anwältin
prospective 3.9	aussichtsreich, möglich, potenziell
prosperity 26.3	Wohlstand
protagonist 23.7	Hauptfigur
protection racket 22.1	Schutzgelderpressung
protective service 2.14	Sicherheitsdienst, Werkschutz
protrude 14.14	hervorstehen
prudish 17.6	prüde
Prussia 7.6	Preußen
public and constitutional law 3.4	Staats- und Verfassungsrecht
public indecency 21.9	Erregung öffentlichen Ärgernisses
public law 10.6	öffentliches Recht
public nuisance 25.5	öffentliches Ärgernis
public order authority 5.3	Ordnungsbehörde
public order offence 2.12	Verstoß gegen öffentliche Ordnung
public order official 5.3	Ordnungsbeamter, -beamtin
public order police 2.12	Ordnungspolizei, Kommunaler Vollzugsdienst, Ordnungsamt, Ortspolizeibehörde, Stadtpolizei
public school 6.6	Privatschule in GB
public security 1.3	öffentliche Sicherheit
public service law 3.3	Recht des öffentlichen Dienstes, öffentliches Dienstrecht, Beamtenrecht
publican 17.1	Gastwirt
pull over 9.5	1 überziehen (*Kleidungsstück*) 2 zur Seite fahren (*Fahrzeug*)
pull someone over 9.1	jemanden anhalten
pulsate 11.6	pulsieren
pumpkin seed 18.9	Meskalin
punch 17.6	schlagen, boxen
punch-drunk 20.5	völlig betrunken
puncture 12.10	Stichwunde
punter 21.9	Freier
pupil 11.6	Pupille
purchase 11.6	1 kaufen 2 Kauf
purpose 2.7	Zweck, Ziel
pursue 1.3	verfolgen, streben nach
pursuit 13.7	1 Verfolgung(sfahrt) 2 Streben
push-up 28.9	Liegestütz
push vessel 25.2	Schubverband
put to death 24.3	hinrichten

Q

qualification requirement 28.7	Einstellungsvoraussetzung
qualified vocational training 3.3	abgeschlossene Berufsausbildung
query 23.3	Anfrage, Erkundigung
quit 28.9	verlassen, ausscheiden
quote 23.4	zitieren

R

radar set 2.5	Radargerät zur Geschwindigkeitskontrolle
radiator 7.13	Kühler
radio call 2.15	Funkspruch
radio call sign 2.15	Funkrufwort, Rufname, Funkcode, Statusgeber
radio patrol 3.9	Funkstreifendienst
raid 15.9	1 Razzia 2 Einbruch 3 überfallen
railroad crossing (*US*) 4.2	Eisenbahnübergang
railway level crossing (controlled or open) 4.2	Eisenbahnübergang (*beschrankt oder unbeschrankt*)
raise 24.2	legen (*Feuer*)
ram 18.8	Schafbock, Widder
ramp 4.2	Auffahrt, Zufahrt
random 6.2	zufällig, beliebig
random check 7.1	Zufalls-, Stichprobenkontrolle
rank insignia (*Plural*) 2.6	Rang-, Dienstgradabzeichen, Schulterstücke
rank patch 2.7	Rang-, Dienstgradabzeichen (*aus Stoff*)
rape 20.3	1 Vergewaltigung 2 vergewaltigen
rapist 21.1	Vergewaltiger
ratio 13.3	Verhältnis, Übersetzung
razor 18.7	Rasierapparat
re 25.3	bezüglich, bezogen auf
readiness to take risks 11.2	Risikobereitschaft
realize 11.2	hier: einsehen
rear-window demister 13.2	heizbare Heckscheibe
rear-view mirror 10.4	Rückspiegel
reasonable grounds 2.13	Anfangsverdacht
recede 14.14	zurückgehen
receipt 5.5	Quittung
receipt slip 14.11	Kassenbon, Quittung
receiver 12.12	(Telefon)Hörer
recent 6.4	relativ neu, kürzlich
recipient 6.2	Empfänger(in)
recognition 26.3	Erkenntnis, Anerkennung
recognize 3.1	1 (wieder)erkennen, 2 anerkennen
recording accidents 2.2	Unfallaufnahme
recording charges / a charge 2.16	Anzeigenaufnahme
recovery position 12.6	stabile Seitenlage
recruit 2.1	einstellen
rectangular 4.4	viereckig
red-handed 17.7	auf frischer Tat
redistribute 9.10	neu verteilen
red oil 18.9	Haschischöl
red-rimmed 14.14	rot umrandet
referee 17.6	Schiedsrichter(in)
reference book 2.15	Nachschlagewerk
reflex silver metallic paint 13.3	silbermetallic
refresher course 6.6	Wiederholungs-, Auffrischungskurs
refuel 14.7	auftanken
refuge 22.1	Zufluchtsraum
refurbish 24.2	umbauen
refuse 8.2	sich weigern
registered owner 7.9	Halter(in)
registration office 1.5	1 Kfz-Zulassungsstelle 2 Einwohnermeldeamt
regular 6.1	Stammgast, Stammkunde
regular police officer 28.7	voll ausgebildete(r) Polizist(in)
reign 7.5	regieren
reimburse 11.6	erstatten
re-integrate 26.2	wieder eingliedern
release 2.16	entlassen
relevant 3.8	betreffend, wichtig, geeignet
reliable 2.14	zuverlässig, glaubhaft, verlässlich
relieve pain 12.8	Schmerz lindern
reluctant 10.7	zögerlich
rely on 9.10	sich verlassen auf
remand custody 13.7	Untersuchungshaft
remand someone in custody 19.3	jemanden in Untersuchungshaft nehmen
remind someone 5.2	jemanden erinnern
remit 2.13	Aufgabenbereich, Zuständigkeit
remote 8.5	entfernt, abgelegen
render assistance 3.9	Hilfe leisten
render unusable 23.3	unbrauchbar machen
rental car 6.1	Leih-, Mietwagen
repeal 16.1	aufheben, ersetzen
repeat offender 24.3	Wiederholungstäter(in)
replica 14.9	Imitation
replica handgun 23.1	unechte / nachgemachte Schusswaffe
reproach 24.6	Vorwurf
reproducible 21.5	nachvollziehbar
reputation 3.2	Ruf, Ansehen
request 2.15	1 Bitte, Anfrage, Verlangen 2 bitten, beantragen
required, be ~ to 2.14	verpflichtet sein, müssen
rescue 11.8	Rettung, Hilfe
resemble 2.12	ähnlich sein
resident 1.5	Einwohner(in), Anwohner(in), Bewohner(in)
residential address 8.1	Wohnanschrift
residential area 1.6	Wohnviertel
residential building 2.10	Wohngebäude
residents only 5.4	nur für Anlieger
residents' registration office 1.5	Einwohnermeldeamt
resort to 13.7	greifen zu
resort to violence 22.1	gewalttätig werden
resource 3.3	Mittel
respective 1.3	betreffend
respond 2.15	1 reagieren, eingreifen, einschreiten (*Polizei nach Anruf*) 2 antworten
responsibility 1.3	Verantwortung(sbereich)
rest area 4.2	Rastplatz
restrain 19.3	festhalten
restrict 2.11	beschränken
ret. (retired) 28.9	im Ruhestand, pensioniert
retail outlet 14.2	Einzelhandelsgeschäft
retail trade 14.3	Einzelhandel
retain 7.5	1 (ein)behalten 2 (Anwalt) nehmen
retirement 28.3	Pensionierung
retrieve 1.4	(ab)holen, abrufen (*Daten*)

retrospective 22.7	im Nachhinein, rückwirkend
reunification 2.6	Wiedervereinigung
rev(olution) counter 13.2	Drehzahlmesser
reveal 3.9	ergeben, enthüllen, aufdecken, zeigen
revenge 24.2	Rache
revenue 22.2	Einnahme
reverse 7.13	1 Rückseite 2 rückwärts fahren, zurücksetzen
reversing lights 7.7	Rückfahrscheinwerfer
ride 27.7	Sternfahrt
ride the witch's broom 18.9	heroinsüchtig sein
right-hand drive (RHD) 7.13	Rechtslenkung
rim 4.5	Rand
riot police 1.3	Bereitschaftspolizei
riot squad 3.3	Bereitschaftspolizei, Einsatzhundertschaft
riot squad department 3.3	Bereitschaftspolizei-abteilung
rising 22.6	Aufstand
risk of escape 19.3	Fluchtgefahr
river police 2.2	Wasserschutz-, Schiff-fahrtspolizei
road hog 10.3	aggressive(r) / rücksichtslose(r) Autofahrer(in)
road licensing regulations 9.4	Verkehrszulassungsord-nung
road policing unit 26.1	Verkehrspolizei
road safety training course 3.3	Fahrsicherheitstraining
road shoulder 4.2	Seitenstreifen, Standspur
road traffic accident (RTA) (*offizielle Bezeichnung in GB*) 3.5	Verkehrsunfall
road traffic authority 7.9	Kfz-Zulassungsstelle
road traffic safety 1.3	Verkehrssicherheit
road user 4.2	Verkehrsteilnehmer(in)
roadworks area / section 2.15	Baustelle
roadworthiness 7.8	Fahrtüchtigkeit
roadworthy 12.3	fahrbereit
roasting (*coll.*) 9.8	Geschimpfe, "Anschiss"
robbery 14.12	Raub(delikt)
rogues' gallery 14.9	Lichtbildstelle, -kartei, -datei, -mappe
roll 9.8	Brötchen
roller bandage 12.8	Verband
rolling pin 23.1	Nudelholz
roof rails 13.3	Dachreling
roofing tile 24.2	Dachziegel
rookie 28.9	Anfänger(in)
rooted 24.3	verwurzelt
rotary (*US*) 4.2	Kreisverkehr
roughly speaking 23.1	ungefähr, etwa
roundabout (*GB*) 4.2	Kreisverkehr
row house (*US*) 16.3	Reihenhaus
rubber bullet 23.7	Gummigeschoss
ruby ale 17.1	*britische Biersorte*
ruddy 14.14	rötlich
rule 2.10	1 Regel 2 Vorschrift 3 herrschen 4 urteilen (*Gericht*)
rumble strips 4.2	Rüttelstreifen
rummage 16.5	durchwühlen
rural 18.5	ländlich
rut 9.10	Spurrinne, Spurrille
ruthless 22.2	skrupellos, rücksichtslos

S

sachet 2.5	Päckchen, Briefchen, kleiner Beutel
sacked, be ~ 20.2	entlassen werden
safety 1.2	Sicherheit (*nach innen, z.B. Vermeidung von Unfallgefahren*)
safety lever 23.6	Sicherungshebel
sag 25.4	zusammensacken
sallow 14.14	blassgelb
saloon 7.4	Limousine, geschlossener PKW
Salvation Army 17.1	Heilsarmee
San Francisco rainbow 18.9	LSD-Tablette
satchel 8.3	(Schul)Ranzen
satellite dish 16.3	Satellitenantenne, Schüssel
satellite-based 6.2	satellitengestützt
satisfied 7.10	zufrieden
satnav (satellite navigation system) 6.2	Navigationssystem, Navi
save 14.9	speichern (*Computer, Handy usw*)
sawn-off shotgun 23.5	Schrotflinte mit ab-gesägtem Lauf
scald 12.10	1 Verbrühung 2 verbrühen
scar 14.12	Narbe
scare someone away / off 16.4	jemanden verscheuchen
scared 21.4	verängstigt
scarf, scarves 1.10	Halstuch, Schal
scene, at/on the ~ 1.4	am Tatort, Unfallort
scene of an accident 3.9	Unfallstelle
scene of the crime 1.10	Tatort
scenes of crime department 26.1	Ermittlungsabteilung
scenes of crime officer 24.2	Ermittler(in)
scheduled 7.16	festgelegt, vorgesehen
scholarship 27.6	Stipendium
school break 7.6	Schulferien
School Resource Officer 28.9	Verbindungsbeamter, -beamtin zu Schulen (*Schwerpunkt ihrer Arbeit ist Drogenprävention*)
school zone 9.5	Schulbereich (*Stück einer an einer Schule vorbeiführenden Straße, auf dem in den USA häufig eine sehr niedrige Geschwindigkeit vorge-schrieben ist*)
scope 2.4	Spielraum, Aufgabenbe-reich
score 6.6	(Tor) schießen, (Punkt) machen
scourge 22.6	Geißel
scrape 25.2	Grundberührung haben (*Boot, Schiff*)
scrape off 23.1	abkratzen
scratch 12.11	Kratzer
sealable 14.9	verschließbar
search warrant 11.6	Durchsuchungsbe-schluss
season ticket 19.1	Monats-, Jahreskarte
secluded 21.3	einsam, abgelegen
second (*Verb*) 3.9	einsetzen, abordnen
secondary school certificate 3.3	qualifizierter Haupt-schulabschluss
secondment 26.1	Abordnung
secure 2.2	1 (ab)sichern 2 sicherstellen

secure evidence 2.2	Beweis(e) sichern / sicherstellen
secure traces 2.15	Spuren sichern
security 1.3	1 Sicherheit (*nach außen, z. B. verhindern, dass Unbefugte in eine Polizeieinrichtung eindringen*) 2 Sicherheitsleistung
security airlock system 2.15	(Sicherheits)Schleuse
security area 2.15	Sicherheitsbereich
security guard 14.2	Wachmann
security service 2.14	Sicherheitsdienst
sedan 7.4	Limousine, geschlossener PKW
seizure 22.4	Sicherstellung, Beschlagnahme
select 6.2	auswählen
self-confident 9.10	selbstbewusst
self-defence and restraint techniques 3.4	Selbstverteidigung und Eingriffstechniken
self-explanatory 4.5	sich selbst erklärend
self-governed 26.1	selbstverwaltet
semen 21.6	männlicher Samen
semi-detached house 16.3	Doppelhaushälfte
semitrailer 7.4	Auflieger, Sattelanhänger
senior citizen 8.3	Senior(in)
senior police officer 12.12	Polizist(in) mit höherem Dienstgrad
senior service 3.3	höherer Dienst
sensible 8.2	vernünftig, einsichtig
sensitive 1.6	sensibel
sentry 28.9	Wachposten
sequence 7.5	(Ab)Folge
sergeant 1.6	Polizeihauptmeister(in)
serial killer 17.10	Serienmörder(in)
serve one's term/time 24.1	Strafe absitzen
service area /services 4.2	(Autobahn)Raststätte, Tank- und Rastanlage
service operations 3.3	allgemeiner Dienstbetrieb
set 9.5	1 Satz (*z.B. Werkzeuge*) 2 Gerät, Apparat
settlement 9.5	1 Entscheidung 2 Regelung, Schlichtung 3 Besiedlung
severe defect 7.3	schwerer Schaden
severe road traffic accident 3.5	schwerer Verkehrsunfall
sexual assault 21.1	Vergewaltigung
sexual harassment 21.9	sexuelle Belästigung
shabby 4.7	schäbig, heruntergekommen, abgetragen (*Kleidung*)
shackles 2.15	(Fuß)Fesseln
shaken 9.1	durcheinander
share a ride 6.5	gemeinsam fahren, Fahrgemeinschaft bilden
shark 1.1	Hai(fisch)
shear off 11.1	abschneiden
sheet (of paper) 9.10	Blatt
shell 23.6	Patrone, Hülse
shell game (*US*) 2.5	Hütchenspiel
shift differential 28.9	Schichtzulage
shift leader 2.16	Schichtführer(in), Dienstgruppenleiter(in) (DGL)
shift work 3.2	Schichtdienst
shin 12.9	Schienbein
shooting competition 23.3	Schießwettbewerb
shooting range 23.3	Schießstand
shootout 24.7	Schießerei
shoplifting 3.9	Ladendiebstahl
shopping arcade 16.5	Einkaufszentrum
shore leave pass 25.1	Ausweis für Landgang
short notice, at ~ 26.3	kurzfristig
shotgun 23.5	Schrotflinte, Jagdgewehr
shoulder 4.2	1 Schulter 2 Straßenrand, Standspur
shower cubicle 16.3	Duschkabine
shuffle 3.1	mischen (*Spielkarten*)
shutter 16.3	Rollladen
shuttle train 14.18	Pendelzug
sideboard 9.10	Seitenwand (*LKW*)
sideburns 14.14	1 Backenbart 2 Koteletten
side lights 7.7	Seitenbeleuchtung
sidewalk (*US*) 4.2	Bürgersteig, Gehsteig
sidewall 7.8	Seitenwand
signals 7.7	Blinker, Fahrtrichtungsanzeiger
significant 3.6	bedeutend, beträchtlich
signify 1.2	bedeuten
signpost 4.7	Wegweiser
signs giving orders 4.4	Ge- und Verbotszeichen
silver bike 18.9	Spritze
similar 2.10	ähnlich
sin 10.2	Sünde
single-chambered 23.6	mit einer Kammer
single-lens reflex camera 16.5	Spiegelreflexkamera
single-track 6.2	einspurig
sink 16.3	Spüle, Abwaschbecken
sip 3.12	nippen, schlürfen
situated, be ~ 5.4	liegen, gelegen sein
sketch 12.11	Skizze
skid 12.6	rutschen, schleudern
skilled 1.6	sachgerecht, geschickt
skimming profits 27.5	Gewinnabschöpfung
skull 4.7	(Toten)Schädel
skull and crossbones 4.7	gekreuzte Knochen mit Totenkopf
skyscraper 6.3	Wolkenkratzer, Hochhaus
slab 16.5	Scheibe, Platte
slacks 14.15	Hose
slavery 17.4	Sklaverei
sleeping policeman 4.2	Straßenschwelle
sleeve 2.0	Ärmel
sliding roof 13.2	Schiebedach
sling 12.8	Schlinge
slingshot 23.1	Schleuder
slip 14.15	(Damen)Unterrock (*nicht Unterhose*)
slip road 4.2	Zufahrtsstraße, Ein- und Ausfahrtstraße (*Autobahn*)
slippery road 4.4	Straßenglätte
sloppy 21.6	nachlässig, schlampig
slot 9.10	Spalt, Schlitz
slot machine 15.2	Spielautomat
slow lane 4.2	rechter Fahrstreifen (*in GB der linke*)
slug 23.6	Geschoss, Kugel
slurred 11.2	lallend, undeutlich
smooth 7.10	glatt, ruhig, ohne Störung
smooth-bore 23.6	mit glattem Lauf
snatch 15.2	entreißen

snort 18.1	schniefen, schnupfen
snow flake 18.9	Kokain
soak 11.5	durchnässen
sob 11.1	schluchzen
sober 3.12	nüchtern
sober up 3.12	ausnüchtern
sobering cell 10.7	Ausnüchterungszelle
sobriety check 11.5	Alkoholkontrolle
sociability 18.1	Geselligkeit
soft body armour 28.9	schusssichere Weste
soft shoulder 4.2	unbefestigter Seitenstreifen
sole 14.13	(Schuh)Sole
sole parent 28.9	Alleinerziehende(r)
solicit 21.9	ansprechen
solvent 18.1	Lösungsmittel
sonic depth finder 25.3	Sonar
sophisticated 2.2	supermodern, auf dem neuesten Stand, hier: raffiniert
sort code 17.4	Bankleitzahl
sovereignty 26.3	Souveränität
spaghetti junction 4.2	komplizierte Kreuzung (*beim Zusammentreffen mehrerer Autobahnen und Straßen*)
span 22.4	umfassen, umspannen
spark(ing) plug 13.2	Zündkerze
sparse 14.14	spärlich, dünn
special 28.1	Hilfspolizist(in) in GB
special agent 28.9	FBI-Beamter, FBI-Beamtin
special branch 26.1	Staatsschutz
Special Events 28.9	besondere Anlässe
special intervention group 1.5	Spezialeinsatzkommando (SEK)
Special Investigations Division 28.9	Kriminaldienststelle für ausgewählte Delikte (*in Tulsa besonders Drogen- und Bandenkriminalität*)
special manhunt 27.5	Zielfahndung
special security law 3.3	besonderes Sicherheitsrecht
Special Subjects 28.9	Sonderaufgaben
specific 14.2	besonders, eigen
speckled 17.1	gefleckt
speed 1.3	1 Geschwindigkeit 2 (*coll.*) Amphetamin 3 (zu) schnell fahren
speed box 13.3	Getriebe
speed camera 9.6	Geschwindigkeitsüberwachungskamera
speed check 1.3	Geschwindigkeitskontrolle
speed control 13.2	Tempomat
speeder 9.1	Raser(in), Autofahrer(in), der / die (zu) schnell fährt
speeding 1.3	Geschwindigkeitsüberschreitung
speeding ticket 2.5	Strafzettel wegen zu schnellen Fahrens
speed limit 4.5	zulässige Höchstgeschwindigkeit (*durch Schilder angezeigt*)
speedometer 9.7	Tachometer
spike a drink 21.2	Getränk mit Zusatzstoffen versehen
spill 9.7	ausschütten
spine 12.9	Rückgrat

spirits 14.14	Schnaps
splint 12.8	Schiene
split 9.10	aufteilen, splitten
spoke 13.5	Speiche
sports badge 3.9	Sportabzeichen
sports utility vehicle (SUV) 7.4	geländetaugliches Straßenfahrzeug
spot 5.5	sehen, erblicken, entdecken
spot, on the ~ 7.1	an Ort und Stelle
spotlight 25.3	Scheinwerfer
spouse 27.7	Ehepartner(in)
spring 13.5	Feder
spur, on the ~ of the moment 24.3	spontan
spyhole 16.3	Guckloch, Türspion
squad 3.3	1 Einsatzgruppe 2 Hundertschaft
square 4.5	Quadrat
squeeze through 5.5	sich durchquetschen, sich durchzwängen
stab 1.10	stechen (mit Messer)
stack 9.10	Stapel
staff 3.7	Belegschaft, Personal
staff party 15.8	Betriebsfest
stage 3.3	Grad, Abschnitt
stage, at this ~ 16.8	zu diesem Zeitpunkt, zum jetzigen Stand (*der Ermittlungen*)
stagger 11.2	schwanken
stag party 11.9	Junggesellenabschiedsparty
stainless steel 13.3	Edelstahl
stalker 20.2	Nachsteller, Stalker
stalking 20.1	Nachstellen
stammer 14.14	stammeln, stottern
stand 13.5	Ständer
standardized material 26.3	einheitliches Lehrmaterial
standard uniform 2.6	Standarduniform, „normale" Uniform, uniforme Dienstkleidung
standby division 5.4	Bereitschaftspolizeiabteilung
standby duty 3.2	Bereitschaft(sdienst)
standby force / police / squad 1.5	Bereitschaftspolizei
start proceedings 8.3	Verfahren einleiten
State Chaplain 28.9	Leitender Seelsorger
state coffers 9.6	Staatskasse
state criminal office 2.8	Landeskriminalamt (LKA)
State Department (*US*) 7.6	Außenministerium
state government 1.3	Landesregierung
state law 10.6	Landesrecht
state level, at ~ 2.1	auf Landesebene
State Office for Vocational and Advanced Training 3.9	Landesamt für Ausbildung, Fortbildung und Personalangelegenheiten (in NRW)
state police service 1.5	Landes-, Staatspolizei (*in D die Polizei eines Bundeslandes*)
state politician 2.10	Landespolitiker(in)
state prosecutor 11.6	Staatsanwalt, Staatsanwältin
state road (*US*) 4.1	Landesstraße
state tax authority 2.13	Landesfinanzverwaltung
statement 5.4	Aussage
statewide 28.9	landesweit, im ganzen Bundesstaat

stationary 2.16	1 fest(stehend), an Ort und Stelle, stationär 2 ruhend, stehend (*Verkehr*)
stationary traffic 2.12	ruhender Verkehr (*als fester Begriff: Ruhender Verkehr*)
station level, at ~ 2.11	auf Inspektionsebene
station sergeant 1.6	Wachhabende(r)
station wagon (*US*) 7.4	Kombi
statute law 10.6	geschriebenes Recht
statutory membership 28.5	Zwangsmitgliedschaft
statutory rape 21.9	Vergewaltigung
statutory rest times 9.9	vorgeschriebene Ruhezeiten
stave off 1.3	abwehren
steep hill downwards 4.4	starkes Gefälle
steering and ignition lock 13.2	Lenkrad- und Zündschloss
stern 14.3	streng
sticker 9.10	Aufkleber, Plakette, Vignette
stimulate 26.3	anregen, in Gang setzen
sting 12.10	(Insekten)Stich
stipulate 7.12	festlegen
stitch 12.8	Stich
stocks 9.7	Pranger
stocky 14.13	untersetzt, stämmig
stop a bank account 14.11	Bankkonto sperren
stop something in its tracks 20.5	etwas im Keim ersticken
stop-and-go 9.8	stockender Verkehr
store detective 2.19	Ladendetektiv(in)
stout 6.1	1 Stoutbier (*z. B. Guiness*) 2 untersetzt, korpulent
straddle the central line 11.4	in der Straßenmitte fahren (*so dass der Mittelstreifen in der Mitte des Fahrzeugs ist*)
strangle 10.7	(er)würgen
streamline 2.8	vereinheitlichen
streetcar (*US*) 7.4	Straßenbahn
strenuous 3.2	anstrengend, anfordernd
stretch limo 7.4	überlanger PKW
stretcher 12.8	Tragbahre
stroke 12.10	Schlaganfall
stroll 15.2	schlendern, bummeln
struts 13.5	Gabel (*Motorrad*)
stubborn 9.12	hartnäckig, widerspenstig
stuck, get ~ 6.2	feststecken
stud earring 14.12	Ohrstecker
study 16.3	Arbeitszimmer
stuff 11.6	hier: Droge
sub-machine gun 23.5	Maschinenpistole
submission 7.13	Vorlage
submit 11.6	vorlegen, einreichen
subsequent 24.2	anschließend, nachfolgend
substantial 10.1	beträchtlich
substantiate 14.7	bestätigen, verifizieren
substitute document 14.11	Ersatzpapier
subway 4.2	1 Unterführung 2 (*US*) U-Bahn
successor 22.7	Nachfolger(in)
sue 6.2	verklagen
sufficient 10. 2	genügend, ausreichend
suffix 7.5	1 Nachsilbe 2 Endbuchstabe (*bei früheren britischen Kfz-Kennzeichen*)
suffocation 12.10	Ersticken
suicide attempt 20.2	Selbstmordversuch
suicide bomber 24.3	Selbstmordattentäter(in)
suitable 3.9	geeignet, passend
sulphur 23.1	Schwefel
summons 11.6	(Vor)Ladung
sunroof 13.2	Schiebedach
superficial 24.3	oberflächlich
superintendent 3.3	Polizeirat
superior 15.6	Vorgesetzte(r)
suppress 17.8	unterdrücken
surface 4.4	Oberfläche
surge forward 20.5	vorwärts drängen
surname 3.8	Nach-, Familienname
surpass 23.2	überbieten, übertreffen
surroundings 11.2	Umgebung
surveillance 2.13	Überwachung
surveillance camera 14.3	Überwachungskamera
survive 14.10	überleben
suspect 2.18	Verdächtigte(r)
suspenders 14.15	Hosenträger
suspicion 2.13	Verdacht
suspicious 2.16	verdächtig
sustain 9.10	aushalten, erleiden
sustainable 26.3	nachhaltig
swallow 18.4	(ver)schlucken
SWAT (Special Weapons and Tactics Team) 2.7	Spezialeinsatzkommando (SEK)
swear at someone 5.4	jemanden beschimpfen
sweater 14.15	Pullover
swerve 9.10	hin und her schwanken, ausweichen
switch 2.7	hier: abändern, sich anpassen
switch on 1.1	1 einschalten (*Licht usw.*) 2 (*coll.*) jemanden zum Gebrauch von Drogen veranlassen
swivel chair 19.3	Drehstuhl
sword cane 23.1	Stockdegen (*historisch*)
sworn police officer 28.9	voll ausgebildete(r) Polizist(in) (*im Gegensatz zu Zivilpersonal*)
sympathy 22.7	Mitleid, Interesse (*nicht: Sympathie*)
syringe 2.5	Spritze

T

tachograph 9.9	Fahrtenschreiber
tachograph chart 9.9	Tachoscheibe, Schaublatt
tachycardia 12.10	Herzrasen
tackle 3.3	bekämpfen, angreifen
tactical behaviour 3.3	polizeiliches Einsatzverhalten
tactical firearms unit 28.4	bewaffnete Einsatzbeamte
tag 7.5	Anhänger, Schild
tailgate 10.3	zu dicht auffahren
tail light(s) 7.7	Rücklicht
take action 5.2	aktiv werden, einschreiten

take into account 24.2	berücksichtigen, in Betracht ziehen
take out 23.7	außer Gefecht setzen
tamper with 6.1	sich zu schaffen machen an
tanker 7.4	Tankwagen
tap 7.13	klopfen
target 17.4	1 Ziel(scheibe) 2 zum Ziel haben
targeted search 27.5	Zielfahndung
tarmacked 25.4	asphaltiert
tarp hoop 9.10	Spriegel
tarpaulin 9.10	Plane
tart card 21.9	Prostituiertenausweis
taser (*Verb*) 23.7	Taser einsetzen
tasked, be ~ 26.3	zur Aufgabe haben, betraut sein mit
tax disc 13.3	Steuerplakette
tax evasion 2.13	Steuerhinterziehung
Tax Investigation Service 2.13	Steuerfahndung
technician 3.2	Techniker(in)
technique 3.3	Technik (*als Methode*)
teetotaller 17.1	Abstinenzler(in), Antialkoholiker(in)
telephone surveillance 24.2	Telefonüberwachung -abhörmaßnahme
temporary 2.9	vorübergehend, zeitweise
ten commandments 24.3	zehn Gebote
tend to 5.2	zu etwas neigen
tendon 12.9	Sehne
tension 9.10	Spannung
terraced house 16.3	Reihenhaus
Texas tea 18.9	Marihuana
text (*Verb*) 9.8	SMS schicken
textbook 28.9	Lehrbuch
thatched cottage 16.3	Haus mit Strohdach
theft 2.5	Diebstahl
theft act 16.1	Gesetz über Diebstahl
theft and handling 17.9	Diebstahl und Hehlerei
theft from a vehicle 13.1	Diebstahl an / aus einem Fahrzeug
theft of a vehicle 13.1	Diebstahl eines Fahrzeugs
thematic area 3.3	Themenbereich
thereupon 3.9	daraufhin
thigh 12.9	Oberschenkel
thorough 18.7	gründlich
thoroughfare 4.2	Durchgangsstraße, Hauptstraße
threat 2.8	Bedrohung
threat assessment 27.1	Bedrohungseinschätzung
threaten 9.10	(be)drohen
three-wheeler 7.4	Dreirad
threshold 2.7	Schwelle
tick off 7.13	ankreuzen
tie-down strap 9.10	Spanngurt
tier 2.3	Schicht, Stufe
tile 16.5	Schindel, Kachel
till 15.6	Kasse
tilted 16.6	gekippt
timber house 16.3	Fachwerkhaus
time switch 16.6	Zeitschalter
time, in good ~ 2.10	rechtzeitig
timing belt 13.2	Zahnriemen
tire (*US*) 5.4	Reifen
tireless(ly) 13.3	unermüdlich
tissue 12.9	Gewebe
to and fro 9.12	vorwärts und rückwärts
toll 4.2	Straßenbenutzungsgebühr, Maut
ton 9.1	hier: hundert Meilen pro Stunde (*160 kmh*)
topic 17.7	Thema, Gegenstand
top layer 7.8	obere Schicht
top tier 28.9	Spitze
torch 1.6	1 Taschenlampe 2 Fackel
tour the country 6.1	durch das Land reisen
tourniquet 12.8	Aderpresse, Tourniquet
tow away / off 5.2	abschleppen
township 28.9	Stadt (*als Verwaltungseinheit*)
town twinning 2.8	Städtepartnerschaft
tow truck 5.7	Abschleppwagen
traction 13.3	Antrieb
tractor (unit) 7.4	Zugmaschine (*Sattelzug*)
trader 2.14	Handelsunternehmen
trade union 28.5	Gewerkschaft
trading standard 2.14	Handelsstandard
traffic check 2.16	Verkehrskontrolle
traffic circle 4.2	Kreisverkehr
traffic commissariat 2.5	Verkehrskommissariat
traffic density 9.2	Verkehrsdichte
traffic enforcement 2.16	Verkehrsüberwachung
traffic infraction 8.3	Verkehrsverstoß
traffic jam 6.2	(Verkehrs)Stau
trafficker 18.4	Drogendealer, Drogenschmuggler
trafficking in human beings 7.1	Menschenhandel
traffic management 3.3	Verkehrslehre
traffic offence 7.11	Verkehrsverstoß
traffic warden 5.2	Politesse *(kann auch ein Mann sein)*
traffic-related matters 2.2	Verkehrsangelegenheiten
trailer 7.2	Anhänger
trailer park 16.3	Wohnmobilsiedlung
trailer truck 7.4	LKW mit Anhänger
train conductor 19.3	Zugbegleiter(in)
trainee 3.3	Auszubildende(r), Lehrling
traineeship 3.11	Ausbildungsplatz
tramlines 5.2	Straßenbahnschienen
transfer form 8.2	Überweisungsträger, -formular
transmit 6.2	senden
transnational 27.4	länderübergreifend
travel agency 6.5	Reisebüro
tread 5.4	(Reifen)Profil
trespasser 16.1	Eindringling
trial 1.7	Strafprozess, Gerichtsverhandlung
triangle 4.5	Dreieck
triangular 4.4	dreieckig
trigger 15.6	1 auslösen 2 Abzug
trivial offence 11.2	geringfügiges Delikt, Kavaliersdelikt
trolley 1.4	Einkaufswagen

trooper 9.5	1 Polizist (*Streifenpolizist einer "State Police" in den USA, unterster Dienstgrad*) 2 berittener Polizist (*Australien*)
truancy 14.1	Schulschwänzen
truck and trailer 7.4	LKW mit Anhänger
truffle 18.8	Trüffel
truncheon 1.9	Schlagstock, Gummiknüppel
trunk 7.10	1 (*US*) Kofferraum 2 Rumpf
trunk road 4.2	Durchgangsstraße, Hauptstraße
trustworthy 14.7	glaubwürdig
tuition 3.3	Ausbildung, Unterweisung
tuition reimbursement 28.9	Erstattung von Schul- und Studiengebühren
tunic 2.6	Uniformjacke
(turn) indicators 7.7	Blinker, Fahrtrichtungsanzeiger
turnover 22.3	Umsatz
turnpike (*US*) 4.1	Autobahn (*gebührenpflichtig*)
turnstile 20.5	Drehkreuz
tusk 18.4	Stoßzahn
tutorial staff 28.8	Ausbildungsbeamte
twenty milligrams of alcohol in 100 millilitres of blood 11.2	= 0,2 Promille
twin town 3.7	Partnerstadt
two-digit 7.5	zweistellig
two-way radio licence 25.3	Sprechfunkzeugnis
tyre / tire (*US*) 5.4	Reifen
tyre monitoring display 13.3	Reifenprofilanzeige

U

umbrella association / organization 22.1	Dachverband
umbrella stand 16.3	Schirmständer
unaccompanied 15.2	ohne Begleitung, allein
unanimous 27.1	einstimmig
unblemished reputation 3.3	einwandfreier Leumund, guter Ruf
unconscious 9.16	bewusstlos
underestimate 11.2	unterschätzen
underlying 28.5	wesentlich
underpass 4.2	Unterführung
underpin 27.3	untermauern, verstärken
undersigned 23.8	Unterzeichnende(r)
unidentifiable 7.5	nicht identifizierbar
Uniform Division 28.9	Revier (*Tulsa hat drei Reviere – East, North und Southwest*)
uniformed police officer 1.3	Polizist(in) in Uniform
unintentional(ly) 12.1	unabsichtlich
unique 26.1	einzigartig
unit commander 2.10	Einheitsführer(in)
University of Applied Sciences: Public Administration and Administration of Justice in Bavaria 3 3	Fachhochschule für Öffentliche Verwaltung und Rechtspflege in Bayern
unkempt 14.14	ungekämmt, unfrisiert
unlawful entry 16.6	unbefugtes Eindringen
unmarked car 2.16	neutrales Polizeifahrzeug, Zivilfahrzeug
unpleasant 2.19	unangenehm
unreasonable 22.6	unvernünftig
unruly behaviour 20.5	rüdes Benehmen
untie 9.10	losbinden, lösen
up-and-over door 16.3	Garagentür (*nach oben öffnend*)
upmarket vehicle 22.1	hochwertiges Fahrzeug
Upper Peninsula 28.9	nördliche Halbinsel des Staates Michigan
Upper Swabia 11.6	Oberschwaben
use deadly force 23.7	von der Schusswaffe Gebrauch machen
U.S. road (*US*) 4.1	Bundesstraße
utility belt 28.8	Dienstgürtel (*mit Ausrüstungsgegenständen*)
utterance 22.1	Zitat, Äußerung
utterly 16.4	äußerst

V

vacant 17.5	leerstehend
vaccination 26.2	Impfung
vacuum 17.4	staubsaugen
vacuum-sealed 18.7	vakuumverpackt
vale 7.5	Tal
valid 5.4	gültig
validate 19.1	entwerten
valuables 2.14	Wertsachen
varnish 14.14	lackieren
vary 2.11	variieren, schwanken
vastness 7.6	Breite
vehicle check 5.4	Fahrzeugüberprüfung, -kontrolle
vehicle defect (rectification) form 5.4	Mängelkarte, -bericht
vehicle registration certificate 7.1	Kfz-Schein, Zulassungsbescheinigung Teil 1
vehicle registration office 13.7	Kfz-Zulassungsstelle
vein 12.9	Vene
verbal cautioning 10.1	mündliche Verwarnung
verge 9.8	Bankett
vest 14.15	Unterhemd
vested with 28.5	ausgestattet mit
veteran 15.6	1 altgedient, langjährig 2 Polizist(in) mit vielen Dienstjahren (*noch im Dienst*)
vice 2.5	Rotlichtkriminalität
Vice 28.9	Einheit zur Bekämpfung von Prostitution, Glücksspiel und Alkohol
vicinity 15.6	Nähe, Nachbarschaft
vicious 10.8	bösartig
victim 12.12	Opfer
vineyard 18.5	Weinberg
vintage car 7.4	Oldtimer (*etwa 1917-1930*)
violence-prone 17.3	gewaltbereit
violent behaviour 13.7	gewalttätiges Verhalten
visibility 5.2	Sicht
vital 3.5	lebenswichtig, -notwendig
V-necked 28.9	mit V-Ausschnitt
vocational baccalaureat diploma 3.3	Fachabitur, Fachhochschulreife
vocational school 6.4	berufsbildende Schule
voluntary 2.11	freiwillig

volunteer 4.7	1 Freiwillige(r) 2 freiwillig etwas tun
Volunteers in Police Service (VIPS) 28.9	Polizeifreiwillige (*sie erledigen ohne Bezahlung Verwaltungstätigkeiten bei der Polizei*)
vomit 11.6	brechen, sich übergeben

W

waiter 1.8	Kellner
waitress 1.8	Kellnerin
waive 8.3	auf etwas verzichten, etwas sein lassen
wake up with a start 14.10	plötzlich aufwachen, aufschrecken
walk one's beat 28.5	Streife gehen
wall cupboard 16.3	Hängeschrank
wall unit 16.3	Schrankwand
wallet 13.7	Brieftasche, Geldbörse
wanted 1.1	gesucht
wanted list 14.11	Fahndungsliste
wanted person 2.18	gesuchte Person
warning fine 5.2	(gebührenpflichtige) Verwarnung
warning triangle 7.10	Warndreieck
warrant 2.16	Haftbefehl
wash basin 16.3	Waschbecken
waste 2.12	1 Müll, Abfall 2 verschwenden
waste water treatment plant 6.4	Kläranlage
water cannon 20.5	Wasserwerfer
water level 25.2	Wasserstand
waterway 3.9	Wasserstraße
waterways authority 25.2	Schifffahrtsbehörde
wavy 14.14	wellig
weaken 25.4	schwächen
weaponry 2.7	Waffen, Bewaffnung
weapons handling 3.3	Waffenkunde
weapons locker 2.15	Waffenschrank
wear and tear 7.3	Verschleiß
wear one's seatbelt 7.1	angeschnallt sein
weave from one lane to another 11.4	den Fahrstreifen wechseln
weave in and out 7.13	immer wieder die Fahrspur wechseln
weld 9.10	schweißen
well-regulated militia 23.4	gut organisierte Miliz / Bürgerwehr
wheat beer 11.6	Weizenbier
wheelchair 5.5	Rollstuhl
whereabouts 14.12	Aufenthalt(sort)
whiplash injury 12.10	Halswirbelschleudertrauma
white-collar crime 22.1	Wirtschaftskriminalität
wide-eyed 9.1	mit aufgerissenen Augen
widespread 16.2	weit verbreitet
wig 14.14	Perücke
wind down 14.9	sich beruhigen
wind jacket 14.15	Windjacke, Anorak
windpipe 12.9	Luftröhre
(window) shutter 16.3	Rollladen
windscreen (*GB*) 5.4	Windschutzscheibe
windscreen wiper 5.4	Scheibenwischer
windshield (*US*) 13.2	Windschutzscheibe
wing 12.11	1 Kotflügel 2 Flügel (*Gebäude*)
wing mirror 13.2	Außenspiegel
wiper(s) 5.2	Scheibenwischer
wipe-wash 13.2	Scheibenwaschanlage
wire brush 17.7	Drahtbürste
withdraw 9.10	herausziehen
withdrawal symptom 18.1	Entzugserscheinung
withdraw money 14.7	Geld abheben
woman police constable (WPC) (*GB*) 1.8	Polizistin (unterster Dienstgrad)
working body 26.3	Arbeitsgruppe
working top 16.3	Arbeitsplatte
works 5.8	Werk, Fabrik
works entrance 4.2	Baustelleneinfahrt
works exit 4.2	Baustellenausfahrt
wounded 23.8	Verwundete(r)
wrap 18.7	einpacken, einwickeln
wrestle 13.7	ringen
wrinkled 14.14	faltig, runzelig
wrist 12.9	Handgelenk
write-off 12.6	Totalschaden
wrongdoer 18.5	Übeltäter(in), Gesetzesbrecher(in)
WW II (World War II) 14.10	Zweiter Weltkrieg

X

Xenon headlights 13.3	Xenon-Scheinwerfer
xenophobia 26.4	Fremdenfeindlichkeit

Y

yell 17.5	(laut) schreien
yellow cab 21.3	gelbes Taxi (*Taxifirma in New York und vielen anderen amerikanischen Städten*)
yellow football 18.9	Meskalin
yield (*US*) 4.5	Vorfahrt gewähren
youth 14.1	Jugendliche(r)

Z

zigzag 11.4	Zickzack / Schlangenlinien fahren
zip, zipper (*US*) 14.9	Reißverschluss
zone 1.5	1 Zone 2 Bezirk, Gebiet

Abbildungsverzeichnis